Herbert B. Edwardes

Memorials of the Life and Letters of Major-General Sir Herbert B.

Edwardes

Volume I

Herbert B. Edwardes

Memorials of the Life and Letters of Major-General Sir Herbert B. Edwardes
Volume I

ISBN/EAN: 9783337018023

Printed in Europe, USA, Canada, Australia, Japan

Cover: Foto ©Thomas Meinert / pixelio.de

More available books at **www.hansebooks.com**

MEMORIALS OF THE LIFE
AND LETTERS OF

MAJOR-GENERAL

SIR HERBERT B. EDWARDES

K.C.B., K.C.S.I.

D.C.L. OF OXFORD; LL.D. OF CAMBRIDGE

By HIS WIFE

IN TWO VOLUMES
VOL. I.

LONDON
KEGAN PAUL, TRENCH & CO., 1, PATERNOSTER SQUARE
1886

DEDICATION.*

"To all my Countrymen who care for India, and especially to the young whose lot is to be cast in it, this Book is dedicated; to show how possible and good it is to unite the Statesman with the Soldier, the Philanthropist with the Patriot, and the Christian with all, in the Government of a Subject Race."

* These lines were written for "The Author's Dedication" to the "Life of Sir Henry Lawrence," by H. B. E.

"Whatsoever things are true,
Whatsoever things are honest,
Whatsoever things are just,
Whatsoever things are pure,
Whatsoever things are lovely,
Whatsoever things are of good report;
If there be any Virtue,
And if there be any Praise,
Think on these things."

PHIL. iv. 8.

PREFACE.

It is not intended to write the "Life" of Sir Herbert Edwardes. That was so full of stirring events and deeds of chivalry that it would be difficult to do full justice to the theme.

My purpose is rather to bring together some letters and speeches that, like a chord of sweet music, may tell something of the harmony and beauty of that lovely mind which has passed away from earth for a while, to find its rest in the Saviour's presence.

The half cannot be told; for there are deeds of noble heroism, acts of truest self-denial ("in honour preferring one another")—great deeds done so secretly that they are known to none but the most intimate sharer of his inner life, which, though they won no honour here, *wait* for that day when the counsels of all hearts shall be made manifest, and God will give the praise.

But besides these, his clear statesmanlike views; his far-seeing, almost prophetic, grasp of the true importance of events, that made his acts so vigorous and his resource so fertile in times of danger, and inspired confidence in those who were around him and dependent on his command; his thrilling eloquence, and the tender pathos and sympathy of his letters;—all these, and the true and fervent devotion of his heart to heavenly things, will shine out in the fragments now put together, and show, if it be but a glimpse, something of the beauty of a great and noble mind—*great* in its humility.

*　　　*　　　*　　　*　　　*

"So it is when a great and good and beloved man departs—sets, it may be, suddenly—and to us who know not the times and the seasons, *too soon*. We gaze eagerly at his last hours; and when he is gone from our sight, we see his image wherever we go, and in whatsoever we are engaged; and if we try to record in words our wonder, our sorrow, and our affection, we cannot see to do it; for the idea of his life is for ever coming into our study of imagination—into all our thoughts—and we can do little else than let our mind in a wise passiveness hush itself to rest. . . .

"We cannot now go very curiously to work to scrutinize the composition of his character; we cannot take that large, free, grand, genial character and nature to pieces, and weigh this and measure that, and pronounce. We are too near as yet to him and to his loss; he is *too dear* to us to be so handled.

"His death (as Hartley Coleridge says) is a recent sorrow; his image *still lives*, in eyes that weep for him." (John Brown, M.D., Edinburgh.)

*　　　*　　　*　　　*　　　*

These words, though written by another, express something of the feeling with which this work has been undertaken, and answer in some measure the question, Why has it not been done before?

EMMA EDWARDES.

41, Onslow Square, London,
1886.

CONTENTS OF VOL. I.

LIST OF ILLUSTRATIONS.

CHAPTER I.

—◆—

1819—1841—1845.

EARLY LIFE TO REGIMENTAL LIFE IN INDIA, AND A.D.C. TO LORD GOUGH.

VOL. I.   B

MEMORIALS OF THE LIFE OF

MAJOR-GENERAL

SIR HERBERT B. EDWARDES,

K.C.B., K.C.S.I.

———•✕•———

CHAPTER I.

SIR HERBERT BENJAMIN EDWARDES, K.C.B., K.C.S.I., was the second son of the Rev. Benjamin Edwardes, Rector of Frodesley, a small country parish in Shropshire, about seven miles from Shrewsbury. The Rev. Benjamin Edwardes was the second son of Sir John Cholmondeley Edwardes, Bart., eighth baronet of Shrewsbury.

Born at Frodesley, 1819.

The family is an old Welsh one, is descended from the ancient kings of Powysland, in Wales, and was seated at Kilhendre, in Shropshire, in the time of Henry I.

The first of the family who assumed the name of "Edwardes" was John-ap-David-ap-Madoc, of Kilhendre, in the time of Henry VII.; and he was great-great-grandfather of the Sir Thomas Edwardes who, for his eminent services to Charles I., was rewarded with the grant of a baronetcy in 1664.

On his father's death, in 1823, at the early age of thirty-one, Herbert was only four years old.

His father's death, 1823.

He and his two brothers (Henry, the elder, and Frank, the younger) were taken care of by their grandmother, the dowager Lady Edwardes, who lived at Moele Brace, near Shrewsbury. It was afterwards arranged that two of the brothers should remain with their grandmother, under whose loving care they were brought up, and educated at the High

School at Shrewsbury, under Dr. Kennedy; and Herbert was taken charge of and adopted by another near relative, the only daughter of Sir Thomas Edwardes, who was married to John Thomas Hope, Esq., of Netley, Shropshire.

Netley. Netley is only a few miles from the home of Herbert's birth, which he left too young to carry away any recollection of; but he always regarded Frodesley with very great tenderness, as the home of his parents and his birthplace.

Frodesley. It is a little village of cottages, with a pretty vicarage house and a tiny church, a few farmhouses, and little besides, close to the Shropshire hills of the "Lawley," the "Longmyund," and the "Caradoc," which he loved so well; for he delighted in all the beauties of that lovely country, and was proud of belonging to it, as all Salopians are.

The little church stands now much as it was when his father ministered in it; and it is the burying-place of most of the Edwardes family still.

Very beautiful was this dear boy of four years old, with curling fair brown hair, and large lustrous and soft-beaming eyes, as I have been told by the daughter of the house * to which he came, who welcomed him to her heart, and loved him thenceforward with tenderest love—a love which he repaid with all the tenderness and devotion of his affectionate nature.

This love came to fill up something of the yearning Herbert always felt for the love of a mother, of which he had no conscious knowledge. For his mother did not long survive his father, and he never remembered her, though he always cherished very tenderly the thought of her.

1828. Herbert was about nine years old when he first went to school. Afterwards he was sent to a school at Richmond, in Surrey, kept by the Rev. Charles Delafosse. It was a large school, and had held a great reputation for many years. But Herbert never thought very much of what he learned there.

He never was very keen about sports and boys' games (being always rather a delicate boy), and liked much better a pleasant book alone, or a quiet walk with a chosen friend.

* This lady afterwards married Herbert's uncle, Sir Henry Edwardes, his father's eldest brother.

His master was a kind, easy, good-natured, clever man, and a good "classical scholar." Herbert was a great favourite with him; for, being fond of a good joke himself, the master enjoyed the wit and talents which were conspicuous even then in his young pupil.

Herbert was always the ready champion of any little boy who was being bullied and unable to defend himself—he would even bear a punishment to save another boy; thus early showing the germ of the noble nature that shone so conspicuously in his after-life.

As has just been said, Herbert was from the first, quick in wit and ready in repartee. He was also fond of poetry and romance, and many a sweet verse he composed in his boyish days; but there was no hand to gather them together and preserve them.

His winter holidays were spent in London, with Mr. and Mrs. Hope; his summer holidays, with them at their country place, Netley, Shropshire.

Thus his youth was lonely. Left much to himself, he fed upon his own thoughts, and books were his companions and his enjoyment. Was this the training that made the roots strike deeper and more firmly, and made him strong and self-reliant, prepared to stand the storm and strain of the battle of life?

He must have left school about the year 1835 or 1836; for, in 1837, he was attending classes at King's College, London.

His dear friend, the Rev. Cowley Powles, writes : " When I went to King's College, Herbert was already there, in October, 1837, and he had been there some time, how long exactly I do not know, but long enough to be among the leaders of the college. His principal forte lay in what would now be called the ' Modern Side.' In classics he did not particularly distinguish himself, nor in mathematics. His taste was more for modern literature. At that he worked hard. I don't think he did work very hard at either of the other subjects.

" He was always thought 'a man of mark,' and in the ' Debating Society ' was decidedly one of the very foremost speakers."

King's College, London, 1837.

He would sometimes amuse himself at lecture with making sketches of figures that struck his fancy. Now and then this was observed, and the sketches called for, when it might be that the lecturer saw a likeness of himself in pen and ink.

With great artistic talent, and a rare facility in drawing caricatures, Herbert had such kindness of nature and such true courtesy and goodness, that he *could* not draw an ill-natured caricature; and a man would see himself caricatured, and yet not be offended. Herbert never made an enemy by it in all his life.

But in after years he could never be persuaded to draw caricatures at all; for he grew more tender and more kind as his character and his nature ripened and mellowed towards perfection; and he thought it was a faculty not good to indulge, because it led to dwelling on the weaknesses or bad characteristics of another, while he liked to search out the *good* qualities in other men rather than their failings.

His friends at King's College.

Herbert's friends at King's College at this time were— Charles Kingsley, Fitz-James Stephens, Walter Dumergue, Nassau Senior, F. W. Gibbs, Benjamin Shaw, Bryan Burgess, and others.

He valued and loved Kingsley always, and they were great together in the "Debating Society;" and they and Walter Dumergue, and Benjamin Shaw, used often to walk home together, arm-in-arm, along the streets, when "college" was over, and carry on their "debates" on their way home.

A close friendship between Herbert Edwardes and Cowley Powles began at this time at King's College, which continued and deepened in after years in loving intercourse that was a perpetual joy, and was only interrupted by death.

To the intercourse between them we are indebted for some insight into his mind in these early days, when congenial friends were few, and his future life lay dim before him.

1839.

In 1839 Edwardes writes to this friend—

"Your habits and mine form part of the 'sympathy' between us (of which —— speaks).

"Owls we are—birds of the moon; and I know you feel

as I do, that the still hour of night, when men, *let us alone*, when the world is, as it were, taken off its hinges, and the noisy machinery of life at rest, then is the time when *individuality*—call it selfishness if you will—comes in upon us, and we look *into* our own hearts and *our own* thoughts, and *feel*, without the alien impulses which other people lend when they run against and jostle with us. To my mind, there is a fascination about night which it is impossible to withstand; there is a mysterious loneliness in it, which quite fixes my whole soul.

"And when there is a moon to look out upon that space of earth, with all its gloomy trees shut in by a thick ' wall of darkness,' on which there is no handwriting but the stars, and those so eternal that they do not break the quiet with idea of motion, oh ! that is indeed a *mass* of solitude which one can enter into and possess with a tangible feeling of happiness, which is poetry to the very heart ! "

＊	＊	＊	＊	＊

Somebody had written to Edwardes to beg him to take more care of himself—"to take more sleep and preserve his constitution." He writes in reply—

"Constitution, indeed ! Life is nothing, time is nothing, but the things for which we live and the things which take place in time are all that is to be regarded ; and if all this, which is the value of life, is to be given up to the furtherance of the mere *process of living*, why, e'en let a vampire suck out my brains, that I may eat and drink, and my body thrive like a beast's ! "

He writes at this time—

"I lead an idle, dreamy, read-y, placid, vegetable sort of life in this country, and never, in a month's time perchance, know the blessing of a thing to *excite* feeling !

"How I do loathe this state of utter inactivity ! but,

thank Heaven, 'tis an intermediate *grub* state, which ends
in emancipation—a ship my chrysalis, the goodly sun of
India my deliverer from cold suspension of existence."

> "No mother's face o'er my cradle smiled,
> No father's love my young cares beguiled.
> They died! My passions all ran wild,
> And hard * was my heart from a little child!

> "I heard men say there were seasons four,
> And each one a different livery wore;
> But summer to me was all frozen o'er,
> And the year was winter for evermore!

> "Yes; I thought for ever it should be so,
> Never to kindle at passion's glow;
> Callous to all things, ay, even woe;
> My life laid aside like a broken bow.

> "But it was not to be. Tho' the sea-waves chill
> And slumber awhile when the cold wind is still,
> Yet, comes but a cloud o'er old Ocean's will,
> Proud man in his ship shall abide it but ill.

> "Long had I slumbered the sleep of the proud,
> But the time was come now when my soul should be bowed—
> When over my fortunes should pass the dark cloud
> Which wakes every passion to struggle aloud."

Written about this time were two little pieces of poetry
which may be inserted here.

> "'Twas autumn! I looked on the leaves as they fell
>   From the bough of an old oak tree,
> And the wild winds whistled a parting knell
>   To the old oak's third jubilee.

> "I watched a red withered leaf yield to the blast,
>   And fly far from the old oak tree;
> While the old oak groaned for the years that were past,
>   And wished, like the leaf, it was free.

> "'Twas summer! I looked on the leaves as they stirred
>   On the bough of that old oak tree;
> The zephyrs were sighing. A beautiful bird
>   Sang the old oak's praise merrily.

---

* This is only an example of how unable he was to do justice to
himself, for his sympathy and tenderness of heart were always remarkable.

"I watched a young severed leaf yield to the blast,
  Which suddenly shook the old tree;
But the old oak laughed at the years that were past,
  And *pitied* the leaf that was free.

                     "H. B. E., 1839."

Here is another—

"Come to the tombs of the ancient men,
  Come there alone at the hour when
  Rest to earthly spirits sent
  Leaves the sepulchre eloquent.

  "Ay, come alone
    When the dark grey stone,
  The bones of the dead concealing,
    Blazons a tale
    In the moonlight pale,
  The deeds of the dead revealing.

"Come to the valley where fairies tread
Heedlessly over the crowned head,
And nature has woven a lily-mask
For the brow that scowled in iron casque.

  "Come there alone
    When the moon has shone
  Her brightest hour, imparting
    A silvery hue
    To the gloomy yew,
  With the tears she sheds at parting.

"Come to me then. I'll tell thee a tale
I've kept so well. Though thy young cheek pale
And I should die by thy father's kin,
Yet *she* shall rest without spot of sin.

  "Come there alone
    When the wassail's done
  And the revellers all are slumbering,
    When sinners sleep,
    And the pious keep
  Dull watch, their bead-roll numbering.

"Come to the valley. Thy mother's there;
Stone there is none to tell she was fair.
But oh! the bones which whiten her grave
Tell she was loved by one who was brave.

"Come there alone.
    Nor sigh nor groan
Break the rest of those departed,
    And the midnight scream
    Of the owl shall seem
To mourn with the broken-hearted.
                "H. B. E., Netley, 1840."

A strain of sadness runs through all these. They are but touches that show the colour of his mind in those young days—a poetic and noble soul, enshrined in a sensitive and delicate frame; the soul impatient of its fetters, and longing to break them and to plunge into a *real* life, for which it felt the aspiration and the capacity, with ever-painful earnestness.

He had no desire to go to India.

But it was not by any choice of his own that Herbert went to India, or that he took to the military life as his profession. He had no associations with India, and had never had any relations or friends there, except the two young brothers who had each joined a regiment there already. But Herbert had never turned his thoughts for a moment in that direction. He desired to go to Oxford and study for the bar. Not that he much cared to be a lawyer either, but he wanted to go to Oxford and *really study*, and to have those opportunities of doing so which never yet had been within his reach, and which he knew that he could use to some purpose if he had the chance; and he considered that he had lost too much time in "school-routine" at Richmond.

Then he was strong in friendship, and his dearest friends were at Oxford, and this made him wish the more to share the advantages they had.

Necessity, not choice, decided his career.

But this not being allowed by his guardians, and finding he must depend upon himself to find some way out of his irksome inaction, he went himself to Sir Richard Jenkins, who was a member of the old Court of Directors, and a friend of the family, and asked him to give him "a direct appointment" to India. To this Sir Richard Jenkins consented at once,* and no time was lost in making the necessary preparations.

* From Sir Richard Jenkins we find a letter, written in 1848, to one

In October, 1840, Edwardes set sail for Calcutta in the sailing-ship the *Walmer Castle*, to go round the Cape.

It was all very distasteful to him, for he entered upon a life that had then no attractions to him, and a country that he had no desire to see. It was, to his own feelings, *an exile*—entire loneliness. So he went *very* sadly; and it was not till he got into "civil employ," and had a field opened before him of a share in the government of the country, that he found the congenial work into which he could throw himself happily.

He spent his twenty-first birthday, November 12, at sea, and landed at Calcutta in the beginning of 1841.

To beguile the monotony of a long sea-voyage (which, in those days, used to take three or four months), he edited a newspaper on board, and called it the *Walmer Castle Gazette*, and in this and in many other ways was the life and soul of the generally dull voyage. For Herbert Edwardes always had great vivacity, and as in all such sensitive, highly-strung, finely-toned natures, there was a play of fancy and readiness of wit that could make sunshine of the darkest day.

He could always extract, out of the passing things of life, the good or the beautiful, the ludicrous or the quaint, and rise with a magic power from the tenderest sympathy of sad thoughts to the sparkle of wit and fancy, carrying his hearers with him, like a well-tuned instrument of lovely chords well handled.

We may say here, in passing, that he never lost this power to the last, in spite of all life's rough storms—

of the family, at the time when Edwardes's name reached England in connection with Mooltân and Bunnoo.

"Gatane, Saturday.

"My dear Sir,

"I fully intended calling upon you when I was in Salop a few days ago, to congratulate you upon the high name young Edwardes has gained for himself by exploits so brilliant and so advantageous to his country. I feel myself much elated with the thought that I have been the means of placing such a man in the East India Company's service; and you may be assured that his conduct is fully appreciated, and I have no doubt will be duly rewarded by those who have the power and the privilege of doing so. I return to London next Monday, and am sorry I was not fortunate enough to meet you.

"Believe me, my dear sir,

"Yours very truly,

"(Signed)   E. JENKINS."

"That loveliness, ever in motion, which plays
Like the light upon autumn's soft, shadowy days;
Now here and now there, giving warmth as it beams,
Now melting in mist and now breaking in gleams."

A fellow-passenger,* who was on board the *Walmer Castle*, has kindly communicated, through a friend, his recollections, which give us a picture of him on board ship. "His figure at that time was slim, and his general appearance gave the impression of delicate rather than robust health. He did not often join in the active games and amusements in which young men on board ship generally engage, but preferred rather to look on. His features were fully formed, and the expression of his face bright and intelligent, whilst his conversation and remarks told of a well-informed and cultivated mind, added to a great sense of wit and humour.

"The monotony of the voyage, which lasted four months, the passengers sought to relieve by the usual expedients of amateur theatricals and the publication of a weekly newspaper. In both, Edwardes was the leading and directing spirit.

"The piece chosen was 'The Rivals,' the principal character, Sir Anthony Absolute, being performed by him with great life and spirit. The rehearsals, dresses, etc., were arranged chiefly under his directions.

"Of the newspaper he was the editor, an 'editor's box' being placed at his cabin-door. This little periodical frequently contained some well-written and witty articles, from that pen which found so vast a field for employment in after years.

"He also possessed considerable talent for etching; and the papers were generally illustrated by some well-executed caricatures of board-ship notables; but so well did he perform the office of editor and censor that nothing which could hurt the feelings of any one ever appeared.

"And so the voyage wore on, until, on reaching Calcutta, those who were then young and full of life separated, each to pursue the unknown road before him, and fight out the great battle of life.

"From these slight reminiscences we cannot fail to be

Letter of a fellow-passenger.

* Lieutenant-colonel Leigh, 7th Bengal Native Infantry.

struck with the fact that he who in after life led on men to
battle, and ruled thousands, was, even then, amongst his
fellow-passengers, in the amusements with which they beguiled the weariness of the voyage, the leader and director.

"(Signed)   R. T. L."

On arriving in India, Edwardes was appointed to the
1st Regiment Bengal Fusiliers (afterwards called the 101st
Bengal Fusiliers, and now the Royal Munster Fusiliers), and
was ordered to join his regiment at Kurnal. He and another
young officer proceeded together up the river Ganges in boats,
as far as Dinapore. Letters are still lovingly preserved of
this time, full of descriptions and sprightly wit, and his
ready pen-and-ink sketches help us to follow him in his
" budgerow " up the river to join his regiment.

His arrival in India.

" On the mighty River Ganges,
" March, 1841.

" MY DEAR COWLEY,

        " My reception in this country has been warm
enough, of course, but I cannot say that it was agreeable ;
for however flattering it may be to have an atmosphere of
mosquitoes waiting round your couch, and printing kisses
on your cheek, I do not think it worth the cost—waking in

En route to Dina-pore.

the morning with your night-cap too small for your head,
which has taken the opportunity (like all bad servants) of
the master being asleep to set up for a swell, and exhibit
in the glass a faithful picture of a spotted pumpkin. For a
week or ten days these horrible creatures confined me in the
house (albeit, my friends declared my features were gnatty
enough for anything), and one of my first reflections was
that if all the natives were to peg into our carcases as these
diminutive light infantry are wont to do, the Honourable
John Co. would be (like many another) in a very bad line
of business.

"But enough of complaints. Let us drop the veil, or
rather the mosquito-curtain, over Oriental plagues. I have
plenty to tell you of Oriental pleasures, and I should be
very far from candid did I not allow that I have experienced
many such since I have been here. Your thoughts will
naturally ask me first how I like the *climate* of my new land
of sojourn ; and I can sincerely answer, that I do not join
the outcry which is made about it. I like it much.

"Were the habits of Europeans here to be the same as
they are at home ; were their vocations of business and
avocations of pleasure to spread over the whole day, and
demand a constant restlessness of body and mind, such as
they do in England ;—I can easily conceive how incompatible such a life would be in such a climate as this. It
would be insupportable.

"But hear what Indian life is, and judge if the reverse
is not nearer the truth. I take my own daily routine for an
example, as I suppose we gentlemen in livery lead more
active lives than our brethren of the pen. (They are the
butlers out of livery—civil servants, and we are regular
flunkies to the company—the running footmen of great
John's establishment.)

"Well, a black rascal makes an oration by my bed
every morning about half an hour before daylight. I wake,

and see him salaaming with a cup of hot coffee in his hand. I sit on a chair and wash the teaspoon till the spoon is hot and the fluid cold, while he introduces me gradually into an ambush of pantaloons and wellingtons—if there is a parade. I am shut up in a red coat, and a glazed lid set upon my head, and thus, carefully packed, exhibit my reluctance to what I am going to do—to wit, my *duty*—by *riding* a couple of hundred yards to the parade.

" Here two or three hundred very cold people, in same condition, are assembled, and we all agree to keep ourselves warm with a game of soldiers, whereupon a very funny scene ensues, and we run about the plain, and wheel about and turn about, till the sun gets up to come and see what the row is about ; and then, like frightened children, we all scamper off and make the best of our way home. Then the packing-case is all taken off again, and I resume my nap after this little interruption as pleasantly as Homer does his epic about Achilles, after a page or two, by-the-by, on the subject of the infernal regions. This, if there is parade ; if not, I take a gallop with the dogs.

" Then breakfast, after which the *intellectual* day may be said to dawn ; for from this till four or five p.m. your occupation must be among your books, your pen, your pencil, and such-like servants of the brain.

" A man whose head has been made out of a turnip, with artificial eyes and a nose stuck thereon, to emulate the outside of a reasoning creature, will tell you that from this time forth your house is not only your castle, but your *prison ;* and if there be not a billiard-table in his house, or a badger in the verandah for his bull-dog to try conclusions with, he is, as it were, dead ; and, indeed, I believe him. But I think it just possible that you may understand that five or six hours laid out before you daily, to do with as you will ('for yourself,' as the schoolmaster said when he gave the head boy a halfpenny), is a thing not so much to be

Opportunities for mental enjoyments afforded in Indian life.

dreaded as desired. I do not fear, then, to acknowledge that I like the regular apportionment of bodily and mental exercise, and enjoy another ride in the cool, clear evening, and the rendezvous at dinner about seven or eight, all the better for having been *alone*—left to my own devices—for a great portion of the day. You see, therefore, that the great feature of Indian life is *quiet*, our portraits of manners and our landscapes of scenery are all mellowed down by what artists call *repose*, and I must own that this is to me a luxury which is bought cheaply by the sacrifice of active out-of-door amusements when the sun is abroad.

"When to this add what, perhaps, you already know; that in all other respects our life in India is one of necessary indulgence—at home among the ever-active miscalled luxury which pervades all the arrangements of our homes, prescribes the cut of our tables and our chairs, models our houses, and presides at our board—I have given you a pretty general idea of the character of a life which would seem to be so congenial to human nature, that a very short time is necessary to habituate the new-comer in all its ways, strange as they must appear at first. But you must not suppose that I am going to wage war from this distance against all that I have left behind me. Fear not that I shall wound thee in thy pride of beef and double stout, and throw thee into a fit of the gout by abusing the good men and things of old England—he must be a bolder and perhaps *colder* man than I am to think of a *comparison*; but I mean to say that the evils of India, like most other evils, have been to me much greater at a distance; its comforts exactly the reverse.

Love of country.

"I cannot express to you the deep feeling of love of *country* which seems spread over all India, and binds stranger to stranger together with that single tie. *Hospitality* is the outward and visible sign of this, and the grand characteristic of the European in the East; and travel where you will,

white face is sufficient passport to good services, wherever
they may be required.

"I am now travelling up the Ganges, with a detachment
of the 65th Regiment of Native Infantry, *en route* for Dinapôre, and have already seen many instances of this good
feeling.

"If we anchor within reach of any European's residence
—a fact of which we are most likely ignorant—the good
man comes down in a fever of delight and exercise to kidnap
the whole of us to dinner ; and if we stop at a station, it is
necessary to write on before to any friends that you may
have in particular, literally to give them the start of the three-
cornered billets which come tumbling down at your arrival.
In short, though you cannot but regret *England*, you meet
with *Englishmen* in perfection. But it is time that I left
off boring you with what most probably you know as well
as I do.

"I demand your gratitude for not dashing over head
and ears into a jungle, and telling you how sweetly every
wild weed smells, and how more than sweetly do the thousand perfumes mingle in the air ; and how the green pigeon
flutters overhead, and *coos* for very joy at the shower of
blossoms which he scatters on one's murderous eyes when
just upon the sight of a deadly 'Westley Richards.'

"I am already posted to the 1st European Regiment at
Kurnâl, the finest regiment in all India, I am told, for
discipline and appointment. It has also the best band and
the best mess in the service. With all these distinctions it
is the last regiment which cadets hope to be posted to ;
they say it is expensive, and the duties laborious—not pleasant things in their way, certainly ; but it seems to me that
if a man enjoys good things, he must be content to pay
good prices for the same. And if he takes any pride in the
discipline of his corps, he must not grudge the labour by
which it is brought about, and which has enabled the regi-

ment to serve with such great distinction all through the late
war, and will enable it, I hope, to gain fresh laurels in the
one now springing up in the part of the country where I
am going.

"This is a cheerful prospect for us *subs*, and I am, at
all events, lucky in being posted to a regiment which is
always called upon when fighting is to be done, and in time
of peace always stationed in the finest and most healthy
parts of India. It is something, moreover, to have your
own countrymen under your command, instead of an ebony
set of soldiers, though of a truth the natives are much
easier to manage."

July, 1842.
At Kurnál.

After staying a few months at Dinapôre, Edwardes moved
with his regiment to Kurnál,* for we find him there in July,
1842. "A delightful station," he writes, "same climate as
a healthy England." A great relief from the heat of Dinapôre.

But he was not idle at either of these places, although the
ordinary routine duties of a regimental officer's life did not
at all satisfy him, and he longed to get into " staff-employ,"
which means being detached from the regiment for special
duties, and being entrusted with the civil and political government of the country.

Study, and
passes in
three
languages.

This was the line for which he desired to fit himself. He
worked resolutely in studying the different languages of
India. He passed in the Hindee, Hindoostanee, and Persian
languages; and in November, 1845, he passed " the Inter-
preter's " examination. All these languages were new to him
before he left England, for he had never turned his attention
to India. But he studied diligently every day with his
moonshee, Sudda Sookh, and did not stop short of pro-
ficiency.

At intervals of leisure he would help in the regimental
theatre (for the amusement of the men), of which he was the
" manager," and would paint the scenes with his own hand
(no slight effort in the hot season); and once, he writes, " I

* Kurnál was afterwards abandoned by the order of Sir Charles
Napier, commander-in-chief, who considered it unhealthy for the troops.

stood six hours a day depicting cottage scenes and lordly castles of the land we still call 'home,' on immense sheets of canvas," at Kurnál, in July, 1842, and took two parts in two different plays at the same time. The consequence of this was a fever that obliged him to take "leave" to Simla, in September. He was dangerously ill, and nearly died. *Fever, and sick leave to Simla.*

His ready wit, wonderfully retentive memory, and powers of oratory, gave him great capacity for these displays of talent; and the amusement to his brother officers and the men was great. To his friend Cowley Powles he writes—

"They may talk of Lord Grey's exertions, but think of a small ensign being slapped on the back with a side-scene, and desired to rise up 'Grand Duke Alexander, brother of the Emperor!' Oh dear me! this is a bad time of the year 'to have honour thrust upon me!' Already has one letter informed you of my theatrical triumphs in the asthmatic and crutch-line as Sir Anthony Absolute; and now while I stand upright, I unroll the seven and twenty towels which gave people to understand that there is gout in the neighbourhood, take off servitude in fact, and don the iron youth of a *Russian autocrat!* I know how it will all end, so write you this last letter—a legacy, and, after that, going to pieces like barley-sugar in a tea-cup, and being swabbed up carefully and sent home to my afflicted relations in a pail. . . .

"And so you think that tidings of you and the good people of Oxford will have no interest for me at the distance of sixteen thousand miles? My dear Powles, I would fain that the same epistle which I am now writing may give you half the pleasure, though that is a poor word, which the bare sight of yours—the recognition of the familiar hand, through all the vile attempts of posts and postmasters to blot it out —communicated to me two days ago when it arrived. But I fear, nay, I *hope*, you cannot understand it. I *know* you will be glad right heartily to tear open another from me;

but, after all, it will be nothing but a *letter*. To me your letter is the fabled horse (not a wooden one) which traverses space in an instant, and sets me down beside you with all familiar things and familiar faces round about you. You know nothing of my habits here, my whereabouts, my every-day οἰκονομί which gives identity to things long after they are out of sight, and when I write to you it is only as if I paid you a visit; you write to me, and I find not only a friend, but a *home*, for so it is in my memory, full of sun-shiny recollections without one single shadow interspersed among them.

"I met with a song the other day. Excuse my copying a verse of it in here—

> "'But when we meet with older years
>   And sadder times that tell
> How sorrowless were those sweet tears
>   Which in our childhood fell,
> Oh, then we feel our own dear land
>   Has some deep charm where'er we roam,
> And *sadly press the stranger's hand*
>   *Who left, like us, his native home!*'

"I know not by whom it was written, but I know that a year ago I should have written 'stuff!' against it; but I shall not do so now. . . . I have been but three months in India, and I know what the last lines mean very well.

"Now, your letter was such a *stranger* to me: you see what I mean? Mine cannot be so to you."

Thoughts of home.

About this time must he have been writing the following lines, which seem to express a similar thought—

> "It was a childish wish of mine
>   To make the earth an evergreen,
> And play all day in warm sunshine,
>   Where winter's face is never seen.

> "I wished to fill the summer trees
>   With poet-birds, like those who sing
> In Eastern Isles, where every breeze
>   Flies back to heaven carolling.

" I long to dwell where spices breathe,
    And lose myself in orange-groves,
Whose gentle task it is to wreathe
    A crown for every maid who loves.

" For I had read that pleasant tale
    Which comes from Araby the blest,
And till I spread the wandering sail
    My foolish heart would not have rest.

" Now, granted is that wish of mine,
    I've found a land that's ever green,
And dwell for aye in bright sunshine,
    Where cold and shade are never seen.

" And are my days all happy now ?
    Youth's dream is life's reality ?
Are there no clouds upon my brow
    Because there are none in the sky ?

" And do I love the matin scream
    Of gaudy parrots in the glade ?
Or nightly mingling in my dream
    The little bul-bul's * serenade ?

" Sing not to me, thou merry bird ;
    Thy song is but an Eastern tale,
I'd give it for the simplest word
    Of England's gentle nightingale.

                              " H. B. E."

Again, in his journey up the country, Edwardes, writing
to the same friend, makes some remarks that might read a
lesson in these days of advocacy of cremation.

" The earth is very prodigal here in her fruits, and
scatters them alike in the paths of the fat baboo and the
skinny pariah ; but you will hardly believe that, day by day
on my journey up the Ganges, I have seen the victims of
this abundance brought down in crowds to die like dogs
near 'the holy river,' or be reduced to ashes by the pious
hands of their relations. . . .

" They have all, or nearly all, died of cholera, and a young
European cannot get a better lesson than he may from these
disgusting obsequies ; though truly, it is getting sermons

        * The Indian nightingale.

from *stones*, for of all men, I suppose the Oriental looks on these things with the greatest apathy. Men swarm, and death is rife; and it seems an everyday thing for them to stretch the limbs of some friend's or relation's corpse.

"I have watched them with my glass throughout the whole process, from laying the first stick of wood to kindling the pile, and seldom indeed have I seen anything which betrayed sorrow or that sort of love which *we* feel for the dead, which shrinks from familiarity with the object and stand aloof as from something belonging to a being more sacred than ourselves. . . .

"I dare say the Utilitarian thinks it well that after death the relation should emerge into the scavenger, and earth be purged as *quick* as may be of what no longer honours it; but I pity the man who would teach us such a creed, and make this *intellectual* age look on their household dead as blots to be washed out, instead of spots to be held sacred in memory."

In these letters may be seen something of the sprightly wit and temper of the writer, and at the same time of the tender gentleness of thought and feeling which distinguished him even as a boy, and was conspicuous in him as a man.

He returned from Simla to Kurnâl, October 20, 1842. His regiment was intended by Lord Ellenborough to join the Army of Reserve, but, Generals Nott and Pollock having returned from Cabul, the Army of Reserve was not wanted and was broken up.

Regiment moves to Subâthoo.

Edwardes's regiment was afterwards moved to Subâthoo, a station in the Himalayan Mountains, on the old road to and not far from Simla, which is the head-quarters of the Government in India in the hot season.

Desires staff-employ.

Books were Edwardes's chief pleasure and his chief recreation. He had friends, and warm ones, too; for he was the life and soul of every society he was in. But India was a sad place to him in those days; for it seemed to open no field in the larger sphere of political work, which he desired, and he felt himself a stranger still.

His chief pleasure was in showing kindness and sympathy to every one who came in his way and needed it—a pleasure which cheered and lighted up his life then, and in all its subsequent stages.

He had always a heart to sympathize and a hand to stretch out to every one in trouble, and many were the prayers that went up to bless him, even when he was only a subaltern with his regiment.

That he was *fitted* for the larger sphere of "political" life that he desired, he showed at this time by writing "The Brahminee Bull Letters."

"The Brahminee Bull Letters," 1815.

These were letters written, of course anonymously, and printed in an ordinary weekly newspaper, the *Delhi Gazette*. They were entitled "Brahminee Bull's Letters in India to his Cousin John Bull in England," and dealt largely and freely with the military questions of the day, then under anxious discussion, relating to our unfortunate disasters in Cabul— the old Cabul War of 1838–1839—all its mistakes, its follies, and its sins, as well as with all questions concerning England's relation with India, and kindred subjects.

These letters attracted great attention, and were looked for eagerly from week to week from one end of India to the other. They were considered to show so much *experience in the field*, as well as so much sagacity and talent, that it was supposed they *could* only be written by some old and long-tried soldier; and Edwardes was often amused at a mess-table, to hear them discussed and well-known names suggested as their author; but he kept his own counsel, and he was not discovered until he chose to reveal their real authorship.

That the author was a young subaltern (still only a lieutenant), with his regiment at a quiet station where he had never had any opportunity of seeing service in the field, no one had ever guessed.

It was reading these letters that first interested Captain Henry Lawrence (then Resident at Nepâl) in their author. He watched for them from week to week, and read them with delight. But it was long before he could discover who wrote them. And when Henry Lawrence was called upon shortly after to take the post of Resident at the Sikh Court at Lahore,

Henry Lawrence appointed Resident at Lahore.

he looked about to find Lieutenant Edwardes, and get him to work with him in his new post.

The vicinity of Subâthoo gave Edwardes frequent occasions of visiting Simla, and these visits afforded him an opportunity of being introduced to Sir Hugh Gough. This was quickly followed by his Excellency making him an aide-de-camp on his personal staff.

Appointed A.D.C. to the Commander-in-chief, 1845.

To this Edwardes always gratefully acknowledged he was indebted for his first step in advancement.

But he had not held this post for many weeks when Henry Lawrence arrived, on his way from Nepâl to take up his new appointment of Resident, wishing to confer with the Governor-General, who was at that time at Simla.

First meeting with Henry Lawrence.

Here Henry Lawrence and Herbert Edwardes first met, and Lawrence soon prevailed with Sir Hugh Gough to give up his new aide-de-camp, and with Sir Henry Hardinge to appoint Edwardes to be one of his Assistants at Lahore.

Asks for Edwardes to be transferred to be his assistant, 1846.

Edwardes had only time to serve with Sir Hugh Gough as his aide-de-camp at the battles of Moodkee and Sobrâon, before taking up the new post at Lahore.

CHAPTER II.

—◆—

1845—1846.

SIKH INVASION OF BRITISH INDIA—BATTLES OF MOODKEE AND SOBRÂON—TREATY OF BYROWÂL.

"Blessed is he who has found his work. Let him ask no other blessedness. He has a work—a life-purpose; he has found it, and will follow it."—CARLYLE'S *Past and Present*.

CHAPTER II.

In November, 1845, Edwardes was selected by Sir Hugh Gough to become aide-de-camp on his personal staff, and on December 11, in the same year, the Sikhs crossed the Sutlej and invaded British India.

"And how was British India prepared to meet them?[*] Suffice it to say that when, after years of empty boasting, the Sikhs at last came as enemies across the Sutlej, they found fifteen thousand more soldiers between that river and Meerut than had been left there by any of Lord Hardinge's predecessors.

The Sikh invasion of British India.

"Now we see the wisdom of the Governor-General's cautious policy. Slowly and silently and by degrees he added to the regiments and gathered them together, and silently strengthened his positions, anxious to avert war, but determined to be ready. Sir Henry Hardinge was something more than an old and experienced soldier, snuffing, like the war-horse, the battle from afar, and preparing for it with exultation. He was the statesman to whose calm and unimpassioned judgment it was given to preserve the peace of India, and he chose that middle course which, the result has proved, united the dignity of forbearance with the necessity of defence.

Sir Henry Hardinge's policy: not to seek war, but to be ready if it came.

"Troops were not massed into an army on the frontier, because this would have rendered *inevitable* the collision

[*] We quote from Herbert Edwardes's own pen.

which Sir Henry Hardinge, his Council, and his Agent on the north-west frontier (Major Henry Lawrence) hoped and believed to be an improbable contingency. . . .

"But the troops, which a wise Governor had spread in peaceful attitude over the surface of the north-west provinces, were yet within bugle-call, and could be summoned to arms in time to repel an enemy. Hitherto Sir Henry Hardinge had been slow, cautious, forbearing almost to timidity; as if peace were a strange but imperative duty that had been imposed on him."

Peace
changed to
war. "The crossing of the Sikhs was like the magic word which woke the Seven Sleepers. It broke the spell upon his nature and disenchanted him. The cold snows of age and prudence melted and disappeared before the rekindled fire and energy of the hero of Albuera; the identity of the accomplished statesman passed away and left a military leader in its place, presiding over the army of the Sutlej.

> "'Telemachus suddenly beheld Minerva,
> She spread her ægis over him!'

"Well was the ardour of the Governor-General at this crisis seconded by the more than youthful energy and activity of the commander-in-chief, whose gallant figure, dashing by the column, was wont to provoke from many a young 'sub.' the hackneyed lines—

> "'Nor slack'd the messenger his pace;
> He show'd the sign, he named the place —
> And, pressing forward like the wind,
> Left clamour and surprise behind.
>
> *   *   *   *
>
> He vanished;—and o'er moor and moss
> Sped forward on the fiery cross!'

Sir Henry
Hardinge a
soldier-
statesman. "It is, however, but just to say that a Governor-General only, and such a Governor-General as Sir Henry Hardinge, happily combining the statesman with the soldier, could have brought the whole resources of the country at a

moment's notice to bear upon the most imminent danger
that has ever threatened British India."

And here it may be well to take a glance at the state of
things in the Sikh kingdom which had brought about this
first Sikh War, after the death of Runjeet Singh, when his
heir was a child and the Queen-mother was regent.

An article written by Edwardes * at this date is full of
interest, and supplies us with many a picture of the events
of these times, when the bold and desperate games of the
reckless Sirdars closed in repeated tragedies,

"and the army became the real rulers, in the (nominal) *Sketch of affairs in the Sikh kingdom.*
government of the Punjab. . . . Trampling upon the
Constitution, they acknowledged no law but their own
interests; and to protect those, combined together, with a
greater singleness of purpose than ever dignified the efforts
of the Mamelukes, the Janissaries, or the Prætorians of the
ancient world. . . . The moving spirit of the rebellion was
undoubtedly the Ráni.† . . . Her infatuation at this crisis *The Ráni at Lahore.*
was complete. Instead of looking around her for some
bold spirits who would seize with vigorous hand the helm
of Government, she threw it, as if it were a bauble, to
Jowahir Singh, her brother, a weak, vain, besotted de-
bauchee.

"She herself plunged into a round of festivities and
voluptuousness with a paramour whom she was now at
liberty to honour. The Court joined in the drunken revels;
and none perceived that, while the Ministry were thus
celebrating the revolution, the Army had stepped into the
Government and appropriated the power.

"The Sikh soldiers now rioted at will; took furlough *The Sikh soldiers.*
to their homes when they liked, and returned as it suited
them; governed themselves and their officers by a parliament of their own, chosen from the ranks; obeyed no other

* In the *Calcutta Review.*   † The Queen-Mother.

orders, overawed the Government, and set the laws at defiance.

"The idiot minister, Jowahir Singh, they openly insulted, with expressions of contempt for his imbecility and drunkenness, and loudly called for Lehna Singh to replace him in the Wizárut. . . . It might be supposed that such a state of things would soon induce so complete a disorganization that the army must dissolve, and disperse over the country in marauding bands. But nothing of the kind occurred. On the contrary, it was the civil and social system which was torn asunder; the executive Government, which was threatened with dissolution; while the army itself, riotous and disorderly to all else around, was only drawn more firmly and compactly together by the bond of mutual interest.

"The very name which they at this time arrogated to themselves, 'Sûrbut-i-Khâlsa Jí,' or, the body of the Khâlsa, breathes the spirit of exclusiveness and unanimity.

"Their acts, wild and bad as they were, were drawn into the focus of a single object; and thus, while plunder and violence were rife at the capital, the provinces were left unmolested, except by their own governors. . . . Rebellion was so regulated that it might be almost called an institution, and military licence had yet its bounds reducing it to conditional liberty.

"Woe indeed to the wretch who disobeyed the will of the *nation!* Expulsion from the ranks, mutilation of a hand, an ear, a nose—even *death* awaited him. Mutiny was the condition of their existence; the Government, the Sirdars, and their own immediate officers, were their proscribed enemies; and the Treasury was their open aim. But to gain these ends, sure never was a debauched army so consistent in its conduct!"

We have not room, nor is it our purpose, to follow all the intrigues of the Lahore Court.

The Sikh Army usurps the place of Government.

"Ministers in the Punjab do not *resign* when they have 'lost the confidence of the people;' nor are they coldly told that 'their services are not required' when they have lost the confidence of the sovereign. In either case, the removal is complete—into another world. The unhappy woman, therefore, could not have blinded herself as to the inevitable tendency of her intrigues."

And now Jowahir Singh was to be the victim.

"On September 1, they led him out in state to the Plain of Mean Meer, and, in the presence of his sister and the Maharajah, he was shot down like a dog. So died the last and the worst Wazir of the Punjab Empire established by Runjeet Singh. Râni Junda evinced some natural affection and remarkable courage on the occasion. She even effected the punishment of the ringleaders in the late tragedy; and, as if roused by her brother's death and her son's danger, assumed the government, sat openly in Durbar, and 'laid aside her debaucheries with her veil.'" ("Papers," p. 10.)

"But the time for prudence had gone by. The vessel of the State, too long unwatched, had drifted to the rapids' edge; and all that skill and courage now could do was to seize the helm, put the barque's head straight, and plunge boldly into the foaming gulf. Finding that it was hopeless to oppose the army, the Râni wisely yielded, encouraged its excesses, called its madness reason, and urged it on in the hope of guiding it to destruction. History scarcely records a conception more bold and able; and while reprobating its unprincipled execution, we cannot withhold our admiration at the design. Runjeet Singh, in the zenith of his power, thought all sacrifices light to preserve the friendship of the British; Râni Junda, in the depth of her despair, when the Sikh nation was at its weakest, sought safety in a war with British India. . . . On December 11,

The Râni Regent yields to the soldiers,

and decides on war with British India.

1845, the enemy crossed the Sutlej and invaded British India. . . .

"Next morning commenced the march on which the fate of two empires hung.

March of the army towards Moodkee. "The whole road from Umballa to Rajpúra, a distance of sixteen miles, was covered with advancing troops and artillery; and the green crops in the fields, on either side of the line of march, were trodden under foot and scattered over by strings of baggage camels and camp followers, who, unable to find room upon the old highway, soon made a new one for themselves, and scrambled on in the dark through gardens and over ditches in a style more sporting than military.

"What a motley and amusing scene is an Indian line of march!

Description of an Indian line of march. "Here, Jack Sepoy, bitterly cold, has tied up his head like a stage-coach traveller, and then stuck his full dress chako on the top of it, much askew. Behind him, rejoicing in the privilege of his rank, jogs along on a miserable bare-ribbed tattú,* a grey-haired súbadar; his very oldest clothes are put on economically for the occasion, but round his throat glitters through the dust his gold-beaded necklace, and on his left breast, perhaps, dangles on a ribbon twice too long, a medal or a star. Next, covering the whole column with dust, canters by, a devil-may-care subaltern, his forage cap cocked knowingly over his ear, and under him the best Bombay Arab that could be got for money, though it would not carry his bills. 'Bless my soul, sir,' croaks a wheezy voice on the other side of the road, 'how often *must* I tell you to keep that beast in the rear?' It is the fat major, who has pulled up in his buggy to spit the ensign's dust out of his mouth and knuckle it out of his eyes.

"On one side of the road a hackery † has fallen in the dark into a ditch, and on the other, a gun. The former

* Pony.   † Native cart.

will be there half the day; for the driver is smoking his
hookah, and waiting till Providence sends some one to help
him.   The other will be all right in ten minutes; for a
dozen strapping Horse Artillerymen have 'put their shoulders
to the wheel,' and are hauling away to a jolly chorus.
Chaque pays, chaque mode!

"Look at that half-clad, knock-kneed wretch shuffling
along at one untiring pace, with a pliant bamboo over his
shoulder, and at either end of it a heavy green box, slung
by ropes. He is a 'banghy-bearer,' and you may take an
inventory of his load without opening the pitârahs; one of
them is always devoted to a guthrí,* and the other to plates,
dishes, and a teapot; for woe betide the khidmutgar who
has not breakfast ready the moment the regiment comes
upon its ground.

"But mind your head, or it will be knocked off by that
half-mad camel, who is overladen with tents and 'tots,'†
and is dancing about the road, furious at the clattering on
his back.

"That red-haired grenadier with the yellow facings is
one of the gallant 9th Foot, and if what he is now swearing
at the camel was not pure Irish, there could not be a doubt
about his country; for at the end of his bayonet he has
slung his boots, and is walking barefoot 'to warm himself.'

"Whose hackery is that with a slipper-bath in it?
There are no ladies in camp.   It belongs to one of the
hospitals, and those three black heads poking out at the
mouth of the bath are the hospital cook's children, who live
in it when it isn't wanted.   Such are some of the queer
incidents and characteristic scenes which cheat the soldier
of a laugh on the Indian line of march.   But let us resume
our knapsack and march on.

* *Guthrí*, the Indian *vade mecum* — a bundle containing a change
of clothes and something of everything that " master possesses."
† *Tots*, tin pots, out of which the European soldiers drink.

An omen.

"For the benefit of those who have a lingering faith in omens, we may as well record here that just before morning broke, on the march to Moodkee, a brilliant star shot from its place in the firmament and fell over the Sutlej, into the dark grave of the earth's horizon. The 'Bright Star' is the highest order in the Punjab, and those who think that the everlasting laws of stellar motion are disturbed by the convulsions of this little orb, imperceptible in space, may confirm their superstition with the coincidence. It is

How fulfilled.

'stranger still,' and much more to the point, that on December 2 died the venerable Fakeer Uzíz-úd-dín, the able minister of Runjeet Singh, and faithful follower of his policy in all the counsels he was called upon to give to the weak successors of his master. He knew our power thoroughly, and his voice was ever for friendship and peace. The last act of his life was a remonstrance against the approaching war; and, without superstition, with him may be said to have perished the genius of the Punjab. . . .

"Three miles from Moodkee, the first indication of the proximity of an enemy reached the army of the Sutlej.

George Broadfoot.

"A note from Major Broadfoot, ever in the front, informed the commander-in-chief that Moodkee was occupied by the Sikhs, in what force it was uncertain.

"Upon receipt of this intelligence, the column was halted, the Artillery ordered to the front, and the Cavalry to support it right and left. Thus 'squaring up,' in pugilistic phrase, the army resumed its march, with intense anxiety looking for the enemy.

"The commander-in-chief, attended by his own staff and that of the Governor-General (made over to him by Sir Henry Hardinge, who reluctantly remained behind), and supported by two squadrons of the 5th Light Cavalry, then made a reconnoissance in front, and soon met Major Broadfoot and a party of Christie's Horse coming back, a little downcast with the tidings that the village now coming into

view had merely been occupied by the advanced picket
of the Khâlsa Army, who had fallen back hastily upon their
own main body; not, however, without carrying off Captain
E. Biddulph, of the 45th Native Infantry, who had the
evening before got so far on his way in a gallant but impru-
dent attempt to join Tait's Irregulars at Ferozepore.

"The momentary excitement over, the weary, foot-sore
troops dragged themselves on to Moodkee, which they
reached at noon; and what a welcome sight then met their
view! Beneath the walls of the fort spread a wide, clear
tank of water; and the reader who has not the memory of
that long march of twenty-one miles, with heavy sand under-
foot and the air thick with dust, disturbed by fifteen
thousand men, cannot paint the eagerness with which men
and horses rushed to the bank, and tried to slake a thirst
which seemed unquenchable.

Halt and refresh-ment.

"In ten minutes the lake was a mass of floating mud,
yet fresh regiments kept coming up, and fresh thirsty souls
kept squeezing their way in, and thinking it was the
sweetest draught they had tasted in their lives. Between
two and three o'clock, the baggage of the troops was
beginning to struggle in, and the men to cook their
breakfast, when Major Broadfoot again galloped into camp
with the news—this time true enough—that the enemy was
advancing in force in front.

"Away with knives and forks, and out with swords and
pistols! Camels, elephants, camp-followers, and other lumber
to the rear! Trumpets sound to horse; bugles, drums and
fifes to arms; and the whole army, which but two hours
ago had made a march of unusual severity, now turned out,
as if fully recruited, to the battle. . . .

How soon disturbed !

"Once more the Governor-General, with a courteous bow
that would have done honour to St. James's, waved his
dashing staff over to the brave chief of that brave army,
and then fell back upon the Infantry.

"The Artillery was in the centre of the front line, and the Cavalry on either flank; the main body of the Infantry, in contiguous columns behind, and a reserve in rear of all. A mile and a half at least from their own camp did the British advance in this order before they came under the fire of the Sikh guns; but then the 'long bowls' came bounding in among them with deadly aim and that peculiar *whirr* which makes the young soldier bob his head. Now tumbrils begin blowing up, and Artillerymen dropping from their saddles; the mutual roar of cannon reverberates over the plain, and smoke obscures the vision. Closer and closer approach the hostile armies; and a staff officer, almost simultaneously from right and left, gallops up to Sir Hugh, with a report that the Sikh Cavalry in clouds are turning both his flanks. Right and left he launches his own Cavalry upon them; right and left their brilliant charge makes the enemy's Horse give way. The British Infantry deploy and advance rapidly in line. A finer sight no man ever saw than that deployment and advance. The jaded men, worn out with forced marches and want of food, forgot all their troubles in their eagerness to close, and nearly the whole of an unusually large staff might at one time have been employed in galloping up and down the line to keep the regiments from doubling into action.

"And now all hands are at it! Cavalry charging cavalry, Artillery thundering on the flanks, and Infantry exchanging a roar of musketry in the centre. The battle is at its height; it rages; but the British *still advance;* and it is a fact, which has not been noticed by any writer yet that we have seen, not even by his Excellency the commander-in-chief in his own despatch, *that the charge of the British Cavalry was the turning-point* of the battle of Moodkee. Up to that moment every arm of the Sikh force, Cavalry, Artillery, and Infantry, had been *advancing*; and though the Artillery and Infantry still stood and struggled manfully after Lal Singh's cavalry had fled, *yet they never* gained another foot of ground, and the last two hours of battle were a series of dogged stands and skirmishing retreats on the part of the Sikh troops, of sharp struggles, gun captures, and pursuits by the British, over five miles of the worst ground that ever two armies fought for. Night closed the contest, or rather the pursuit, and the British army was left in possession of the field and nineteen of the enemy's guns.

"Thus ended the battle of Moodkee, and the victory of December 18, 1845, must be acknowledged to have been no mean achievement. It is no easy matter, at any time, for fourteen thousand men to thrash between thirty and forty thousand; nevertheless, as was the case in our early Indian battles, the discipline was all on the side of the minority. Those days have long passed away. We have now been teaching the art of war to Asia for upwards of a century; and though not exactly reduced to the sad pass of that celebrated grandfather who taught his grandson draughts, 'until at last the old man got beaten by the boy,' yet there is no longer that vast disparity between the discipline of the native and British Indian armies that we can afford to give them, as of old, the odds which Clive thought very fair at Plassy."

Unequal numbers.

It was at this battle of Moodkee, when carrying Sir Hugh Gough's orders to recall the flank detachments back to their line, that Edwardes was severely wounded by a bullet through his thigh.

Edwardes wounded.

The following incident will be worth recording, as illustrating the feeling of brotherhood and kindness of which Edwardes has written in the former chapter *—one of those tender things to which even the stern scenes of a battle-field can often bear witness.

Edwardes was riding along, on this occasion, on a line

* At end of chap. i.

chesnut Arab charger that he had lately bought. The
blood was streaming from his thigh, and he was getting
faint, when he met a friend and brother officer * who
stopped him, and said, " Edwardes, you are badly wounded ;
get on a gun-carriage, and go into hospital. You can't ride
off the field." " No," said Edwardes ; " if I throw the reins on
my Ruby's neck, I shall never see him again. I will ride
on." And his friend, in a moment, tore off the long turban
he had twisted round and round his helmet, and bound up
his thigh with it to staunch the bleeding—no trifling act at
such a time, and in the midst of the exposure of a battle-
field on the plains of India.

A friend on
the battle-
field.

With help of this, Edwardes rode safely off the field, and
went into hospital for his wounds.

As it is not our purpose to write a history of the Sikh
War, but only to touch upon those points and events of it in
which our biography is concerned, we need not pursue the
subject further than to tell, that when the second battle
(Ferozeshah) was fought, Edwardes was still in hospital ; but
he was sufficiently recovered to take part in the battle of
Sobrâon, which closed the Sikh campaign.

He writes—

A final
contest ap-
proaches.

" It was yet dark, on the morning of February 10th, 1846,
when the army of the Sutlej moved out at last from their
lines at Nialki, and advanced to a final contest with the
invading Khâlsa.

" Halfway between the British outpost at Rhodawâla
and the Sikh camp stood three trees, the only ones upon
the plain. In the upper branches of these trees, the Sikhs
had erected munchâns, or platforms, for sentries to sit in, and
watch the movements of our troops at Rhodawâla.

" A deep ditch and bank were thrown round the spot,

---

* The name of this officer deserves to be recorded. But alas! he is
gone from amongst us, and in a sad and cruel way. He was the Colonel
Holmes who, with his wife, was shot by his own men whom he trusted,
during the Mutiny of 1857. His wife was the daughter of Lady Sale.
Both were driving together in an open carriage, when one of his own
troopers rode up and shot them both dead, without a warning.

and it was easy to see from the British outpost that the place was strongly occupied during the day.

"About half a mile to the right of the muchâns was the village of Little Sobrâon; and here also the enemy had posted a strong picket within an entrenchment. It was necessary to drive in both these pickets before Sir Hugh Gough could push forward his heavy guns within range of the great Sikh entrenchment, and when detachments of her Majesty's 62nd Foot stole cautiously down upon them in the darkness and mist of the morning, they were both found unoccupied, and were taken possession of without firing. It was afterwards ascertained that these posts were held during the day, and abandoned after dark in the evening; and this circumstance, added to a thick fog which deferred the dawn, was very favourable to the British, enabling the commander-in-chief to bring up his several divisions in order of battle, and post his Artillery without any alarm to the enemy, in whose camp might plainly be heard the light song and rolling note of the nukaruh,* which told of deep and false security.

"Sir Hugh Gough's plan of attack was as follows:—The heavy guns were to commence operations by a cannonade upon the entrenchment, into which, crowded as it was with upwards of thirty thousand men, their fire was expected to carry confusion and dismay. Sir Robert Dick's division, on the extreme left of the British line, was then to advance and storm the right or western corner of the Sikh position; General Gilbert's division, on the centre, and Sir Harry Smith's division, on the right, were simultaneously to make false attacks, with the view of diverting the enemy's attention from the real attack of Sir Robert Dick.

"Brigadier Cureton, with a brigade of Cavalry and a troop of Horse Artillery, was directed to threaten the ford of Hurrikí Puttun, about a mile distant from the eastern

The battle of Sobrâon.

* A kettledrum.

corner of the entrenchment, on the opposite bank of which the enemy's Cavalry were posted.

"Agreeably to this plan, at about seven o'clock a.m. the Artillery opened; the fog rolled off, as if it were a curtain, and the surprised Khâlsa at once heard and saw that the avenger had come upon them. In an instant the Sikh drums beat to arms, and many rounds had not been fired from the British guns before an answering thunder from the entrenchment told that the works were manned and the struggle had begun.

(margin) The struggle begins.

"At nine o'clock the Artillery officers reported that the ammunition of the heavy guns was well nigh expended; and it is a fact that when Sir Robert Dick was hastily ordered to advance, he moved up in the face of a furious cannonade from the enemy, and under *cover of a slackened fire* from his own side. (This was not the fault of the Artillery officers, who had prepared as many rounds as the shortness of the time between the arrival of the guns and the battle would permit.)

"The attack was led by Brigadier Stacy, with her Majesty's 10th and 53rd Regiments, and the 43rd and 59th Native Infantry, supported on the flanks by Captains Horsford and Fordyce's batteries, and Lieutenant-Colonel Lane's troop of Horse Artillery.

"Beyond all comparison, this was the finest attack of the campaign.

"The Field Artillery galloped up and delivered their fire within three hundred yards of the enemy's batteries; and the Infantry charged home with the bayonet, and carried the outworks without firing a single round—'a forbearance,' says the Governor-General, 'much to be commended, and most worthy of constant imitation.' As it was the finest attack, so also did it meet with the most determined hand-to-hand resistance which the Khâlsa soldiers had yet opposed to the British.

" Like lightning, the real plan of the attack seemed to flash on the minds of all the desperate men in that entrenchment, and, disregarding the distant feints of Gilbert's and Smith's divisions on their left and centre, they rushed to the right to repel the real danger that was upon them.

" In vain Stacy's brigade tries to withstand the mass, which every moment is growing denser; in vain Wilkinson's brigade comes up to the support; in vain Ashburnham's reserve swells the furious tide of the assault. It was like the meeting of two mighty rivers, one swifter and one deeper than the other; and as the swifter for a moment penetrates its duller neighbour's stream, then, yielding to the overpowering waters, is rolled back and swept away, so would the conquered trenches of the Sikhs have been wrested again from the brave division of the British had not Sir Hugh, with the intuitive quickness of a general's eye, marked the crisis and the struggle, foreseen its issue, The crisis. and ordered up Gilbert's and Smith's divisions to the rescue. They advanced; the enemy beheld it, and, returning tumultuously to the posts they had abandoned, poured upon these new enemies from every foot of the entrenchment a destructive fire of grape, round shot, and musketry.

" In spite, however, of a loss unprecedented in so short a time, these two indomitable divisions persevered in storming what proved to be the strongest part of the enemy's position ; and the entrenchment being thus carried by the British at three different points, the gunners, who drew their swords when they could no longer fire, were bayoneted beside the guns they had so murderously served, while the Cavalry and Infantry, driven from three sides into a confused and disordered mass, but fighting to the last, were inch by inch forced to retreat where alone retreat was possible.

" Preferring death to surrender, they recklessly plunged

Death pre-
ferred to
surrender. into the river. The bridge of which they were so proud, and to which they had so confidently trusted, broke down under the first party of flying horsemen, and became impassable; while the Sutlej, having risen seven inches in the night, had flooded the ford. 'In their efforts to reach the right bank,' says the graphic narrative of the commander-in-chief, 'through the deepened water, they suffered from our Horse Artillery a terrible carnage.'

"Hundreds fell under this cannonade; hundreds upon hundreds were drowned in attempting the perilous passage. Their awful slaughter, confusion, and dismay were such as would have excited compassion in the hearts of their generous conquerors, if the Khâlsa troops had not, in the earlier part of the action, sullied their gallantry by slaughtering and barbarously mangling every wounded soldier whom, in the vicissitudes of attack, the fortune of war left at their mercy.

"Sixty-seven pieces of cannon, upwards of two hundred camel-swivels, numerous standards, and vast munitions of war were left in possession of the victors." ("Papers," p. 77.)

"At half-past ten o'clock p.m. not a Sikh soldier was left alive upon the British bank of the Sutlej; and thus, in little more than four hours, was fought the bloodiest battle, The victory
complete. with the worthiest foe, and gained the completest victory, recorded in our Eastern annals. . . .

"Thus ended, also, in awful and disastrous tragedy, the Sikh invasion of British India. On the side of the British there were killed 320, and wounded 3063. . . .

"The very *lowest* estimate of the Sikh loss is eight thousand; we have heard survivors of that routed host lament the death of *twice* that number. And those who, in cooler mood, when the unsparing passions of war were still, revisited next day the silent battle-field, and looked into those trenches where their dead defenders lay in heaps; or saw the Sutlej fords choked with human bodies, and its swelling waters still covered with bloody garments and the wreck of a great army—recalling in awful vividness the mind's picture of God's last judgment upon Pharaoh—will remember the spectacle of destruction to the last day they have to live. . . .

"The Governor-General, though suffering from a severe fall, and after riding all day about the field, returned to Ferozepore on the afternoon of the 10th, within a few hours after the action had ceased, to superintend the passage of the Sutlej by our troops." ("Papers," p. 68.)

"Six regiments of Native Infantry crossed the Sutlej that very evening. Our troops cross the Sutlej.

"The commander-in-chief broke up his camp next day and marched to Utari; and on the 14th the whole army of the Sutlej was encamped at Kussúr, in the Punjab, within thirty miles of the capital. . . .

"That evening there arrived from Lahore a strange triumphal procession of three elephants and a buggy, loaded with European prisoners, who had been taken by the Sikhs in the affair of Buddowál, and now sent in by Golâb Singh as a peace-offering to the victors, at whose feet his country was prostrate. Deputies from Lahore had arrived at Ferozepore, and peaceably demanded an audience of the Governor-General two days before the battle of Sobráon. They were told with becoming dignity that *they would be received after the battle.* On the 11th they had the audience they desired, posted back to Lahore, and returned again to the British camp at Kussúr. They were followed, on the 14th, by Rajah Golâb Singh, Dewan Dinanáth, and Fakeer Núr-úd-dín, with full credentials from the Maharajah, and empowered to agree, in the name of the Maharajah and the Government, to such terms as the Governor-General might dictate." ("Papers," p. 68.) The Sikhs sue for terms of peace.

"'I received the Rajah in Durbar,' writes the Governor-General himself, 'as the representative of an offending

Government, omitting the forms and ceremonies usually
observed on the occasion of friendly meetings, and refusing
to receive, at that time, the proffered nûzzurs and com-
plimentary offerings.'" ("Papers," p. 68.)

Complete
submission.
"Thus humbled, the chiefs were handed over to the
chief secretary and Governor-General's Agent, Mr. Currie and
Major Henry Lawrence, to learn their fate. Closeted with
these, they remained the greater part of the night in conference; but before they separated, a paper was signed by
them to the effect that all that had been demanded would
be conceded." ("Papers," p. 69.)

"On the 17th, the Maharajah himself came in to make
his submission; but the Governor-General had appointed
the meeting to be at Lullcâni, ten miles further on, and
Alexander was in no haste to see Darius humbled. An
account of the interview is given in the 'Papers' so often
quoted (p. 70), and all that is essential to note here is, that
the offending sovereign came in disgrace, and went away in
honour. Negotiations stopped not the advance of the
British army, which, unopposed, pushed on to the capital.
The Sikh army, indeed, was broken in every sense, body
and soul. Some eight or ten thousand—doubled, quad-
rupled by report—still held together, about twenty miles
from Lahore, but herding rather like frightened deer than
Khâlsa warriors. The *invaders were invaded;* and those
who, in the intoxication of their pride, talked so lately of
carrying their baby-king to Delhi, had now not a sword to
draw in defence of their native land. . . .

"On February 20, the army of the Sutlej encamped on
the plains of Mean Meer, in the suburbs of Lahore, the
scene of Jowahir Singh's murder; and it is impossible not to
contrast *our* conduct in victory with what would have been
Con-
querors'
forbear-
ance and
discipline.
theirs had they reached the capital of Hindostan. We had
just cause, most assuredly, to feel resentment against a
people who had invaded our territories, and endangered

even the safety of British India; yet *there* might be seen our generals forbearingly encamped, three miles from the rich city which the fortune of war had placed at their mercy, and punishing with dismissal or flogging any soldier or camp-follower who dared to enter it for the gratification even of his curiosity.* And is there any one who doubts that if the Sikh army had been successsful at Moodkee or Ferozeshah, and penetrated as far as Delhi before another army could be brought to oppose them, the streets of the imperial city, though no longer offering the same gorgeous temptation to a lawless and greedy soldiery, would have run with the blood of the inhabitants and been as completely and brutally sacked as ever it was by the army of Nâdir Shâh? The lofty, dignified, and magnanimous attitude of the British army before Lahore did honour to the European character; and the forbearance of the troops, to British virtue and discipline. Proclamations were issued to calm the terrified people of the Punjab; and as one by one the chiefs and officers came in, they were received by all in the British camp with the kindness and consideration their gallantry deserved.

"Dark looks there were among them, bespeaking broken hopes and smothered longings for revenge; but oftener there was a subdued yet manly bearing, as free from boasting as from bending, which none could behold without admiration. In later days, this was more especially remarkable among the Sikh sepoys, who, coming to their pay-tables through or near our ranks, bore themselves with a soldierly resignation which could scarcely have been expected from the vaunting, conceited Khâlsa.

"The Durbars and the Treaties therein ratified; the stately restoration of the young Maharajah to his throne; and the leaving of a British force at Lahore, at the earnest

* See Government Order, Army of the Sutlej, of date February 20, 1846.

solicitation of a timid Ministry ;—is it not all put before the reader with graphic vividness in the minutes of Mr. Currie* and the despatches of the Governor-General (Lord Hardinge) ? . . .

"The country was at his feet, and few people, when they come to consider the details of the story, will deny that the Governor-General was wise to refrain from annexing the Punjab. To us his forbearance seems more than *wise;* it is eminently magnanimous, merciful, and patriotic." †

Treaty of
Byrowâl,
1846.

The Treaty of Byrowâl was ratified on March 11, 1846, and by this treaty the independence of the Punjab was prolonged, subject to the continued occupation by the British troops.

"The interposition of British influence," so the Governor-General declared in a subsequent despatch, "will be exercised for the advantage of the people, and the success of their interposition will be assisted by the confidence and cordiality with which the Sirdars will co-operate with the British Resident.

"That officer, Lieutenant-Colonel Henry Lawrence, is well known to the chiefs by his energy, talent, and integrity; by these qualities he has conciliated their good will and respect. . . .

"A Council of Regency, composed of leading chiefs, will act under the control and guidance of the British Resident.

"The Council will consist of eight Sirdars; and the members will not be changed without the consent of the British Resident, acting under the orders of the Governor-General.

"The power of the Resident extends over every depart-

---

* Afterwards Sir Frederick Currie.
† From Edwardes's article in the *Calcutta Review*, No. 46, "The Sikh Invasion of British India."

ment and to any extent. A military force may be placed in such forts and posts, and of such strength, within the Lahore territory, as the Governor-General may determine.

"The terms give the British Resident unlimited authority in all matters of internal administration and external relation during the Maharajah's minority, which would terminate on September 4, 1854." *

By this treaty Henry Lawrence was left, in all but the name, the reigning power of the magnificent realm of the "Five Rivers" (or Punjab), the ancient kingdom of Porus, the original "India" of the Greeks and Persians.

As regards the country, Mr. Arnold, in his "History of Lord Dalhousie's Administration of British India," thus sums up the results of Lord Hardinge's Government—

"Writing on the Ganges in the last month of 1847, the Governor-General was able to report the Punjab (to the Secret Committee) as perfectly tranquil; but for the perilous passions of the Queen-Mother, he could boast to make over the peninsula free from any disturbing cause. Our supremacy beyond the Sutlej was declared to be as real as if it were loaded with the real responsibilities of annexation." *Results of Lord Hardinge's arrangement.*

Well aware that the Sikhs were to be trusted only as far as they were under control, Lord Hardinge doubled the garrison of the north-west. He left on this side and on that side of the Sutlej more than fifty thousand men and sixty guns.

This digression seems necessary to explain the position of increased power and responsibility in the affairs of the Punjab at this time, and also to give a picture of the people and of the country in which Edwardes's lot is now cast.

Life has made a great stride with him. He is in stirring times, and invested with great responsibilities; and his was a nature that rejoiced in difficulties, and, when danger showed

---

* At this time the Jullundur Doâb was annexed, and Henry Lawrence made his brother John its Commissioner.

itself, seemed to spring up with even greater vigour, energy, and resource. He has now found the field he sought for, and it proved a training-ground for the after-life which follows.

Before this chapter is closed, that tells the story of the conquered Sikh nation, it may be of interest to quote from a local journal an account of the " Koh-i-noor " or Mountain of Light, the great jewel of the Lahore treasury, which fell, at the end of the Sikh Wars, into the possession of her Britannic Majesty ; for it seems by its history as if the Koh-i-noor carried with it the sovereignty of Hindostan.

It was consigned to the care of an English officer, Major Mackeson, to be brought home to the Queen ; and we quote from the *Times'* account of his arrival in England, July 1, 1850—

" Her Majesty's steam-sloop *Medea* has just arrived at Portsmouth, with a freight more precious, in nominal value, than was ever carried from Peru to Cadiz. Major Mackeson, one of her passengers, a meritorious and distinguished officer, brings with him that famous diamond of the East called, in the fondness of Asiatic hyperbole, the Koh-i-noor, or Mountain of Light, which after symbolizing the revolutions of ten generations by its passage from one conqueror to another, comes now, in the third centenary of its discovery, as the forfeit of Oriental faithlessness and the prize of Saxon valour, to the distant shores of England.

" It was in the year 1550, before the Mogul dynasty had been established by the prowess of the great Akbar, that this marvellous stone was first brought to light in the celebrated mines of Golconda. The kingdom of this name constitutes one of the five Mohammedan States which towards the close of the fifteenth century had been formed in the Deccan. The diamond-mines which have rendered it so famous in story were situated at some distance to the east of the capital city, near the present station of Condapilly, and are now in our possession, though they have long ceased to reward or invite the labours of treasure-seekers. When the Mogul Princes extended their pretensions to the sovereignty of the Deccan, Kootub Shah, the King of Golconda, was brought into collision with Shah Jehaun, the reigning Emperor, and father of the great Aurungzebe. Kootub Shah's Prime Minister at this period was the famous Meer Jumla, a statesman who to political abilities of unusual excellence added a singular knowledge of precious stones. He had, in fact, been at one time a diamond merchant, and was, therefore, peculiarly competent to appreciate the treasures of Golconda. It happened, too, that Shah Jehaun himself was a connoisseur of scarcely less skill, insomuch that when at a later period he had been dethroned and imprisoned by his father, and a doubt had been created respecting the value of a certain ruby in the Imperial treasury, the gem was actually transmitted to the deposed Prince for his inspection and decision. Two such characters were well fitted for the transaction which ensued. Shah Jehaun took up the cause of Meer Jumla against his sovereign, and the Koh-i-noor passed from Golconda to Delhi.

"While the kingdoms of the Deccan were successively absorbed in the culminating dominion of the Moguls, the Koh-i-noor rested among the treasures of Imperial Delhi, where, on November 2, 1665, it was seen by the French traveller Tavernier, who, by the extraordinary indulgence of Aurung-zebe, was permitted to handle, examine, and weigh it, being the first, and till now, probably, the last European who had ever enjoyed such a privilege. The Great Mogul sat on his throne of State, whilst the chief keeper of the jewels produced his treasures for inspection on two golden dishes. The magnificence of the collection was indescribable, but conspicuous in lustre, esteem, and value was the Koh-i-noor. Sometimes worn on the person of the Moguls, sometimes adorning the famous peacock throne, this inestimable gem was safely preserved at Delhi until, in 1739, the empire received its fatal blow from the invasion of Nadir Shah. Among the spoils of conquest which the Persian warrior carried back with him in triumph to Khorassan, and which have been variously estimated as worth from thirty to ninety millions sterling, the Koh-i-noor was the most precious trophy, but it was destined to pass from Persia as quickly as that ephemeral supremacy in virtue of which it had been acquired. Nadir Shah had entertained in his service a body of Afghans of the Abdâllee tribe under the leadership of Ahmed Shah, who also served his master in the capacity of treasurer, and when the Persian conqueror was assassinated by his subjects, the Afghans, after vainly endeavouring to rescue or avenge him, fought their way to their own frontiers, though only four thousand strong, through the hosts of the Persian army. In conducting this intrepid retreat Ahmed Shah carried off with him the treasures in his possession, and was probably aided by these means as well as by his own valour in consolidating the new State which, under the now familiar title of the Doorânnee empire, he speedily created in Cabul. *It seemed as if the Koh-i-noor carried with it the sovereignty of Hindostan,* for the conquests of Ahmed were as decisive as those of Nadir, and it was by his nomination and patronage that the last Emperor ascended the throne of the Moguls.

"At the beginning of the present century the treasures and power of Ahmed were vested in the person of Zemaun Shah, subject to the incessant assaults of his kinsmen. One of these at length proved successful, and in the year 1800 Zemaun Shah *found himself a prisoner at the disposal of his brother Shah Shuja, the identical puppet, forty years later, of our famous Cabul expedition,* so that we are now brought down to modern times and characters. Shah Shuja presently ascended the throne of his brother, but the treasury of Cabul was wanting in its most precious ornament, till at length, ingeniously secreted in the wall of Zemaun Shah's prison, was discovered the Koh-i-noor. It was eight years after this, while the Doorânnee monarchy was still formidable enough to inspire the Powers of the East with uneasiness, that *Mr. Elphinstone, accredited by Lord Minto to the Afghan prince, betook himself to what was then the remote and unknown town of Peshâwur, where, at his state reception, the Koh-i-noor again flashed, after an interval of so many years, upon the dazzled eyes of a European.* Shah Shuja, afterwards the client and pensioner of the East India Company, was dressed on this occasion in a green velvet tunic, fitting closely to his body, and seamed with gold and precious stones. On his breast was a cuirass of diamonds shaped like two flattened *fleurs-de-lis,* and in a bracelet on his right arm blazed the priceless jewel of Golconda. The Prince gave a gracious audience to the Ambassador, and Mr. Elphinstone retired, but the Koh-i-noor was not fated long to continue in the divided and tottering family of the once-powerful Abdallees.

" The Embassy had scarcely recrossed the Indus when Shah Shuja was expelled from Cabul, though he contrived to make this far-famed diamond the companion of his flight. After many vicissitudes of exile and contest, he at length found an equivocal refuge under the protection of that powerful chieftain who had now consolidated the dominions of the Sikhs into a royal inheritance for his own family. Runjeet Singh was fully competent either to the defence or the restoration of the fugitive, but he knew or suspected the treasure in his possession, and his mind was bent upon acquiring it. He put the Shah under strict surveillance, and made a formal demand for the jewel. The Doorânnee Prince hesitated, prevaricated, temporized, and employed all the artifices of Oriental diplomacy; but in vain. Runjeet redoubled the stringency of his measures, and at length June 1, 1813, was fixed as the day when the great diamond of the Moguls should be surrendered by the Abdâllee Chief to the ascendant dynasty of the Singhs. The two Princes met in a room appointed for the purpose, and took their seats on the ground. A solemn silence then ensued, which continued unbroken for an hour. At length Runjeet's impatience overcame the suggestions of Asiatic decorum, and he whispered to an attendant to quicken the memory of the Shah. The exiled Prince spoke not a word in reply, but gave a signal with his eyes to a eunuch in attendance, who, retiring for a moment, returned with a small roll, which he set down upon the carpet midway between the two chiefs. Again a pause followed, when at a sign from Runjeet the roll was unfolded, and there in its matchless and unspeakable brilliancy glittered the Koh-i-noor.

" In this way did the 'Mountain of Light' pass in the train of conquest, and as the emblem of dominion, from Golconda to Delhi, from Delhi to Mushed, from Mushed to Cabul, and from Cabul to Lahore, verifying by the esteem which it everywhere commanded the perspicacity and judgment of Meer Jumla (who is the Mirsimola of Tavernier's travels) and the Prince Shah Jehaun. Excepting the somewhat doubtful claims of the Brazilian stone among the Crown jewels of Portugal, *the Koh-i-noor is the largest known diamond in the world.* When first given to Shah Jehaun it was still uncut,

weighing it is said, in that rough state, nearly eight hundred
carats, which were reduced by the unskilfulness of the artist
to 279, its present weight. It was cut by Hortensio Borgis, a
Venetian, who, instead of receiving a remuneration for his
labour, was fined ten thousand rupees for his wastefulness by
the enraged Mogul. In form it is ' rose-cut '—that is to say,
it is cut to a point in a series of small ' facets,' without any
tabular surface. A good general idea may be formed of its
shape and size by conceiving it as the pointed half of a small
hen's egg, though it is said not to have risen more than half
an inch from the gold setting in which it was worn by
Runjeet. Its value is scarcely computable, though two
millions sterling has been mentioned as a justifiable price,
if calculated by the scale employed in the trade. The Pitt
diamond brought over from Madras by the grandfather of
Lord Chatham, and sold to the Regent Orleans in 1717 for
£125,000, weighs scarcely one hundred and thirty carats ; nor
does the great diamond which supports the Eagle on the summit
of the Russian sceptre weigh as much as two hundred. Such
is the extraordinary jewel which, in virtue of conquest and
sovereignty, has passed into the possession of England. It
was prudently secured among the few remaining valuables of
the Lahore treasury at the commencement of the last insurrection, and although even its nominal value would be an
inadequate compensation for the cost of the Sikh Wars, we
may look upon its acquisition as a fitting symbol of that
supremacy which we have so fairly won."

CHAPTER III.

———◆◇◆———

1846.

THE "RESIDENT" AND HIS "ASSISTANTS"—CASHMERE—
GOLÂB SINGH.

" Chase brave employments with a naked sword
    Throughout the world.   Fool not; for all may have,
  If they dare choose, a glorious life or grave."

GEORGE HERBERT.

CHAPTER III.

EDWARDES'S experience of war as Sir Hugh Gough's aide-de-camp was of short duration; for Henry Lawrence, coming up to Simla on his way to take up his post at Lahore, met Edwardes there for the first time, and asked him to go with him to Lahore as Assistant-Resident.

Lahore was the capital of the Sikh kingdom of Runjeet The state of affairs at Lahore. Singh. Runjeet Singh had died, and his heir, Dhuleep Singh, was a child. The actual government devolved upon a "regency," which was, as has been seen already, most disastrous for the country—composed of the Queen-Mother, and corrupt Sirdars, whom she ruled in profligacy and vice.

Henry Lawrence undertook the post of Resident at this Sikh Court with the earnest desire of guiding the Sikh Government to learn how to govern themselves, and to build up an Empire in the midst of violence and intrigue, by teaching them to rule wisely, for the good of their country.

To assist him in his labours, he looked out for himself a band of young men, chosen wherever he could find them, who he thought would enter into his views and work heartily with him in this chivalrous endeavour to raise the Sikh Government to govern wisely and justly, and to protect the weak and the oppressed from tyranny. And in this aim and object Herbert Edwardes sympathized most truly.

He thus became the first Assistant to the Resident of Lahore, in 1846. The rest of the Assistants were John Reid Becher, John Nicholson, James Abbott, Reynell Taylor, Edward Lake, George McGregor, Arthur Cocks, Harry Lumsden, George Lawrence, L. Bowring (afterwards from time to time added to)—all rare men, who have done great

deeds for India's good, and who live in history ; so that the
bare mention of their names here will suggest to the reader
who has only studied India as a matter of history a long list
of noble deeds and services ; while, to those who are living
still, it speaks of a noble brotherhood of brave men and true.

Henry
Lawrence
on his
Assistants.

Henry Lawrence, writing to his friend Sir John Kaye,
said, "I was very fortunate in my Assistants, all of whom
were my friends, and almost every one was introduced into
the Punjab through me. George Lawrence, McGregor, James
Abbott, Edwardes, Lumsden, Nicholson, Taylor, Cocks, Hodson, Pollock, Bowring, Henry Coxe, and Melville are men
such as you will seldom see anywhere, but, when collected
under one administration, were worth double and treble the
number taken at haphazard. Each was a good man ; the
most were excellent officers."

Of this band of young men, all whom Colonel Henry
Lawrence personally attached to himself, and by whom he
was always greatly beloved, he made Edwardes the first,
placing him in the position of a private secretary, for closer
personal intercourse and working together ; and so they were
generally found occupying one room, and were drawn together in great affection, and in a growing admiration of each
other's qualities.*

This was the congenial work that Edwardes had been
longing for, and it opened the door at once to the larger
sphere of work and interest that he had desired to find.

Heart and soul he threw himself into it, sympathizing
entirely with the large views and unsparing philanthropy
with which Henry Lawrence entered upon his work for the
good of the people, seeking to elevate them, to teach the
rich and the powerful *how to govern*, and to protect the poor
and the oppressed against their oppressors.

---

* There is a note of this time written by Henry Lawrence's wife, who
was then in England. Writing to Edwardes's aunt, she says, "Your
nephew is a very highly valued assistant and friend of my husband, who,
in writing to me, says, 'Edwardes has left me. We have now been five
months together in close fellowship, the last three months even sleeping
in the same room. Taking him all in all, bodily activity, mental cultivation, and warmth of heart, I have not met his equal in India.' . . . We
had admired 'Brahminee Bull' long before we knew Mr. Edwardes.

"(Signed)   HONORIA LAWRENCE."

These days were like the olden days of chivalry—like nothing that *can* be now in the country.

Great power and great opportunities for accomplishing great good, this was just the field for developing great men with large desires for good, and this was just the field that Herbert Edwardes had sighed for, and had wondered where he should find it. He always liked to call Henry Lawrence "the father of his public life," and he loved to trace the influence for good that he received from him. The affectionate interest then begun, ended only with the death of Sir Henry Lawrence, in 1857.

If it is asked why such days cannot be again, it may be answered, because the Punjab is governed in a totally different manner now. These were its early days. At this time the Punjab was the scene of the anarchy and misgovernment that ensued upon the death of Runjeet Singh, and the mission of Henry Lawrence was to steer the ship of the Punjab out of those troubled waters into calmer seas. And honestly he strove to do it; and this brave band of young men put all their strength and power to the work with him. *(marginal note: Early days of the Punjab rule.)*

But nothing could stave off the annexation of the country beyond a few years; and it was with real sorrow that Henry Lawrence found his chivalrous scheme of leading the Sikhs to good government fail at last, and the necessity arise for England to take the government on herself.

Then Colonel Lawrence became the President of a board * appointed by the Governor-General, and ruled the magnificent province with the wisdom with which he had been unable to inspire the corrupt and vicious Court at Lahore to govern their country for themselves.

But in these early days (even after annexation) things were in a very different state to what they can ever be again. These were the days of the Court of Directors and Board of Control in England, and not the Secretary of State in Council, under her Most Gracious Majesty's Government. The countries have been brought nearer together. *England* now governs, and India is governed *from England*. The Secretary of State for India, at Westminster, now rules the Governor-

---

* The "board" consisted of three members, Sir Henry Lawrence being President.

General, or Viceroy, and sends his orders through the telegraph, or cancels orders which the Viceroy may have given if he does not approve of them.

In former days it was the Court of Directors who appointed the Governor-General, and he was an *autocrat.* He did what he pleased, and if the Court of Directors did not approve of any of his acts, and thought the matter of sufficient importance to interfere, they would, with the sanction of the Board of Control, recall him, and send out another. But they did not interfere with his authority *ex officio.* And as the Governor-General was despotic under this old *régime*, so, in every grade, the members of the Government of India were more independent in their respective authorities, and rulers had more power for good (and perhaps for evil too).

And so the Punjab, being a new country, was in a wild and free state, and uncivilized, and Colonel Henry Lawrence was free to make his own laws, and to give his own rules and orders to his subordinates unfettered to a great extent; giving *them* also powers and liberty to act for themselves, in the same relative proportion, in carrying out their duties. And he laid out before them great ends to accomplish, leaving them entirely to their own discretion and resources how to bring about the desired result.*

Now everything is done in a perfectly different way. Everything is tied up with *red tape*, and is done by "rule," and all the rules are numbered, and men *can* be machines. There is, consequently, less of that personal individuality that so strongly stamped the Government in those early days. This is why Henry Lawrence *chose* his staff, and gathered such a band of young men around him as he could *trust*, in command and power.

And here we see how the Punjab came to take such a

---

* Only the other day, in conversation with one of these "old assistants," he remarked, "What days those were! How Henry Lawrence would send us off to great distances; Edwardes to Bunnoo, Nicholson to Peshâwur, Abbott to Hazâra, Lumsden somewhere else, etc., giving us a tract of country as big as half of England, and giving us no more helpful directions than these, 'Settle the country; make the people happy; and take care there are no rows!'" And how well they carried out his orders has become "the early history of the Punjab."—E. E.

high stand of honest and chivalrous work, stamped as its government was from the first with the impress of the noble and chivalrous and heroic character of Henry Lawrence.

Henry Lawrence puts his stamp upon the Punjab.

The sense of *responsibility*, so congenial to a noble nature, roused all the energies of these young men; and *this* was just the field to call out all the great qualities of a man, and to make him fertile in resource and self-reliant; to draw out, in fact, all that was *in* him.

Never was a man more willingly, more ably, and more heartily served than was Henry Lawrence, by all this chosen band of assistants; and never was such a bright band of noble spirits raised up and called forth to any work, as was seen in these early days in the Punjab.

One secret of the attraction that there was about Henry Lawrence, as the leader of this chivalrous band of young men, was the *generosity* of his nature. His heart *took delight* in awarding praise where praise was due, and in acknowledging the value of every man's work; not only applauding it himself as he thought it deserved, but letting the Government in Calcutta know the value of the services done by their hand. This sympathy cheered them on and encouraged them; and his personal influence on them served to inspire their devotion both to him and to their work.*

One secret of attraction in the leader.

Edwardes now laid aside the routine of regimental life, which was never to be taken up again; and the desires and aspirations after a larger field and a deeper life were about to be satisfied.

An extract from a letter of his, at this time, may serve to encourage some young reader in similar circumstances. Edwardes writes—

"I landed in India in January, 1841, without either friends or interest, and for the instruction of those who think it is of no use to study either the languages, history, or policy of British India, unless the Governor-General

---

* This quality was one great difference between the two brothers Lawrence (Sir Henry and Sir John); and it explains the *difference* in the feelings with which they inspired those who loved them and who served under them both. Both men had great qualities, but the two characters were totally *different.*

happens to be their grandfather, I record the fact that at the close of 1845 I was promised the first vacancy in the Judge Advocate-General's Department of the Bengal Presidency, and have good reason to believe that I was to have had the second under the Governor-General's Agent on the north-west frontier. But before either of these occurred, his Excellency the commander-in-chief, then Sir Hugh Gough, Bart., honoured me by making me an aide-de-camp on his personal staff—a step to which I gratefully acknowledge that I am indebted for all the opportunities of succeeding years."

Deputed to the Court of Cashmere. In the autumn of 1846 Lieutenant Edwardes was deputed by Colonel Henry Lawrence to the Court of Jummoo, to aid Maharajah Golâb Singh, the Governor of Cashmere, in the suppression of Sheikh Imam-úd-dín, who had revolted, and headed a rebellion against the new governor, to whom the country of Cashmere had lately been assigned by the English for a large sum of money (a crore of rupees), as part of the indemnity for the war, which the bankrupt Sikh Court at Lahore was unable to pay to the conquering power in any other way.

The Resident was bound to support Golâb Singh's rights against the rebel chief; and Edwardes was sent by Henry Lawrence to give him assistance. To effect this, Edwardes opened negotiations with the Sheikh himself, whom he induced to submit and to deliver up the secret orders to rebel, which he had received from Rajah Lal Singh, the favourite of the Queen-Mother at Lahore.

On this the Sheikh was permitted by Henry Lawrence to surrender, and, giving himself up to Edwardes at the foot of the Cashmere Hills, was by him conducted to Lahore.

On the evidence of the papers thus obtained, Rajah Lal Singh was brought to trial under the walls of Lahore, was deposed from his place in the Sikh Ministry, and banished from Lahore to Hindostan.

A vivid picture of the intrigues of the Sikh Court, and a graphic picture of the Cashmere events of this period we find in a letter of Edwardes, written to a friend in England, dated Rihássee, a mountain fortress above Jûmmoo, the capital of Maharajah Golâb Singh's dominions.

"September 21, 1846.

" MY DEAR POWLES,

"I have not heard from you again since I wrote *Cashmere affairs.* last, but I have got hold of such a *character* here, such a rare specimen of human nature, that I must add him to your gallery of life's experience and send him home, as naturalists would a unicorn or a flea with two sets of teeth.

"You know how much it has been the fashion of late years to discover that oral tradition has been acting on a deliberate system of deceit, and handing down to us as historic personages mere men of straw. We have been reared up amid an atmosphere of biographies, inhaling and calling it life; and now these wicked chemists insist on analysing it in our very lungs, and swear it is destitute of the oxygen of truth. *Experience*, familiarity with the *actual*, has certainly a sad tendency to shake one's confidence in history. It shows us that real events are always wanting in that *completeness* and *roundness* with which they are recorded.

"The historian never gives you one or two acts of a play without all the others; he would be ashamed to take your money at the door of a revolution and not show you every scene, from the ringing of the prompter's bell to the fall of the curtain.

"This is not *life;* the world, as Tom Moore sings, is 'half in shade and half in sun,' and we see, at best, but one-half of anything upon it. The rest is guesswork. But to apply these rambling observations. In our childhood there was no character in history supposed to be better established than that of hump-backed Richard of Gloucester. Shakespeare was history. Latterly, however, doubts have been thrown upon the fidelity of his picture, and Bulwer in a late work (of fiction truly, but such fiction as an imaginative mind weaves out of facts) has boldly put forth his likeness of the young Prince, painted in very different colours.

"One of the arguments for disbelieving Shakespeare has been the *incredibility* of so deep a villain as his 'Richard.' Now it has fallen to my lot to become the best of friends with just such a man in the flesh—a real, live villain. I feel as proud as Professor Buckland when he picked up the enormous ammonite.

"In my last letter I think I must have told you that I was expecting to be sent to Lahore, to relieve Major McGregor. It happened as I thought, and in the hottest and most feverish month of the year, when the Spirit of Water has shot his last arrow at him of Fire, and the Sun comes forth again like aroused Achilles, flaming across the plain and withering up the souls of the rivers, I bid adieu to the Himalaya (region of eternal spring), and plunged into the seething plains. A man leaping from an iceberg into Hecla may, if he survives it, appreciate my public spirit! I reached 'the bloody capital' on September 3, and on the 7th was ordered off again to Jûmmoo.

"Without meaning to be insulting, but determined to be communicative, I take it for granted that, like the rest of the English gentlemen who live at home at ease, you are profoundly ignorant of Oriental geography. I take upon myself, therefore, to inform you that Jûmmoo is about seventy or eighty miles north of Lahore, which latter city I assume as a given point of knowledge in your brain; for I'll lay my life you looked it out in Carey's atlas last winter, and referred to Dr. Butler for its alias amongst the Macedonians.

"Well, Jûmmoo is the residence of Maharajah Golâb Singh, King of the Kohistan (hill country) and Cashmere countries, which, I dare say you have not forgotten, were acquired by our brave armies in the last campaign as indemnity for invasion, and afterwards, with that strange mixture of political wisdom and imperial generosity which makes the English in India incomprehensible to natives,

were given away again to their present possessor, a subject
formerly of the state from which we took them.

"By the treaties then concluded at Lahore, the Sikhs
were bound to make over all the ceded districts to us,
or whomsoever we might appoint. We appointed Golâb
Singh. Now you can easily imagine the jealousy which
would be felt by a native power at giving over, in sackcloth
and ashes, a rich tract of its territory to one who, yesterday,
was a subject of its own—a powerful subject, all but
independent, but still a subject acknowledging, perhaps,
a more perfect allegiance than he paid. Hence began
intrigues, and month after month passed away without—for
some *reason* or other which was quite *reasonable*—Golâb
Singh being in possession of Cashmere.

"By a singular fatality also, Golâb Singh commenced
an intrigue with the Sikh Governor of that province. His
name is Sheikh Imâm-úd-dín, and he is supposed to be
immensely rich from the accumulated plunder of his own
and his father's administration.

"Golâb Singh is a miser, and contemplated with regret
the approaching departure from his dominions of so much
wealth. It seemed to him like rooting up the mountain
in which lie his mines of iron, lead, and other precious
metals, and transplanting it into an enemy's country. So
he spoke the Sheikh fair, and offered to keep him on
as Governor of Cashmere. Here, then, was the former lord
of that province telling the Governor that if he wanted
to prove his fidelity he must not come away, and the
present lord begging as a favour that he would stop! He
took them both at their word, and set up for himself!

"He is a young man, with all the qualities which win
popular applause, and less than the usual share of those
vices which, in the East, make governors detested.

"The people, who looked forward with horror to the
rule of Golâb Singh, declared like one man in his favour,

and the refugee scions of old depressed and ruined royal
families in the surrounding hills flocked round him with
their scanty band of faithful ruffians, and determined to win
back, under his banner, some of their ancient lands.

"This revolution, or rebellion, broke out in the end
of August; and scarcely had I reached Lahore when the
news came in that the rebels had set upon a small body
of the royal troops, murdered 'the Lord-Lieutenant,' and
driven the rest of the Maharajah's army to take refuge in
the '*Hurree Purbut*,' the Acropolis of Cashmere.

"Our Government was aroused. Interference could no
longer be deferred, and I was ordered off to Jûmmoo to
offer the Maharajah aid, and (how you will laugh!) 'advise
him at the present juncture!' A lieutenant of Foot
advising the King of the Mountains!

"Such is India. It is, however, I am aware, no ordinary
chance, and I am the more grateful to Colonel Lawrence,
the Governor-General's Agent, for entrusting me with the
mission.

"I arrived here on September 20 (this is two marches
from Jûmmoo, a mountain villa of the Mountain Cæsar),
and hard at work have I been ever since, stirring up the
sleeping lion.

"To show you that I have not much leisure, I began
this on September 24, and am now writing this line on
October 6.

"What have I effected since I came? I have forced
Golâb Singh to abandon intrigue and take to a sharper
arbiter of quarrels—the sword. He is collecting his army,
and marched from here yesterday on his road to Cashmere.

"Our Government has made the Sikhs send two divisions
to assist him; and an army of our own is coming up in the
rear to menace or to strike, as circumstances may require.

"I follow and join the Maharajah's camp to-night.

"You are a man of peace, and will naturally ask somewhat gravely if I have made no effort to settle this matter without bloodshed? Yes, I have offered the Sheikh his life, and a fair trial for his property, if he comes in to me without striking another blow. But I have not waited for his answer.

"There is no arguing in this country without force to back you. A rebel never gives in till the avenger is within a march of him. If you have his life at heart, threaten to take it. 'Make a pass' at your enemy's liver, and your sword goes over his shoulder; for he kneels to escape it.

"This very day ought to bring me the Sheikh's reply, and it is in an anxious interval that I am now writing to you.

"As far as my own judgment goes, I think he will come in; but the more I see of Asiatic character and European diplomacy, the more convinced am I that we have no means of judging correctly of the conduct of natives.

"The principles on which they argue are so widely different, the axioms from which they start are so opposed to ours that it is impossible we can ever come to the same conclusions. Long experience and familiarity with the natives may and must do something to give us a clue to their modes of thought; but it does very, very little.

"When we think we have estimated them rightly, some new prejudice, or some old superstition, an almost impossible suspicion, or a downright mad contrivance, flits before their eyes, and leads these grown-up children in full chase after a *feu follet*.

"Their utter depravity is one thing which always involves natives in a mesh of their own spinning. They cannot imagine such a thing as honesty for honesty's sake. The English in India are renowned for *truth*; *i.e.* in its narrow sense—truth of the tongue, not of the heart and mind. They say we always perform our promises and make good our threats. But when we perform some romantic act of good faith (such as paying a banker who has lost your note of hand), they look puzzled, shake their heads, and say, 'Well, it is very funny. I wonder what his *reason* was.'

"Thus, in great affairs of State, when a Governor-General with slow dignity keeps on the even tenor of his way in all integrity, marching upon a point of diplomacy which he has openly avowed, the native Prince with whom he deals cannot believe that he wants what he asks, or is going where he says, but suspects treachery, and becomes guilty of it himself. He perishes, and with his last breath says, 'That *cunning* Governor-General!'

"I have laid it down, therefore, as a rule on which I mean invariably to act, so long as health and fortune keep me in the political department of this country, *never to assume that a native* will do anything, but hope that he will *do the best, and prepare for his doing the worst.*

"But 'Where is the villain? Let me see his face!' I think I hear you exclaim. My dear Powles, I could not think of showing you my royal tiger till I had kept you standing at the door of his den for some while, to excite your curiosity. But now you may 'walk up,' as the showmen say, and behold *Maharajah Golâb Singh.*

"I shall describe him to you like the little guide at the Bodleian, whom well do I remember standing before the picture of King William and Queen Adelaide, and informing us accurately, in the same breath, of their birthday and the price of the frames. When shall I again stroll with you through the Bodleian?

"It is now nearly forty years ago since a courtier in some favour with Runjeet Singh, the old lion of the Punjab, made interest for a young relation of his own, named Golâb Singh, and got him enlisted in one of the Cavalry regiments, on the humble pay of Rs.20 a month.

"The Punjab Cavalry was famous; it had earned for

itself a name, and for Runjeet a kingdom; and its ranks
were filled by the yeomen of the land, who took a pride in
their leader, and were in turn regarded with partiality.

" On a spring morning, when the green meadows between
the palace at Lahore and the Ravee River invited Runjeet
out to see these troops at exercise, a more gallant spectacle
could perhaps not have been imagined than the Sikh
Ghorchurruhs pouring in clouds along the plain, with
their long tapering bamboo lances bending in the air, their
many-coloured scarves flaunting saucily about, their silver-
bossed shields rattling against sword and pistol, and their
large well-managed horses gaily caparisoned, bounding to
the spur or curvetting at the rein. 'Wah! Wah! Shah-
bash!' ('Well done!') 'Bravo!' would shout the energetic
Runjeet, as his keen one eye watched the lightning wheels
of two young scamps who, with Oriental licence, had escaped
from the ranks, and were chasing each other with quivering
spear across the grass.

"'Let them be rewarded. The young fellows ride
well!'

" For one service or another there was scarcely a trooper
(in the later years of Runjeet Singh) who had not one or
more grants of land, from a *well's-watering* of the ground
to a village. ('*A well of land*' is an idiom in this country;
it means as much as can be cultivated with so much water.
It is Oriental, and, I think, *picturesque*.) It must not be
concluded, therefore, because our hero Golâb Singh enlisted
as a common trooper, that therefore he was a peasant or of
low extraction.

" On the contrary, he was a young cadet of an old but
poor family in the Kohistan or hill country, the Highlands
of the Punjab; and to this day I know not whether he is
prouder of having gained a kingdom for himself, or of
having had a royal great-grandfather.

" He was a remarkably fine and powerfully made man,

with a handsome face, and a head of hair and beard like a
lion, and as black as the plumage of the raven. He could
sit like a Centaur on an unbroken colt ; and at fifteen, killed
five men in a skirmish with his own sword.

"Runjeet contemplated him with delight. He was just
the stuff of which a conqueror makes up his army.

"Golâb Singh had two brothers younger than himself,
Dhyân Singh and Soochèt Singh. They were cast in the
same mould, and, when old enough, found no difficulty in
joining their brother Golâb in Runjeet's Guards.

"If these men had had but only common sense, they must
have risen in such a service, where the sword cut every
courtier's way to fortune. But they had more—two of them,
at least. Golâb and Dhyân Singh had rare though rude
abilities, indomitable ambition to turn them to account,
and few scruples to stop them in their path. From troopers
they became commanders; from commanders, generals; from
generals, governors; from governors, kings. A Maharajah is
a king of kings, and kings are his chief servants.

"The three Jûmmoo brothers, as they were called, were
the ministers of Runjeet. He conferred on them, bit by bit,
a large portion of the Kohistan; they held his most
profitable governments; they conquered provinces, and
shared the spoils. In short, they became the three chief
men in the warrior-court of Runjeet Singh; they were all-
powerful in the Punjab; and when Runjeet, full of honours
and disgraces, worn out with years, and toils, and debaucheries, died, and left his kingdom to an idiot son, the father's
prime minister, Dhyân Singh, became, in fact, the head of the
Empire.

"Then began that series of political crimes which ended
the last campaign, in the extinction of national independence ; for who can call the Punjab independent now ?

"Now, Nihâl Singh, the heir-apparent, poisoned his dotard
father. Golâb Singh was the young Prince's chosen mentor,

and is not above the suspicion of having instigated the deed.
But mark the speedy retribution.

"Now, Nihâl Singh had been out to the burning of his
father's corpse, and, mounted on an elephant, in a golden
howdah, *with Golâb Singh's son* at his side, was passing under
an archway of the palace gates, on his return—a King! A
sudden crash, a beam falls from the arched roof, a scream,
and the Prince and his companion lie bleeding on the
ground, the former dying, the latter dead.

"Who did the deed? *Chance! says* everybody in the
crowd. *Dhyân Singh! thought* everybody in the kingdom.

" He was an ambitious man, and Nihâl Singh showed as
a boy that he would not ' brook a rival near the throne.'
He died, therefore, of his wounds.

" Dhyân Singh then made common cause with one of
Runjeet's wives, who had a son of more gentle disposition,
named Sher Singh.

" Golâb Singh and his party shut themselves up in the
palace, and resisted his entrance. The army sided with the
young Prince. A storm ensued. Three days did the stout
Golâb maintain himself against the Sovereign and his army,
and not till the gardens beneath were strewn with dead
did he agree to compromise. A short time passed on, and
again the minister intrigues to change the Sovereign, and
hires Ajeet Singh, a Sikh Sirdar, to ' do the deed.'

" There is a review, and Sher Singh sits at the window of
a summer-house to see the manœuvres of his troops. Ajeet
Singh's regiment performs to admiration. He approaches,
and presents a double-barrelled gun in grateful acknowledgment of the Prince's praise. Sher Singh stoops to receive
it ; and the assassin, turning the muzzle round, discharges
the contents of both barrels into his breast! Dhyân Singh,
by a strange coincidence, arrives, *not knowing what is going
on.* He is astonished—shocked, but takes the murderer into
his carriage, and drives him home. They quarrel on the

road. Ajeet Singh stabs Dhyân Singh to the heart. Dhyân
Singh's son, a bold boy named Heera Singh, summons the
Army round him to avenge his father's death.

"The murderer takes refuge in the palace, is pursued,
attempts escape by letting himself down by a rope from a
window, and is shot by twenty bullets before he reaches
earth.

"The throne is vacant. Another mother is sought in the
harem of the great Runjeet, and forth comes the Râni
Junda (whose name for ambition and debaucheries will be
recorded with those of Messalina, Faustina, and Catherine II.)
and her son Dhuleep Singh, the present boyish Maharajah of
the Punjab.

"Heera Singh, the son of the late minister, becomes
minister himself, and lover of the Queen. He rules ably,
but is intoxicated with pride at his own success.

"The soldiers call for his uncle, Soochèt Singh, whose
daring gallantry and coxcomb loves have made him their
darling. He hastens down from Jûmmoo to pluck his
nephew from the council board. Heera Singh wins the
army back again with gold ; they surround the man they
have invited ; he disdains to fly, and dies upon a heap of his
treacherous assailants.

"One alone of the three great brothers then remained—
the subject of this narrative, Golâb Singh.

"Had he less ambition than Dhyân or Soochèt Singh
that he remained in his mountain fastness, and ventured not
into the arena where the Sikh chiefs, like gladiators,
contended for political power? I should say that he had
more. But though he had as much courage as his brother
Soochèt, he did not, like him, court danger for the
pleasure of the strife ; and fully as covetous of power as his
brother Dhyân, he did not, like him, think that it could
be won at Court ; which was a sand too shifting for the
foundation of a fortune, and where there were so many

enemies to be removed that to escape them all would have been a miracle. His was the cunning of *the vulture.* He sat apart in the clear atmosphere of passionless distance, and with sleepless eye beheld the lion and the tiger contending for the deer. And when the combatants were dead, he spread his wings, sailed calmly down, and feasted where they fought.

"Detestable as I think the character of Goláb Singh, I cannot but admire the unity of design, strength of purpose, and untiring patience of his career. He began struggling with the world as a boy, and his beard is now grey; yet he has watched and waited, waited and watched, the ups and downs of life till he saw that it was his *turn.* He knew it *must come,* from the signs of the times; and, without fretfulness or impatience, he let youth and manhood both fleet by, certain of age bringing the *opportunity.*

"The last struggles of the Sikh empire are briefly chronicled in an article I have written for the *Calcutta Review,* No. XI., just published. From it you will see the events that led to the war with the British in 1845–46.* In this place I will merely add that the love of Heera Singh for the Queen-Mother ceased when he had made it a steppingstone to the Vizárut.

"She supplied his place with a clerk in the Treasury, named Lal Singh. Heera Singh was ass enough to flout him.

"The woman—piqued woman!—rose in arms, compassed his death with a revolution, and set up her brother, Jowáhir Singh, in his place. Jowáhir Singh was drunk all day and worse all night. The state was ruled by the Queen-Mother and Lal Singh, no longer clerk, but King, a Rajah of the Empire.

"Disgusted with his excesses, the Army rose and murdered Jowáhir; and the Queen, to save herself and

* From this we have seen extracts in chap. ii.

lover, with matchless courage and resource incited the mad
soldiery to carry their arms across the Sutlej.

"A curious spectacle was then presented—the Queen
at Lahore, watching the destruction of her Army; Golâb
Singh at Jummoo, watching the destruction of the Queen!

"You know the rest. The British, in a brilliant campaign
of sixty days, drove back the Sikh army, after beating them
in four pitched battles, and crossed the Sutlej marshes of
the great empire of the Punjab.

"I know not in all history a parallel to the generosity
then displayed by the British Government. Reflecting on
the long and sincere friendship of Runjeet Singh and the
childhood of his descendant, the present Maharajah, the
Governor-General waived the conqueror's right, and reseated
Dhuleep Singh upon the throne.

"The Cis-Sutlej territory of Lahore, on which the
invaders had landed, and the Jullundur Doâb, a rich tract
of country adjoining the British hills, was taken by the
British as indemnity for the war; and the fertile province
of Cashmere was conferred on Golâb Singh as a reward for
not aiding in the invasion.

"Here, then, is our Hero — the sagacious, far-seeing
time-observer—an independent King at last! nay, a king
of kings—for he is a Maharajah!

"This is the *outline* of his career, but how fearful is the
filling-up!—the crimes of duplicity, treachery, abuse of
power, and savage destruction of human life with which he
has cleared his way step by step and left himself alone—
infamous even in the Punjab!

"He has himself recounted to me how, when sent by
Runjeet to subdue a turbulent province, he seized '*a few*'
of the chiefs, flayed them alive, stuffed their skins with
chaff, and hung them up *pour encourager les autres*. 'Sometimes when I wished only *to frighten* a man,' he says, 'I had
him scalped, *all but a little piece*, and just as he thought he

was *really* going to be killed, I put his scalp on again,
and let him go!' This he tells with a bland smile, as if
talking of peeling apples. On another occasion, when the
men of a district ran away, he set a price upon their heads
and had them hunted down. And when the wives of the
murdered men, now left destitute, came to beg for mercy
in a body, he sold them to his soldiers, and so recovered the
money which he had paid for their husbands' heads.

"There is hardly a noble family in the hills into which
he has not carried, at one time or another, death by poison,
assassination, or intolerable imprisonment.

"And now that you have read all this, doubtless you
think that cold-hearted ambition is the ruling passion of
this man's mind. Strange to say, he has one stronger still
—that of *avarice*, which, if possible, has led him to inflict
more misery than his ambition, because it has found
vent in his Government, and has *soaked down to the poor*,
like salt water overflowing a meadow and withering the
roots of the green grass, long after it has disappeared from
the surface.

"His appetite for money is perfectly insatiable. Already
his riches are not to be counted; stored here and there,
some in forts, and some in the forest or the mountain-side,
and those who stored disappearing, so 'tis said, and dying
unaccountably, leaving him sole possessor of the secret of
his hoards. And now he *is a King*, and has a wide field
wherein to reap.

"Every living man is to him a blade of golden corn,
which he will never leave till he has gathered, and threshed,
and winnowed, and garnered.

"He has declared himself the great factor of his kingdom. Everything between heaven and earth, and the
metals under the earth, are his. Everything made for
produced goes to *him* at an insignificant cost, and is *retailed*
by the *agents of the Emperor* at hundredfold profit. Thus

producer and consumer are at once oppressed, and the
Sovereign, as an individual, thrives!

"In this country it is the custom for a subject never to
approach his lord without an offering called a nûzzur.
Maharajah Golâb Singh understands this well, and, instead
of doing as the English do to the poor or the middle
classes, viz. *touch* the present as a symbol of acceptance,
without taking it, you see him riding about on a little
ambling pony through the by-lanes of his hills, catch
sight of a poor wretch ploughing in the distance, and beckon
him up to him *on purpose to get his nûzzur.*

"The miserable man feels in his waistband for a piece
of silver. Ah! there is a rupee! He runs up to the Maharajah, and presents it trembling. Golâb Singh, *in an absent
manner,* slips the money into his girdle, asks after his wife
and family, exhausts all the resources of his accomplished
manner on making the man think he really cares a fig for
him; and then, riding on, he tells you, with a chuckle, that
'that poor devil's field only produces five rupees,' so that
he has just robbed him of one-fifth of his harvest! *That*
he considers a feat; and certainly it is the legerdemain of
the devil!

"Having now thrown off the picture of the King of
Cashmere for your own private gallery of human nature,
I think you will exclaim, 'How *could* the English make
a *King* of such a scourge?' The answer is that it was
one of those political necessities which are deplored, but
cannot be avoided without embracing a still greater evil.

"The chief person in the framing of the Treaties which
ended the campaign in February, 1846, was Colonel Henry
Lawrence, whose assistant I am now; and I am sure *the*
public voice will bear me out in asserting that he is the
most benevolent and philanthropic man in India. It is fair
also that I should add that *he* does not (or did not) believe
Golâb Singh to be the monster I have above depicted.

"In his own book, 'The Adventurer in the Punjab,' he

describes him to be a bad man; but most Sikh chiefs were
bad men; their *school* was one of tyranny and barbarous
disregard of human life and all finer human feelings. In
the course of my late residence at his Court, however, I
saw the *beast in his lair;* and I prophesy that Cashmere,
now reduced to nearly the lowest point of misery which
men endure before they expatriate themselves for ever,
will, under his iron rule, be depopulated in a few years!

"Oh, what a field is that valley at this moment for that
noble animal, *a just ruler!* In five years I would undertake to raise its revenue to a million, and its people from
Irish poverty to what Providence designed them to enjoy—
scriptural milk and honey.

"This brings me back to the unfinished thread of the
Cashmere Insurrection.

"On October 19, Meêrza Fukeêr Oolluh of Rajâwur,
the mainstay and ally of Sheikh Imâm-úd-dín, came in to
me and submitted.

"The army still advanced, and had reached the foot of
Barangulla Pass into Cashmere, when the rebellious Sheikh
wrote to say he would meet me at Barangulla, on October
30. This was a march ahead of our Army.

"I went with two regiments to guard against treachery.

"Late at night, Imâm-úd-dín, worn out with a forced
mountain-march of forty miles, in the course of which he
had been drenched in a snowstorm, arrived; and, surrounded by his officers, made his submission to the British
Government (which I hope you can imagine me representing!).

"On November 1, I had the pleasure of conducting him
to the tent of Colonel Lawrence, the Governor-General's
Agent, who had a few days before come up with the army.

"And thus ended the rebellion.

"At this present (November 11), I am on my road to
Lahore, in charge of the Sheikh and his army—leading, in
fact, my own bear into town.

" Now, you know, if I were an ancient Roman I should
be entitled to 'a triumph,' and should enter the city in
a gold chariot (the original of our 'glass fly'?) with
Sheikh Imâm-úd-dín and his lieutenants darbied and
muffled, and a shopful of Cashmere shawls held up on
yard-measures waving gloriously cheap in the air. A band
of Cashmere virgins—or mayhap old women, for lack of
them—would announce my advent with songs of ' Io
triumphe ! Io triumphe !' and the senators (now called
Lal Singh, Tej Singh, Deena Nâth, Bhuggut Râm, and
other unpatrician names) would be Maulii and Fabii,
coming out in snowy togas—or what moderns vulgarly
call clean shirts—to welcome my return !

" As it is, I shall be challenged by a black sentry, who,
ten to one, won't let me into Rome—I mean Lahore—
without the countersign.

" This comes of not being one's own ancestor ! . . .

" Before closing this enormous budget, let me acknowledge your kind letter of July 29, written in the sunny
isle of Jersey; which reached me when I was up to my
elbows in the Rebellion. . . . It set me thinking about
our different lots—yours all peace; mine all unrest, excitement, struggle, and turmoil ! . . .

" These barbarous phases of society, into which an
educated man descends as into a pit of lions, have, after
all, a wild, almost terrible interest. There is something
noble in putting the hand of civilization on the mane
of a nation like the Punjab (if I may borrow Spenser's
allegory), and *looking down* brute passions.

" What a victory ! to bind a bullying people with a
garland—to impose security of life, good order, and law
as fines, upon a whole nation, for their offences against the
tranquillity of the human race !

" Yours ever affectionately,

" (Signed)   HERBERT B. EDWARDES."

THE TOWN OF SRINUGGER, THE CAPITAL OF CASHMERE.

The great Mosque, entirely of deodar, or cedar-wood, built A.D. 1500.

Is it necessary to say something, before we pass on, on the subject of giving over the beautiful province of Cashmere to Golâb Singh, of whom we have been reading how cruel a character he bore? (But of which of the Sirdars could the historian paint a fair and unsullied picture?)

We can find some explanation in Edwardes's words on this subject.

" It is often asked, Why was Rajah Golâb Singh so highly honoured and so lavishly rewarded for his *double* treachery— to *us*, in sending food and ammunition to the Sikhs; to his *countrymen*, in betraying the cause he volunteered to advocate?

" The premises assumed being incorrect, it is only logical that the conclusion should be false.

" Rajah Golâb Singh sent *no* supplies to the Sikh army; he only promised to do so—in itself almost a warrant that they never went, even if we knew not, from other sources, that he sent not a man, nor a grain of corn, nor a pound of powder. He only came to Lahore after repeated and pressing calls; and when there he told the Durbar, the chiefs, and the soldiers that ' they were asses; that, if they wanted peace, he, *who had taken no part in hostilities*, would plead for them; and, if they wanted war, they might go to ruin their own way.' {Rajah Golâb Singh.}

" He was taken at his word, and yet not trusted. Nominally *plenipotentiary*, he was associated with the most astute servants of the Durbar, and the fault, therefore, is not his, if the terms they jointly made were such as the Maharajah found himself unable to fulfil, except by the cession of more territory.

" And when the British Government had become possessors of Cashmere and Jümmoo, Golâb Singh had an undoubted right to purchase, as they to sell it. In exchange for a crore of rupees they took it; and in exchange for a crore of rupees they parted with it again. . . .

"Two things are at all events certain. First, that the Durbar, though publicly poor, was privately rich; as ministers, they had an exhausted treasury; as individuals, they had stores of wealth. . . .

"To talk of the want of *patriotism* or treachery of Goláb Singh—the last of a Sikh-murdered family—is worse than idle. . . .

"Second, it was infinitely better, not only for *us*, but for the people of all ranks in the Punjab, that Goláb Singh should be *out* of it. He could only have wished to be Wazir, that he might realize at last the schemes of aggrandizement which his ambitious heart had for years been scarcely able to contain. It is, indeed, difficult to conjecture whether wisdom would have prompted him to aim only at the independent sovereignty of the hills, which, as a subject, he had so long monopolized; or avarice, his ruling vice, have tempted him to sit upon the throne before which he was once proud to bow. But his road to either object would have been the same.

"The impoverishment of the Punjab would have prepared the way for its division or its conquest, and the hearts of all classes of the people, from the Sirdar to the ryot, would have been gradually broken by fines, confiscations, and extortion."

While Edwardes was conducting Sheikh Inám-úd-dín to Lahore to take his trial, Colonel Lawrence proceeded to Cashmere to see Goláb Singh established in his new possession. During his absence Edwardes was left in political charge at Lahore; and for his exertions in appeasing a second religious tumult in the city, he received the thanks of the East India Company.

CHAPTER IV.

1847—1848.

BUNNOO—TREACHERY AT MOOLTÂN—BATTLE OF
KINYÉREE.

"I have asked you to hear this story to-day, not that we may learn only how battles may be won (we find out generally with more or less of blunder how to do that), but that we may learn the happier lesson, how *man* may be won; what affection there is to be had for the asking; what truth for the trusting; what perennial honour for a moment's justice; what life-long service for a word of love."—JOHN RUSKIN.

CHAPTER IV.

THE chivalrous scheme of guiding the Sikhs to govern their own country, which Henry Lawrence strove so hard to carry out, was found to fail so far, that it became necessary to exercise a more firm control for the suppression of anarchy, and to prevent, if possible, impending ruin. Henry Lawrence's chivalrous scheme fails in part.

But this was *not* possible, even with the energy and chivalry of Henry Lawrence and his band of assistants, who all worked heart and soul with him.

When the catastrophe came, it was (in Edwardes's own words)— The causes of failure.

"Not brought about by the natural process of gradual decay. India has not been looking on at the affecting spectacle of an ancient dynasty sinking feebly and peacefully into the grave, but at the violent agonies of a young and profligate state, which has died by its own hand in the mad moments of a national debauch."

Kaye describes the position of affairs thus: "Ill supported by a corrupt and selfish Durbar, Lawrence and his assistants had been gradually compelled to come forward, far more than they desired, in the character of administrators. Instead of confining themselves to the work of advising and instructing the Sikh officers, and preparing them to take, on the withdrawal of the British, the entire government into their own hands, our English officers had often been necessitated, in spite of their honest endeavours to remain in the Pressure of affairs. Forcing the English administration of affairs.

background, to assume a more prominent position in the actual direction of affairs.

"The formality of the Sikh Durbar was there, but the real administration was our own; and the broad stamp of British beneficence was upon it.

Efforts to develop the resources of the country.

"After the maintenance of general tranquillity, the development of the resources of a neglected country was the chief thought of the English officer; and he worked as strenuously towards the attainment of this great end as though the country had been actually our own.

"The whole country had been surveyed and the system of taxation laid down on fixed principles; the fiscal and excise systems had been readjusted, and oppressive duties and Government monopolies of all sorts abolished. A census had been made, and the population and trades of Lahore determined; and the Durbar had sanctioned the outlay of £30,000 on roads and bridges, to be increased to £60,000 when the state of the country allowed." (Buist's "Annals of India" for the year 1848.)

New code of laws.

To this it may be added that Colonel Henry Lawrence, anxious to have a very simple code of laws, founded on Sikh customs, reduced to writing, and administered by the most respectable men from their own ranks, assembled for the purpose, at Lahore, some fifty Sikh heads of villages—greybeards, of good local reputation, under the immediate superintendence of Lèna Singh, one of the Sikh Sirdars; and they had prepared a code, when Colonel Lawrence was compelled by ill-health to proceed to England for a time.

Henry Lawrence takes leave to England.

Edwardes had not been long at Lahore when he was detached on special duty to Bunnoo, by Colonel Lawrence.

Edwardes deputed to Bunnoo.

It was in February, 1847, that he was deputed, in command of a Sikh force, to make, if possible, an amicable financial settlement of Bunnoo, an Afghan valley, west of the Indus, which had long been in arrears of revenue, and had failed to pay its annual tribute to Lahore; and Runjeet Singh, "The Lion of the Punjab," as he was called, had been unable, for a quarter of a century, to bring them to obedience.

Object of the expedition.

Plans proposed.

Edwardes proposed to the Resident the plan of a regular military reduction and occupation of the valley; and this plan, recommended by the Resident, and approved by the Governor-General (Sir Henry Hardinge *), was at once entrusted to Edwardes to carry out.

He was despatched with five hundred men and two troops of Horse Artillery, and in the brief space of three months he levelled the walls of four hundred fortified villages, built a strong fortress in their stead, and ran a military road through the heart of the valley, by these means entirely subjugating it.

His own words tell the story best, and the details are fully described in "A Year on the Punjab Frontier," which he published when he was at home in 1850. He says in the preface—

"This book is simply what it professes to be—the result of a busy year, on an important frontier, in a country and at a crisis which have excited the national attention of Englishmen. In writing it, the object I have in view is to put on record a victory which I myself remember with more satisfaction than any I helped to gain before Mooltân —the bloodless conquest of the wild valley of Bunnoo. It was accomplished, not by shot or shell, but simply by balancing two races and two creeds. For fear of a Sikh army, two warlike and independent Mohammedan tribes levelled to the ground, at my bidding, the four hundred forts which constituted the strength of their country; and, for fear of those same Mohammedan tribes, the same Sikh army, at my bidding, constructed a fortress for the Crown, which completed the subjugation of the valley.

"It was a year of intense labour in great public duties, with never any certainty of life for four and twenty hours."

This peaceful subjugation of the valley of Bunnoo demands our attention.†

* He became Lord Hardinge in May, 1846.

† From "A Year on the Punjab Frontier" we extract a description of Bunnoo. "In spring it is a vegetable emerald, and in winter its many-coloured harvests look as if Ceres had stumbled against the great Salt Range, and spilt half her cornucopia in this favoured vale. Most of the

Marginal notes:

Military force.

A bloodless conquest.

Balancing two races and two creeds.

Description of the valley of Bunnoo.

In the district of Bunnoo, at Akra and Khâfr-Khôt (by
translation "The Infidels' Fort"), and profusely scattered
over other provinces of the Punjab, occur the remains of
Græco-Bactrian cities, vestiges of the conquering steps and
permanent dominion of Alexander and his Macedonians.

In the second Cabul Campaign, the monument erected by
Alexander over his favourite horse Bucephalus, was passed
by the British army in nearly as perfect a state as the day
when it was erected, and Greek coins were found on the
spot.

These ancient "mounds" are frequently met with in
different parts of these wild frontier lands, and mark the
course of this great warrior of old.

Some of the pieces of ancient stone-carving found distinctly show the mingling of the stiff figures of Indian
sculpture with the more graceful lines of Grecian art.

A photograph, representing some of these Buddhist and
Græco-Bactrian heads, collected and placed in the museum
at Lahore—some of them dug out of ruins at Taxila (now
"Shah-ki-deyree," or the Mounds of the Kings), in the Rawul
Pindee district—will enable the reader to trace this for
himself.

What a pity that such treasures as these, and others like
Akra, in Bunnoo, whether Greek or Buddhist, should lie
at our feet, as full of meaning as the obelisks of Egypt, and
not, like them, be forced to give up their secrets!

About this time, a friend, having felt inclined to shrink
from the first proposal to undertake a certain responsibility,
draws from Edwardes a letter on the subject, which exhibits

fruits of Cabul are found wild, and culture would bring them to perfection.
As it is, the limes, mulberries, and melons are delicious. Roses, too,
without which Englishmen have learnt from the East to think no
scenery complete, abound in the upper part at the close of spring.

"Altogether Nature has so smiled on Bunnoo that the stranger thinks
it a paradise ; and, when he turns to the people, wonders how such spirits
of evil ever found admittance.

"The Bunnoochees are bad specimens of Afghans. Could worse be
said of any human race? They have all the vices of the Puthâns rankly
luxuriant, the virtues stunted. The introduction of Indian cultivators
from the Punjab, and the settlement of numerous low Hindoos in the
valley, have contributed, by intermarrying, slave-dealing, and vice, to
complete the mongrel character of the Bunnoo people."

Mingling of the lines of Buddhist and Grecian art.

Its people.

GROUP OF GRÆCO-BACTRIAN HEADS.

a phase of his own character; and the circumstances that called it forth need not to be further entered upon here.

"Camp Bunnoo, December 17, 1847.

" My DEAR ——,

". . . Concerning the other matters treated of in your letter, I am not offended that you felt uncertain of my sympathy or ridicule. In this world we know little of our neighbours, and, as it was in the days of Wickliffe, so it seems to be pretty much now, that those who have Bibles are obliged to hide them.

"To me the principles you avow seem the highest on which either a public or private person can act in all situations of life ; and if you have succeeded in so disciplining your mind as to see God in everything, and realize His *presence* around and about you at every hour of the day, and refer all questions of life and duty, great or small, to the awful tribunal before which you thus perpetually are standing,—why, you are, in my opinion, as much to be respected as envied by every right-thinking man.

"But excuse me if I ask you whether the fears you express of encountering responsibility are consistent with your reliance on the overruling Power which drives events before it like so many straws? Are you not, with so happy a *morale*, the *last* man who should feel a moment's uneasiness under any amount of responsibility imposed upon you ?

" I do not say that it follows that, because you trust in God, you must *succeed*. The inscrutable laws which are made for a *world's* conduct cannot turn aside for an *individual ;* and it is well known that the best men are often most unfortunate in life. *Means* also are prescribed for the working out of *ends ;* and the plans of a fool, however good his intentions, by accident only occasionally meet with the same success as those of a wise and prudent man.

"The reverse would be a *miracle,* and the infatuated bigot who, on the strength of his intense trust in God ,should

undertake to accomplish ends without the visible material
means (such as an uneducated man to read Hebrew, a
civilian to manœuvre an army, a tailor to make shoes,
a divine to excel in handicrafts which he had never learnt,
or a woman to lift up the Pyramids), would assuredly, in
these days of no-direct Divine interference, be doomed to
bring shame on himself and ridicule on his religion.

"But to take the instance in point. Possessed of sound
sense by nature, and more of the advantages of education
than fall to the lot of most men, you are furnished with
adequate *means* for the accomplishment of any *ends* short
of the highest flights of that semi-inspiration *genius*. And
therefore I think you should have more self-confidence than
I; and while I blame you greatly for the feelings you
entertain upon this particular point, I feel ashamed almost
at the calmness—no, not calmness, more than that, the
enthusiasm—which possesses me whenever great trust is
laid upon me.

"For the first time I begin to ask myself if this is
presumption and windy self-conceit? If the result of my
self-examination is to make me a moral coward, I shall
never forgive you! . . .

"The result will very likely be that . . . *will* come,
and I gather from your note that you will accuse yourself
of having thus interfered with your destiny, instead of
leaving it to be decided for you by others. . . .

"That lack of confidence and those misgivings I hold,
in your case, to be self-imposed delusions, which you might
blow away like tobacco-smoke; which you *ought* to and *will*
conquer; for, depend upon it, my dear ——, they will else
be frightful stumbling-blocks in your public path; and that
a continual mental struggle, however lofty and virtuous
be its aspirations, is not the frame of mind in which to
watch over the 'respublica.' . . .

"I have written this in the midst of a thousand interruptions, and if any expression seems harsh, pray pass over it the sponge of forgiveness.

> " Believe me, ever, my dear ——,
>> " Yours very sincerely,
>> "(Signed)   HERBERT B. EDWARDES."

On December 17, 1847, the powerful, brave, and hitherto unconquered Vizeeree tribes resigned their independence and consented to pay tribute. On December 18, the foundations of the fort of Dhuleepgurgh were laid. On May 5, the people and chiefs were ordered to throw down their forts, about four hundred in number. *{The tribes resign their independence.}*

These chief results had been accomplished in less than three months; but besides these, a new town had been founded, which to this day is flourishing; a military and commercial road made through a roadless valley; tracts of country, from which the fertilizing mountain streams had been diverted by lawless feuds, had been brought back to cultivation by the protection of a strong Government; others, disputed and lying waste, had been settled and occupied and sown once more; canals had been designed and cut, turning a desert into a fruitful land; while, still nearer to civilization, a people who had worn arms as we wear clothes, and used them as we use knives and forks, had ceased to carry arms at all, and, though they quarrelled still, had learnt to bring their differences to the bar of the civil courts, instead of the sharp issue of the sword. In a word, the valley of Bunnoo, which had defied the Sikh arms for twenty-five years, had in three months been peacefully annexed to the Punjab and subjugated without a shot being fired. This was a conquest of peace, won by influence — personal influence — such influence as every political officer should exercise in the country under his charge. As Edwardes says— *{Results.}*

" Such I am proud to think every other assistant to the Resident at Lahore had acquired in his own district. See how the Hazára tribes took James Abbott for their Khan! See how the Eurofzáes loved Lumsden! See how the men *{Personal influence.}*

of Rawul Pindee followed Nicholson! When the Mooltán
Rebellion first broke out, I had been, off and on, about a
year among the Trans-Indus people. I had gone to them
at the head of great armies, on great errands, and met with
great success. A master who had confidence in me entrusted
me with almost despotic power, for good or evil; and I trust
the people never saw me wield it except for good. I found
five different countries oppressed by one tyrant, and removed
him. I found three chiefs in exile, and restored them.
Those countries and those chiefs rallied round me in the
hour of need, and were my army.

Civilized
and un-
civilized
govern-
ment con-
trasted.

"Another source of influence was fixedness of purpose
—a determination to make many barbarian wills give way
to one that was civilized. In British India, the mind of
Government is registered in laws and regulations for the
people's good. . . .

"Far different is the condition of the half-subdued
frontier of an ill-governed native state. There laws exist
not, and he who rules must rule the people by his *will*.
If his will be evil, the people will be far more miserable
than it is possible for any people to be in the corner of
British India which is administered with least ability; but
if his will be good as well as strong, 'happy are the people
that are in such a case;' for a benevolent despotism is the
best of all governments.

"In my little sphere I gave my whole soul to the
establishment of that vast and priceless blessing, peace;
and can truly say that no man assisted me without being
rewarded, and no man opposed me without being punished.
This was well known; and when I held up my hand for
soldiers, the soldiers came; and when I turned my back
upon the province during an imperial war, peace still
reigned undisturbed behind me." *

* A local journal, called the *Indian Public Opinion and Punjab
Times*, makes the following comments upon these times and events:—
"The success with which Edwardes reduced the turbulent valley of

In illustration of the foregoing remarks may be quoted   In illustra-
the following happy ending of a long-sustained "boundary   tion.
feud : " *—

"Knowing their superstitious natures, I called in a holy   Settling a
priest, and explaining to him my earnest wish to put an end   boundary
to this bloody strife, I bade him take up his Korán, and   feud.
follow me to the bank of the Indus, where I had already
assembled the chiefs and followers of the contending sides.
Then, leading in the priest, I addressed the assembly,
recounted the forays of the last few years, and the barren
fields and desolate hearths they had occasioned ; the con-
sequent poverty of the people, and resentment of the
Government ; and my own determination to treat either
party as an enemy who should in future bring disgrace
upon my head, by appealing to the sword, instead of me,
for justice.

"'You *know* your own boundaries well enough,' I said ;
'they are written down in your hearts, though you say you
have got no papers ; and Allah sees them, though I cannot.
This holy man will swear you both on the Korán. Tell him
a lie at your peril. Declare your boundaries now, once
for all, and I will see you stick to them. Then there will
be peace ; and you will all cultivate, and get rich, and be

Bunnoo to obedience, persuaded the wild tribes to pay revenue, and pulled
down the four hundred forts in the valley, was, in our opinion, a greater
proof of genius than all his victories over the troops of Dewan Moolraj.
  "The difficulty of the undertaking can hardly be exaggerated. The
Bunnoochees had never, voluntarily, paid a rupee of revenue. A Sikh
army, it is true, every two or three years, made a raid upon the valley,
and carried off whatever they could plunder ; and this they called
collecting the revenue. And yet, at the persuasion of Edwardes, these
wild, lawless people submitted, and beat their swords into ploughshares.
The forts were all pulled down by a certain day ; and Bunnoo has, ever
since, been as peaceful as any district on the frontier. Edwardes had
immense influence over natives ; and it was a remarkable sight to see
him in a 'jirgah,' or council, arguing with the chiefs, persuading and
gesticulating with such good humour and skill, that he generally won
them to his side of the argument before he had finished."
  * Their quarrels are generally about land.

good friends with Government, and there will be no
necessity for an army to come with guns, and blow all
your villages away like a whirlwind. As for the past,
everybody's honour is satisfied. The Kusrânees pride
themselves on being thieves, and they stole the Ooshturânnees' cattle; the Ooshturânnees pride themselves on
being brave, and they killed the Kusrânees in the fight.
Now begin a new score; shake hands; and when you
have done swearing, come along to my tent, where there
is a new turban for every follower, a shawl for every chief,
and a good dinner for everybody.' I then left them to the
priest, who frightened them dreadfully, I was told; and
then made them swear on the Korân to keep the peace
and their own boundaries; after which they all got dresses
of honour, and dined together without stabbing any one.'

"Once only during the war did I hear of this peace
being disturbed. Futteh Khan, Ooshturânnee, followed me
to Mooltân, with all his retainers, and one day he came
to me, boiling with rage, and requested a furlough—so
many days to go home, a day to stay and shoot a Kusrânee
who had stolen one of his goats, and so many days to
come back again. On his honour he wouldn't overstay his
leave, and hoped there would be no fight while he was
away!

"I had very great trouble to prevent his going, and he
was sulky for a long while afterwards at having been made
to pocket an affront; however, I have little doubt that he
has shot the man since."

Terms of
the Treaty
of Byrowâl.

By the Treaty of Byrowâl, which was concluded in March
1847, Lord Hardinge had undertaken that the Punjab should
be managed during the minority of Maharajah Dhuleep
Singh. Lord Hardinge engaged to control the civil internal
administration of the country and to maintain tranquillity
within, as well as to provide for its external security; and
this he engaged to do at the especial instance of the Lahore
Sirdars.

The consequence of this arrangement was that a peace ensued in the Punjab to which it had long been a stranger. _{Peace ensued.}

But in April, 1848, occurred the treacherous murder, at Mooltân, of two young Englishmen, Mr. Vans Agnew, of the Civil Service, and Lieutenant W. A. Anderson, of the 1st Bombay Fusiliers— _{How disturbed.}

"Young men of great promise and who had already distinguished themselves. The former is described by the Acting-Resident at Lahore, Sir Frederick Currie (Henry Lawrence was obliged by sickness to take leave to England in 1847–48), as 'the oldest political officer on this frontier, and a man of much ability, energy, and judgment, with considerable experience in administrative duties.' . . . And Lieutenant Anderson is spoken of as an excellent Oriental scholar, who was for some time Deputy-Collector in Sindh under Sir Charles Napier, and has travelled through the whole of the Mooltân districts." * _{Agnew and Anderson.}

These two young men were chosen at Lahore to proceed to Mooltân on special duty. And here comes in a romance of history, more vivid and exciting than any romance of fiction. _{Truth stranger than fiction.}

Moolraj was the Governor of Mooltân under the Sikh Government; but failing in his payment of tribute or in his faculty for wielding independent authority, and, from the protection afforded by the English power at Lahore, being unable to oppress his people to his heart's content, he came to Lahore and pressed upon the Durbar his proposal to resign. _{Moolraj proposes to resign.}

Every opportunity was given to him to recall his wish to be relieved of his office as Dewan or Governor of Mooltân, but he persisted in it.

It was therefore arranged that two English officers should go to him two months before his resignation; that he should instal them in charge, and initiate them himself.

It was at his own earnest desire, and not in any way to take his government from him, that they were sent. And

* See Blue-Book, page 120.

this, after repeatedly giving him the option of retracting his first voluntary proposal.

These remarks are made to show the *treachery* of the deeds that follow.

As Edwardes says—

" Into the clear hearts and open acts of the British officers you may look for ever, and find no cause for the rebellion.*

" The hot weather was beginning, and they were induced by the heat to proceed by water, while their escort marched by land. The Sikh escort† consisted of about fourteen hundred men, the Goorkha regiment of Infantry six hundred strong, seven hundred Cavalry, and one hundred Artillery-men with six guns.

Arrival and encampment.   " They all met together at Mooltân on April 18, and encamped in the Eedgah, a spacious Mahommedan building within cannon-shot of the north face of the fort, and about a mile from Moolraj's residence, which was a garden-house outside the fort, called the Am-Khâs.

" Early on the morning of April 19 the two British officers and Sirdar Khan Singh‡ accompanied Moolraj into the fort. They were shown all over it; received the keys; were invited by Moolraj to install their own Goorkhas in possession, and plant their own sentinels. They mustered Moolraj's garrison, who seemed angry at the prospect of losing employment; allayed their fears with promise of service, and prepared to return, Mr. Agnew speaking kindly to them, and assuring them that they should be kept in their present service and their present grades.

" The whole party then mounted, Mr. Agnew going on with Moolraj, followed by Lieutenant Anderson with Khan Singh. They passed forth, and on to the bridge over the ditch. Two soldiers of Moolraj were standing on the bridge.

---

* " A Year on the Punjab Frontier," vol. ii. page 58.
† All natives.   ‡ The new Nazim.

"One of them, named Umeer Chund, gazed for a moment at the two unarmed Englishmen, and then struck Mr. Agnew so unexpectedly with a spear in the side that he unhorsed him, and Agnew sprang to his feet; at the same instant Moolraj's horse reared, and he forthwith rode off to the Am-Khâs, making no attempt to interfere.

"Agnew, who was ignorant of fear, struck his assailant with the riding-stick in his hand. The ruffian threw away his spear, and, rushing in with his sword, inflicted two severer wounds. He would probably have killed Mr. Agnew on the spot had he not been knocked into the ditch by a horseman of the escort. The scuffle was now known; the crowd pressed round to see what was the matter. News was carried back into the fort that swords were out on the bridge; an uproar rose within; and in another moment the whole garrison came pouring forth.

"Moolraj had got safe back to the Am-Khâs. Nor was this all; his own personal Sowars turned back *half-way*, and pursued Lieutenant Anderson, who had, till now, escaped.

"Who can tell now who ordered them to go back? These men sought out Anderson, attacked and cut him down with swords, so that he fell for dead upon the ground, where he was found afterwards by some of his own Goorkha soldiers, who put him on a litter and carried him back to the Eedgah. Meanwhile Sirdar Khan Singh extricated Agnew from the mob, lifted him on his own elephant, and hurried away, roughly binding up his wounds as he went along.

"The road lay past the end of Moolraj's garden, but finding guns were being drawn out and matchlocks fired, they took another road. Moolraj was inside. If *he had not ordered them to fire*, how came they to do so? — Moolraj's conduct.

"At the Eedgah, whence they had started, the two friends met. A sad meeting for them, who had gone out full of life, and health, and zeal to do their duty. Their wounds dressed, Mr. Agnew drew up a report of these occurrences to — Meeting of the two friends.

the Resident at Lahore ; addressed a letter to Moolraj,
expressing a generous disbelief in his participation, but
calling on him to justify this opinion by seizing the guilty
parties, and coming himself to see them at the Eedgah."

This was at eleven, and at two Mr. Agnew wrote off to
Edwardes and Cortlandt for assistance.*

" Moolraj briefly sent a message he could neither give up
the guilty nor come himself. Agnew behaved with con-
summate calmness and heroism. He pointed out to the
messenger how absolutely indispensable it was for Moolraj
to come to them, if he wished to be thought innocent. But
Moolraj never came, and his message briefly advised them
to see to their own safety.

" The messenger on his return found his master now
presiding in a war-council of his chiefs. The Puthâns of
the garrison were setting their seals to an oath of allegiance
on the *Korân*; the Hindoos, on the *Shastras* ; the Sikhs, on
the holy *Grunth*.

" The Sikhs were fastening a war-bracelet on the wrist of
Moolraj himself!

" On the evening and night of April 19 the whole of the

* A transcript of poor Agnew's last words may be added in a note.
The original is still preserved, scrawled in a hurried hand.
                                        " Mooltân, 2 p.m. April 19.
    " MY DEAR SIR,
            " You have been ordered to send one regiment here. Pray let
it march *instantly*, or, if gone, hasten to top speed. If you can spare another,
pray send it also.
    " I am responsible for the measure. I am cut up a little, and on my
back. Lieutenant Anderson is much worse. He has five sword-wounds ;
I have two in my left arm from warding sabre-cuts, and a poke in the
ribs with a spear.
    " I don't think Moolraj has anything to do with it. I was riding with
him when we were attacked. He rode off, but is now said to be in the
hands of the soldiery.
    " Râm Singh and his people all right.
                            " Yours in haste,
        " (Signed)   P. A. VANS AGNEW.
    " To General Cortlandt, or Lieutenant Edwardes, Bunnoo."

carriage-cattle of the officers and their escort, which were
out grazing, were carried off. No flight was possible. But
these brave men thought not of flight.

"Morning broke, and Mr. Agnew made one last effort to
avert the coming tragedy.

"He forwarded to Moolraj's officers the purwánnas of the _{Last appeal}
Maharajah, ordering them to make over the fort to Sirdar ^{to Moolraj.}
Khan Singh, and obey all Mr. Agnew's orders.

"The messengers found Moolraj again engaged in council
with his chiefs and organizing the rebellion.

"These messengers were told Moolraj was their master,
and they would only obey him. This extinguished hope.

"Agnew wrote to the British Agent at Bháwulpoor to
bring troops to his assistance, intending to hold out in the
Eedgah till this reinforcement could arrive.

"All disguise was now cast aside. The guns of the
fort opened on the Eedgah. The Lahore Artillerymen
refused to serve the guns. The fire of the rebels never
slackened. . . .

"And now arrived an Embassy from Moolraj in return
for Mr. Agnew's. Moolraj invited the escort to desert the
British officers, and promised to raise the pay of every
soldier who came over.

"One Goláb Singh, commandant of the Ghorchurruhs of
the escort, led the way, and went over to Moolraj, who
tricked the traitor out with gold necklaces and bracelets,
and sent him back as a decoy. In vain Mr. Agnew
bestowed money on the troops to hold out for three days
only. It was honest money.

"The troops went over—Horse, Foot, Artillery ; all had
deserted by the evening, except Sirdar Khan Singh, some
eight or ten faithful horsemen, the domestic servants of the
British officers, and the moonshees of their office.

"Beneath the lofty central dome of that empty hall, so
strong and formidable that a very few stout hearts could have

defended it, stood this miserable group, around the beds of the two wounded Englishmen. All hope of resistance being at an end, Mr. Agnew had sent a party to Moolraj to ask for peace. A conference ensued, and in the end it was agreed that the officers were to quit the country, and that the attack upon them was to cease. Too late!

"The sun had gone down, twilight was closing in, and the rebel army had not tasted blood.

A cry for blood.

"An indistinct and distant murmur reached the ears of the few remaining inmates of the Eedgah, who were listening for their fate. Louder and louder it grew until it became a cry—the cry of a multitude for blood!

"On they came, from city, suburbs, fort—soldiers with their arms; citizens, young and old, and of all trades and callings, with any weapon they could snatch.

"A company of Moolraj's Muzbees (or outcasts, turned Sikhs) led the mob.

A cruel mob.

"It was an appalling sight, and Sirdar Khan Singh begged of Mr. Agnew to be allowed to wave a sheet and sue for mercy. Weak in body from loss of blood, Agnew's heart failed him not. He replied, 'The time for mercy is gone; let none be asked for. They can kill us two if they like, but we are not the last of the English. *Thousands of Englishmen will come down here when we are gone,* and *annihilate Moolraj and his soldiers, and his fort.* . . .

"'The crowd now rushed in with horrible shouts, made Khan Singh prisoner, and, pushing aside the servants with the butts of their muskets, surrounded the two wounded officers.

"Lieutenant Anderson from the first had been too much wounded even to move; and now Mr. Agnew was sitting by his bedside, holding his hand, and talking in English. Doubtless they were bidding each other farewell for all Time.

"But the time was short.

"Goodhur Singh, a Muzbee, so deformed and crippled with wounds that he looked more like an imp than mortal man, stepped forth from the crowd with drawn sword, and, after insulting Mr. Agnew with a few last indignities, struck him twice upon the neck, and with a third blow cut off his head. Some other wretch discharged a musket into the lifeless body. *The end of the tragedy.*

"Then Anderson was hacked to death with swords; and afterwards the two bodies were dragged outside, and slashed and insulted by the crowd, and left all night under the sky. . . .

"Morning assembles the crowd again; no longer furious, but content. Whither go they? To the Am-Khâs, Moolraj's palace, for he is now a king. . . .

"There sits the arch-rebel, in High Durbar, taunting Sirdar Khan Singh, late his rival, now his prisoner. Goodhur Singh, the murderer, approaches, and presents a head—noble still in death. The crowd make way for him as for some good man, and call him the second prophet. Umeer Chund, who assaulted Agnew at the fort, is called the first. *Scene in Moolraj's court.*

"Moolraj rewards the second prophet with an elephant, some money, and the horse his victim rode; and long afterwards poor Agnew's servants, peeping from their hiding-places in the suburbs, could see their master's assassin capering through the street on their master's well-remembered horse.

"The head was then thrown into the lap of Sirdar Khan Singh, who is told to 'take the head of the youth he had brought down to govern at Mooltân.'

"The Sirdar, thinking over many kindnesses and benefits he had received at the hands of Mr. Agnew, burst into tears. The head was immediately taken from him. It was not allowed to be wept over. Indignities followed which it can serve no good purpose to repeat. Suffice it that, as all things pall in this world, so Moolraj and the multitude *Indignities to the murdered Englishmen.*

outside at last grew weary of dishonouring the murdered Englishmen.

"Moolraj ordered them to be buried, and they were laid in a hasty grave among the tufts of grass by the Eedgah, near the place of their murder.

"Twice the people of Mooltân tore them up, to rob them of the clothes that wrapped them. A third time they were buried, and a sentry placed over the spot till they were forgotten by their murderers.

Moolraj's rebellion in its rise.
"Such was Dewan Moolraj's rebellion in its rise. Can any one pity such a rebel in his fall?

"Moolraj is not less a murderer because he was one on a large scale, and murdered with an army instead of a kitchen-knife. He was the assassin of his invited guests; the traitor who dethroned the dynasty under which his family rose from insignificance to honour; the rebel who, striking selfishly for his own independence, rivetted the chains of his country."

The commotion caused by this event was not limited to Mooltân, but spread from thence into other provinces, and resulted in a general insurrection of the Punjab.

Agnew's letter reaches Edwardes.
While this terrible scene was enacting at Mooltân, poor Agnew's letter, written on April 19, 1848, was making its way to Edwardes's camp. It reached him on the 22nd, and at once he hastened to their succour.

Edwardes tells the story—

"It was towards evening of the 22nd, at Dera Futteh Khan, on the Indus, that I was sitting in a tent full of Beloochee zamindars,* who were either robbers, robbed, or witnesses to the robberies of their neighbours, taking evidence in a trial. Loud footsteps, as of some one running, were heard without, came nearer as we all looked up and listened, and at last stopped before the door. There was a whispering, a scraping off of shoes, and brushing off of dust from the

* Owners of land.

wearer's feet, and then the purdah (curtain) of the door
was lifted, and a kossid (running messenger), stripped to the
waist and steaming with heat, entered and presented a letter-
bag, whose crimson hue proclaimed the urgency of its
contents.

"'It was from the Sahib in Mooltân,' he said, 'to the
Sahib in Bunnoo; but as I was here I might as well look
at it.'

"I took it up, and read the Persian superscription on the
bag: 'To General Cortlandt, in Bunnoo, or wherever else
he may be.'

"It was, apparently, not for me, but it was for an officer
under my orders, and the messenger said it was on important
public service.   I had, therefore, a right to open it, if I
thought it necessary.   But there was something in the
kossid's manner which *alike* compelled me to open it and
forbade me either to question him before the crowd around
me, or show any anxiety about it.

"So I opened it as deliberately as I could, and found an
English letter enclosed, directed to either General Cortlandt or myself.   It was a copy taken by a native clerk of a
public letter addressed to Sir Frederick Currie by Mr. P.
Vans Agnew, one of his assistants on duty at Mooltân, with
a postscript in pencil, written by Mr. Agnew and addressed
to us.

"Appended is a faithful fac-simile, which will be regarded with mournful interest as the last tracings of a hand,
ever generous, ever brave, which held fast honour and public
duty to the death.

"During the perusal of this letter I felt that all eyes
were upon me, for no one spoke, not a pen moved, and there
was that kind of hush which comes over an assembly under
some indefinite feeling of alarm.   I never remember in my life
being more moved, or feeling more painfully the necessity of
betraying no emotion.   After lingering over the last few

sentences as long as I could, I looked up at the kossid, and said, 'Very good! Sit down in that corner of the tent, and I'll attend to you as soon as I have done this trial.' Then turning to the gaping moonshees, I bade them 'go on with the evidence;' and the disappointed crowd once more bent their attention on the witnesses. But from that moment I heard no more. My eyes, indeed, were fixed mechanically on the speakers, but my thoughts were at Mooltân, with my wounded countrymen, revolving how I ought to act to assist them." *

His design for relief. Although he had at his disposal only a single Infantry native regiment, and an inadequate force for such an enterprise, he conceived the daring design of driving the rebel Moolraj into his fortress of Mooltân, and of rescuing the whole of the country around Mooltân from his grasp. But his first act was to send off a letter in reply to Agnew, to assure him that he should lose no time in hastening to his assistance.

"Camp, Dera Futteh Khan, April 22, 1848.

Reply to Agnew. "MY DEAR AGNEW,

"Your letter of April 19 to General Cortlandt reached my camp at three p.m. to-day, and I fortunately opened it, to see if it was on public business.

"I need scarcely say that I have made arrangements for marching to your assistance at once. I have one Infantry regiment and four extra companies, two Horse Artillery guns, twenty zumbooruks;† and between three and four hundred horse. This is a small force, but such as it is you are welcome to it, and *me*.

"Your position is one of immense peril; but God will bring an honest man out of worse straits, so trust in Him, and keep up your pluck. . . . Rely on it, it shall not be my

* "A Year on the Punjab Frontier."
† Camel-mounted guns.

Lt Anderson to
give Anderson
myself come to
and asked him to
I cannot throw
to do with it
when he is
off, but to now-
hands of the State

Grant

All right

Mooltan 19th April 1848

My dear Sir Frederick

You will be sorry to hear that as Anderson
and I were coming out of the Fort Gate after
having received charge of the Fort from Dewan
Moolraj; we were attacked by a couple of
soldiers, who taking us unawares succeeded
in wounding us both pretty sharply. Anderson
is worst off poor fellow, he has a severe
wound on the thigh another on the shoulder,
one on the back of the neck, and one in the face
I think it most necessary that a doctor should
be sent down this I hope not to need him
myself. I have a smart gash in the left shoulder
and am this the same arm. The whole
Troop have multimed, but we hope to
get them round. They have turned our
two Companies out of the Fort

Yours in haste

fault if we are a day later than the 27th; but the very
sound of our approach will be a check to your rascally
enemies; and to *you* as refreshing as the breeze which
heralds the rising sun at morning.

"If you are pressed, pray bring away Anderson, and join
me. With all my heart I hope you are both safe at this
moment. Write—write; and believe me, with the sincerest
wishes, in weal or woe,

"Yours aye,
"(Signed)   HERBERT B. EDWARDES."

The cheery ring from this glowing heart would have
encouraged the brave fellows if it had ever reached them.
But they were past all succour before Edwardes's return-
messenger reached Mooltan.

Too late!

Startled from his plans of legislative improvement and
moral regeneration in Bunnoo in this rough way, Edwardes
quickly set himself to raise the mountain tribes, to discipline
raw levies, with the view to drive back the rebel chieftain
behind the very walls of the fortress from whose citadel
he had long oppressed the surrounding country, and within
which he had now crowned his oppression of his own people
by murder and rebellion.

Measures
taken
against
Moolraj.

How Edwardes gathered his army, and maintained and
paid his soldiers, may best be told in his own words. We
have already noted how, when he held up his hand for
soldiers, the soldiers came; and now he had real need of them.
The force that he raised, was fed and paid out of the revenues
of the country which it conquered.

How fed
and paid.

"I commenced the war," he says, "with a few thousand
rupees in hand, and maintained it for nine months with
an expenditure, civil and military, of two lakhs of rupees
a month, without receiving more than one lakh from the
Sikh and another from the British Government.

"Commissariat I had none at first; but the war was
in a fat country, and to find corn we had only to find money.

General
Cortlandt.

"In the extensive financial arrangements which such wants and expenditure required, I was assisted more than I can sufficiently express by General Cortlandt, one of the best coadjutors ever man had. The soldiers, being poor, were paid regularly every fortnight throughout the war.

Wild dis-
cipline.

"As to discipline; there was no time to attempt what regular soldiers call discipline. The men had to fight the day after they were enlisted, and they could only fight their own way. All I did was to make the best of their way; to draw tight such discipline as they had.

"So while Foujdar Khan gathered all his Mooltânee Puthâns around him, I encouraged Futteh Khan To-wannuh to summon his father's friends.

Existing
rivalries
controlled.

"Bitter and deadly hatreds and jealousies raged between them; but separate ends of the encampment were assigned to each, and morning and evening, when I held Durbar, native fashion, on the ground, to please my men, the various officers of either party ranged themselves behind the young Mullick or Foujdar, on opposite sides of the carpet, and viewed each other with subdued resentment. Occasionally a rush would be made by both parties to get on my right hand, but by equal kindness and access to both, by equalizing their pay, and advising them in their squabbles, I soon got them to lie down together like the lion and the lamb, and at last, little more of their former enmity remained than served as a useful rivalry in the field.

Concerning
plunder.

"With regard to plunder; discipline was steadily enforced. Had the smallest offence of this kind been overlooked, the whole force would have become a band of robbers, and I made instant and severe examples of every offender. If a soldier *wanted* his discharge without pay, he had nothing to do but to go to a field and steal a sugar-cane, when he was followed by the screaming husbandman to my tent, and took the consequences.

"It is a pleasing reflection to me that, under the protection of the irregular force, while blockading Moolraj, *Moolraj's tenants saved the fields around Mooltán.*

Effective discipline saved the crops to Moolraj's tenants.

"As to fighting; this is a very easy matter if men are brave, and on the Indus frontier the population lived in a state of feud. . .

"As for a reserve; I never permitted such a thing. A regular army may rally and return to the charge.

Reserve.

"I have seen my own glorious corps, the 1st Bengal Fusiliers, return a third time to the attack of a Sikh entrenchment higher than their heads, after two cruel repulses, and with two hundred of their men and officers down on the ground. That was at Sobrâon. Did they get in? *Of course* they got in. *Such* troops *must* get in! But it is a very different thing with undisciplined armies.

"They are either successful or defeated at once. There is no middle course; no doubt about the matter. No reserve will ever stop their flight; but the 'reserve' will run, and run, with the advance that has been repulsed.

"The force was kept together during nine months of varying success, by regular pay and kind treatment.

"The officers I learnt to know well—their characters, their circumstances, and their wants; and by living the same life they did, wearing the same dress, talking the same language, and sharing with them all dangers and fatigues, they became attached to me and I to them.

Influence.

"I believe that, when the war was over and we had seen our mutual enemy subdued, to part was a mutual sorrow.

"Wild, barbarous, indifferent to human life, they were yet free, simple as children, brave, faithful to their masters, sincere towards their God. During the whole war I never lost by desertion one man of all whom I had enlisted. . . .

"The crowded city has its virtues, but so has the desert and the mountain; and he who walks the world aright will find something good wherever he finds man, and nothing barren from Dan to Beersheba." *

This was the material with which Edwardes prepared to do his work. The generous confidence, as well as the vigorous hand and the masterly intellect with which he performed it, tell their own tale.

He saw the disastrous consequences of *defeat* on the frontier and of *delay*, which would allow Moolraj to get possession of the country, collect the revenue, gather recruits, and strengthen himself at Mooltân. And if the British army could not take the field till after the rains, all our difficulties would only increase.

---

* Archdeacon Hare, in his "Guesses at Truth," p. 411, has noticed with approval Edwardes's confidence in his fellow-men. He says, " I cannot deny myself the pleasure of confirming what is here said, by the authority of one of those great soldiers and statesmen whom our Indian empire breeds, and who has exemplified the power of these principles by his own wonderful achievements, both pacific and military, on the banks of the Indus. Major Edwardes, in his 'Year on the Punjab Frontier,' after speaking of an expedition he undertook into the country of the savage Vizeeree tribes, relying on the honour of one of their chiefs, adds, ' I pause upon this apparently trifling incident for no foolish vanity of my own, but for the benefit of others; for hoping, as I earnestly do, that many a young soldier, glancing over these pages, will gather heart and encouragement for the stormy lot before him, I desire above all things to put into his hand the staff of confidence in his fellow-men.

> " Candid and generous and just,
>   Boys care but little whom they trust,—
>   An error soon corrected ;
> For who but learns in riper years
> That man, when smoothest he appears,
>   Is most to be suspected ? "—

is a verse very pointed and clever, but quite unworthy of the "Ode to Friendship," and inculcating a creed which would make a sharper or a monk of whoever should adopt it. The man who cannot trust others is, by his own showing, untrustworthy himself. Suspicious of all, depending on himself for everything, from the conception to the deed, the ground-plan to the chimney-pot, he will fail for want of the heads of Hydra, and the hands of Briareus. If there is any lesson that I have learnt from life, it is that human nature, black or white, is better than we think it, and he who reads these pages to a close will see how much faith I have had occasion to place in the rudest and wildest of their species, how nobly it was deserved, and how useless I should have been without it ' (from ' Year on the Punjab Frontier ')."

"The only move which can save this frontier," Edwardes writes, "is, in my opinion, the advance of Bháwul Khan's army across the Sutlej, so as to threaten Mooltán, and oblige Moolraj to recall his frontier expeditions."

He writes to the Resident at Lahore—

"I see by the papers that the idea has got about that Moolraj has sixty thousand soldiers; at present he has not more than ten thousand. But if Mooltán is not invested, however slightly, and a few months elapse before any steps are taken to check his present career of impunity, those who best know the military resources of this frontier are quite of opinion that he may gather fifty thousand; from what I see, I quite agree with them." *

The scenes rapidly deepen in interest, but they are fully told in Edwardes's own book; and our space obliges us to content ourselves with a glance only at some of them—a hasty sketch and a few extracts. Those who want to follow him closer through these nine months of scenes of danger and of chivalry, should take up his "Year on the Punjab Frontier," and they will not be disappointed.

"General Cortlandt was already co-operating nobly with Edwardes, and none saw clearer than he to what end events were tending; none new better the value of every hour."

Now comes a letter from the Resident at Lahore (June 5, 1848)—

"The account you give of your force is highly satis-

---

* In the *Calcutta Review*, No. 43, April, 1854, there is an article by Sir Henry Lawrence (in answer to some assertions made by Sir Charles Napier), in which he says, writing of Edwardes, "Since the days of Clive no man has done as Edwardes, nor do I know many who could and would have acted as he did, on the Mooltán outbreak. Few indeed, with his means, would have taken the same decided step, and fewer could have carried it out."

factory, and reflects the greatest credit on your zeal and perseverance, which have raised the greater part of it and made it what it is in the short space of a month."

And to the Secretary of the Government of India, by the same, and same date—

"I forward a letter from Lieutenant Edwardes. His Lordship will perceive that this enterprising and energetic officer has entirely succeeded in performing the duty assigned to him of getting possession of and holding the whole of the Mooltân districts Trans-Indus."

Edwardes writes to the Resident—

Nawâb of Bhâwulpore co-operates.

"I have urged Bhâwul Khan to put his troops across the Sutlej, and co-operate. . . . The Nawâb has a very fine little force of from ten thousand to twelve thousand men, well equipped and disciplined, and composed almost entirely of fighting Puthâns. . . . He is desirous that a British officer should be with his force."

Lieutenant Edward Lake (Engineers), Acting Deputy-Commissioner at Jullundur, was deputed to Bhâwulpore.

The Resident writes: "He is a very intelligent, active officer, with great knowledge of the natives, and peculiar tact in managing them and gaining their regard."

Here, then, were two brother-assistants of Henry Lawrence's old band at work together again.

An old friend comes on the scene.

"Lieutenant Lake was, in fact, constituted the Commander-in-chief of the Dâoodpootra army," says Edwardes.

How well he justified that unusual trust, to the mutual honour of his own Government and that of the troops he led, appears abundantly in Edwardes's reports.

He gives the following testimony to his friend, and the insertion of it may be pardoned now.

"By his instructions from the Resident, he was not put

under my command. It seemed enough to tell him ' to
co-operate according to his own judgment and discretion.'
But he did more. Events brought us irresistibly together.
Before Lieutenant Lake could reach his army, I had crossed
the Chenâb, and saved the Dáoodpootras from a disastrous
defeat at Kinyéree ; and, finding me in the successful
execution of my own plans, Lake at once put himself under
my command, and, without one selfish thought, devoted his
rare abilities and energy to second the operations of another.
I felt the generosity of the action then ; but I do more full
justice to it now, when I can look back calmly on those
stormy times, and remember how impossible it was that two
young heads should always think alike, however true their
hearts kept time; yet never was there anything but unity of
action in the field.

Friends in council.

"Seldom, indeed, did we differ, even in the council-tent ;
but if we had two plans, Lake manfully exposed the weaknesses of mine, and if I was not to be convinced (as I own
I very seldom was), he gave up his own better judgment,
and made mine perfect by the heartiness of his assistance
in giving it effect.

" My peaceful readers, whose experience of ' heroes ' has
happily been confined within the limits of the biographical
dictionary or the smooth historian's page, may think so
well of soldier-nature as to deem Lake's magnanimity and
lack of jealousy a thing of course; but others who have
lived in camps will know both its rarity and its value, and
esteem it the most unfading of the laurels won by Edward
Lake under the walls of Mooltân. ' Better is he that ruleth
his spirit than he that taketh a city.' "

Nothing so mean as jealousy could exist between two
such noble spirits and firm friends. It is dwelt upon here
in a parenthesis, as a pleasant picture of Indian life.
But it was one only out of many; for all the band of
noble brotherhood gathered at Lahore under Henry Lawrence

A glimpse of some of

in 1846, and since scattered over the wild country, are doing glorious work—Lieutenant Reynell Taylor in Bunnoo; Major George Lawrence and Nicholson in Peshàwur; Captain James Abbott in Hazàra; John Becher at Batàla, and all rejoicing in each other's success. There was no rivalry, but in achieving good results.

On June 10 the Resident at Lahore wrote to Edwardes, giving him *carte-blanche* to act as he thought best, and on June 18 was fought the first battle with Moolraj's troops— the battle of Kinyéree.

"The rebel army of from eight to ten thousand Horse and Foot and ten guns, commanded by Moolraj's brother-in-law, Rung Ram, and the Dâoodpootra army of about eight thousand five hundred Horse and Foot, eleven guns and thirty zumboorahs, commanded by Futteh Mahommed Khan, were on the left bank of the river.

"My force, consisting of two divisions (one of faithful regulars, Foot and Artillery, of the Sikh service, about fifteen hundred men and ten guns, under General Cortlandt; and another of about five thousand irregulars, Horse and foot, and thirty zumboorahs, under my own personal command), was upon the right bank, on June 17.

"A strong division of three thousand Puthân Irregulars crossed that day, and Foujdar Khan (who by this time had become the Adjutant-General of the Puthân levies) led them on to join the Dâoodpootras, which they did a little before sunrise."

Edwardes determined to cross with the rest of the force the following morning. His own pen will tell the story best.

"I slept that night on the right bank, intending to take over a second division as soon as the fleet returned from its first voyage. But at six a.m. on the 18th no fleet was to be seen. Two little ferry-boats had, however, come up from another ferry, and getting into these, with a few horsemen and servants, and leaving General Cortlandt to pass the rest of the force over as rapidly as he could, I pushed off for Kinyéree.

"About a hundred yards from the left bank I was roused from a ' brown study '—not unnatural amid plans so doubtful in their issue, so heavy in their responsibility—by a burst of Artillery within a mile or two of the shore. A second cannonade replied, was answered, and replied again, and two tall opposite columns of white smoke rose out of the jungle, higher and higher at every discharge, as if each strove to get above its adversary; then broke and pursued each other in thick clouds over the fair and peaceful sky. . . . *Opening of the fire.*

"Gazing at this unmistakable symbol of the fight below, I could scarcely forbear smiling at the different speculations of my companions in the boat. The servants, men of peace, declared and hoped it was only a salute fired by the Dáoodpootras in honour of the allies who had just joined them; but the horsemen knit their brows, and devoutly cried, ' Al-láh ! Al-láh !' at every shot, with an emphasis like pain on the last syllable. They quite *felt* there was a fight going on· *Different speculations caused thereby.*

"For my own part I felt so too; and as I stepped on shore, and buckled the strap of my cap under my chin, I remember thinking that no Englishman could be beaten on June 18.

"Nor am I ashamed to remember that I bethought me of a still happier omen and a far more powerful aid—the goodness of my cause, and the God who defends the right. *Trust.* A young lieutenant, who had seen but one campaign, alone, and without any of the means and appliances of such war as I had been apprenticed to, I was about to take command, in the midst of a battle, not only of one force whose courage I had never tried, but of another that I had never seen ; and to engage a third, of which the numbers were uncertain, with the knowledge that defeat would immeasurably extend the *Discouragement.*

rebellion which I had undertaken to suppress, and embarrass
the Government I had volunteered to serve. Yet, in that
great extremity, I doubted only for a moment—one of those
long moments to which some angel seems to hold a micro-
scope, and show millions of things within it. It came and
went between the stirrup and the saddle. It brought with
it difficulties, dangers, responsibilities, and possible consequences terrible to face; but it left none behind.

A critical moment.

"I know I was fighting for the right. I asked God to
help me to do my duty, and I rode on, certain that He would
do it.

Who shall be the guide?

"On the shore not a creature was to be seen; so we had
to take the smoke and roar of guns for our guides to the
field of battle. But how to find out my own side was a
difficulty, and not to fall into the hands of the enemy. On
one side the firing was regular, and apparently from guns
of equal calibre; on the other side, irregular and unequal,
as if from guns of different sizes. Obliged to choose between
them, I paid the enemy the compliment of supposing their
guns would be the best, and those of Bháwul Khan the
worst, and rode straight through the jungle to the latter.

"At the village of Kinyérce I got a wretched peasant to
put us on our road, though he would not go a yard along with
us; and soon we met a horseman who had been despatched
by Foujdar Khan to tell me what had happened and conduct me to the field. . . .

"From him I learnt that Rung Ram, the rebel commander, had taken up a strong position on the salt-hills of
the village of Noonár, and then opened on the allies. Hot-
tempered, brave, but ignorant of fields, and consequently
rash, the Dâoodpootra levies lifted up their voices in one
vast shout of their master's name, then rushed impetuously
forward, without waiting for an order or asking for a plan.
Their very baggage was mixed up with them; the Artillery
was entangled; and the fire which poured down upon them

from the heights of Noonár was so different from the matchlock volleys of their own border warfare, that they staggered,
stopped, and finally fell back in a mass of confusion upon a
village in their rear. . . .

" It was at this moment of confusion that I arrived at the
field—a plain covered with jungle, amongst which loaded
camels were passing to the rear, out of range of the enemy's
guns, and detachments of wild-looking warriors, with red
hair and beards,* were taking up a line of posts. Suddenly
a European stepped out of the crowd, and advanced in a
hurried manner, wiping his forehead and exclaiming, ' Oh
sir, our army is disorganized !'—a pleasing salutation on
arriving at a field of battle ! He then told me his name
was Macpherson, and that he commanded one of the
Nawâb's two regular regiments. I asked him where his
general was. He laughed, and pointed to a large peepul
tree, round which a crowd gathered. I galloped up, and,
looking over the shoulders of the people, saw a little
old man, in dirty clothes, and with nothing but a skull-cap
on his head, sitting under the tree, with a rosary in his
hands, the beads of which he was rapidly telling, and
muttering in a peevish, helpless manner. ' Ulhúmdoolilláh !
Ulhúmdoolilláh ! (' God be praised ! God be praised !')
apparently quite abstracted from the scene around him,
and utterly unconscious that six-pounder balls were going
through the branches, that officers were imploring him
for orders, and that eight or nine thousand rebels were
waiting to destroy an army of which *he* was the General.

" He had to be shaken by his people before he could
comprehend that I had arrived ; and as he rose and
tottered forward, looking vacantly in my face, I saw that
excitement had completed the imbecility of his years, and
that I might as well talk to a post.

Marginal notes: A pleasing salutation.   TheGeneral of the allies

* The Dáoodpootras are fond of staining their hair red, as others are
of staining it black.

"Turning, therefore, to the many brave and experienced officers of his staff, and to Peer Ibraheem Khan, who now came up, I learnt the general nature of their position ; and then struck out a plan for the day. 'Nothing,' I said, 'can be done with an army so disorganized as this, or with guns such as Peer Ibraheem describes yours to be. The enemy has taken up a strong position, and will probably prepare to be attacked. It is not likely that he will attack us until he thinks we don't mean to attack him. I will write to General Cortlandt to send over the guns, and not a move must be made till they come. In the meanwhile, occupy yourselves with recovering the order of your force, make the whole lie down in the jungle, keep them as much under cover as possible, and let your Artillery play away as hard as they can on the enemy's guns. Above all, stand fast and be patient.'

A critical emergency.

Faces the position.

"I then betook myself to the left where my own three thousand men were posted; and as I rode down the Dâoodpootra line, and received the loud greetings of the soldiers, I saw how timely had been my arrival. I had not joined them in a moment of triumph, but of trial. They found their ally for the first time when (in Asia at least) allies are most seldom found—in the hour of difficulty ; and seeing a single British officer come amongst them to share dangers they were encountering for the British Government, they felt its justice, and took heart again. . . .

Foujdar Khan a good ally.

"I found my own three thousand men, who had stuck their standards upright in the turf, and were lying down in a beautiful line between them. This was the work of Foujdar Khan, and I loudly praised all the other officers as they flocked around me.

"I now dismounted from my horse, and asked, without much hopes if any one had got pen and paper.

"'Sahib!' replied a well-known voice behind me, and, turning, I beheld Sudda Sookh, the moonshee of my office, pulling out a Cashmere penbox from his girdle, just as quietly as if he had been in Cutcherry. He had no sword or other implements of war, but merely the writing materials, with which it was his duty to be furnished; and, though he looked serious and grave, he was perfectly calm amid the roar of hostile cannons and men's heads occasionally going off before his eyes.

"'What are you doing here, Sudda Sookh?' I asked in astonishment.

"He put up his hands respectfully, and answered, 'My place is with my master. I live by his service; and when he dies, I die!' A more striking instance of the quiet endurance of the Hindoo character I never saw.*

"Seating myself under a bush, I wrote two short notes to Cortlandt, informing him of our critical position, and my belief that I could hold out until three p.m., by which time he must send me guns, or the battle would be lost.

"They were written at eight, and what I had engaged to do was to stave off Rung Ram's army for seven hours. Those seven hours I should never forget if I lived seven centuries.

"The firing on both sides continued for six hours without slackening; and though the Dâoodpootra Artillery drew the heaviest fire to the right of our line, yet my Puthâns got so much more than they were ever used to in the petty raids of their own frontier, that they were continually springing up and demanding to be led on against the enemy. 'Look here!' they cried 'and there, and there!' (pointing to men as they were hit). 'Are we all to be killed without a

---

* This fine fellow was the moonshee who first taught Edwardes languages when he was a subaltern with his regiment, and he became so attached and faithful that he never left his service, but was the head moonshee in his office to the last day of Edwardes's labours in India. He was a man of noble bearing and the strictest probity, never taking a bribe nor falling into any native vices. He was renowned as a good man, and universally respected.

blow? What sort of war do you call this, where there is
iron on one side and only flesh and blood on the other?
Lead us on, and let us strike a blow for our lives!'. . . Then
the officers crowded round, and every one thought he was a
general, and if only I would listen to *him* (pulling me by
the sleeve to interrupt my rebuke to some one else), the
battle would be mine.

"But of all the advisers, I must do them the justice to say
that none counselled a retreat. Every voice was for attack.

Wait for the guns.

"Foujdar Khan and one or two others alone supported
my opinion, that we must wait for Cortlandt's guns.

"Happily I had no doubt or misgiving in my own mind.
I never had a clearer conviction in my life than I had that
day that I was right, and they were wrong; and with a
patience, which in the ordinary affairs of life I never had
possessed, I strove hour after hour to calm the rash and
excited throng, and assure them that when the proper
moment should arrive, I myself would lead them on.

The strain.

"And so I sat out those seven hours under a June sun,
with no shade but that of a bush, and neither a drop of
water nor a breath of air to lessen the intolerable heat. . . .

"The enemy at last were not to be kept back, but
advanced with such an overpowering strength in Cavalry
and Artillery that a desperate expedient became necessary.

"Imploring the Infantry to lie still yet a little longer,
I ordered Foujdar Khan and all the chiefs and officers who
had horses, to mount, and, forming themselves into a
compact body, charge down on the rebel Cavalry, and
endeavour to drive them back upon the Foot. 'Put off the
fight,' I whispered to Foujdar Khan, 'or not a man of us
will leave this field.'

"Gladly did these brave men get the word to do a deed
so desperate; but with set teeth I watched them mount,
and wondered how many of my choicest officers would come
back.

"Spreading their hands to heaven, the noble band solemnly repeated the creed of their religion, as though it were their last act on earth ; then passed their hands over their beards with the haughtiness of martyrs, and, drawing their swords, dashed out of the jungle into the ranks of the enemy's horse, who, taken wholly by surprise, turned round and fled, pursued by Foujdar and his companions to within a few hundred yards of the rebel line, which halted to receive its panic-stricken friends. A moment of devoted bravery.

"In executing this brilliant service Foudjar Khan received two wounds, and few who returned came back untouched. Many fell.

"The purpose, however, was completely answered. . . . At that moment of moments might be heard the bugle-note of Artillery in the rear. 'Hush!' cried every voice, while each ear was strained to catch that friendly sound again. Again it sounds, again, and there is no mistake. The guns have come at last, thank God! The welcome guns.

"Quick, quick, orderlies, and bring them up. There's not a moment to be lost! Now, officers, to your posts ; every one to his own standard and his own men. Let the Infantry stand up and get into as good a line as the jungle will allow; let none advance until I give the word, but when the word is given, the duty of every chief is this, to keep the standard of his own retainers in a line with the standards right and left of him. Break the line, and you will be beaten ; keep it, and you are sure of victory.*

"Away they scattered, and up sprang their shouting brotherhoods. Standards were plucked up and shaken in the wind, ranks closed, swords grasped, and matches blown, and the long line waved backwards and forwards with agitation as it stood between the coming friend and coming foe.

* This is the only manœuvre I ever attempted to instil into that impatient mass."

The clash.

"Louder and louder grew the murmur of the advancing rebel host, more distinct and clear the bugles of the friendly guns. And now the rattling of the wheels is heard, the crack of whips and clank of chains, as they labour to come up. The crowd falls back, a road is cleared, we see the foremost gun, and amid the shouts of welcome it gallops to the front.

"Oh, the thankfulness of that moment! the relief, the weight removed, the elastic bound of the heart's mainspring into its place, after being pressed down for seven protracted hours of waiting for a reinforcement that might never come! Now all is clear before us. Our chance is nearly as good as theirs; and who asks more?

Cortlandt's relief.

"One, two, three, four, five, six guns had come; and panting after them, with clattering cartridge-boxes, might be seen two regiments of Regular Infantry—Soobhan Khan's corps of Mussulmans, and General Cortlandt's Sooruj Mookhee. It was well thought of by the General, for I had only asked for guns; but he judged well that two regiments would be worth their weight in gold at such a pinch.

"There was scant time for taking breath, for the enemy was close at hand; so, bidding the guns come with me, the two regiments to follow on the guns, and the whole Irregular Cavalry line advance steadily in rear, under command of Foujdar Khan, I led the Artillery through the trees on to the cultivated plain beyond. There we first saw the enemy's line. . . .

The crash.

"Round went our guns, and round went theirs, and in an instant both were discharged into each other. It was a complete surprise; for the rebels believed truly that all the guns we had in the morning had left the field with the Dāoodpootras,* and of the arrival of the others they were ignorant. Down sank their whole line among the long

---

* Who had slipped away and retired towards the river without any orders or necessity.

stalks of the sugar-cane; and, as we afterwards learnt from
a Goorkha prisoner, the fatal word was passed that 'the
Sahib had got across the river with all his army from Dera
Ghazee Khan, and led them into an ambush.'

"To and fro rode their astonished and vacillating
colonels; and while the guns maintained the battle, the
intelligence was sent by swift horsemen to the rebel general,
Rung Ram, who, seated on an elephant, looked safely down
upon the fight from the hills around the village of Noonár.

"Meanwhile the Sooruj Mookhse and Soobhan Khan's
regiments had come up, closely followed by the line; and I
made the two former lie down on the left and right of the
Artillery, and the latter halt under cover of the trees.

"The gunners were getting warm. 'Grape! grape!'
at length shouted the commandant; 'it's close enough for
grape.' And the enemy thought so too, for the next round
rushed over our heads like a flight of eagles.

"And there, for the first time and the last in my short
experience of war, did I see hostile Artillery *firing grape into
each other.* It was well for us that the enemy were taken
by surprise, for they aimed high and did little mischief.
General Cortlandt's Artillery were well trained and steady,
and their aim was true.

"Two guns were quickly silenced, and the rest seemed   A charge.
slackening and firing wild. A happy charge might carry
all. I gave the order to Soobhan Khan's regiment to attack;
and away they went, Soobhan Khan himself, a stout heavy
soldier, leading them on, and leaping over bushes like a
boy. Before this regiment could reach the battery, an
incident characteristic of Irregular troops occurred : a cluster
of half a dozen horsemen dashed out from the trees behind
me, and, passing the regiment, threw themselves on the
enemy's guns. Their leader received the ball full in his
face, and fell over the 'cannon's mouth.' It was Shah
Niwaz Khan of Esaukheyl, whose family I had recalled

from exile to rule over their own country. The regiment followed, and carried at the point of the bayonet the only gun which awaited their assault.

"Another gun lay dismounted on the ground.

"While this was doing, our guns poured grape into the cover where the rebel Infantry were lying, and these, hearing their own Artillery retire before Soobhan Khan's charge, retreated hastily through the high crops with which the fields were covered, but suffered heavily from the fire behind them, and formed again in great confusion when they reached their guns.

"At this point a small body of Cavalry were approaching, and I asked an orderly if he knew who they were.

A narrow escape.

"He thought they were Foujdar Khan and the mounted chiefs of the Puthâns, and I had just turned my horse to ride towards them with an order, when a single horseman advanced, and, taking a deliberate aim, discharged a matchlock at me within fifty or sixty yards.

"The ball passed first through the sleeve of the brown holland blouse which I had on, then through my shirt, and out again on the other side through both, and must have been within a hair's-breadth of my elbow.

The crash of conflict.

"And now I gave the word for the whole line of wild Puthâns to be let loose upon the enemy. One volley from our battery, and they plunged into the smoke-enveloped space between the armies, with a yell that had gathered malice through hours of impatient suffering. The smoke cleared off, and the Artillerymen of two more rebel guns were dying desperately at their posts; their line was in full retreat upon Noonár, and the plain was a mass of scattered skirmishers.

"Once more our Artillery galloped to the front and harassed the disordered enemy. In vain the rebels tried to rally and reply. Our Infantry was on them, and another and another gun were abandoned in the flight.

"Rung Ram, their general, had long since fled. Mool-raj's Puthán Cavalry, who had stood aloof throughout the battle, were supposed to have gone over; the regular regiments, and especially the Goorkhas (who had deserted Agnew and Anderson at Mooltán, and now fought with halters round their necks), had borne the brunt of the day, and suffered heavily. More than half the Artillery had been lost.

"The pursuit was hot, and fresh and overwhelming numbers seemed to be pouring in upon both flanks; for at this juncture the Dáoodpootras had come up again, and were burning to retrieve their place.

"Thus, without a general, without order, and without hope, the rebels were driven back upon Noonár; and, having placed its sheltering heights between them and their pursuers for a moment, they threw aside shame and arms, and fled, without once halting, to Mooltán.

Complete rout of the enemy.

"But of ten guns that the rebels brought into the field of Kinyérce, but two returned to Mooltán.

"Their camp at Noonár and all their ammunition fell into our hands, and the former furnished many of our Irregular levies with tents for the first time.

"And so ended the battle of Kinyérce, which began a little after seven a.m., and was not decided till half-past four p.m.

"At five p.m., after nine hours' constant exertion of mind and body under a fiery sun, I leave the reader to imagine the feeling of thankfulness with which I sat down at Noonár, on the very ground occupied by Moolraj's army in the morning, and penned a hurried despatch to the Resident, announcing our victory."

Happy conclusion.

Edwardes ends his despatch to the Resident—

"God be praised for a most signal victory, gained under the most discouraging circumstances; but to be followed, I hope, by most encouraging results."

This battle of Kinyeree has been called "the Waterloo of
the Punjab," having been fought on the glorious anniversary,
June 18; nor can we fail to notice a second coincidence in
the timely arrival of Cortlandt's guns, which, like Blücher's
at Waterloo, turned the tide to victory.

Moolraj was thoroughly disheartened. This force was his
"all;" he had more guns, but not any more field-pieces.

Another account of this battle has been given by an eye-
witness,* an officer attached to Edwardes's Brigade, who
writes—

"There can be no doubt, had not Moolraj met with defeat
at this time, the whole of the Punjab would have been in a
blaze, and all the richest districts of Mooltân would have
fallen into the hands of the enemy. But, happily, Edwardes
was in the country, on the right bank of the Indus, opposite
Leiah, with two guns, three hundred Horse, four companies of
Foot, and one disaffected Sikh regiment.

"Edwardes crossed to Leiah, and commenced collecting
the revenue, whereupon Moolraj sent ten thousand men and
ten guns to attack him. Edwardes was naturally obliged to
retreat, and take up his old ground on the right bank of the
Indus, securing all the boats. At the same time, he wrote to
General Cortlandt (Nizâm of the district of Bunnoo) to come
to his assistance, which he did in six days, with six guns, one
regiment of Foot, and one hundred Horse.

"At Dera Futteh Khan, Edwardes added, in ten days,
two thousand men to his force, and Cortlandt moved towards
Sungur with six guns, two regiments of Foot, and a few Horse;
Edwardes remaining to prevent the enemy from crossing the
river at Leiah On the day Cortlandt marched down the
right bank of the Indus towards Sungur, the enemy made a
corresponding movement on the left bank, and encamped
opposite to Cortlandt at Sooltan Khan. Next day Edwardes
dropped down the river in boats, and joined General Cortlandt. In this way Edwardes and Cortlandt reached Dera
Ghazee Khan, where a small friendly force was quartered:
the enemy, as before, encamping on the opposite bank.

* Copied from a letter written by an officer attached to Lieutenant
Edwardes's Brigade to an English newspaper, dated Camp, Sooruj Koond,
Mooltân, October 26, 1848.

"On the march to Dera Ghazee Khan, Edwardes raised four thousand men, his whole force amounting to seven thousand.

"Early on the morning of the 18th, Edwardes hastened to cross the Chenâb himself, but before he had reached the opposite bank the enemy commenced the battle of Kinyéree by attacking the Bhâwulpore army. Edwardes soon joined his men, and took up his ground on the left of the line. At seven a.m. the whole of the Bhâwulpore and enemy's guns were engaged, and a well-directed fire was kept up for six hours, when the enemy advanced, pouring in grape and musketry, which compelled the Bhâwulpore force to fall back and withdraw their guns.*

"Edwardes's small force was consequently (three thousand men) left to maintain its ground between the two armies, and the enemy immediately brought all his guns and Infantry against it. Edwardes had the greatest difficulty in keeping his men from advancing; but by riding up and down the line, and constantly assuring the native officers that the guns were being brought up, and by ordering the men to lie down, he succeeded in holding his position until nearly three p.m., when, finding that all must be lost in a quarter of an hour if something were not done, he collected the few Horse he had (about a hundred) and made a headlong charge into the enemy.

"For a few minutes they were checked, or rather surprised,

---

* This rather exaggerates the valour of the Bhâwulpore troops, who "retired" into safety, and came up at the end of the fight, and in time for the victory. We have seen the true picture, sketched by Edwardes's own pen, of the entire inefficiency of their General in command to lead them in the hour of difficulty. But the allies were soon to be reinforced, and their value secured, by the arrival of Lieutenant Lake to command them. On June 28, he started to ride from Bhâwulpore into Edwardes's camp; broke down in the heat and had to halt, and reached it in the evening of the 28th, "with the thermometer at 120 degrees inside our tents,"—"a very valuable acquisition," says Edwardes.

Lake had written, "Don't fight any more battles, like a good fellow, till I join you," adding, "Let me know if there is any *immediate* prospect of a fight, and I can join you in one night." Edwardes adds, "This was indeed delightful news. Old Futteh Muhommud would be now put on the shelf. I should get an able colleague in his stead, and many a weary hour would be wiled away in the society of one of my best and most accomplished friends."

and the remaining Horse had scarcely returned to their ranks when two of General Cortlandt's regiments, with six guns, came up. No time, as may be supposed, was lost in bringing them to bear; no gun discharged that did not make dreadful havoc amongst the enemy, Edwardes himself pointing some of the guns, and riding everywhere to encourage the men.

"It was soon apparent that the enemy's fire began to diminish, and Edwardes, thinking this a favourable moment, ordered the whole of his men to charge; and then began one of the fiercest hand-to-hand fights—short-lived, it is true, for the enemy were soon completely routed and driven off the field, leaving eight guns and the whole of their baggage in the hands of the victors. For want of Cavalry the pursuit could not be carried far; but the enemy did not attempt to make head again, but retreated upon Mooltân, with all the haste he could make, whither Edwardes and Cortlandt followed him."

CHAPTER V.

—◦—

1848–1849.

BATTLE OF SUDDOOSÂM—RETRIBUTION—THE FALL OF MOOLTÂN.

"Some say that the age of chivalry is past, that the spirit of romance is dead. The age of chivalry is never past so long as there is a wrong left unredressed on earth, or a man or woman left to say, 'I will redress that wrong, or spend my life in the attempt.' The age of chivalry is never past so long as we have faith enough to say, 'God will help me to redress that wrong, or, if not me, He will help those that come after me; for His eternal will is to overcome evil with good.'"—CHARLES KINGSLEY.

CHAPTER V.

On June 29, 1848, the allies were encamped near Sooruj Koond, about three miles from Mooltân, to the west of a large deep canal. The enemy had taken up his ground within two miles of the city, and to the east of the same canal, defending the two bridges with his remaining guns.

Early on the morning of July 3 Edwardes moved towards Tibbee, on the north-west of the fort, and Moolraj marched in the same direction, to prevent Edwardes attacking the city of Mooltân.

The allies were about to encamp at Tibbee when the enemy crossed the canal, and offered them battle. This was at noon.

Lieutenant Lake, commanding the Bhâwulpore troops, forming the left of the army, immediately marched to secure some high ground in his front; General Cortlandt, commanding the centre, marched on the enemy's flank, and Edwardes moved to the left, threatening the enemy's rear.

This battle of Suddoosâm commenced by Lake opening his guns at grape distance, the enemy returning his fire with great spirit, which was kept up for some time. When Cortlandt and Edwardes got into position, the battle became general, and lasted for six hours. The enemy fought with desperation; and, although compelled to retreat early in the day, they took advantage of every favourable position, and did not relinquish it without a struggle. Battle of Suddoosâm

About four p.m., orders being given for the whole line to advance,* and a shower of grape being thrown in, the enemy

---

* " At Suddoosâm, Moolraj commanded in person. He got a fall from his elephant from a shot catching his howdah, mounted his horse, and retreated precipitately from the field. Once moved, the day was ours;

were routed in every direction, and driven into Mooltân, leaving two guns and numbers of killed and wounded en the field.

An extract from the *Times* of that period may be interesting here—

"We cannot forbear from a few words of congratulation and acknowledgment upon the admirable, but not extraordinary, service which a young subaltern has just rendered to the Indian Government, in the revolt of Mooltân. We say, not 'extraordinary,' because the history of British India is full of examples showing how individual resolution and abilities are developed by the noble opportunities and the munificent encouragement which the service of the Company combines.

"Otherwise this summary termination by a single lieutenant of a war for which an army of ten thousand men was expeditiously mustering, is an achievement as well entitled to be termed extraordinary as any which our columns have ever chronicled.

"Lieutenant Edwardes, who is the same officer whose intuitive sagacity and acquaintance with native character rendered his services so useful during our demonstrations against Cashmere and our negotiations with its mysterious chieftain, chanced to be stationed in the Lower Punjab at the moment of the outbreak in Mooltân.

"Acting as officers are expected to act under the traditions of Clive, and in a country where an isolated subaltern is frequently the responsible Governor of a province, he advanced at once with the little troop under his command, on the unexpected duty of saving two of his countrymen, overawing the great city (of Mooltân), and chastizing an insurgent chief, Moolraj, at the head of an unknown force.

for the native army that retires is lost. The enemy are said to have suffered very heavy loss, increased by a cruel and treacherous act of the Dewan's. Between the field and the city runs a large nullah (ditch, or stream), and there is but one bridge at that part of it which is nearest Suddoosâm. No sooner had Moolraj got across this bridge himself with his Artillery, than he planted two guns upon it, to stop his own soldiers from retreating. The majority of the enraged fugitives forced the barrier with some loss, but many of them tried to swim the nullah, and were drowned. Hundreds never re-entered Mooltân, but struck off into the country, and have probably gone to their homes."—H. B. E., "Year on the Punjab Frontier."

" He was too late to effect his main object (which was to save the lives of Agnew and Anderson), but he held his own against every attack, destroyed by detached encounters the prestige which the successful murders of these two officers was lending to the insurgents, and zealously availed himself of his peculiar skill and opportunities to recruit by extempore levies the force under his disposal.

" Out of the mixed population of these hosts it seems that the Sikhs alone displayed any inclination to the cause of Moolraj; and these mainly, we doubt not, were of the disbanded and broken troops of the Queen-Mother's army.

" The Puthâns, or Afghans, from the west frontier, and the Beloochees, or people of Beloochistan, who preceded us in the conquest of Sindh, and who form a considerable element in the present population of that province and of the Southern Punjab, both Mohammedans by creed, evinced a decided preference for our standard, and took service so freely under Lieutenant Edwardes (or other district commanders) that that officer soon counted a disposable force of six thousand men, heartily inclined to the work in hand.

" Thus strengthened, he assumed at once the character with the capacity of a general, and commenced operations by opening communications with our steadfast ally Bhâwul Khan, who had already crossed the Sutlej against Moolraj, but so indiscreetly that the superior forces of the latter had caused him some losses.

" Lieutenant Edwardes, however, contrived to cross successively the Indus and the Chenâb, effected his junction with the Bhâwulpore force, and deliberately awaited the formidable enemy, against whom all the cantonments between Lahore and Umballa were busily contributing their contingents.

" Nor did he wait in vain. On June 18, a day of brilliant omen (for, as he said, ' no Englishman can be beaten on June 18 '), he was attacked by the whole force of Moolraj, and after a battle, of which the duration shows the severity, he remained master of the field, having utterly routed the enemy, captured more than half of his guns, and finished the war.

" Few battles of Indian history will be more remarkable

than this. Several of the most famous engagements of our early career were decided by the mere manifestation of courage. Plassey was a cannonade, far more bloodless than that of Valmy; its characteristic was the then unwarranted resolution of Clive to assault an army which could have buried his six battalions under their turbans. And, even in the more costly conflicts of Munro and Wellesley, there was actually a European regiment to bear the brunt and do the business of the day.

"But Lieutenant Edwardes, like Clive at Arcot, appeared first to have made his army, and then to have led it to victory. He successively attracted, enlisted, organized, and manœuvred his army, and led it to triumph, within the compass of a few weeks.

"These are the events that teach us that our service wants nothing but what we trust it may long want—opportunity; and that we shall have Pictons and Crawfords again in plenty, if ever the first trumpet of war should unfortunately sound."—(*Times* quotation.)

Results of the battles. "The result of these two battles is, it is said, that Moolraj distrusts the whole force which fought on the 18th, and is not inclined to let them into the fort, but means to encamp them under its walls. So treated, they will probably melt rapidly away.

"In a few days the task assigned to this army will be accomplished; and Moolraj and his rebels will be confined to the fort of Mooltân." (Lieutenant Edwardes to the Resident at Lahore.)

In generous praise, Edwardes forwarded to the Resident a notice of the services of the officers who were with him at this time.

To the Resident at Lahore.

"July 2, 1848.

Lieutenant Lake. "Lieutenant Lake will himself give you an account of the share taken in the battle of Suddoosâm by the Dâoodpootras, but it is for me to inform you how much their good service was due to the judgment with which he took up their successive positions, and the confidence which they could not but imbibe from witnessing his personal intrepidity under the hottest fire. To him and General Cortlandt your warmest praise is due. General
Cortlandt.

"The latter maintained a solid and unshaken centre throughout the day, and handled his regular regiments and Artillery like a good soldier and a brave man.

"To Foujdar Khan Alizye, who has throughout these operations acted as my adjutant-general, and who, in spite of a severe sword-wound received at Kinyéree, on June 18, took command of the Cavalry yesterday at Suddoosâm, and directed their movements, I feel under the greatest obligation, and at some future time shall lay his services more particularly before you. Foujdar
Khan.

"Nothing could well be more different than the battles of Kinyéree and Suddoosâm.

"The battle of Kinyéree was, for a long while, one of endurance; that of Suddoosâm, though it lasted from noon to sunset, was one of incessant action. In the former, it was my painful duty to keep still and quiet my men; in the latter, I did nothing but ride up and down the line, encouraging the different divisions to advance from point to point, now driving skulkers out of a village or a corn-field, now reproving a standard-bearer for letting other colours go ahead of him, now hurriedly thanking Cortlandt for pointing his own guns, now dashing off to keep an eye on Sheikh Imâm-úd-dín. Differences
between
the battles
of Kinyéree
and Sud-
doosâm.

"The equestrian vicissitudes I underwent that day are truly ludicrous to remember, though very serious matters at the moment. I commenced the action on a big chesnut Arab named Zál; but, sulky at being so long without his dinner, he refused to leap a canal, which had brought the Artillery to a halt, and fell with me right into the middle. Nor, with all my pulling and hauling, could I get him Equestrian
vicissi-
tudes.

out, and I was obliged to leave him till the fight was over. General Cortlandt then got me a bay horse from an officer in his Artillery; but I had not gone two hundred yards when over he came backwards, and bruised me dreadfully on the ground. A shot had grazed his nose.

Native servants "faithful to their salt."

"Fat Sâdik Mahommed Khan, who was my aide-de-camp all that day, next put me on a grey, belonging to one of his own followers, and this beast I had fairly ridden to a standstill, when up came one of my own 'syces' (native grooms), with a grey Cabul horse of my own, called Punch.

"'What are you doing here?' I asked, for I had mounted Lake on this horse in the morning. 'Lake Sahib has sent it with his compliments, as he hears you have lost Zâl, and he has borrowed another horse for himself!' So I finished the day upon Punch, and when the fight was over I thanked Lake for the timely thought. Lake burst out laughing, and said, '*I* send the horse back? Never! That villain of a syce walked off with it, and left me without any horse at all!'"

This is a good characteristic story of native servants, who are "faithful to their salt," and will often serve their own masters well, but have no idea of doing the same to another servant's master; and this good syce seems to have acted upon that idea, and could conceive no reason why his master shouldn't ride his own horse. His master's desire to horse his friend was quite too romantic an idea, he thought, for these times, to be indulged.

Another amusing and characteristic incident, romantic in another way, may be told in Edwardes's own words.

Sâdik Mahommed Khan.

"I have mentioned Sâdik Mahommed Khan. He was a servant of the Maharajah, appointed to do duty with the Nâzim of Mooltân, and, when the rebellion broke out, was drawing pay from both. . . . Moolraj expected him to side with him, but, though unable to escape, on account of his house and family, he refused to set his seal to the oath of rebellion on the Korân, and the very day that I arrived before Mooltân, Sâdik and his father took their hawks on their wrists, and, under pretence of hunting, issued forth from the city and joined me. It is an incident illustrative of those strange uncertain times that, two days afterwards, he was my faithful henchman at Suddoosâm, and, being well mounted, was often the only man by my side.

"Had he been a traitor, he might have killed me at any moment. But I heard his story, believed it, trusted him, and was rewarded by invaluable service throughout the rest of the rebellion.

"Yet it was as hard to trust in those days as it was necessary.

"The very moment before this battle of Suddoosâm I was dipping my head into a pail of water, preparatory to putting on a thick turban, so as to keep my brains cool as long as possible in the sun, when Sâdik Mahommed's own uncle insisted on speaking to me. *Incidents of the war.*

"Lifting my dripping head out of the pail, I listened to the old man's solemn warnings to be on my guard; 'for,' said he, 'all these men, like my nephew, who have come over from the enemy are here by Moolraj's orders and consent. You are drawn into a trap. Half your soldiers are friends, and half are foes, and, like rice and split peas, they are all mixed up in one dish. If there is not some treachery in this day's fight, my name is not Sûrbulund Khan!' *Unheeded warnings of traitors in the camp.*

"The idea was not pleasant, and I soused my head under water again, desperately; but soon came up, wrung out the water, clapped a turban over my wet hair, and thanked the old gentleman for his information, which was too late to be useful, mounted my horse, and—never found out any of the traitors from that day to this!"

Another incident of the field about this time had a more painful ending, but before we close this chapter it must be told.

"I was in the very act of writing, when a horseman rode in from the picket, and reported that Moolraj's army was crossing the bridge in the same order that they had done before, and were coming on again to give us battle.

A real disaster.

"Astounded, but unable to disbelieve, I beat to arms, summoned the chief officers, ordered the line to be turned out at once, and was holding a hurried conference with Lake and Cortlandt in my tent, while all three of us were jumping into boots or buckling on swords or pistols, when a second horseman from the picket entered. I had just loaded my pistols, and went on cramming them into my belt, while listening to the man's report. The hammer of one got entangled, but, without looking to see what was the matter, I seized the barrel in my right hand, and pulled the pistol into its place. A loud report, a short pang, and I had lost the use of my right hand for life! The ball had passed through the palm, and lodged in the floor at my foot. But there was no time for regrets.

A false alarm.

"The line had turned out, and Lake rushed to the field to take my duty and his own. Nobly he would have done both; but I must own it was a great relief to me to hear that, as our line advanced, the enemy retreated again behind the city walls, and proved to have been only a party of Cavalry sent out to reconnoitre our position. Had Moolraj given us battle that day, the result must have been more doubtful than it had ever been before. All Lake's attention and guidance was demanded by his own undisciplined Dáoodpootras. He had had no time to become acquainted with my men or they with him, and the accident which had happened at such a critical moment to their customary leader would have been an omen of certain defeat to their superstitious minds.

"Even as it was, the occurrence was unfortunate, for while it prevented me from being surrounded by my officers, as I was wont to be all day, and confined me like a prisoner to my bed, in Moolraj's 'hall of audience' it was a subject of loud rejoicing and congratulation. At first I was reported dead, and Moolraj made a present to the messenger who brought the news, burying me with the decent remark, that I was 'a stout youth, and it was a pity I should be cut off so young!' On hearing that I had only lost my hand, he probably took the present back again and thrashed the messenger."

Moolraj's disappoint-ment.

The good right hand could never use *a sword* again, though for other purposes it healed right well; so the consequences were serious, but the Directors of the Honourable East India Company honoured Edwardes with "a special grant" of £100 annuity, 'with reference to his eminent services.' (The wound not having been received in action, the grant had to be made "special.")

Great were the troubles brought about by the deed of treachery at Mooltán, and long-sustained were the labours by which Edwardes succeeded in defeating Moolraj when he came out to fight, or in keeping him shut up in his fortress; until the time came when the siege of Mooltán was undertaken by the army of Regular troops under command of General Whish, with which Edwardes and his force of six thousand men cordially and effectually co-operated.

Then, too, followed retribution for the great crime which on January 3, 1849—nine months afterwards—*redeemed the promise* of the dying Agnew and his brave companion, when, in the certainty of his country's honourable regard for blood so shed, the words rang out, "Thousands of Englishmen will come down when we are gone, and will annihilate Moolraj, his soldiers, and his fort."

The retri-bution for the crime.

"When the fort of Mooltán was taken by the English army, three companies of the very same regiment to which Lieutenant Anderson belonged (the 1st Bombay Fusiliers), under Captain Leith, assaulted the 'Bloody Bastion' or Khoonee Boorj, . . . and soon made the city of Mooltân their own.

"Then arose, from every crowded height and battery, whence the exciting struggle had been watched, the shouts of applauding comrades; and through the deafening roar of musketry which pealed along the ramparts and marked the hard-earned progress of the victorious columns through the streets, both friend and foe might hear that sound, never to be forgotten, the 'hurrah!' of a British army after battle.

Fall of Mooltân.

"Thus fell the blood-stained city of Mooltân! Where are now the citizens who hooted on the murderers of Anderson and Agnew?—the idolaters who, with fresh-painted foreheads, and garlands of flowers in their hands, prostrated themselves with joy before their unconscious gods, and thanked them for the death of the Christians?

"Shame—shame-stricken; hiding in holes and corners; invisible, or kneeling in the mud for mercy—mercy from the Christian conqueror, to whose countrymen they had shown no mercy! . . .

Moolraj's cruelty to his own defenders.

"No sooner did Moolraj see that the breach in the city walls was carried by the British, than he closed the gates of the fort upon the unsuccessful defenders of the city, and thus left three-fourths of his army at the mercy of their enemies.

"The indignant garrison of the city, deserted on one side by the master whose miserable existence they had prolonged, and pursued on the other up every street and alley by the British, saw no hope left for them in Mooltân; and, scrambling over the western walls or issuing at the Loharee gate, concealed themselves till night among the Afghan suburbs; then, under cover of the darkness, dispersed and fled, without gain or honour, to their distant homes.

"Never did broken vessel, left high and dry on some *The city* inhospitable shore after a storm, exhibit a more perfect *of the dead.* wreck than the city of Mooltân on January 3, 1849. Its streets were strewn with slain, chiefly Sikhs, whose long religious locks, spread wildly out on the bloody ground, gave their dead a demoniac look, which no one who has walked over a Sikh battle-field can forget. So might some Michael Angelo portray the hosts whom 'the spirits of devils' shall gather together to be destroyed at Armageddon.

"Soon, however, was this city of the dead alive again with armed men. For it was determined to attack the fort. On January 4, a brigade of the Bombay division marched round and encamped on the north of the fort; and, communicating by pickets and patrols with the Bengal division on the east, and with a detachment of Irregulars on the west, completed, for the first time, the investment of Mooltân.

"Fast now were the toils closing in around Moolraj; his heart began to fail, and on the evening of January 5 he made his first overture to surrender."

"*Dewan Moolraj to Major Edwardes.*

"January 5, 1849.

"Having sundry representations to make before you, I *Moolraj seeks the* write to say that, with your permission, I will send a con- *mercy he* fidential person of my own to wait on you, who will tell *could not show.* you all."

"*Major Edwardes to Dewan Moolraj.*

"January 5, 1849.

"I have received and perused your urzee. You say you have sundry things to represent, and with my leave will send a confidential person for that purpose. This I ·cannot assent to. It is quite impossible. The time for that was April last. You then preferred war; now go through with it, or, if you are unable, surrender yourself to General Whish. After which you can represent anything you like."*

Thus refused a parley by Edwardes, Moolraj appealed to General Whish, but still made Edwardes the medium of communication.†

Moolraj's petition.

At last, seeing his condition desperate, Moolraj determined to surrender. He sent in his submission to General Whish: "I ask only for my own life and the honour of my women. You are an ocean of mercy. What more need be said?"

The general's reply.

The British general answered, "I have neither authority to give your life nor to take it, except in open war. The Governor-General only can do this; and, as to your women, the British government wars with men, not with women. I will protect your women and children to the best of my ability."

Moolraj surrendered.

Moolraj still delayed. All night the guns thundered on. At seven next morning Moolraj at last surrendered, and the British batteries ceased firing.

Edwardes writes to the Resident at Lahore—

"Camp, Mooltân, January 22, 1849.

Retribution complete in victory.

"It is with heartfelt satisfaction that I announce to you the surrender of Dewan Moolraj to Major-General Whish at nine this morning, and the occupation by British troops of the strong fortress of Mooltân, without the bloodshed of an assault. . . . The flag of old England is now flying out

---

* Blue-Book, p. 531.

† The full details of the military conduct of the siege are not attempted here, and it is not necessary to follow all the steps, neither can space be afforded to do full justice to all the bravery of the arms engaged.

The reader is referred to the full details recorded in the "Year on the Punjab Frontier."

Not only was it shared in by Regular and Irregular troops, but by British seamen too. Commander Powell, of the Honourable East India Company's Navy, had, from the first, largely assisted the operations against Mooltân.—E. E.

in the fresh breeze and bright sunshine from the highest
bastion of the citadel.

"Dewan Moolraj is a prisoner in the tent of the Chief
Engineer.

"The troops intended for the assault are now disarming
the garrison and protecting the women and children.

"I congratulate you and the Government of British
India on the extinction of the firebrand which raised this
flame in the Punjab." *

Thus ended the second siege of Mooltàn.

And were the two brave Englishmen forgotten in the
flush of victory? Never. Edwardes writes—

"The bodies of those officers were carefully—I may say
affectionately—removed from the careless grave where they
lay, side by side; and, wrapped in Cashmere shawls (with
a vain but natural desire to obliterate all traces of neglect),
were borne by the soldiers of the 1st Bombay Fusiliers
(Anderson's own regiment) to an honoured resting-place
on the summit of Moolraj's citadel.

"By which way borne? Through the gate where they
had been first assaulted? Oh no! Through the broad and
sloping breach which had been made by the British guns
in the walls of the rebellious fortress of Mooltàn."

Crowning honour to the dead.

They had safely trusted themselves to the honour of their
Government, the bravery of their country's troops, and the
affectionate remembrance of their brother officers; and the
besieging army did not march away to other fields without
performing its last melancholy duty to the memory of Agnew
and Anderson.

Their services, their death, and its avenging were com-
memorated by Edwardes on a monument which he was
instrumental in getting erected, "by the surviving Assist-

* Blue-Book, p. 553.

ants to the Resident at Lahore, to the memory of their friends."

The following inscription on it was written by Edwardes:—

"On this, the farthest frontier of the British Indian Empire,
which their deaths extended,
lie the remains of

PETER VANS AGNEW   WILLIAM ANDERSON
of the   and   Lieut. 1st Bombay
Bengal Civil Service   Fusilier Regt.
Who, being deputed
by the Resident at Lahore, whose Assistants they were,
To relieve Dewan Moolraj
(Viceroy of Mooltân under the Sikh Empire),
at his own request,
of the Fortress and Government which he held,
were assaulted and wounded by the Garrison
on the 19th of April, 1848;
and, being basely deserted by their Sikh escort,
were, on the following day,
with a signal breach of national faith and private hospitality,
most barbarously murdered
in the Eedgah, under the walls of Mooltân.
Thus fell these two young public servants,
full of youth, rare talents, high hopes, and promise of utility;
even in their deaths doing their Country honour.
Covered with wounds, they could not resist,
but hand-in-hand awaited the onset
of a bloodthirsty rabble:
calmly foretelling the day when
'thousands of Englishmen
should come there to avenge their death,
and destroy Moolraj, his army, and his fortress.'
History records how the
prophecy was fulfilled.

After two separate sieges,
The Fort of Mooltán was surrendered to the British troops,
and the bodies of the two murdered officers
(which had been treated with the most savage indignities)
were, in all righteous vengeance,
carried through the breach
made by the British guns,
and buried, with military honours, on the summit
of the Citadel.
'Thousands of Englishmen'
stood round the grave.
Dewan Moolraj
was brought to trial at Lahore, convicted of
murder, and sentenced to be hanged;
But was recommended to mercy, and
finally ordered to be transported for life.
His Rebellion
was followed by an insurrection of the
Sikh people, and brought on
the Second Sikh War;
which resulted in the Annexation of the
Punjab to British India,
and the restoration of peace,
after many years of anarchy
(with a brief interval),
to the countries between the Sutlej
and the Indus.

Thus did an overruling Providence
bring good out of evil.

The surviving Assistants to the Resident at Lahore
erected this monument to the memory of their friends."

News of these successes were gladly received at head-
quarters, and it may be a fitting close to this chapter to note

the terms in which Edwardes's services were acknowledged, by a few extracts from letters received at this time.

From his Excellency Right Hon. Lord Gough, G.C.B., Commander-in-Chief, to Sir Frederick Currie, Bart., Acting Resident at Lahore.

"Simla, June 27, 1848.

" I received yesterday copy of Lieutenant Edwardes's letter to your address of 18th inst., and I beg to congratulate you very warmly on the complete success of all your combinations, which have led to the very important victory gained by Lieutenant Edwardes on June 18—a victory that does so much credit to all employed, especially to Lieutenant Edwardes.

" I feel doubly interested in the career of this officer, who served with so great satisfaction to me upon my personal staff; and the sacrifice I made in giving him up is amply compensated for by the benefit the public service has derived from his ability, energy, and self-devotedness.

"(Signed)   HUGH GOUGH."

From the Governor-General follows extract—

From the Secretary to the Government of India, to the Resident at Lahore, Sir Frederick Currie, Bart.

"Fort William, July 8, 1848.

" The account of the successful action has afforded the highest satisfaction to the Governor-General in Council, . . . and his Lordship desires me to convey to you, and to request that you will convey to Lieutenant Edwardes, the cordial expression of the approbation with which the Government of India have regarded his proceedings ; their recognition of the foresight and skill by which he effected a junction with the Nawáb's troops; and their high sense of the steady gallantry by which he made good his opportunity, and achieved the important success which merits these thanks."

*From the Acting-Resident at Lahore, Sir Frederick Currie,
Bart., to Lieutenant Edwardes.*

"Lahore, July 10, 1818.

"MY DEAR EDWARDES,

"It falls to the lot of few men to have the
opportunity of rendering such brilliant and useful service
to their country as you have been enabled to perform ; and
the gallantry, skill, and self-devotion with which you have
improved the opportunity afforded you must command the
admiration, while the great value of the services effected
will call forth the grateful thanks, of the Governor-General
in Council, as they do, in an eminent degree, my own.

"You have, indeed, performed most eminent and valuable
services, which his Lordship in Council will, I am sure,
appreciate as I do, and will greet with some hearty acknowledgment.

"This second victory * is a very important one. It will,
I doubt not, have the effect of disheartening the followers
and partisans, open and secret, of the rebel Moolraj, and of
enabling you to confine him and his remaining army to the
city and the fort till a British force shall put a period to the
rebellion by crushing him in his stronghold.†

         "(Signed)   F. CURRIE."

When the news reached England, Edwardes's masters, the
Court of Directors, were not behind in kind and appreciative
congratulations.

*Extract of a despatch from the Honourable the Secret Committee
of the Court of Directors, to the Right Honourable the
Governor-General of India.*

"London, August 21, 1818.

"'Para. 8.—Of Lieutenant Edwardes it is impossible to
speak too highly. Commencing with a small body of troops,

   * Of Suddoosâm.   † Copied from Punjab Blue-Book, pp. 46–49.

scarcely trustworthy, he raised, within a month, a considerable force, whom he inspired with confidence, and animated by his own example to the most daring and successful undertakings.

" ' No dread of responsibility, no rumours of widespread disaffection, no danger from open mutiny, no delay on the part of allies, subdued his dauntless spirit nor slackened for a moment his indefatigable exertions.

" ' We have perused all the details respecting the brilliant exploits of that gallant officer, and do not hesitate to say, to him we consider to be due the whole merit of the result; and that to him we are indebted for the favourable position of British interests in the Punjab.

" ' We know not which most to admire, the prudence or the energy, the skilful combination or the cool courage, by which Lieutenant Edwardes, under circumstances most discouraging, and with means apparently inadequate, has performed services which will be for ever memorable in the annals of British India.

" ' We most cordially concur in the praise bestowed upon him by Sir F. Currie, and we desire that this expression of our high approbation and esteem may be forthwith conveyed to him.'

" True extract.

" (Signed)   — WHYLIE,

" Assistant-Resident."

It was very gratifying to him to receive from England a letter from the late Governor-General, Lord Hardinge, who, having given up the reins of government, was not officially required to notice his deeds. He writes—

" South Park, September 4, 1848.

" MY DEAR EDWARDES,

" I have followed you in your glorious career with the deepest interest and highest admiration. You have shown, in the midst of great difficulties, a mind full of resources and a heart resolute to execute plans, in which prudence and skill have been admirably combined with boldness and gallantry.

"I congratulate you most heartily on your heroic deeds, which place you at once in the rank of the most distinguished officers which the Indian or any army have produced.

"My anxious desire is that you may be able to complete your exploit, which has rendered the name of Edwardes so honourable, without one leaf of your laurels being shared by any other man; and, as you use the pen as skilfully as you wield the sword, I shall in my retirement enjoy the perusal of your journal at once attesting your well-earned fame and stimulating others to follow your noble example.

"I am also gratified that my anticipations of your character should be verified. Two years ago, I wrote to Colonel Sykes my opinion of my young *political;* and I trust that the Government and the Court of Directors will mark by liberal and appropriate distinctions the sense which the people of England, and the army, entertain of your eminent services.

"It is not necessary that I should interfere, but I could not refrain from expressing my confident expectations that the rank of field-officer, the honour of the Bath, and some token of public approbation, may be conferred upon you; and I know they will.

"My object in writing is merely the gratification of my own feelings in expressing to you my appreciation of the great merit and splendid qualities which you have shown, and again most cordially to congratulate you on your success and well-earned fame,

"Always, my dear Edwardes,

"Very sincerely yours,

"(Signed)   HARDINGE."

The reply to this is so interesting, so genial, and so full of life, that a few extracts may be made from it.

"Camp before Mooltân, November 14, 1848.

"My dear Lord Hardinge,

"I have, as you may suppose, received many congratulations and kind letters of approbation from England since the news of my humble victories crossed the seas. Our own great Indian Government, a Cabinet Minister, and troops of affectionate friends, have tried their best to spoil me with overpowering thanks for merely doing my duty.

"But I can sincerely say that, setting aside out of the comparison the effusions of dear relatives, deliciously ignorant of facts, and who would probably have praised me just as highly had I cleverly run away 'from the horrid rebel,' no letter has so gratified me as your Lordship's of September 4.

"Many and mixed feelings entered into this. Your Lordship was Governor-General when I first entered the Bureau Diplomatique; and what a big word 'Governor-General' is!"

"You were *the giant* that stalked over the great field of the Punjab, and through the glorious scenes on the Sutlej; and I was one of the dwarfs who panted by your side—in short, you were my *master;* and scarcely have I worked out my apprenticeship ere you condescend to take in me the interest of a friend. But it is not this merely which has made me get almost every word of your letter by heart.

"Naturally, I look upon your Lordship as the type of a policy, as the conceiver of the glorious experiment of honesty which will now annex the Punjab to British India without one reproach of ambition, without even a Frenchman's sneer at the 'improvement of a bad boundary;' and when the Mooltân Rebellion first broke out, I felt certain that, in all England, yourself and Colonel Lawrence were the two men who understood its *meaning*, its bearings on our relations with the Sikh people, and *how you had provided* for such an *event being met.*

"I need not scruple to say that I do not consider the way in which the crisis was met at its commencement in April last, as in accordance with your Lordship's policy, the breathing spirit of which was *vigour;* nor with your Lordship's *intentions and arrangements,* as fully and minutely laid down in a military memo. of the defence of the Punjab, which I have often read over with Colonel Lawrence—of which I have no copy, but which must be in the office of both the Resident at Lahore and the General commanding the Punjab division.

"A leading feature in that minute was its providing a movable brigade for any possible emergency; and I am one of those who believe to this day, and perhaps ever shall, that had that brigade, under a fine soldier like Brigadier Campbell, marched *at once* upon Mooltán (say on April 25), the rebellion would have been nipped in the bud by the escape and surrender of Moolraj. He never contemplated resistance to poor Agnew, who was first assaulted by a sulky sentry, and murdered afterwards in a vindictive outbreak of a garrison which expected to be thrown out of service.

"As for a ' Punjab conspiracy '—a ' matured insurrection of the Sikh people,' etc., my belief is that they never existed until called into life by the timid policy which presupposed them. Moolraj did not rebel because the Sikhs were ready to back him up. The Sikhs backed up Moolraj because the British Government did not put him down.

"Intriguing truly never was wanting in the Punjab, and the Queen-Mother, in particular, never ceased to 'agitate;' but there was only an evil *animus*—there was no unity, no head, no oligarchy even, no confidence among the aristocracy in each other, nor among the soldiers in the aristocracy.

"The *Sikh Insurrection* was created out of the *materials collected to put down the Mooltán Rebellion.* .

" It began with squadrons and companies, and grew into regiments, whose impurity begot armies; but at last it remains an unwieldy disorder, without a leader, without a plan of campaign, without money to carry on one. Yet there could have been no conspiracy without these things.

" Entertaining these views (which I may say here were shared by every Assistant in the Residency), I cannot describe to your Lordship the sorrow, shame, and impatience with which I thought of our Government enduring, not only a rebellion, but the murder of its magistrates, from April till October! I felt humiliated as an Englishman in the presence of every native round me; and the exclamation which rose to my lips a hundred times a day was, ' It was not so in Lord Hardinge's time!'

" At last I could stand it no longer, and conceived the idea of first wrestling all the Trans-Indus provinces from the rebels, by recruiting the warlike tribes whom Moolraj had called to join him at Mooltân; and, having effected that, and put myself, in so doing, at the head of six thousand men, to get the Bhûwulpore Nabob given me as an ally, and concentrate his forces and my own on Mooltân, so as to keep Moolraj at home until the troops could come.

" It seemed to me that, with Moolraj a prisoner as it were in his fortress, his rich provinces in my possession, and my army at his threshold waiting for him to come out, the spectacle would not be humiliating to our name, nor the Sikh people have any encouragement to rebel.

" In these political feelings I know myself to have been much influenced by the memory of your Lordship and Henry Lawrence; and though I found, amid the life-and-death struggle which then ensued, no leisure *to write*, I often thought that both of you would hear through official channels of my *essay*, and recognize your young pupil in its spirit.

" And this, my Lord, is the peculiar pleasure which I

have derived from your letter. You could not have so
warmly thanked me for what I have done, had you not felt
sure I had done what you would yourself have ordered me
to do had you still been at the helm. . . .

"I cannot gather from your Lordship's letter whether
you shared the hopes of many sanguine friends that Moolraj
would surrender to me, of his own free will, a stronghold, in
July, which he has since been able to maintain against a
British army until November. Certainly you would not
forget the existence of the Mooltân Fort in the background,
and therefore will not be so disappointed at subsequent
events as those who did—who thought it a matter of course
that, if I could drive Moolraj *into* Mooltân, I could certainly
drive him *out;* and to do so it is true that I only wanted
heavy guns.

"After the battles of June 18 and July 1, so thoroughly
dispirited was Moolraj, that any ragamuffin in my irregular
levies felt that we only wanted a few battering guns and
mortars to add the renowned fortress to our conquests; and
this I wrote to the Resident.

"He also saw now a chance of closing the Mooltân
Rebellion, and betook himself to the military authorities.
Little did either he or I anticipate the delay which
followed.

"The guns could not be sent without British troops to
take care of them, and they could not get carriage under a
month.

"Ultimately it was the last week in August before
General Whish's force was assembled at Mooltân, and the
first week in September before the heavy ordnance arrived.

"Meanwhile, not only had Moolraj recruited, *but a Sikh
force* * *had found its way into Mooltân.*

"To this latter we owe the failure of the siege. It
fraternized just as we had established a battery within

* Shere Singh's.

breaching-distance of the city wall; and, in a moment, the garrison was nearly doubled.

"This defection of Rajah Shere Singh has not failed to bring much odium on me, and I have been compelled to reflect in my own mind that the disappointment of a brave Division naturally seeks something on which to wreak itself; and, as naturally, seizes on the nearest 'political,' and it must ever be the painful lot of political officers to be tongue-tied in their own defence.

"I cannot stand in the market-places exclaiming, ' Rajah Shere Singh and his army came not to Mooltân at my bidding, but *against* it.' My remonstrances to Sir Frederick are extant; my written orders to the Rajah to halt, wherever he might be, bear the date of June.

"The Rajah marched on, in spite of orders, and when he came I could only make the best of him.

"From July to September I was encamped on a plain, between Moolraj in my front and Shere Singh in my rear, with pickets watching both!

"Bitterly did I regret, too, that they did not both attack me then; for Lake would have taken one, and I the other, with the utmost pleasure, and fought them, as Lord Nelson said, 'fore and aft.'"

Then follows further filling-up of details of the causes of delay and the siege, into which we need not further go, and concludes—

The gap filled up between Moolraj's crime and punishment.

"I must confess I have been much consoled by the receipt of a long and most kind letter from Lord Dalhousie, written long since the siege was raised, and in a strain of unaltered satisfaction, so that, if I have not realized all the expectations of friends at home, and economized a winter campaign, I may still feel happy in having been useful in a less degree—in having filled up the gap between the crime and the punishment of Moolraj, and staved off the

Sikh Insurrection by my successes from May till September.

"Lord Gough believed that to do this it was merely
necessary to gazette the army of the Punjab for this latter
month; but insurrections cannot be postponed, like tea-
parties, with a note, nor enemies be bound over to keep
the peace until it is quite convenient to you to fight.

"In self-defence, and not in boasting, I express my conviction that 'Kinyéree' and 'Suddoosâm' alone permitted
the British troops to pass the hot season in barracks.

"This much I have thought due to the interest your
Lordship has taken in my career. Now let me tell you more
general news. . . .

"My Lord, yours sincerely,
"HERBERT B. EDWARDES."

This letter has an interest in its personal bearing which
will excuse its admission here, for it brings the subject into
a focus, and speaks for itself, explaining simply and honestly
the position that was forced upon Edwardes by circumstances,
and how he held it.

And when the army joined him, how cordially and effi-
ciently he co-operated with it, and brought his well-trained
levies to swell the regular forces and to complete the retribution—all this is known in history. But while we write, it
is amusing to remember a little incident which shows how
nearly it dropped out of history altogether.

When the siege was over, and the despatches had to be
written, General Whish called Edwardes to his tent, and
asked him pleasantly (as he was so ready with his pen) if he
would kindly frame his despatch for him.

This Edwardes did, with careful accuracy and pains; and
when he took it to him, the general was pleased to see how
well the despatch read. Of course it told of everybody's
deeds except Edwardes's own. But what was Edwardes's
astonishment to find, when the despatch came out of the
office of the copyist, that the general had only topped and
tailed it, and there was not a word in it about himself and

all his force.   Edwardes might have passed the injustice over
for himself alone, but he could not for them; and he took it
to the general, and pointed out the omission.

"Dear me!" said he; "and so it is! Well, shall I add
a postscript to it now?"

"Well, general," said Edwardes, "I don't think you *can*
get six thousand men well into a postscript, if you tried!"

And so the general had to put them into a separate
despatch, and give an efficient and valuable portion of his
force before Mooltân the acknowledgment they deserved
so well.

So much for the chances of war—and history!

The accounts of Edwardes's successes and exertions, when
they reached England, were met not with acknowledgment
only, but with rewards.

The letters we have quoted from were followed quickly
by the communication of honours conferred by her Majesty—
a majority and the Companionship of the Bath.

*From the Right Honourable Sir J. C. Hobhouse, President
of the Board of Control, to Major H. B. Edwardes.*

"India Board, London, September 7, 1848.

"Sir,

"I have great satisfaction in announcing to
you that, in consideration of your distinguished services
in your late actions with the Mooltân rebels, you have
been recommended to her Majesty by the Duke of Wellington for a majority in the territories of Lahore.

"I beg you to accept my cordial congratulations on this
well-deserved promotion.

"I have the honour to remain,
"Your very faithful servant,
"(Signed)   John Hobhouse."

And to this letter succeeded another—

To Major H. B. Edwardes, C.B.

" India Board, London, October 24, 1818.

" Dear Sir,

" I have again much satisfaction in announcing to you an additional honour conferred on you for your distinguished services at Mooltán.

" The Queen has been graciously pleased to ordain a special statute of the Order of the Bath, for appointing you an extra member of the military division of the third class, or Companion of that Order.

" I congratulate you cordially on this distinction,

" And remain, dear sir,

" Your very faithful servant,

" (Signed)   John Hobhouse."

A resolution was also passed at a meeting of the Court of Directors to present Edwardes with a special gold medal, to mark their estimation of his services.

From the Court of Directors of the Honourable East India Company.

" At a Court held Wednesday, September 13, 1848.

" The Chairman having called the attention of the Court to despatches from the Government of India, announcing the military operations carried on against the rebel forces of the Dewan of Mooltán, by Lieutenant, now Brevet-Major Herbert B. Edwardes, of the Bengal Army, as communicated to the Court by the Secret Committee, on the 23rd and 30th ult.;

" Resolved, unanimously, that this Court do present to Major Edwardes a gold medal, in testimony of their high approbation of the important services rendered by him, in raising and organizing large forces in a foreign territory, under circumstances of the greatest difficulty; in wresting, within a very brief period, an extensive tract of

country from the power of the rebels; in skilfully combining
his forces with those of an ally; and in completely defeating
the troops of the enemy in two pitched battles; thus
evincing the possession, in the flower of his youth, of all
those qualities which form and ennoble the character of the
British officer."

This was communicated to him as follows :—

" India Board, September 21, 1848.

" Sir,

"I am directed by the Commissioners of the
Affairs of India to acquaint you that they cordially
approve of the resolution passed by the Court of Directors,
on the 13th inst., proposing to grant to Brevet-Major Herbert
B. Edwardes a gold medal, in acknowledgment of the
distinguished services lately rendered by that officer in
the territories of Lahore.

" (Signed)   THOMAS WYSE."

These unsolicited honours could not fail to be gratifying
to Edwardes, but his nature would not allow him to be
satisfied unless they were shared by others; and, in his
reply to Lord Hardinge's letter of congratulation, he wrote—

Edward Lake.

. . . "Another of your Lordship's 'young politicals' joined
me in the middle of all this fighting, Edward Lake, who was
deputed by Sir Frederick Currie to accompany the Bhâwulpore army, and who ultimately (by the infallible working
of Sir Robert Peel's principle of civilization swallowing up
barbarism whenever they come in contact) superseded its
commander. Lake justified every favourable opinion you
ever formed of him; and in the fight of Suddoosâm, on
July 1, made a bad army as good as the best. It has been a
source of great regret to me that as yet no notice has been
taken at home of either Lake or Cortlandt. I feel almost as
if I had been the means of injuring both, though I lost no

opportunity, in my public or private letters, of acknowledging how much of the success was due to them.

"General Cortlandt's situation is most peculiar, and his General
conduct in it admirable. I declare that I consider him the Cortlandt.
only servant to the little Maharajah who has been 'true to his
salt.' If ever it should lie in your Lordship's power, may I
hope that you will say a good word for a man who combines
in no ordinary degree the qualities of a good soldier and a
good civil officer."

Although Edwardes was not at this moment satisfied by
the promotion of his friend Edward Lake, he had abundant
reason to be so afterwards; for he lived to see him win
honours and renown, and rise to be Financial Commissioner
of the Punjab, which office he gave up when he left India to
retire to England in 1866.

Nor does it appear that either he or General Cortlandt
were left out in the public thanks; for there is a letter—

From the Resident at Lahore to Lieutenant Lake.

"Lahore, July 10, 1848.

"I have received the description of this second victory
gained by the forces of our ally, Nuwâb Bhâwul Khan. . . .
While I request that you will communicate to Futteh
Mahommed Khan Ghoree and the officers of the force my
appreciation of their courage and services, I feel that to yourself my thanks and admiration are peculiarly due, for the skill
and gallantry with which you directed the movements and
operations of the force, to which Lieutenant Edwardes bears
such ample testimony, and to which the success of the
Bhâwulpore army is in an eminent degree attributable.

"I am satisfied that the Governor-General in Council
will appreciate and acknowledge the great value of your
services on this important occasion."

*From H. M. Elliot, Esq., Secretary to the Government of India,
to the Honourable Sir F. Currie, Bart., Acting-Resident
at Lahore.*

"Fort William, Calcutta, July 29, 1848.

" I am directed to request that you will convey to Lieutenant Edwardes and to Lieutenant Lake the highest approbation of the Governor-General in Council of their conduct in the action, and the strong sense the Government entertain of the gallantry, energy, determination, and skill which these officers have displayed." *

Of General Cortlandt, the Resident writes in a public letter to Edwardes—

"Lahore, July 10, 1848.

" General Cortlandt has again distinguished himself. His skill in managing his troops, and his intrepidity in action, are in the highest degree creditable to him, and entitle him to the warmest thanks of the Maharajah and myself. . . .

"The Durbar have at my instigation, addressed a purwánna to the officers and men of General Cortlandt's regiment ; and have, in a proclamation to the troops of their army, spoken of the conduct and services of these corps in terms which will, I trust, be gratifying to them, while it is to be hoped that their conduct, with its reward, may have the effect of stimulating the other Durbar troops, to the exhibition of similar fidelity to the Government." †

Reward to Foujdar Khan, 1849. The services of Foujdar Khan, whom we have seen acting as Edwardes's adjutant-general at Kinyéree, and, in spite of his wounds, leading the Cavalry at Suddoosâm, were eventually rewarded by Lord Dalhousie with the title of Khan Bahadoor, for we find the copy of a letter from Edwardes, in which the honour was conveyed to him (dated Lahore, July 12, 1849), which we will here insert.

* Blue-Book page 248.   † Blue-Book, p. 247.

Draft of a Persian letter to Foujdar Khan (Alizye), forwarding his sunnud of "Khan Bahâdoor-ee" from Lord Dalhousie.

"Lahore, July 12, 1849.

" MY FRIEND,

"I feel as great pleasure in sending you this sunnud of Khan Bahâdooree from the Governor-General as I did in receiving my own honours from the Queen of England.

"Together we shared the danger of our position at Leiah, when we had few soldiers, and most of them traitors; together we shared the labour of raising an army to meet the rebels and defend the frontier under my charge; we sat under one bush at Kinyéree throughout that fiery day in June, waiting for our guns; we fought together at Suddoosâm and throughout the siege of Mooltân; and it is right that you should share, not merely in the victory, but its rewards.

"I rejoice, therefore, in the title that has been conferred on you; I think you earned it well by your bravery, fidelity, wisdom in council, and equanimity in trouble; and I hope you will long live to enjoy it and the jageer * which Lord Dalhousie has promised you.

"Thus, my friend, have the exertions of one year enriched you for life, and put you out of the reach of want and the caprice of a Maharajah or his Sirdars. A year ago, when commander of only twenty-four horsemen, you could never (even in your dreams) have hoped for such good fortune. Let the rest of your life, therefore, justify the reputation of your tribe for fidelity and gratitude.

"In time of peace speak well, among your countrymen, of the British Government, and in time of war be ever ready with the good sword Sir Henry Lawrence gave you to assist it.

* A "jageer" is a grant of land given by Government as a reward for services.

"Thus shall I ever be proud that you were my officer, Sir Henry Lawrence that he recommended you to honour, and the Governor-General that he conferred it upon you.

"(Signed)   HERBERT EDWARDES."

Value of personal influence.

Such words as these, and such generous appreciation of services, it is that build up most securely our influence in the East, and *cement* our country's rule with the *personal influence* which a strong and generous mind (such as this we are studying now) brings to bear upon its work, with these brave untutored races.

The strong personal attachment which they are capable of forming is the secret of many of the great deeds of faithful service, and even chivalry, with which our Indian history in the past is filled.

And Edwardes was an example of this, which young soldiers would do well to mark for their own imitation. His brave, genial, generous, noble nature made the natives love him; his confidence in them bred confidence in return; and his good judgment taught him where it was safe to *trust.* And they knew that if he had a strong hand to punish the guilty, he had an open, generous hand for those who were deserving.

Fruits gathered in after-years.

Years afterwards, when the stormy days of difficulty at Peshâwur came, it was seen how the *fruit* of this time we are passing through now was *gathered.* When Edwardes and Nicholson raised their flag in 1857, at Peshâwur, and called for "Levies" to take the place of disarmed mutineers, up sprang readily the men of this same country to answer to the call; and at their head we shall see again Foujdar Khan, ready to go to the front and serve again in Afghanistan the master whom he served so well at Kinyéree.

CHAPTER VI.

—◦—

1849—1850.

RETURN TO ENGLAND—MARRIAGE—WRITES "A YEAR ON
THE PUNJAB FRONTIER."

"As cold waters to a thirsty soul,
So is good news from a far country."

ROV. xxv. 25.

"All blessedness of heaven, and earth beneath,
Of converse high, and sacred home
Are yours, in life and death."

KEBLE.

WHEN the "year on the Punjab frontier" was completed, and the Mooltân Campaign was at an end, Edwardes proceeded to Lahore to make his official returns, and to put affairs into order, to enable him to take his furlough home to England.

Sir Henry Lawrence had now returned from England. He had received the honour of a K.C.B.-ship at home, April 28, 1848. He had hurried back to India when the news of the siege of Mooltân reached him, anxious to be at his post at Lahore again; disappointed to find that his generous policy and labours for Sikh independence and good self-government were being thwarted by the recklessness and faithlessness of the people themselves.

Sir Henry Lawrence returns to Lahore.

His disappointment at the failure of his efforts for Sikh independence.

Edwardes had gone through great exposure under canvas at Mooltân and Bunnoo during the whole summer heat, and at a time when the commander-in-chief thought it impossible to bring British soldiers into the field, and made this a reason for delaying the siege of Mooltân.

Throughout this time Edwardes had kept the field, fought Moolraj, and defeated him in two pitched battles, shut him up in his fort, and kept him at bay till the army could be assembled.

In the course of this service Edwardes had many hair-breadth escapes and wonderful deliverances. Once, as was told in chap. iv., a bullet passed through his sleeve, entering at the wrist and passing out at the elbow, without touching him. Again, when the muzzle of a gun was held up against him in a *mélée*, and he thought that nothing *could* have saved him, it flashed in the pan and he was unharmed, and, putting

Hair-breadth escapes.

spurs to his horse before his antagonist could draw his sword, he escaped. At another time, when an assassin came into his tent for murderous purpose, and there was only the small camp-table he was writing at between them, the sentry rushed in and seized the man before he could touch him.

Moolraj had set a price on his head, and had sent spies into his camp to bribe his servants to poison him. The plot was discovered by Edwardes and all his guests becoming at the same time very sick one day, after partaking of dinner together; and through accidentally overhearing the conversation of some natives in the verandah of his tent, he discovered the cause, that the soup was poisoned. Some emissary of Moolraj's had offered himself to fill a vacancy in the kitchen establishment, and had been accepted unwarily by the head servant.

Out of such and many other dangers he had been safely brought; but now, when the duty was done, and he had come with great honour and unexampled success from the field of Mooltân—Moolraj defeated, Mooltân taken, and the campaign over;—the return to Lahore, and hot weather in the plains in one of the hottest stations of the Punjab, and the very hard grind of office-work there, were more than he was physically equal to endure.

Sir Henry Lawrence urged him, however, to try and carry the official work connected with Bunnoo and Mooltân through the office before he left India; and he was himself anxious to bring to notice the services of those natives and officers who had served under him. But it was working the willing horse too much, and it was no wonder that, soon after taking up the heavy office-work at Lahore, he was struck down with fever, and was for some time very seriously ill.

Illness.

Furlough to England. On recovering from this fever sufficiently to travel, there could be no longer any further delay, and Edwardes was allowed to take his "leave" to England. He had private reasons, too, for desiring it; for his own personal happiness (and not only his own) was deeply concerned in this journey.

From such a sacred and holy shrine it is difficult to lift the veil. But yet the story of Edwardes's life would not be truly told if we were to leave out of it that one true, deep, earnest, and guiding passion of his whole existence. From a boy his heart was set and fixed in one true love, and it was the pole-star that led him on to realize his hopes. Determined that, till he saw what his future was to be, his lot should be unshared, he waited only to feel his foot upon the ladder, and this he did when Sir Henry Lawrence selected him for Lahore.

Then he took Sir Henry Lawrence into his counsel, and a story so like his own readily won Sir Henry's chivalrous sympathy and approval. There need have been no more delay; but then came the expedition to Bunnoo, and after that swept in the rebellion of Moolraj, the siege of Mooltân and all the stirring and absorbing events connected with it.

Unhesitatingly Edwardes could set aside his own personal wishes and objects to follow a course of duty; but now, with his duties accomplished, he longed to be free.

One would expect, in a nature so rare in depth of tenderness, so strong and true, so romantic and at the same time so noble, so keen in enjoyment, so sensitive to pain, so finely-strung with Nature's keenest sensibilities, and yet so towering above all the littlenesses and cruelties of man—one would *expect* that in a nature such as this, a *home* was a necessity, and that he would be as rare in love as he was in other things —rare in the constancy of one great affection.

And will the reader wonder if now the truth is not withheld by her who all her life has owned so rich a wealth of possession, and owns it still?

But before passing on, it may be permitted to take a parting look at the life of the "Old Residency" at Lahore, presently about to pass away in the change and struggle of the coming days; for it will never come again! When Edwardes returned to India, all had changed into a more regular form of life.

One wave courses over another with all the freshness and power of the present; but there is no time to gather up the lessons, unless we learn them as they pass.

It was a wonderfully *real* and happy life in those early days of the "Old Residency" at Lahore. Here was a band of strong, and young, and earnest men, all bent on doing good, with their minds clear, and strong, and full of hope; and

Picture of the "Old Residency" days.

at their head is Henry Lawrence, a giant in the battle of life,
fighting against evil and wrong, and guiding all, and quicken-
ing into life and usefulness all bright thoughts and schemes
that came to any of that earnest band of friends.

Honoria
Lawrence.

And among them a few fair, gentle women, wives and
sisters—very few. But the ministering angel of them all
was Honoria Lawrence, the brave and noble wife of Henry
Lawrence, who was ever the inspiring genius of her husband's
higher life, the glad sharer of his every thought, and the
softening and the refining element that glided through and
pervaded that "Old Residency," and gave a charm to the
wildness and roughness of this frontier-life to all its inmates.
For hers was a mind that loved the wildness, and rejoiced in
the unconventionality of the life; and her room was the
natural rallying-point for all the wit and talent that was
among them—and there was no lack of that.

We will give a specimen of her thoughts at this time.
She writes—

"There is something unspeakably solemn in the *status* of
our household now. That young fellow just leaving earth;
the young couple full of hope and joyance; Harrie, with her
sore grief drawing daily nearer; 'Bulbul,' all restless with
hope and fear; the P——s newly launched, and beginning, I
think, to feel the bitterness of the waves; and then, how we
go regularly on, eating and drinking, sleeping and waking, as
if there were no care or trouble in life!

"I try to keep before me that all is but a *training* (these
present things), not the object of our being, but only the
discipline for our real being. Words easily *said*, and, in a
certain sense, believed; but oh! the difference between the
dead and the living faith in them! . . .

"I feel how short the time is that rests to any of us,
and then the blessed calm—the meeting, never to part, on
the other side of the stream—when all the pettinesses and
earthlinesses that fetter and embitter the intercourse of
friends here will be swept away, and there will be an ever-
growing, still-beginning peace! *Safe, safe, safe,* that blessed
and comfortable word! the cold dark valley passed, with the
Saviour for a comforter."

Did we call her a ministering angel just now? Yes,

truly, for she ever pointed upwards; while, with a large share of wit and originality, and a mind well stored by reading, she was always ready to lend a charm and brightness to every discussion.

There is no sphere like India for a completely happy *woman's life*—her husband's helpmeet—and Honoria Lawrence filled it perfectly. What more need be said?

But the time approached when Edwardes could take his longed-for rest at home. His friends, John Lawrence and his wife, urged him to take charge of their two little girls. Their ages, of six and seven, made the first parting from their parents necessary. And Edwardes undertook the unusual charge confided to him, and never had any little girls more loving and careful protection. Children always loved him. His bright, genial nature always attracted them to his side, and he was ever ready with some bright story or fairy-tale to tell them that riveted their love; or he was ready for a game of play with them on the shortest notice. So it was like a holiday to take a journey with Edwardes, and the tears of parting soon dried up with them.

In the end of the year 1849, Edwardes left Lahore, and his friend John Nicholson also intending to take his furlough home, the two friends gladly agreed to start together.

They dropped down the Indus in boats to Bombay (which was the slow way in which the journey then was made), stopping every night to let the boatmen rest, and to give the little girls a run on the land to hunt for tiger's footprints on the sandy shore.

Edwardes and Nicholson leave Lahore together.

The pleasant companionship of the two friends beguiled the tedium of the river-journey, and gave time for thought; and we can fancy how these two earnest, brave men would exchange their thoughts about the country they had been ready to give their lives for, and fight their battles over again. Both had been trained by the same master, Henry Lawrence; both were in entire heart-sympathy with each other.

This is the first time we have had occasion to notice the friendship of these two men, which remained strong and deep throughout their lives, as friendship in such strong and noble matters must be, when founded, as in this case, upon the profound respect and admiration in which each held the other. Knowing each other most intimately in the trying and difficult circumstances in which their lives had been cast in these stormy days of the early history of the Punjab, they were more than brothers in the tenderness of their whole lives henceforth, and the fame and interests of each other were dearer to them both than their own.*

Indian friendship.

One great charm of Indian life is the fast friendships that it makes for life. Being thrown into circumstances of difficulty and danger that can never be experienced in quiet lives at home, men have a *need* they never know in the case of home life, and find that need is answered in some brave and noble friend whom it has been their good fortune to be linked with in their public duty.

And thus these two brother-assistants of Sir Henry Lawrence's choice were welded together in the strong, true love and friendship that was a mutual joy in their whole after-lives, interrupted only by death, when, in 1857, this same John Nicholson—at the time we are *now* speaking of soon to be made major and C.B. for his services in the Punjab, *then* the General John Nicholson to whom so large a share of the honour of taking back Delhi from the mutineers is due—fell, in leading the assault of that city.

This may seem a digression somewhat out of place, but may be pardoned; for it is impossible to those who know and love him to leave the name of John Nicholson with only a passing mention.

To return, we left the travellers gliding down the river

---

* As an instance of this, we may copy from a local paper. "We may mention here an instance of Major Edwardes's great and singular modesty with respect to his own high merits. When he was the 'Lion' of the day in 1849, and was on one occasion fêted at the Mansion House, his name coupled with 'The Health of the Indian Army,' proposed by the chairman as one of the toasts of the evening, the Duke of Wellington and other distinguished officers being present . . . rising to speak, and turning towards his friend Major Nicholson, he said, 'Here, gentlemen, here is the real author of half the exploits which the world has been so ready to attribute to me.'" The effect was instantaneous and almost electrical, and will never be forgotten by those who witnessed it.

"In the interesting Parliamentary Papers relating to the Punjab, which were published in May, 1849, we find not a word of self-laudation or assumption of credit, but much of prudence, intelligence, and foresight, and a deep insight into the native character."

to Kurrachee, and beguiling their way with books and talk. Dropping down the river, 1849. It was at this time that Edwardes wrote a curious foreshadowing of a storm that *really* burst in terrible force over India in 1857.

It is a mere memorandum written by him in his commonplace book, and is copied as it stands.

" *Memorandum.*

" A good story might be written by way of *prophecy*, or I would rather say *warning*, of the sudden and unexpected overthrow of the British Indian empire by the British Indian army.

" Scene.—Lahore. Time—Fifty years hence, or A.D. 1900. Materials as follows :—

" The native army, according to a system introduced by a Lord Napier, who was commander-in-chief about 1850, has been for the last forty-five years *massed* upon great points, such as Cabul (annexed about 1880), Peshawur, Lahore, Umballa, Delhi, Dinapore, and Calcutta, in Bengal ; in Madras, . . .; and in Bombay . . . The extension of the empire by the annexation of Khorassan has rendered a vigorous economy necessary, and prevented the increase of the European army. Pressure of parties in England has transferred the Government of India from the East India Company to the Crown, which has introduced the same colonial system as prevails over its other dependencies, and has lately lost Canada.

" ' Lord Frederick Verisophts ' are now Commissioners of provinces, and young barristers come out as magistrates. To meet their convenience, law is administered in English, and English education has superseded vernacular through all the Government schools. The people, in consequence, are oppressed and discontented.

" The courts, in the hands of a few Bengalee Baboos, are not resorted to, except by the rich.

" The country is consequently ripe for evil designs.

The army, for the sake of economy, has continued to be increased from the same classes of Hindoostanees, and the only balance is between the Hindoos and the Mussulmans.

"About the year 1855, an extensive scheme, organized by Râni Junda, Bhaie Maharaj, Rajah Déena Nâth, and others, to restore the Râni to the throne of Lahore by means of our own soldiers, was discovered by Bhaie Bikrumah Sing (jealous of Bhaie Maharaj) to the British Government, and the ringleaders hanged or imprisoned.

"But the secret of unlawful organization could not be so easily unlearnt; and the ambitious spirits of the country, who could nowadays find no native court to which to resort for service, commenced and gradually matured a secret confederation of the whole native army, which was much favoured by the system of military centralization now in force.

"The large European society in the great cantonments has withdrawn the officers more than ever from their men, and few are now left who can discourse with them in their own language.

"Still, indications of the conspiracy creep out through officers of irregular corps, which at first hold aloof, though tempted.

"Midnight meetings of the Native Divisional Committees, under pretence of native festivals, should be described. Their correspondence in Persian, which has become 'cypher.' The outbreak on the first of a month at muster; massacre of all European officers at parade; ineffectual stand of few European regiments; retreat to the sea and embark; division of the empire; upstart princes, etc."

"This sketch of a prophetical Indian novel was written on or about December 21, 1849, in my boat, dropping down the Sutlej River, with John Nicholson, on our way to England after the second Sikh War. The inspiration of it was drawn from the experience we had lately had in the Punjab of the Sikh army; the fear of similar results in our own

native army, on which Sir Henry Lawrence was so often
talking to us all; and the views of discipline entertained
by the then commander-in-chief, Sir Charles Napier.

> "(Signed)   HERBERT B. EDWARDES."

This reads like a prophecy of 1857, for the reader must
remember that it was written eight years before the event.
It shows, at least, what anxious questions were burning in
the minds of these men.

John Nicholson, not having the same motive for urgency
in his return to England, thought it a good opportunity to see
Constantinople, and turned aside in Egypt. So the two
friends parted for a few months, to meet again in England.

Edwardes landed in England on January 27, 1850. He
was received with great enthusiasm everywhere as "the hero
of Mooltàn."

He had taken ship in the same steamer at Bombay that
brought home the commander-in-chief, Lord Gough; and it *Arrival in England.*
is amusing to see how entirely unconscious he was of the
reception he was to receive, for he was standing on the
paddle-box of the steamer, watching the approach to his
native land with very different thoughts, when Lord Gough
called to him, "Edwardes, come down; you're called for."
And he was surprised to find that some of the cheers on the
English shore, which he counted all for his chief, Lord Gough,
were intended for himself; so little was he thinking of
anything but the private hopes and longed-for meetings that
awaited him.

A lieutenant in his regiment (then the 1st Bengal Fusiliers,
afterwards called the 101st), he had been promoted to major,
and the Queen had awarded him the Companionship of the
Bath ere his arrival in England.

He received the "thanks of the House" and the marked
approval of the Duke of Wellington, expressed both privately
in a most gratifying way, very shortly after his landing in
England, and publicly.

It was remarked on one occasion, in the House of Lords,
when the rewards were being discussed, "these would be
unprecedented honours for so young a man." Upon which
the Duke of Wellington rose, and said, "Gentlemen, Lieut.

Edwardes's *services* have been *unprecedented*, and his rewards must be unprecedented too." This stopped the discussion.

Edwardes used to tell with pardonable pride of the reception he met with at Apsley House, from the aged Duke of Wellington.

He had received an intimation that he would be expected to call; so, as soon as the pressure of engagements allowed, he drove to the door and sent in his card. The old porter at the door, looking at it, said, "Major Edwardes! Oh, Major Edwardes; we have been looking for *you* ever so long—every day. Come up, sir, and I'll take in your card." Then he ushered him upstairs and went in. In a few moments out came the aged Duke of Wellington and led Edwardes in by the hand, warmly welcoming him. Seated on a sofa by his side, he took out the map and went through all the campaign with remarkable clearness and discrimination, showing that he had followed him closely in all his movements, and cordially approving, from point to point, of the measures he had taken.

It was pardonable for a young soldier to be proud of being so welcomed and so approved by the first military authority, and a veteran in the art of war.

Publicly also were many expressions of approval, and we may extract from a few of the records before passing on.

In the House of Lords, April 25, 1850, the Marquis of Lansdowne moved votes of thanks to the Governor-General of India, the Commander-in-chief, and the officers and men engaged in the late military operations in India, mentioning with especial praise the conduct of Major Edwardes, thus—

The Marquis of Lansdowne in the House of Lords.

"That officer having then been recently appointed assistant in the management of the country in the neighbourhood of Mooltân, and, finding himself at the head of a single native regiment, conceived the design of driving Moolraj into his fortress and rescuing the whole of the country round Mooltân from his grasp. He effected it, and he effected it without the assistance of a single European force.

"Such was his character, such was the confidence which he inspired among the natives, such was the means that he used, and such the revenue that he raised at the moment, in this very country that he was rescuing from the grasp of the treacherous Moolraj, that he was enabled to unite a very considerable force — that force entirely native, composed entirely of new levies. He was enabled to pay those levies, to arm them, and to drive back that chief within the very walls of that fortress from which he had issued to obtain possession of the surrounding country. He did so, after defeating him in successive actions, in every one of which Edwardes was himself personally engaged, inspiring confidence among the troops by his exertions; in more than one instance actually seizing the guns with his own hand, and, by his uniform good conduct and ability, commanding the affections and the respect of the natives, who followed in his army." . . .

Viscount Hardinge. "The daring manner in which, led only by that heroic young officer, Major Edwardes, the Sikhs had attacked a particular fort, was beyond all praise." . . . *Lord Hardinge.*

Sir John Hobhouse. "It was only yesterday that the Government received the news of a great exploit, performed by a British officer, young in years, and only a subaltern in rank, who performed it under every disadvantage, unaided, and, it might be said, alone; for he had not the assistance of a single fellow-countryman, or even of one of his own colour.* *Sir John Hobhouse.*

"In one month alone, and, as he had said before, quite unaided, with levies which he had raised himself only a month before, and which he had himself disciplined—under a burning sun, in countries inundated by great rivers—that young man overthrew a formidable foe, and by his own right hand and sagacious head saved, he might say, from great peril, a distant part of our Indian empire. The honourable gentleman would, he was sure, find satisfaction in adding to the praises which would be for ever, he thought, bestowed on Lieutenant Edwardes.

"It was not necessary for him to detail the services of the gallant Major Edwardes. It will be sufficient to say that her Majesty, in her royal condescension, had thought it right to depart from the common forms, and had commanded that, before the end of the campaign, he should receive the appointment of major, together with the Companionship of the Bath.

* True of early Bunnoo times, at first, but afterwards he was aided by Lake and others, as we have seen.—E. E.

"On the 27th, they made the first attack on Mooltân, and on January 2 they carried the fortified city of Mooltân.

"The first letter was from Major Edwardes; it contained this sentence, 'I take the liberty of informing you that the city of Mooltân, after a week's storming, has been taken, and I hope to raise the flag of England over the walls of the citadel before three days are over.'

"It appeared that the British forces had to contend against an army of thirty-six thousand men, and when the citadel was entered, three thousand were still among the ruins, who could only be dislodged with difficulty.

"No less than thirty-six thousand shot and shell had been thrown into the citadel, and so thick was the fire that the only place which the chief of the besieged was able to find shelter in was under a gateway. He mentioned those circumstances to show that the capture of a citadel, so bravely and resolutely defended, was no trifling event." . . .

The Duke of Wellington.

The Duke of Wellington was heard to say, at a farewell dinner given to Major-General Sir Charles Napier, that "he considered that, by the capture of Mooltân, the object of the war was accomplished; that it was one of the great events of the campaign, and, he hoped, the end of it." The Duke of Wellington added that "in the early period of the war, Major Edwardes and other officers under the Government of Lahore had generally distinguished themselves in collecting and disciplining certain disbanded forces; and he was happy to say they had performed their duty with advantage to the country and with honour to themselves. They had immortalized themselves by their conduct. It was impossible to speak too highly of that young officer, Major Herbert Edwardes." . . .

This discussion ended in the thanks of the House being given to the Right Hon. the Earl of Dalhousie, Governor-General, etc., and many others.

Lord Hardinge.

Praise from the lips of such military judges need not be suppressed, and these quotations justify themselves. It is only necessary to add that Lord Hardinge rose and corroborated all that had been said, adding, "He had heard with great pleasure and infinite satisfaction the allusions made to Major Edwardes. He was a most sensible, clever young man. During a portion of the period that he" (Lord Hardinge) "served her Majesty in India, Major Edwardes was in command of eleven or twelve thousand men, and most cleverly did he keep them together, displaying great tact, judgment, prescience, and coolness. It was his wish to notice the exertions of other officers—Lake, Pollock, and Nicholson —who, in conjunction with Major Edwardes, had rendered such signal services in that memorable action." . . .

Nor was Edwardes overlooked by his masters, the Court of Directors; for these were the days before the government of India was taken over by the Crown.

A "special gold medal" was struck for him, and presented to him in full Court, with a special address. This was a peculiar honour which he might well value, as such a medal had never been given in a similar way before.

The medal was a very handsome one, and beautifully wrought. The design was entrusted to Wyon. It consisted of an inscription in the centre, " To Lieutenant Herbert Benjamin Edwardes, Brevet-Major and C.B., for his services in the Punjab, 1848."

SPECIAL GOLD MEDAL GIVEN BY THE COURT OF DIRECTORS, 1848.

The inscription was surmounted by his family arms, supported by the figures of Valour and Victory holding a laurel wreath over the arms. Below, the figure of the infant Hercules strangling the serpent (emblematical of his youth, and the lotus leaves as emblematical of India). On the reverse side is the head of the Queen, the fountain of all honour.

The medal was shown to her Majesty by the Chairman

of the Court of Directors, and her Majesty graciously sanctioned the bestowal.

When completed, the die was broken, never to be used again.

This unusual honour was announced to Edwardes in the following letter from the Chairman of the Court of Directors:—

"East India House, February 7, 1851.

"MY DEAR MAJOR EDWARDES,

"With reference to your note of the 4th, I shall be happy to present to you personally, at a meeting of the Court of Directors, the gold medal which the Court have resolved to confer on you. Wednesday next at 2.30 will suit me, if it will be convenient for you.

"On the occasion I shall merely express the pleasure it affords me to have an opportunity of presenting it to you personally.

"I shall read the 'minute' of the Court, in which the grounds of their 'resolution' are briefly but comprehensively expressed.

"I shall then allude to the deep interest we take in the honour and interests of our officers; congratulate you on the great honour and success which have hitherto attended you; confidently anticipate that the same energy, skill, and bravery will distinguish your future career; and that the medal now presented, in commemoration of your youthful heroism, will prove the harbinger, under the blessing of Providence, of a long-continued career of honourable and useful service to India.

"To make a long speech would be contrary to practice on such occasions, and a very brief reply in acknowledgment will be all that is expected.

"Very faithfully yours,

"(Signed)   JOHN SHEPHERD."

According to this bidding, the gold medal was personally presented to him in full Court, and Edwardes, in acknowledgment, replied—

" Mr. Chairman and members of this honourable Court,— Standing as I am in the presence of the great Government of which I am a servant, in whose vast charge of territory the Punjab is but a speck, and before whose high calling in the East the fleeting services of one humble individual shrink into insignificance, it would be both disrespectful and absurd if I were to occupy your attention for more than the few moments which gratitude may claim.

" But it would be ungrateful to be altogether silent while holding in my hand a reward so rarely conferred upon any public servant—never, perhaps, before on a subaltern of your army; and therefore it is that, not only in my own name, but in the name of all my brother officers in the whole Indian army (an army whose past services you *know*, and whose present efficiency I earnestly beg you to *believe*, will stand comparison with that of any army in the world), in their names, not less than my own, I gratefully thank you for this medal, which conveys to all of us an assurance, immortalized by art, that there is no officer in your army, however humble, who may not render useful service to the British-Indian Government and the British-Indian people by warring only to re-establish peace; and whose endeavours in that cause this distant but watchful Court will not observe and mark with its utmost approbation.

" For my own part, I have only to declare that I regard this brilliant trophy less as casting lustre on the past, than as throwing a kind, a cheering, a supporting, and a guiding light upon my future labours in your service."

These were only some of the public honours that greeted Edwardes on his return to his native land. His name had become a household word in England, and go where he would, he was received with acclamation and honour. Especially in his own county, Shropshire, and in the town of Shrewsbury, was a very hearty and cordial welcome accorded him.

As he entered the town he found it was *fête*-day in Shrewsbury. He was met by the mayor and town councillors, who conducted him in procession to the town hall, where a public reception was prepared for him. The streets were crowded, flags and banners waving.

An address was presented of most warm and hearty welcome, amidst a crowded audience of sympathizing and rejoicing friends, and relatives, and fellow-countrymen.

Among others who spoke, Dr. Kennedy, the Head-Master of Shrewsbury School, said he hoped he might be allowed to quote the description of "the happy warrior," for to the high standard therein exhibited he thought none approached more nearly than Major Edwardes.

It seemed to him that Wordsworth had by anticipation there drawn a vivid and faithful portrait of the young "hero of Mooltân."

> " Who is the Happy Warrior? Who is he
> Whom every man in arms should wish to be?
> Who, if he rise to station of command,
> Rises by open means, and there will stand
> On honourable terms, or else retire,
> And in himself possess his own desire;
> Who comprehends his trust, and to the same
> Keeps faithful, with a singleness of aim;
> And therefore does not stoop, nor lie in wait
> For wealth, or honour, or for worldly state;
> Whom they must follow; on whose head must fall,
> Like showers of manna, if they come at all;
> Whose powers shed round him in the common strife,
> Or mild concerns of ordinary life,
> A constant influence, a peculiar grace;
> But who, if he be called upon to face
> Some awful moment to which Heaven has joined
> Great issues, good or bad, for human-kind,
> Is happy as a lover; and attired
> With sudden brightness, like a man inspired;
> And, through the heat of conflict, keeps the law
> In calmness made, and sees what he foresaw;
> Or, if an unexpected call succeed,
> Come when it will, is equal to the need;—
> This is the Happy Warrior; this is he
> Whom every man in arms should wish to be."

Brave words and beautiful, but not too beautiful to be true; for, though the ideal of a poet, it is no flattery, nor the heightened colouring of affection, to say that they are wonderfully true of Edwardes in all particulars.

And singularly in the last, for he never was depressed

when things went wrong and great public difficulties had to be confronted; but it seemed as if his nature rose buoyantly above the storm, and his fertility of resource in times of danger made him great in council, while his cheerfulness was an encouragement and support to those around him.

He replied to this cordial welcome in the following genial words:—

"Mr. Mayor, ladies and gentlemen of Shropshire,—When I left London this morning, I was quite unprepared for the honour you have now paid me, and I hope you will accept of the unstudied but heartfelt thanks of a soldier.

"I have been ten years away from my own country, and I need not expatiate to you on the pleasure I feel on my return home, or on the feelings which I entertained in my absence, of the miseries of the one, or the pleasures of the other. The return to one's native county, I should say, is the very centre, core, and kernel of the joy of returning to one's native land. I have travelled over many lands since I set my foot last on English soil—over a great part of the globe.

"I have seen the ocean in its anger and in its repose; I have seen the sun set in that gorgeous land and over those beautiful waters of the Indian Ocean; I have been through the whole of the Upper Indies; I have seen that beautiful range of mountains so celebrated in Afghan story;—but not for one moment, in viewing those enchanting scenes, did I forget my Salopian land.

"Even among that splendid range of the Himalaya Mountains, whose grandeur is said to exceed the Alps and the Pyrenees, I assure you I never forgot, even in their magnificence, to call to my memory the blue mountains of my beloved Shropshire and beautiful Wales. How truly could I say with the poet!—

> " 'He who first met the Highland's swelling blue
> Will love each peak that shows a kindred hue,
> Hail in each crag a friend's familiar face,
> And clasp the mountain in his soul's embrace.'

"With reference to the services so kindly alluded to, it little becomes me to speak. They have been described in words too flattering; but I hope you will excuse me if I thank you for them as if I deserved them.

"But of all the honours I have received, the dearest to me have been the cheers which have greeted me this day in my native county."

On another occasion, at this time of "welcome home" at Shrewsbury—we quote from one of Edwardes's speeches—he says, describing some of the scenes at the battle of Moodkee:

"This was the beginning of November, 1845, and in a few days afterwards, the Sikh army invaded British India, and we were plunged into the first Sikh War. Here was I, then, at once placed in a position to study war practically, on the largest scale, and under the greatest advantages, at the right hand of Sir Hugh. And I can tell you that the man who rides by the right hand of Hugh Viscount Gough through a campaign is, as the Irishman would say, 'in a mighty convanient place to see a good dale of fighting.' If a young soldier wants an insight into the principles of war, I would advise him to volunteer to such a situation, and he will meet with a good many eye-openers in it. I can tell you a story in illustration of this.

"At our very first battle of Moodkee, on December 18, before the two hostile lines of infantry had met, two staff officers simultaneously dashed in from right and left, and rode up to the commander-in-chief.

"'The enemy's Cavalry, your Excellency, have outflanked us on the right,' said one. 'The enemy's Cavalry have outflanked us on the left,' said the other.

"So there were fifteen thousand horsemen on the one hand, and fifteen thousand on the other, turning both our flanks at the same moment, and our small army in the middle. Without one moment's hesitation, Lord Gough gave directions that charges of Artillery and Cavalry should be made to both flanks; and it was in this movement to repulse the Sikhs that her Majesty's 3rd Dragoons commenced that series of remarkable achievements which have since stamped them as the noblest Cavalry regiment that ever went out to India.

" The charges were made, and the repulse was complete on both flanks. Our Artillery and Cavalry went through the enormous line of the enemy and got into the rear, so as to become an object of the deepest anxiety to Sir Hugh Gough.

" It was at that time he turned to two of his aides-de-camp, and commanded them to recall the flank detachments back to their own line.

" I was one of them, and I leave you to judge whether it was a pleasant office. However, it was performed, and I, perhaps, shall bear with me the memorial of it to the grave, in the scar of a musket-ball through my thigh.

" Such was my introduction to the art of war at the hands of my earliest patron in India, Hugh Viscount Gough.

" I recovered from that wound in time to serve as his Lordship's aide-de-camp at the closing fight of Sobráon. That battle was one of the most noble sights which, perhaps, man ever saw, and it was most complete in its results.

" An extended plain was in front, and a broad and rapid river at the back of the enemy's position. To use a soldier's phrase, which all military men will understand, we turned our right shoulders to the enemy and drove them into the river.

" It was a most magnificent and instructive sight for a young soldier. Thus the campaign closed.

" Lord Gough recommended me to Lord Hardinge, the Governor-General, for promotion to the great political staff which was then required for the Punjab, and for this great step in life I am materially indebted to those two illustrious men.

"But while I express my gratitude to those powerful friends who gave me these great opportunities, let me never forget the master who taught me how to use them—Sir Henry Lawrence, who at this very moment * but a captain of Artillery, has made himself, by his high purposes and indomitable energies, the foremost man in India, and a bright example to every Indian soldier. He it was who, through three years of the British occupation, was my political master and my private friend. It was sitting at his feet, amid great political events, that I trust I learned this noble lesson—to live, not for myself, but for my country."

But all the public honour with which he was welcomed home could never dull his heart, or make him forget or be careless towards his old friends; and a sprightly, genial letter was written about this time to his old and valued college friend, which is very characteristic.

"Sansaw Hall, March 4, 1850.

"It is more than probable, my dear Cowley, that Octavius Cæsar would have cut Tully dead, in the Via Sacra, had he met him in the triumphant moment of his entry to Rome, with Antony and Lepidus. As it was, he sent slaves to do it at Tusculum.

"Therefore, reasoning in the fashion of Arnold from ancient to modern times, I have little doubt you are, this blessed moment, expatiating on the vices of ingratitude and ambition as deadening the heart, stifling the finer feelings, etc., of your old friend Herbert Edwardes.

"And truly, Tully, I have treated thee abominably in not answering thy 'De Amicitia;' but let it be some expiation

* 1850.

that, before setting off to Netley to be dragged in triumphal
chariot, I now have sat down to tell thee that I yearn to see
thee as much as if I had written it and paid the post.   I
would have written from London if I could, but, believe me,
it was not possible.

"I came home for peace and repose, and find a campaign
of hospitality. My hand aches with 'How d'ye do's;' my
lips with kisses; and my ear with praise. One while I feel
repaid for many hardships and many strivings after service
to the Government; and then, again, *afraid* of some great
evil overtaking me after all this pride and adulation. It is
not wholesome; but I must try and *think* large quantities of
salt to season it.

"I have no time to say more now than that I shall leave
Shropshire on Tuesday night to be present at the *levée* on
Wednesday, and if you can manage to meet me, we can
both have the happiness of meeting after ten years of
separation.

"Believe me,

"Ever yours,

"H. B. E."

In May, 1850, he received the honorary degree of D.C.L.
at Oxford, among others to whom that honour was awarded
at the Commemoration of that year. There he was warmly
received and hospitably entertained at Exeter College by his
friend Cowley Powles, who was then Fellow of that college.

Another interesting letter of Edwardes, kindly given by
Archdeacon Browne, may be inserted here. It was written
in return for kind congratulations on his successes at Mooltân, and shows the warmth of affection he preserved for
King's College, London.

"Camp, Mooltân, January 13, 1849.

"My dear Sir,

"I believe it is something of the same feeling
which makes us through life love our own village better

than all the world, that implants in every man's mind a lower 'faith' that there never was any school or *alma mater* like the one where *he* was birched or philosophized.

"Shelley and Byron have declared themselves exceptions to this rule; but then, poor people, they were expelled!

"For my own part, I have ever been ready to do battle with all heathens upon two cardinal points of my belief, that there never was seen the like of Delafosse's school at Richmond, or the equal of King's College, London.

"The former, to be sure, was a point of affectionate honour with me, partly because the Rev. Mr. D——, or 'Charles,' as we irreverently called him, never flogged me without making a pun, to show he was not angry in his heart; and partly because his daughter Theresa won my young love with bread-and-jam and kisses.

"But the latter tenet, the peerlessness of King's, was, I assure you, a pure conviction of reason, unsullied by jam, and unrevealed by the light of azure eyes, unless, indeed, she, the real γλαυκῶπις Ἀθηνῆ, may have looked kindly on at the argument.

"Judge, therefore, my dear sir, how *very* happy I must have been to receive the congratulations of one so intimately associated in my memory with the excellences of King's College as yourself; for it showed that the tie between the pupil and professor was felt by both.

"It gave me very great pleasure to learn that the scholars of King's have gone forth successfully into the arenas where academic prizes are contended for. One of my most valued friendships was formed at King's with Cowley Powles, now tutor of Exeter, a scholar whose accomplishments Oxford has long since acknowledged. He has, from time to time, given me most interesting accounts of the eminence of Cayley in mathematics, Kingsley in the wide sphere of metaphysics, and others of my term, whose track I follow with solicitude through life.

"I do not know whether you will agree with me, when I own that it is not in the records of Oxford and Cambridge that I should look for the proofs of the soundness of the system you pursue at King's.

"Peter the Great studied all trades, that as a king he might think justly of the classes who pursue them, and it is said that he even laboured at shipbuilding; yet he could not have gone into a dockyard and striven for wages with a common shipwright, though the shipwrights knew nothing of other handicraft as Peter did.

"The education at our two old universities is, in my opinion, a class education, and those who aim at its prizes must concentrate their faculties into a *focus* on one or two subjects.

"At King's your *academia* is built on a broader basis, and you throw open all the windows of knowledge—north, south, east, and west—admitting floods of light from wherever they may come.

"Your students are attracted to the history of their own country as well as that of the old world; to compare Bacon with Aristotle, not translate the latter for a degree. In one hall you read to them the periods of Cicero, and in another teach them that it is not ungentlemanly to *spell* English correctly, nor unscholastic to write their own language as elegantly as that of Athens.

"Poor Daniells is no more; but when I was at King's, the student might pity the punishment of Prometheus in one room with *you*, and sin with him in the next among Daniells's electric wires. It is impossible, I think, that science and knowledge, in so many forms could be forced upon the student's mind without giving it a more catholic tone of utility than if it had only been taught to scan and calculate.

"In a word, I would seek the King's collegians *in the world*, not in the Tripos or the Double First.

"At this moment there are two students of King's far

ahead of their contemporaries on the road to fame in this
very country of the Punjab.

"One is Frederick Pollock,* son of the great lawyer, and
nephew of Sir George, a subaltern in his corps, but commanding thousands as a political officer. When General
Whish, on September 16, 1848, retired from the siege of
Mooltân, Pollock, with two thousand of my Horse and six of
my guns, covered the rear all through the day. He promises
to be a fine officer, and the college may be as proud of him
as an *élève* as I am of him as an assistant.

"The other is Herbert, of the 18th Native Infantry, who
was an assistant to Major George Lawrence at Peshâwur, and,
when the rebellion broke out, was put into the fort of
Attock, on the head of the Indus, a post which he has
since most nobly defended with a handful of Afghans against
a Sikh army of besiegers.

"The feat is so extraordinary that I hope to see him
knighted as a reward, in spite of the envious cries of older
men, who were never kissed by the sweet maid Opportunity!

"The siege of Mooltân, you will be glad to hear, is now
drawing to a close. Before a week the breach will be
stormed and—God willing—carried. General Whish's army
will then move up to join Lord Gough's, and I shall be left
in quiet possession of my pro-consulate.

"And now, having strayed so long among the quiet
cloisters of the past, I feel loth to issue out again into the
din of 'hammers closing rivets up;' but each to his own, so,
as of old, I reverently touch my cap, and beg you, my dear sir,

"To believe me ever,
"Your very grateful pupil,
"(Signed)   HERBERT B. EDWARDES,
"Associate of King's College.

"To the Rev. R. W. Browne, M.A.,
Professor of Classics, King's College, London."

---

* Now Sir Richard Pollock. F. R. being his initials, he must have
been called "Frederick" by his early friends.—E. E.

With these feelings we can understand that amongst many welcomes and public entertainments was one much prized from his own college (King's, London). He writes—

"They have made me an Honorary Fellow, which was the highest honour in their power, and has pleased me sincerely. In my own heart, amidst my great and unexpected successes, I have owned that I owed much to the *catholic* sort of learning I got at King's."

A public dinner was given to him by the College on May 15, with a great gathering to welcome him as a new Fellow, at which his speech will show the feeling he bore towards them.

"My Lord Feversham and gentlemen—Your cheers are not only one of the heartiest, but one of the most gratifying, welcomes which I have met with in England, coming as they do from the voices—and I hope *hearts*—of six hundred gentlemen, who are more or less connected by past or present associations with King's College, an institution which must ever be dear to me for many reasons—because it was within those walls that I passed three happy years of student life; reading, as none but the young book-lover ever reads, with a thirstiness of curiosity and reverent enthusiasm for the great fathers of knowledge, whose bodies lie embalmed in russia upon the shelves of libraries, and whose memories are canonized in the calendar of learning; because it was within those walls that I formed friendships which I hope will accompany me through life; and lastly, but not least, because it was within those walls that I received the most valuable part of my education, to which I should be ungrateful indeed if I did not acknowledge that I owe any success I have obtained in life.

"Yes, the smiles of Venus may coax even Vulcan to forge arms for Achilles; but be sure that the patron goddess of all soldiers is Minerva. Her armoury is the

Speech at King's College, 1850.

bibliotheca; her forge, the study; and *practical knowledge* is
the trenchant blade which she puts in the tyro's hand, and
says, 'Go forth and conquer.' And if we search the
academic halls of England for practical knowledge, I know
of no institution where it can be found in the same perfection
as at King's College.

"There, the future physician learns from nature, in a
laborious course of chemical manipulation, the hidden
secrets of amalgamation which make poisons blessed balm
in the hands of the adept; and balms, jealous of each other's
virtues, poisons from the hands of the ignorant.

"There, that great magician of the age, the civil
engineer, begins his course; and what an interesting sight
it is, low down in the stone galleries of the college, to see
the students' academic cap bending over the whirling lathe
or fiery forge, moulding thus early to his will the iron
which is to be his future slave!

"There, the future pastor, no longer satisfied with
Polemic lore, studies the statistics of public health and
principles of sanitary reform amongst the poor.

"There, the younger soldier, compass in hand, imagines
to himself a foe (some desperate murderer, perhaps, and
rebel in his stronghold), and draws around him the investment and the sap, which by slow but inevitable approach
will surely enable justice to overtake him.

"There, lastly, may students destined for any walk in
life, lay that best foundation for success of any kind—knowledge of their own language, of their own glorious literature,
and of the free and happy laws of their own country.

"The course of education in all these branches has been
rendered much more practical than it was in my time; but
even then, twelve years ago, it had begun to meet the
wishes of the age in a wise spirit, and lead the love of
usefulness into healthy channels; and I would adduce, as
proofs of it, the names of Major Herbert and Lieutenant

Pollock, two officers who obtained an honourable fame
during the late war by defence of important posts. It was
indeed impossible that the shadows of such spirits as Otter,
Hugh James Rose, and Lonsdale should not rest for life on
the character where they fell; and in proportion as I for
one gratefully remember the instruction which I gained at
King's College, so do I rejoice that life has furnished me
with an opportunity of doing anything to benefit the
College.

"Nero is said to have wished that all Rome had but
one head, in order that he might cut it off. The liberty I
am about to take is a more human one, though the victims
have bled like Romans in our cause. I must beg you to
unite together in your own minds the three hundred
gentlemen who have extended us their patronage, and drink
Lord Feversham's health as their single representative.

"I have now to propose to you a toast which requires no
recommendation whatever from any one. It is that of the
Council of King's College and Lord Harrowby.

"This is the illustrious and learned body of men by
whose ability and zeal the affairs of this great institution
are conducted, and anybody who glances over their names
will feel a national pride in the reflection that so many
noblemen and gentry, so many dignitaries and lawyers,
should take delight in promoting religious education. The
best commentary on their labours is the rising prosperity
of King's College in every department. Like the architect
of St. Paul's, they may stand amidst the work of their own
hands and say, 'Circumspice' ('look around'). I give you
the Council of King's College and Lord Harrowby."

Speech at a public reception and banquet in Liverpool
Town Hall.

"Mr. Mayor and gentlemen of Liverpool,—I thank you
warmly for the distinguished honour you have paid me on

Speech at Liverpool.

the occasion of my visiting your neighbour, Sir Edward Cust, by inviting me to dine with the mayor and corporation of the second city of the kingdom. To be the honoured guest of that city under any circumstances would be felt to be a great distinction by any Englishman who understands and values the municipal institutions of this country and the rights of self-government, which those institutions at once recognize and represent. But when I remember what it is that has made Liverpool the second city in the kingdom; when I reflect that it owes its importance to its commerce; that its ships are in the ports of all our colonies, giving them what they cannot produce in exchange for what they cannot consume; that, as the *capital* of the British colonial empire, it is dependent on colonial prosperity, and has the deepest interest in our foreign policy and possessions;—then, indeed, I feel as one who has laboured for that policy, and fought for those possessions, that there is a peculiar honour in the approbation of your citizens.

"No man can bear greater or more grateful testimony than myself to the warm interest taken by all classes of our countrymen at home in the affairs of British India; but in no other part of England can these affairs have been lately watched with the same anxiety and attention, or be so fully understood, as in the city of Liverpool; and, attaching, therefore, the highest importance to your opinion, I feel, I assure you, that the approval of my conduct implied in this hospitable reception is the highest honour.

On colonies and their use.

"There are few changes which strike me more, after a ten years' absence from England, than the change of feeling on the subject of England's colonies. 'New kings have arisen who know not Joseph;' and it has become a moot-point, whether colonies are of any use at all. As a matter of history, I should have thought it sufficient to appeal the question to either Rome in her prosperity or Spain in her decline.

" In the court of St. James's the other day, when I looked around on all the great men of this generation, I thought that England could ill spare to blot one of those great names from out her records, as this day I think she could not afford to blot this city from her map.

" The experience of other nations and our own have ceased to be convincing, alike fail to avert the novel question, What is the use of colonies?

" Citizens of Liverpool, I would answer that question thus—The use of colonies is *not to abuse them.* A colony well treated and liberally governed is certain to repay the mother-country with interest and honour, with commerce in peace and sympathy in war.

The use of colonies.

" If such is the condition of many of England's colonies at this moment; if many of them seem to be bound to us by bonds which they would fain break, instead of ties which they would willingly draw closer; if irritation in time of peace threatens separation in time of war; if, in short, there be any of our dependencies which remind us of America, and which reproach us with not having profited by American experience;—then can I with pride, as a servant of the Honourable East India Company, ask you to turn with me to the administration, condition, and prospects of British India.

" There are doubtless many men at this table who know India much better than I do, and I gladly call upon them to add their testimony to mine, that in no other dependency of the British crown is there to be found the same proportionate amount of good government, improvement, prosperity, and contentment.

" Yet British India is not a colony, it is only a dependency. It is not peopled with our citizens, but with our subjects; it is not a land which has been freely given, but an empire which we have grasped. What is the reason of this anomaly?   It is this, that the administration of

India as a dependency. Not a colony, but an empire.

British India is wholly and solely grounded upon *the welfare of the people.* Yes, I fearlessly assert that the prime and motive principle of the Anglo-Indian Government is to secure the prosperity of the native population. Any other benefit, any other ulterior advantages that may be derived by this country are secondary to that great end.

India ruled for the benefit of India.
"True, thousands of our countrymen are, year by year, deriving wealth and honour from that distant land; but that wealth is the wages of a life-time spent under a burning sun in administering the justice of which I speak; that honour is given to England (let the Peace Society say what it will), not to those who carry fire and sword into distant lands for their own ambition, but to those who willingly give their own blood to maintain in Asia that best blessing —peace, which Asiatic rulers never gave it.

"I may be told that this is not the origin of the East India Company's charter—that the merchant princes spread their wandering sails in ships freighted with long-cloths, not with laws; inspired by commerce, not with philanthropy. But this is the very conclusion and the moral which I would wish to draw.

"The Government of India was indeed not so begun, but it has so ended. It commenced in selfish policy and selfish legislation; but it has grown into better things, and lives and lasts by making home dividends secondary to colonial welfare.

"And I rejoice most heartily to have had this opportunity of expressing before the first citizens of Liverpool, whose welfare is so intimately bound up with our colonial empire, the deep conviction which I as a colonial servant feel, that the time has come when the whole colonial policy of the Crown of England must be remodelled or fall into decay. We must take a deeper interest in colonial legislation. We must deem the smallest colonies deserving of the best men of our aristocracy for governors, and not insult them with our worst; not deem that British India is the only dependency which cannot safely be misruled by a King Log or a King Stork.

"We must cease, once for all, to look upon them as inalienable possessions, as so much property entailed on England in perpetuity. That relationship can never be maintained longer than the youth and weakness of a colony; and we should, of our own free will, prefer that more beautiful relationship of parent and child, which exhibits the mutually noble spectacle of kindly protection during infancy, separation without asperity in youth, lasting attachment during manhood, and grateful assistance in old age."

What is the ultimate result of our rule?

Speech at a festival in aid of the building and endowment funds of King's College Hospital, London, April, 1850.

"My Lords and gentlemen,—I believe there is no day in the year in which the health of her Most Gracious Majesty Queen Victoria would not be a most welcome toast at any table, public or private, in the happy land over which she rules; and it must be a matter of congratulation to all Englishmen that the toast, which would always by courtesy head the list, is spontaneously lifted to that position by the prayers of a religious people, who hail with enthusiasm on a throne the virtues which make private life illustrious.

Speech at King's College.

"To-day, however, there is a happy felicity in the toast, for it is the day on which our Sovereign's birthday is celebrated, and I am sure you will all heartily unite in wishing that her life may long be spared to our country. The Queen.

Queen's birthday speech.

"My lords and gentlemen, having wished long life and happiness to her Majesty, I am sure we must not separate her from that royal consort in whose union is found so bright an example for our English homes.

"I give you the health of Prince Albert and the Royal

Family, among whom let us gratefully remember the Duke
of Cambridge for his active assistance this morning, and
their Royal Highnesses the Duchesses of Kent, Cambridge,
and Gloucester, all of whom are patronesses of our concert.
His Royal Highness Prince Albert.

"The next toast is one which will be received with
reverence by every well-wisher of King's College; for it
is the very foundation on which that college stands, the
key-stone of its every arch—The Church.

"The head of the Church seems, *ex-officio*, to be the
head also of King's College; but it would have been impossible for the present primate to have so heartily assumed
the connection of his lamented predecessor with King's
College, unless a deep bond of union had been found in a
community of high and holy objects. May they long
continue to be a mutual support. The Church.

"The toasts which we have already drunk—the Queen,
the Royal Family, and the Church—are used by established
custom at the anniversaries of all public bodies as so many
steps whereby to climb to the great object of the day, which
stands conspicuous on this moral elevation.

"The object with which it is my duty to-day to crown
this basis of loyalty, reverence, and national pride is one
well worthy of the eyes of this great assembly. It is, next
to a temple, the noblest piece of moral or national architecture of which man is capable—a hospital for his suffering
fellow-men.

"The festival which we are assembled to celebrate in
part this day is in aid of the building and endowment
funds of King's College Hospital. This hospital has been
sustained through ten years of infancy by the annual
contributions of a very large body of charitable friends,
and having survived its early troubles and struggled on to
a vigorous youth, it now demands a more permanent and
certain provision for its support. Its parents are beginning

to be ashamed of its poor appearance. It is too big to be
running about the streets of the Strand with so little clothes
on ; too old to be begging sixpences from every well-dressed
gentleman who enters the gates of King's College. In the
language of fathers and mothers, it is high time that it was
provided for.

"Now, it is my duty to-day, in as few words as I can, to
point out the claims which this hospital has upon the public
for such provision, and I beg the kind indulgence of this
large assembly while I endeavour to do this.

"And, first, let me ask you to fix in your minds and
remember one fact, that the office of the King's College
Hospital is *twofold:* first, as a charity, as a simple hospital ;
second, as a school of practice and illustration for the
medical students of King's College.

"And first, as a hospital. During the past nine years no
less than 11,747 patients have been admitted and treated
within the walls of the hospital, and 138,448 outside the
walls, making a glorious total of 150,195 cases of suffering
poor whom this hospital has relieved.

"It is impossible that you can have read that without
feeling the liveliest gratification at so much good having
been accomplished; but it *is* possible that you may also
have felt satisfied with that amount of good, and soothed
your minds with the belief that nothing remained here to
do—no sickness unattended to. But it is my painful duty
to disabuse you of so pleasing a delusion, and to inform
you that in the course of every year hundreds of cases fit
for admission are obliged to be refused admittance to the
hospital for want of room " (with further details, which were
interesting at the time, but need not be repeated here).

"Coming as I have from a foreign country, after ten
years' absence, it has been a source of the greatest happiness
and patriotic enthusiasm to me to mark the very prominent
increase of benevolent institutions in this country, and

especially in the neighbourhood of London, since I left England. It is impossible to go out of London by any railroad without being attracted by the numerous asylums, almshouses, and provident institutions which stud the road-side. There is scarcely a company or a trade which has not got its refuge for broken and superannuated brethren. Look, too, at the public baths and washhouses, the lodging-houses for artisans of both sexes, and the ready sympathy which the grievances of any class of poor are certain to attract. This surely is a new and a delightful spirit, a genial change in public feeling, which is awakening daily more and more to the responsibilities of wealth to poverty and of the strong towards the weak. And if we need any further instance of this awakening, we surely have it here this day.

" It 1847 it is recorded that 'nearly three hundred people sat down to the anniversary dinner.' But three years have passed, and those years not years of prosperity or accumulation of wealth, but years of social and commercial trouble, in which the classes who support such charities as these may be supposed to have suffered great diminution of private wealth. Yet, notwithstanding all this, we have on this occasion as many *patrons* as in the anniversary of 1847 there were *guests.*

" What does this show but that the heart of educated man is expanding under the influence of extended know-ledge, that true Christian charity is increasing with our need of it, and that the rich and poor are, in our day, drawing nearer to those mutual relations so classically pictured by a modern poet.

> " ' Then none were for a party,
>   But all were for the State ;
>   Then the rich man helped the poor,
>   And the poor man loved the great.' "

Most gratifying to Edwardes was all this unlooked-for appreciation of his services, and his public welcome at home.

But his own personal happiness, and not only his own (as we have said), was very deeply concerned in this coming home.

His *duty* (which he had put first) was *done*; the desire of his heart could now be accomplished.

Long years, weary waiting, and an anxious and prolonged campaign had swept in between him and a long-cherished dream of happiness—the happiness that his noble, pure, true, and devoted heart had nursed tenderly in full confidence of hope ever since he was a boy.

And now the clouds had swept away, the weary time was over for both!

On July 9, 1850, he was married at Petersham Church, near Richmond, in Surrey, to Emma Sidney, the youngest daughter of James Sidney, Esq., of Richmond Hill, Surrey— the wife who mourns him still, and whose hand traces this outline-story of a most beloved life.

"Nothing is sweeter than love, nothing more courageous, nothing higher, nothing more pleasant, nothing fuller nor better in heaven and earth; because love is born of God, and cannot rest but in God, above all created things." *

> " Thrice blest, whose lives are faithful prayers,
>   Whose loves in higher love endure;
>   What souls possess themselves so pure,
> Or is there blessedness like theirs ? " †

During this, which he used to call his "first happy year," he wrote, 'A Year on the Punjab Frontier,' for happiness could never mean idleness with him. This gives a full account of his work in Bunnoo and Mooltán; and to that we would refer the reader who may wish to follow the details of that year's work further than the scanty sketch that has found its place in this volume will enable him to do.

Writes " A Year on the Punjab Frontier."

But he found it difficult to find a quiet corner to write it in, and his time was short, for he was soon to be back in India.

The desire for quiet was at last satisfied at Festiniog, North Wales, and the book was written there.

We will close the chapter with a sprightly note of invitation to his wedding, written to his faithful friend and correspondent, who had just taken the step in advance of him.

* Thomas à Kempis.   † Tennyson.

"MY DEAR COWLEY,

"Where are you? Whence shall I summon you? Into what bowers of bliss am I intruding, to drag you down from the empyrean of love to the lower heaven of friendship?

"Go forth, O, postman! and do what postman may, in search of my lost friends. And if (as is not impossible) thou shouldst arrive at their retreat, when, hand-in-hand, sitting all silently, they shall have presumed to undo all creation since the Fall, and in their spirits' crucible reduced the world to Eden, and mankind to Cowley and Mary; then, be not weak or human, but with the stern unbending righteousness of a Wesleyan preacher, startle them with a stout rap! rap!

"Cowley, you must come, and Mary too, if you *can*; but if you *cannot* without great wrestling with railroads and post-chaises, then, nevertheless, shall I know that you are present in heart, and wish Emma and myself all the happiness which you yourselves know how to value.

"Ever yours affectionately,
"HERBERT B. EDWARDES."

This slight extract, given as a specimen, serves to show the sprightly genial nature of the man, and the easy and rapid way in which his thoughts flowed when he took pen in hand to answer even the simplest note or write of ordinary things, ever lighting up with wit and fancy even the most prosaic subject, or beautifying with deep feeling and tender pathos from the storehouse of his own true heart the *real* things of life.

These letters might be greatly multiplied did our space allow it.

CHAPTER VII.

——•◦•——

1851—1853.

RETURN TO INDIA—LIFE AT JULLUNDUR.

"The nobleness of life depends on its consistency, clearness of purpose, quiet and ceaseless energy."—JOHN RUSKIN.

CHAPTER VII.

On March 20, 1851, Edwardes and his wife returned to India. He found time to write his farewell to his friend Nicholson, whom he left behind, intending to extend his tour in Europe before returning to India.

" Radly's Hotel, Southampton, March 20, 1851.

"My dear Nicholson,

"Good-bye; we sail to-day. May you have a *séjour* in Europe, as pleasant as I know you will make it *profitable*.

"If possible, take our station in your way through the Punjab. A late letter from India tells me I am to go to *Jullundur*.

"It is a principle of mine to go wherever I am sent; so say no more.

"My *judgment* also opposes my *wishes* in the matter; for I feel sure that this arrangement has been made by *friends* who wished me to go through a course of *regulations*, and so promote my more speedy fitness for a Commissionership.

"There was nothing said about Peshâwur. Probably Lumsden keeps it; and I am sure he will do well there. If Lumsden has it not, *you* ought to get it. Perhaps there may be some prejudice against married men in my exclusion. If you return a bachelor, this may be in your favour; but, if your heart meets one worthy of it, *return not alone*.

"I cannot tell you how good it is for our best purposes

to be *helped* by a noble wife who loves you better than all men and women, but God better than you.

"Adieu, and believe me ever, my dear Nicholson,

"Your sincere friend,

"HERBERT EDWARDES."

Appointment to Jullundur as Deputy-Commissioner.

Edwardes's first appointment was Deputy-Commissioner of Jullundur. This was a rich tract of country called the Jullundur Doab, adjoining the hills in British possession, which had been taken (with the Cis-Sutlej territory of Lahore) as indemnity for the war at the end of the first Sikh War.

It was a fertile and beautiful country, and the people were happy and peaceful.

First home at Jullundur.

Nothing could be happier than our lives were there. Dangers and anxieties, long waitings, and the heart-sickness of hope deferred, all past! It was "as the days of heaven upon earth." His time fully occupied and well spent in raising and ameliorating the condition of the people, he made himself accessible to all, and even the poorest man who had "a grievance" knew that he could bring it into a court where the judge would himself give him a hearing, and not allow a bribe to be taken by one of his official attendants; and if it became necessary, in order to settle the dispute fairly, to see the ground (the people's quarrels are generally about land), he would ride out and investigate it for himself.

Description of his court of justice.

So the people soon came to know him as their best friend and protector, and his Commissioner, Mr. Donald McLeod (afterwards Sir Donald, his immediately superior officer in command), put on record (in sending up to Government the usual "report" on Edwardes leaving that appointment) that Major Edwardes's court was so renowned among the people for its purity and justice, and his decisions were *felt* by themselves to be so accurate, that, in a difficult decision, the guilty person had been known to betray himself by *trembling* when brought before him for his opinion; the fame of his justice and discernment had spread so much among the people over whom he ruled.*

* This is given on the authority of Mr. McLeod himself.

The return to work was in itself welcome; and to return to work among the many friends who had together laboured in the early days of the new province of the Punjab was very congenial to his taste.

And if any one ever thought that the reception he had met with at home, or the public honours that had been awarded him, had raised him in his own estimation or had made him careless of his old friends, they had made a great mistake; for every success, and the increase of the world's honours, had on him the effect that they have on all truly great and noble characters, and made him more really humble in his estimation of himself, and very notably to the end of his life only more considerate and generous in his estimation of others.

Result of prosperity and honour upon character.

There is a characteristic letter on this subject, written to a friend soon after arriving at Jullundur.

"July 3, 1851.

" My dear ——,

" Your lengthened peck at your own breast to feed hungry friends, assures me that *you* are still the good 'Pelican' * of former days, and therefore I am both sad and sorry that you should have been found in the same plight with those commoner birds, who hate the lark as much as the eagle, and believe that up—up there in the clouds, where the high winds have borne it, it despises the whole feathered race, instead of 'singing at heaven's gate' its own humble song of gladness. How could you, who *have* seen something of me, believe that I should have been rendered indifferent to old friendships in this country by having met with universal kindness in England?

* This allusion to "Pelican" may need some explanation. In the happy days of the times of the Old Residency, when Sir Henry and his wife, Honoria Lawrence, were the centre of a large and merry party of Assistants, all living together in one large house, and where the intervals of heavy work were relieved by the most cordial and friendly intercourse, it pleased the fancy of Lady (Henry) Lawrence to choose familiar names for most of them, which she thought suited them; and so it happened that this correspondent was the one to whom she had attached the name of "Pelican." Hence the allusion.

" That I was much gratified by all the honours I received, is true ; how could it—why *should* it be otherwise?
The more so that I really did not expect it; for having
been vilely abused by half the press and two-thirds of the
army in India for daring to serve my country, I had retreated
within myself, and begun to fancy that I truly had been in
a dream of imaginary utility, but was, in sober earnestness, a
most scurvy knave, whom it was every man's duty to kick.

" That was the kind of mood in which I left Lahore, and
it was only disturbed at Bombay by the most generous and
unjealous hospitality.*

" I was prepared to sneak into England very quietly, and
go and ' shoulder my crutch, and show how fields were won,'
by my own fireside.

" Dickens tells us of a squire who was reckoned a great
poet by his wife and six children in Yorkshire.　There was
yet hope, therefore, that I might, among my own dear ones,
so far at least approximate the ideal of a hero as to be
acquitted of cowardice, lying, and a few other infirmities of
the flesh.

" If I ever thought of it at all, *this* was the outside of
my English hopes—to find a haven from abuse, jealousy,
hatred, malice, and all uncharitableness. The overwhelming
shouts of thousands on the pier at Southampton, which, after
crowning the venerable head of Lord Gough, were turned
upon *me*, awoke me for the first time to the fact that there
was a whole class of persons in the world who deemed that
I had done well.

" It was pleasant in such a case to find them my own
countrymen, the English ; and so long as I remained among
them I enjoyed such immunity from slander that only one
libel appeared against me, and that was extracted out of
the *Mofussilite!* †

* This was from Sir Bartle Frere, who entertained him at Bombay in a
most kind and cordial manner.
† An Indian newspaper.

"Much indebted, therefore, am I to the English people—
whether to the nobles for letting me behold the great, the
beautiful, and the luxurious in their own unequalled halls;
the merchants for their hospitable feasts; the unwashed for
their hoarse good-will; the women for their smiles, copies of
verses, locks of hair and acrostics.   Yea; why should I
exclude that tear, dropped by the Welsh chambermaid over
my wounded hand, when she reflected that, but for the
major, she might have been that moment making the ' charpoy ' (or bed) of a great horrid Sikh ?

"In short, my dear ——, everybody did what he or she
could, to make me forget that I was mortal—to fill me with
conceit and pride.   This I grant; but I do. . . .

"*July* 8.—'Here the manuscript is blotted,' as the novelists
say.   A tide of horrid necessities has come in between the
nominative case and the verb; and every day's delay in
this reply is confirming you in your opinion.

"I was going on to say that I do not plead guilty to the
moral wreck to which I was exposed.   I believe my soul
has performed no transmigration, but still inhabits that
old body with the long nose and beard, which men call
Herbert Edwardes.

"My dear ——, can there be a meaner dog than he who
runs mad on good victuals, and behaves like a hound when
he is starved ?   Answer me that, an' you be a student of
character!   Prosperity is doubtless a severe touchstone, and
men, observing that it often leads to arrogance, go a step
too far, and lay down the axiom that all who rise *are proud.*
Herbert Edwardes has risen, *therefore* he is proud.

"It is certainly very difficult to know ourselves.   Juvenal
says 'it comes from Heaven' to do so; and so I may be
mistaken; but if I know anything of myself, I am a far
humbler man now, far more conscious of my own short-
comings and of the true source whence all merit comes,
than I was when ensign in the Honourable Company's 1st

European Light Infantry—conscious of powers above the
moistening of pipeclay, and writing 'Brahminee Bull' letters,
to get away from my regiment.

"At least I feel so; and God is my witness. But I
know that this is not the opinion of that large majority of
the Indian world who have no personal knowledge of me,
and judge only on general principles; and it is, I confess,
a sorrow in my lot that envy, and jealousy, and miscon-
struction pursue me wherever I go, *in my own presidency.*

"It is a trial, probably, which every *public* man should
aforehand be taught to contemplate as the natural consequence of his own ambition.

"Let no man leave his own fireside for the arena of
public life unless he is prepared to be hated by two-thirds
of his fellow-beings. Speaking from my own *Indian* experience, I should pray for any child of mine to be blessed
with common sense—*very common* sense, a contented mind,
and a humble heart. Let not any one whom I love be
afflicted with the ability to rise.

"It is only the ability to inflict fancied injury on those
left below—the ability to be envied, misconstrued, and
deeply wounded. If you *must* rise, *live* yourself up to the
mark; and when the deaths of your contemporaries have
left you a major-general and a dotard, you may hope to be
recognized as a good public servant. The ghost of your
former self will be admitted to be a most proper man!

"Now let us have done with this. It is seldom I give
way to such gloomy views of human nature; but finding
you ('mine own familiar friend, whom I trusted') on the
world's side, made me angry.

"Many, many thanks for your lively panorama of old
associations at Lahore. Your running commentary is almost
equal to that of Mr. Stocqueler, who is showman to the
'Overland Route to India,' in Waterloo Place, London.

"Gladly would I seize any opportunity of revisiting

those old haunts in the Sikh capital. There is no more beautiful alchemy than that by which time turns by-gone days of toil, and danger, and sickness into pleasant memories. Those very jahgeer statements seem jests in re-trospect; and I laugh as I read them backwards, and see Runjeet's Sirdars proving their rights in a back parlour to a Feringee in a flannel waistcoat and pijâmahs.

"Thanks to you for your kind congratulations on my marriage. It has, indeed, added much to my happiness, or rather created it. I wish you could find time to come and pay us a visit in the cold weather or any weather. We would make you quite as happy as a bachelor is capable of in our spare room. . . .

"Your affectionate friend,

"HERBERT B. EDWARDES."

In the summer of 1852 this happy life at Jullundur was disturbed by apprehensions of a war with Burmah; and the 1st European Fusilier Regiment being under orders for service, there was no certainty that Edwardes would not be called upon to join it—a call which no soldier would wish to disobey.

A fever had forced his wife to the hill-station of Dhurum-sálah in advance of him, and this separation made the anxiety fall heavier on both. But this danger passed away.

Edwardes, writing to a relative at home, says, dated Jul-lundur, September 3, 1852—

"I write to set your minds at rest about the Burmah trip, which seemed to threaten me when last I wrote.

"The anxiety about it continued till the very end of August, when Government announced to the Board at Lahore that I should not be required. . . . I cannot say how thankful I am that my dear wife has been spared the lengthened separation, and painful anxieties, and rumours of death, and wounds, and defeat which a campaign brings so ruthlessly home to *all who are not in it.*

"This news has been to Emma like permission to get well, and free leave for the first time to see the mountains, and watch the lights and shadows carrying on their, from time to time, everlasting struggle on the hills and vales of this world. From that moment she has begun to feel quite well, and when I reach there, and she gets out with me to ramble along the hill, the exercise and air and happiness of our being once more together, will, please God, all help to restore her strength.

"She is determined to return to the plains when I do, and says she will never leave me any more, though October is the loveliest of all the months in the year in the Himalayas. . . . Henry Lawrence left Lahore on September 1, and goes by Chumba to meet us at Dhurumsâla, where we shall all be together under the roof of Mr. McLeod, the Commissioner, who only left me the day before yesterday, after staying a few days. He is a rare and excellent character, one whose life is one even career of duty to God and man, and whose mind and heart do not apparently contain one selfish thought. He is by nature blessed with at once the best of intellects and the kindest of dispositions; and an industry of study, stimulated by the desire to be useful, has given him a range of knowledge on all subjects bearing on the welfare of the people of India, such as I do not know that I ever saw equalled. Yet few people hear of him, and in the noisy world the ripple of his gentle stream of goodness is altogether drowned. But it fertilises, nevertheless, and when I come to compare my own brawling fame with the secluded usefulness of this good man, I quite shrink with shame, and positively rejoice that there will be a light in which the true value of things will stand revealed.

Donald
McLeod.

"Yours very affectionately,
        "H. B. E."

There is also an interesting correspondence, preserved by

Sir Donald McLeod, which shows the affectionate terms on which they worked together, the Commissioner and the Deputy-Commissioner, from which a few extracts may be made here.

"Jullundur, February 11, 1852.

" MY DEAR McLEOD,

"Just as I had prepared all for moving into camp, a tremendous case sprang up against one of the vukeels here, named Ahmud Hoossein, who had got an unhappy village into mortgage, and was determined to keep it there, with or without law. I have a great feeling against vukeels in general, believing they are only another obstacle interposed between the people and their rulers, increasing litigation, protracting decisions, and swelling costs. The late orders of the Board seem to show a similar feeling in higher quarters. My attention was therefore rather attracted to this particular case, and though it has greatly fatigued me, I am very glad for the general weal that it came into my net.

Vukeels, or agents.

" It is beyond all comparison the worst case I have seen in these courts, and it has ended in my committing A. H. and his accomplice to your sessions for trial, with, as I believe, an irresistible mass of evidence. If my view is correct, any punishment I could have given him would have been ludicrously inadequate.

" This, however, leads me to consult you on a wider question. Have I the power to dispense with all the vukeels? I mean professional practisers, not private servants.

" The Board says discourage them. But why permit them? I have eight in my court, and I will, if you allow me, tell them all to seek their fortunes in more genial climes. If you think this principle must be recognized of affording a professional adviser to the suitor, then at least there will be no objection to reducing the eight to two.

On native vukeels in our English courts.

" But if ever we are to be honest with ourselves and throw aside all shams and humbugs, it is in a new country.

Why be fettered in the Punjab with a principle which is allowed to have worked unmitigated evil in Hindoostan? The genius of the East is not yet honest enough for this link of English procedure, and it is a pity to perpetuate the errors of our older provinces.

"If it is the *honest* suitor who is to be considered, I am quite sure he will prefer the stream of justice from the source, such as it is, rather than be filtered through the fingers of a vukeel. If it is the dishonest suitor who wants advice, I say at once, let him want!

Choongee arrangements.

"The much-talked-of choongee (octroi, or town dues) has been at last arranged for Jullundur, and starts on June 1. I have arranged that there shall be a parish meeting every Monday to audit accounts, and these I shall attend myself. We had a full meeting of the citizens at Cutcherry yesterday to discuss the details, and everything was done with the good will and voice of the majority.

"I trust the choongee may become a bond to bind up the parties in this ill-conditioned city, and elicit the virtue of public spirit. The interest evinced yesterday was very great, and I took pains to show them that all were interested in preventing evasion of the duty.

"I return you John Lawrence's memo. on the Doáb Jageers * with many thanks. They are marked with the seal of Cromwell, a truth and determination which one cannot but consent to and admire, but an absence of the tenderness to spare, which is often to be regretted."

First Christmas at Lahore.

The first Christmas was spent at Lahore; and a happy visit to Sir Henry Lawrence was heavily clouded by the crash which fell about that time upon the Punjab, in the change of the Government by the loss of Sir Henry Lawrence, who was transferred to the post of Governor-General's Agent in Rajpootana, leaving his brother John Lawrence, with Mr. Robert Montgomery and Mr. Mansel, as the Governing Board at Lahore.

* Government assignment of land.

This was nothing less than a personal grief to the many who loved their chief; for few had a greater power of attaching men with chivalrous devotion than Sir Henry Lawrence. And now that he was taken from the country that he had made his own, where he was surrounded by the men he had gathered about him by his own choice, who had looked on him as the father of their public life, and had caught from him their inspiration, and felt sure at all times of his support and approval, and his generous acknowledgment of all their services, what *could* the Punjab be to them without their head? It seemed at the time like a watch in which the mainspring was broken, and with a heavy heart the journey back to Jullundur was undertaken, to return to work again. Loss of Sir Henry Lawrence.

But the spirit that Sir Henry Lawrence had evoked and cherished would continue with them still; and the province that he had started so brilliantly and successfully had caught a fire that could not easily be put out. And so the brave, bright spirits went forth again with fresh energy to carry on the labours that had been begun so well under their beloved chief, and knowing in their hearts that it would please him best that they should stay and work where he had placed them. The feeling throughout the Punjab.

One of the pleasant duties of an Indian official's life is the winter march into the interior of the country. Taking up house and home under canvas, and marching on from day to day, or resting in one place for a few days, as the work may require,—a district officer is brought face to face with all the people under his government; and, pitching his tents outside a village or a town, he opens his court amongst them, and they can flock in and explain their grievances, their difficulties, or their quarrels, and he can judge for himself of the facts of a case that might be greatly misrepresented at a distance. Camp life.

Edwardes's bright, genial nature gave the people confidence and trust; and they soon understood that they had a friend as well as a governor in their midst.

This work goes on for most of the cold-weather months. Riding on in the early morning, fifteen or twenty miles, you find the tents pitched in a pleasant place (for the native servants are very clever in selecting good ground), perhaps in some shady corner, under beautiful trees, near some running water or some shady garden; breakfast laid; and the sun Its enjoyments.

having just begun to be hot enough to make shade welcome, you get off your horse, thankful for the home-like tents prepared to receive you. There you are well sheltered during the heat of the day; and, when the sun goes down, you can come out and enjoy the gipsy life and the surroundings of the country.

Then the tents you left behind you are carried on to the next encampment, so that you can spend the night quietly where you are, and go on next morning, to find the same accommodation awaiting you, if there is nothing to detain you more than one day. Or, sometimes, several days may be spent on the same ground. "Wonderfully good servants," the

Indian servants.

reader will say. And so they are, for there is no lack of any comfort on the table or in any other place; and you may ask a number of friends to dinner if they come across your path (as they often do), and you will find no difficulties of supplies.

(It would be well if our pampered English servants could sometimes learn a lesson from these good servants!)

And this was the life to which Edwardes and his wife now returned in the Jullundur District.

Edwardes writes to a dear friend in England—

> " Camp Nakdôur, in the District of Jullundur,
> " Night of February 19, 1852.

" My dear Powles,

　　" How ill I have treated you! and with what a gentle hand you 'heap coals of fire on my head'!

　　" Such a reproof should never have come to me before I had written to you in answer to your last, and yet it has found me only surrounded by regrets and good intentions. Let me not waste the precious time, however, but say how welcome your affectionate letter was to us, and how reciprocally we had ourselves felt for you at Christmas-time. We went for a true English holiday to Lahore, and I took there with me a long list of home letters to be written, as a duty well fitted to that season of remembrance.

　　" Among the list no name pressed more upon my thoughts than yours; and I had hoarded up the idea of writing to you quite childishly and freshly, and for all the world as if I were not thirty-two!

"But when I got to Lahore, Sir H—— gave me so much work to do that my 'holiday' proved only a 'change of legs,' like the poor cab-horse's *bait*.

"And so the days went on among the hard demands of the present, and I saw the dear past no more, except at cake and pudding time, with a flickering of childhood round the burnt mincepies.

"I brought my unanswered letters back with me to Jullundur, and laid them by with a sigh. But now I must and will write to you, and confess, for the good of my soul, how much wrong I have done you. Very, very welcome, my dear friend, were your Christmas wishes and your wife's to me and mine. May God, indeed, bless them to us, and b'ess ours in your behalf. It is, without going farther, a blessing to be thankful for that we can all four think thus, and feel thus, for each other. It is a stout staff this, in our hands, as we go plodding on, that we have a friend. And what a paltry obstacle is space in such meditations, which defy the isolation of the exiled body, and are at home again with a distinctness that may be sworn to in the witness-box!

"At this moment I am at home with you, and have left my mind's clothes sitting upright in a chair at Nakôdur.

"Now, then, let me sit with you both on the sofa, on the left hand of the fire in the library, and tell you my story. . . .

"Of myself I have much that I could tell you if time permitted, but now shall only say that, after having had charge of wild provinces, it is now my singular lot to have the least barbarous and most quiet district in the Punjab. The one was ruled with justice in the rough; the other is administered with a highly-finished system of civil, criminal, and revenue laws.

"The days of Alfred and Victoria present an analogous

comparison, and the transition from one to the other could not but be a great mental exertion.

"Fortunately, I was not too old; the versatility had not all left my thoughts and faculties; and, being willing to learn of every one who had anything to teach, I have struggled through the technicalities, and once more feel equal to my work. (I had written 'master of' it, but this I am not; I only hope to be.)

"It has been very uphill work, as you will easily conceive, and the last six months of 1851 were as laborious as any almost that I ever underwent.

"Now I am in a condition to look back and be thankful for feeling every way a better servant of Government; and, strange as it may seem to say so, I believe I could reduce Bunnoo easier now that I know more of settled government; while settled government comes easier to me for my familiarity with lawless tribes. Each has its experience to teach, and one reflects a light upon the other. Nor do I know which duty may be called the higher, or which has more of that fascinating interest which lightens long days of never-ceasing toil. To be flung into a country where anarchy prevails, and introduce the rights of man to man, and all to Government, is doubtless high employ. But to succeed this rough pioneering, and build on the space that has been cleared; to civilize those who have been subdued; to perpetuate peace by registering all rights, and thus transferring the strife of aggression to the arena of a law court instead of a bloody plain; to lay the broad foundations of national prosperity, by limiting taxation to a fixed demand for a quarter of a century, and so securing to industry all its earnings and to capital all its interest; to open schools and dream of plans of education; to effect, in short, a social change which the missionary alone can crown, must be allowed to be a lot of exceeding great utility, such as the largest heart might be occupied in fulfilling.

" And these are our labours now in the Punjab. And
this brings me to that part of your letter where you mention
Archdeacon Hare's kind present, and kinder expressions
of interest in my book. It has gratified me more than
I can say, and I shall myself write and thank the archdeacon as soon as his book reaches me. The longer we
live, the more we value the good opinion of the few and
are indifferent to that of the many. Emma is writing a
long letter to you, but, for fear she may leave herself out,
as she always does, I shall tell you that she got through the
hot weather with only one week of fever, but has now had
another in the cold weather, which is quite unauthorized. . .

" We have a delightful plan in our heads, if it please
God to enable us to effect it—to take two months' holiday
in September and October next, and plunge into the depths
of the Himalayas. Will not this be charming—to be happy
amid Nature's grandest works, and have leisure to enjoy
their contemplation ?

> " Yours ever affectionately,
> " HERBERT B. EDWARDES."

What can be told more about the Jullundur life? It
was *his* first "home" in India—*our* first "home together."
The desire of our hearts, long delayed, at length accomplished. It was "sweet to the soul !" We thought—never
on earth was there such a paradise before !

He had busy, useful work, in peaceful times, and in a
pretty, rural, quiet country—busy in bringing justice and
security into the homes of the people, protecting the weak
and the oppressed, and punishing the evil and the tyrannous.

Peace and
happiness.

Fifteen months passed away very quickly in such works
as these ; and yet it may all be put into few words—that he
was a great administrator.

We had a charming house (filled with all the pleasant
things we had brought out from England—pictures and books,
piano, and English comforts, which were more rare in those
days in the Punjab than they are now) and a delightful large

garden full of many kinds of orange trees and lovely flowers

And when his day's work was done, he came in from his office, and we had our happy evenings to spend together, in whatever way we liked best.

It was a time of peace and joy, after the storms of war and anxiety. It is, indeed, not too much to say, these were " as the days of heaven upon earth "—most blessed.

Suddenly disturbed. Out of this happiness we were startled one morning at breakfast by a letter from the Governor-General, Lord Dalhousie, ordering Edwardes to take charge of Hazára, a wild hill-country near the frontier of Cashmere, where the government was more difficult, and the Governor-General desired, on that account, to have Edwardes's services. His power of ruling wild races (and attaching them too) had been well tested and proved at Bunnoo, and to no one were they better known than to his Lordship.

He was ordered to move to Hazára as quickly as possible —Lord Dalhousie "hoped within ten days."

This was, indeed, a sudden uprooting. House and furniture had to be sold off; whatever could be packed had to be packed at once in boxes, to take with us on camels—the home we had made so pleasant to be broken up, and most of the things we had brought out from England dispersed to the four winds of heaven; for we were going where there was no house to live in, and where an Englishwoman had never been seen before.

It was my first lesson on the uncertainty of an Indian life. But it was a happy lesson to learn (as I learned it) that the happiest of homes consists in the companionship and fellowship of the being who is the most dearly-beloved on earth; and home and the very best of society can be comprised within the four canvas walls of a tent, in the jungle, and far from the sight of another white face, even with the thermometer at 100° Fahr.

This sudden break-up and departure was a source of universal regret. About this time Mr. Donald McLeod writes to the Chief Commissioner, at Lahore (Mr. John Lawrence), for Sir Henry had by this time started for his new post at Rajpootana.

"I regard Edwardes as a loss altogether irreparable— regarding him as the very best and most unexceptionable officer I have as yet been brought in contact with, from which I make *no* exceptions. It is not his ability that I admire so much as his weight of character and high tone and principles altogether. There is not a corner of the district where his impress has not been already felt, and always in the most salutary manner. The clearing of the atmosphere which has taken place in one year is marvellous, and in another two years I am quite certain Jullundur would have been the pattern district of the Punjab—not as regards clap-trap appearances or symmetrical nukshurs * (although in a little time he would not have been behind-hand in these), but as respects all that is requisite for a healthy and honest administration. I grieve over his departure more than I can tell, and cannot refrain from thinking that he is thrown away upon those demi-savages, valuable though his services will no doubt be, there or elsewhere.

Donald McLeod's estimation of his Deputy-Commissioner's value.

"Yours sincerely,

"(Signed)   D. F. McLEOD."

And Mr. Robert (now Sir Robert) Montgomery, the Judicial Commissioner of the Punjab, after reading this, writes—

"I return Mr. McLeod's letter. Such a testimony from *such* a man is of greater value and worth than all the praise Edwardes has ever had, whether from the Governor-General, the Court of Directors, or the British Senate.

"This is *real*, by a man who is a competent judge ; much of the other was mere eloquence.

"Yours ever sincerely,

"(Signed)   R. MONTGOMERY."

* Official forms or reports.

Such was the estimate set upon his work when the time
came for him to leave Jullundur. And what was it to himself? In writing to convey the news to Mr. McLeod, he
says—

"Camp, Phillōr, February 9, 1853.

Duty ac-
cepted.

"The enclosed will cause you as much surprise, if not
so much regret, as it causes me. I accept it because it is a
duty to do so; and have written to beg that I may be
relieved forthwith.

"I shall march back to Jullundur at once—at least in
a day or two—and commence tying knots in all the loose
ends. Tell Abbott that I will come over and bid farewell
to him and you, before we turn our faces to the north. . . .

"Tell me if there is any particular piece of duty you
wish me to do before going. I cannot say *how* sorry I am
to leave many, many plans for the good of this district
unfulfilled."

Again, on the way to Hazára—

"Camp, Scalkote, March 10, 1853.

"MY DEAR McLEOD,

Regrets at
leaving
Jullundur.

"I cannot enough thank you for the kind farewell
public letter in which you have recorded your satisfaction
with my labours at Jullundur. It has been, naturally, a
great consolation to us; for we know how high a standard
you judge by, and how sincerely you speak or write. I
know too, that your heart is in the welfare of the people;
and therefore, that, if you are pleased with my work, the
work itself has been really for the people's good, which I
can truly feel to have been my end and aim in all that I
have done.

"You cannot feel more regret than I do at this removal,
for it is impossible to be in earnest in an undertaking and
not feel pain at leaving it unfinished.

"*Finis coronat opus;* and aspirations that never reach that end, how weak and miserable they all look, as they come tumbling down, and lie in broken heaps of good intention!

"The district seemed to me, when I first came, rotten to the core, and striving only to pass muster with a fair outside. What I set out to do was to purify it—to cut the bad away and have honest work done, however little there might be of it to show. In doing so, under a system of checks, by periodical statements, I was, temporarily, at a disadvantage, and felt it at times keenly; but I was always sustained by the conviction that I was doing the best for the people, and therefore for Government, whether the latter knew it or not; and I always found in my district a full reward for comparisons made beyond it, on paper. In the end, rapidity would have followed integrity, and the Jullundur nukshurs (forms) might have looked as well as others.

"Now it is impossible to say what turn things will take. Farrington cannot possibly take things up at the point where I left them. He would be an angel if he could. But if he has the one faculty of controlling his subordinates, all will be well. He has nothing to conquer, nothing to root out, very little to regret; he has only to prevent relapse and to carry on an impulse. His doing or not doing so depends more on his character than on his ability. . . . I trust he may water and reap where I have only been permitted to sow. . . .

"We leave here to-morrow, and expect to be at our destination by the end of the month. . . . When I have seen something of the country, I shall write to you again. . . .

"It is a great source of regret to us, this break-up, but I have the consolatory reflection that it has been neither sought nor avoided. We are not going of our own accord. . . .

"Where I am going John Lawrence describes all things in confusion. Everything to be done and much to be undone; police and revenue divisions to be remodelled altogether;

stations, civil and military, to be fixed; roads to be made; and the *details* of a summary settlement to be entered upon —I mean, arbitrating between the malgoozar * and the community.

" Yours,
" H. B. E."

This was the report that reached us of the land that we were going to.

The march was long, and the hot weather was approaching, and there was no time to be lost, whatever might be the regrets. On the way some letters were written that tell the tale of regret from his own pen.

" Lahore, March 4, 1853.

The march. "The heading of this letter will show you how far we have got on our journey. It has been a sad uprooting for us both, publicly and privately. There is not a corner of the district of Jullundur which I do not know, not a road which I have not traversed, not a cluster of villages which I have not visited, not an official of whom I have not taken the measure. The good and the evil of it all is in my heart, and, having swept and garnished it with great labour, I was just beginning to furnish it with improvements and fit it up with useful measures. To be torn away at such a moment, and sent to begin all over again in a new charge, leaving the people in whom I had such interest to be learnt afresh by my successor, and the officials I had tightly grasped to be clutched firmly or weakly, as chance may be,—all this makes up a trial very painful and hard to bear.

Prospects. "But it is over now, and our faces are towards Hazâra; and I have already taken an interest in its grand physical features, and pored over the map, and gathered some insight into the *locale*, and rummaged its records out of the Board's offices, and plunged into a correspondence with the Commissioner at Peshâwur as to the proper place for

* The rent-payer.

the military cantonments, on which I think I have made up my mind without having seen the place! So here you see how elastic the mind is, and how the best way to be happy is to be active and useful. . . .

"The country is described as most beautiful; hills and valleys tossed together, and man turning the mountain streams into plenty of food and wealth! Hazâra,

"But they say that the valleys for the three months of autumn—August, September, and October—are very feverish, from the exhalation of vapours by the soaked earth in the drying-up of the rains. These three months, then, make the drawback to an otherwise healthy climate, and the remedy is, if possible, to live, during that season at least, on the heights.

"This autumnal unhealthiness is not peculiar to Hazâra; it is characteristic of the whole lower range of the Himalayan chain, and is no where more strongly perceptible than in the much-coveted and favourite district of Kângra.

"The inhabitants of Kângra relate that those months 'the cats cannot catch the rats, nor the rats get away from the cats, but lie prostrate together;' and they of Noorpoor, in the same district, where we have also a military cantonment, say 'the stones in their streets get fever and ague and chatter audibly.'

"I hear the only house worthy of the name is at Tundiânée (which being translated means 'the place of coldness'), on a mountain nine thousand feet above the level of the sea, 'among goodly cedar-trees.'

"It sounds like Lebanon . . . to Emma it cannot but prove a happiness, coming in at her eyes like light, to look out for ever upon such a scenery of glorious hills. . . . And now I think you know as much about it as I do, and I hope, like me, see enough in the prospect to reconcile you to it, though wishing we could have been let alone.

"H. B. E."

CHAPTER VIII.

1853—1855.

HAZÂRA—PESHÂWUR—THE AFGHAN TREATY.

" My friend, all speech and rumour is short-lived, foolish, untrue.
Genuine work alone—what thou workest faithfully—that is eternal.
Stand by that, and let Fame and the rest of it go prating."—CARLYLE,
Past and Present.

CHAPTER VIII.

THE hot weather of 1853 had set in by the time that Hazára Hazára reached, 1853. was reached, and the long march had become somewhat tedious.

The country of Hazára is charming. Wild roses and clematis grow in the hedges—a welcome sight.

The people were very wild and untamed, and as yet, in 1853, were totally unaccustomed to the sight of Europeans. They had been little invaded by them, as their country lies off the high-road to Peshâwur, and stands on the borders of Cashmere.

They had been placed under the government of Colonel James Abbott (now Major-General and C.B.), a man greatly and deservedly beloved by them, who had made their yoke so easy that he went about amongst them like a patriarch with his flock; and his name among them generally was " Kâka Abbott," or " Kâka Sahib " (" Uncle ").*

---

* A tribute of praise to Colonel James Abbott, written by Edwardes may be inserted here: "James Abbott became Deputy-Commissioner of Hazára in 1847, and remained so till 1853, when he resigned the charge. Thus he was six years in Hazára, and he left it amidst the unfeigned regrets of the people. During his rule, exiles driven out by the Sikhs, ten, twenty, thirty, forty years before, had flocked back again from behind the border and been re-settled on their paternal lands; Hazára had passed from a desolation to a smiling prosperity. It was *he* who had worked the change—a single Englishman. He had literally lived among them as their patriarch—an out-of-door, under-tree life. Every man, woman, and child in the country knew him personally, and hastened from their occupations to welcome and salute him as he came their way. The children especially were his favourites. They used to go to ' Kâka Abbott ' whenever their mouths watered for fruit or sugar-plums. He literally spent all his substance on the people. . . . His last act was to invite the

It was doubly hard to be uprooted ourselves to disturb *such* a man in such a far-off place; but Government can afford no space for private feelings, and Colonel James Abbott was now to let the light of his genial sympathy and kindness shine upon a larger sphere of English life at Ishapore, near Calcutta (where he took the appointment of the charge of the large Government gunpowder factory there), and we had to bury our regrets and put our shoulder to the new wheel.

The first desire of the Government was to place a regiment in the heart of the country, in Hazára; and the first duty was to find a site for a cantonment.

A lovely valley, surrounded by hills, at an elevation of about four thousand feet above the sea, was fixed upon by Edwardes.

The hills rose from the plain, first gently, and covered with verdure and stunted trees; then they rose higher and higher, and, bearing on their bosoms loftier foliage of fir, oak, and chestnut, opened out at last into a distant view of the high mountains of Kaghán and Cashmere, which is just across its border on the other side of the river Jhelum, that divides the two countries of Hazára and Cashmere from each other.

Abbotta-bad.

Edwardes named it "Abbottabad," to preserve in the country the memory and name of the man who was so greatly beloved by the people over whom he ruled.

The valley was full of rice-fields and other crops, which the people were ready enough to sell; so the crops were purchased and the land laid out, and the 3rd Sikh Regiment was brought up and ordered to "hut" themselves.

Tents were lived in here for six months, in too much heat

country—not the neighbours, but all Hazára—to a farewell feast on the Nárá Hill; and there for three days and nights he might be seen walking about among the groups of guests and hecatombs of pots and cauldrons— the kind and courteous host of a whole people.

"What is the result? The district of Hazára, which was notorious for its long-continued struggles with the Sikhs, is now about the quietest, happiest, and most loyal in the Punjab."—(H. B. E.)

Sir Henry Lawrence also wrote of him thus: "Major James Abbott is of the stuff of the true knight-errant; gentle as a girl in thought, and word, and deed, overflowing with warm affections, and ready at all times to sacrifice himself for his friend or his country; he is at the same time a scientific, courageous, and energetic soldier, with peculiar power of attaching others, especially Asiatics, to his person."—(H. M. L.)

ABBOTTABAD (IN 1853).

to *be desired*, without the shelter of a house ; and meanwhile the people were got with difficulty (for they were the roughest of workmen, and had no idea of English requirements), by liberal and daily payments, to build us a small cottage.

Hazâra was a very peaceful, happy home—a region of sweet flowers. Wild rose in the hedges, the hawthorn blossom, clematis, blackberries, oleander, and the cuckoo's note reminded us of England ; and, except just in the hottest season of the year, the climate was very temperate in a good house. But this we had to do without, for we were the first on the ground. *Description of Hazâra.*

Very different is the state of things now (in 1885), and no one could recognize it for the same place where we arrived and pitched our tents, at the end of a long march from Jullundur, in May, 1853, just as the hot weather was beginning. Then nothing but rice-fields ; now with good houses, barracks, a pretty little church, and other marks of civilization, and filled with the busy sounds of European life.

Still, it is a happy, sweet retreat, and fortunate are the people who are ordered *there* to make their dwelling-place in India !

Four thousand feet above the sea-level is high enough to be called a delightful climate. It would seem as if here, indeed, was Rasselas's "Happy Valley" to be found—as if, cut off from all the world besides, it must needs be peace and quietness.

And it was a very small English community that found themselves assembled there. One Sikh regiment, numbering four officers (two of whom were married), with Edwardes and his wife, formed the whole society.

It is pleasant now to recall the friendly intercourse and kindly deeds with which those few months were filled. Great need there was for sympathy, for trouble soon found its way to us, and death was busy in the little company, and sickness and sorrow called for tenderest ministry.

The story can be simply told. The Sikhs were ordered to "hut" themselves—no unreasonable order, for the heat was coming on quickly, and there were no barracks to be built without workmen. But simple huts would protect them from the heat, and the occupation would keep the men *Mutiny in Hazâra.*

in health, far better than idleness. But the men didn't think
so, and they refused to do it, and said "they were not coolies."
This was mutiny, and Government, thinking the men could
not be in a good state of discipline, called for a court-
martial upon the commanding officer. He, a young man of
twenty-seven, thinking it would go against him and that he
would be disgraced, lost all control over himself; and, to
make a long story short, he died before the court-martial
was concluded, leaving a young wife and two very young
children.

Then the medical officer of the regiment died of fever.
He was Dr. Keith, a son of the eminent writer on prophecy;
and the sympathies of all in this small party of isolated
friends were especially awakened for him, preparing to receive
his bride, who was just about leaving Scotland to join him.
The news arrived only just in time to stop her on the eve of
starting.

So out of this little community of four officers, two were
gone—one leaving a widow and two little children to claim
the sympathy and care of those that were left.

A dark
cloud.

It was as if a dark wave of trouble had indeed passed
over this beautiful valley of peace, where we had pictured
such different things! We could only bind up the bleeding
wound with all the help and sympathy that we could bring
to aid.

Another officer was sent up to command the regiment;
and the men, ashamed of themselves, set to work under his
orders, and built up their huts without more delay.

This was a sad interlude in the few months between summer
and autumn, when Edwardes was called to leave Abbottabad
again; before the roof was on the little house that had been
begun.

Short, however, as the time had been, it sufficed for forming some acquaintance with the lovely scenery that abounds
in Hazâra; and a march to Khaghân showed him the beauties
of the Nynsook River. The name "Nynsook" means
"eye's delight," which suggested these lines—

HAZÁBA, FROM DÓNGA GULLY. MOUNT "Sir HERBERT" ON THE LEFT.

From a drawing by Colonel H. B. Crimston.

THE NYNSOOK RIVER.

"Among the streams which wander near,
And lave the foot of fair Cashmere,
There rushes one, by lone Koonnhâr,
Unlike what all its sisters are;
Not clear and musical and mild,
But dark and hoarse and madly wild—
Now whirling round, now foaming on
Like molten silver in the sun;
Anon, beneath the forest-shade,
Gloomy, yet fierce as molten lead;
In vain the mountain stops its way,
Aloft it leaps in angry spray,
And long the glen repeats the shock
With which it triumphs o'er the rock.
And still with fear do peasants tread
The path which overhangs its bed,
Knowing no mortal aid can save
The stoutest swimmer from its wave.
Well, then, may stranger, shudd'ring, look
Down on the torrent of Nynsook.

"Yet, should it be his mood to find
A moral in each whispering wind,
An angel-face in every gleam
Which lights the earth, in every stream
A nook which overflows with love
To men below from Heaven above,—
Then will he view Nynsook aright,
And own 'tis well called 'Eye's Delight.'
Its forest name was Laloo-Sir,
Till Delhi's greatest emperor,
Flying from state to still Cashmere,
O'erspread his gay pavilions here.
Nor silken tent nor regal ease
Can shield the high from low disease,
And underneath that proud display
The favourite child of Ukhbâr lay,
Feverish and sick and dim of sight,
A pain to her each ray of light!

"Vainly from Ind to Khorassân
The father sought each holy man,
Each wise hakeem, each famed fakeer,—
Still drooped the lid, still flowed the tear.
Magic and medicine, alms and prayer,
All offered hope—all left despair;

Till on the banks of Laloo's water,
All blind and sad, sat Ukhbâr's daughter,
Listening, in melancholy mood,
The solemn sayings of the flood.
It seemed the spirit of the deep
Cried, ' Maid, arise ! no longer weep,
But thrice thy burning eyeballs lave
Within the Laloo's icy wave ! '

" O glorious Trust ! O holy Faith !
Which shows men life when all seems death,
'Twas thou who led'st that sightless maid
Where those who saw, shrank back afraid ;
'Twas thou who fixed her slender hold
On slippery rocks, so wet, so cold,
And taught her bend securely o'er
The river, heedless of its roar.

" Twice has she bathed those burdened eyes,
Twice have their lids essayed to rise,
Undoubting still, she bathed again,
And light flows in upon her brain !

    *   *   *   *

Just so with life ! the even lot
Is often one which gladdens not,
While toil, by which we are deterred,
Proves a Bethesda—angel-stirred."

                         "H. B. E.

" Khaghân, September, 1853."

But, as has been said, there was not much time allowed him to enjoy the comparative rest that the peaceful retreat of Hazâra seemed to promise amid its natural beauties and its healthy climate among its hills. He was soon called to stormier scenes.

In October, 1853, the news came that Edwardes's Commissioner, Colonel Mackeson, had been attacked by an assassin at Peshâwur, and so severely wounded that he was scarcely expected to survive many days.

Murder of
Colonel
Mackeson.

It happened in this way. Colonel Mackeson was hearing the appeals of the people in the verandah of his house at Peshâwur, when a man, who had been remarked all day as very earnestly engaged at his devotions—his carpet spread within sight of the house, and making repeated and continued prostrations—came up to him towards evening, and presented a paper.

Colonel Mackeson, supposing it to be a petition, raised his arm to receive it from his hand, and the man ran a dagger into his chest.

The man was seized by the attendants, and Colonel Mackeson had just strength to call out, "Secure the man, but don't kill him," before he was carried into his house. He died of the wound in a few days. The man was supposed to have been instigated by the people of Cabul to commit the act, as he was traced to have just come from that country, where he had been for some time "sitting at the feet" of one of their fanatical "moolahs" (religious advisers), and it was supposed that he had thence drawn his inspiration.

Peshâwur is a large city in that portion of Afghanistan which was annexed to the Punjab by Runjeet Singh, and is one of the most fanatical cities of India. In has a large, and busy, and thriving population of wild and warlike people, all armed with knives and daggers, and naturally inclined to think little of pointing their arguments with the sword.

Having so lately belonged to the Afghans, these were not likely to be very pleasant neighbours; for they had never been reconciled to the loss of the city and province, and dearly longed to get them back again.

On the death of the Commissioner, Colonel Mackeson, the excitement in Peshâwur was great, and the place was in a panic—officers sleeping with their boots on and their swords by their sides, ready for danger.

It was in this state of affairs that Edwardes was ordered to Peshâwur, the Governor-General, Lord Dalhousie, considering him the most fit man to meet the crisis that had so suddenly arisen. The order was accompanied by a private letter from Lord Dalhousie.

Ordered to Peshâwur.

"Government House, October 17, 1853.

"MY DEAR EDWARDES,

"I have much and real pleasure in acquainting you that the Government has selected you to fill the very important and difficult office so sadly vacated by the slaughter of my poor friend Mackeson.

Lord Dalhousie's letter of appointment.

" In the whole range of Indian charges I know none which at the present time is more arduous than the Commissionership of Peshawur.

" Holding it, you hold the outpost of Indian empire.

" Your past career and your personal qualities and abilities give me assurance that, in selecting you, I have chosen well for its command. I feel confident that your tenure of it will advance you by another and a long stride towards the third letter G., which I once already anticipated for you, and towards the high and solid reputation of which that letter will be the sign.

" You have a fine career before you. God speed you in it; and for your own sake, and for the sake of this empire,

"Believe me to be,

" Very truly yours,

"(Signed)   DALHOUSIE."

The post was promotion to him from a Deputy-Commissioner to a full Commissioner, and " Governor-General's Agent on the Peshâwur Frontier," one of great responsibility, as it combined, with the ordinary civil administration of the division, the political relations of our Government with the kingdom of Cabul, or Afghanistan, from which country the plain of Peshâwur, a valley sixty miles long, is only divided by the high mountain ranges of the Afreedee Hills, and Swât, and the Sulimanee Mountains.

Edwardes faces his position.

Edwardes set himself at once to work to understand our position at this important point of the British rule in India. And he soon convinced himself of the falsity and the weakness of it, standing, as we were, at the very door of Cabul, and at open or secret enmity with its people—the natural outcome of all the bloodshed on both sides in the old Cabul War of 1839–42.

This was work that was very congenial to him. He had, as he had already shown, a great power of ruling wild races. A frontier officer * who knew him well writes—

"The genius—for it was nothing less—that Edwardes

* Dr. T. Farquhar, of the Guides.

displayed in dealing with the hostile and independent tribes around Peshâwur was very remarkable.

"Guiding the genius there was deep Christian principle, and a combination of head and heart-work which, when well balanced, have an irresistible effect on civilized as well as on savage communities.

"In all his dealings with natives the thoughtful expressiveness of face, and the manner with which Edwardes listened patiently to their views and difficulties, assured them of his sympathy and gained their confidence. He seemed to see at a glance the true motive that influenced them, and, by a happy turn of the conversation or a timely jest, would brush away the little artifices cleverly or clumsily adopted, warily to approach the difficulty on their minds. *Mode of dealing with the Frontier men.*

"With the people about Peshâwur especially the chivalry of his character enabled him to sympathize with the manly independence of the Frontier men, and in a peculiar way he fascinated their eager and impressible dispositions. . . .

"Edwardes found that the policy of his predecessor had been, to have paid spies moving about among the independent hill tribes, reporting regularly to him all that was going on of interest to the Indian Government. *The spy system.*

"The people knew they were watched, and necessarily felt uneasy and suspicious.

"The unfaithful character of the men employed rendered their services often worthless, if not worse than useless. Frequent raids into our territory were unreported, often, it was believed, through complicity or fear, and mischief was worked through partial dependence for information on unreliable agents.

"The hostility of the frontier certainly did not decrease under the system, and indeed the frequency of incursions and open-day murders seemed to increase, Edwardes's predecessor himself having just fallen a victim to an assassin's knife.

"Edwardes, on taking up the reins of political power, felt a strong aversion to the policy, as much perhaps from its want of the true ring of fair, open dealing with the people which was natural to him. The money, too, he felt to be misspent on men of such doubtful allegiance to their employers. *Edwardes's views on the system.*

"He, therefore, called together the chiefs and representatives of the different tribes, and, in his statesmanlike way, spoke of the power he represented and wielded. He warned the evil-disposed and hostile that swift punishment would be meted out to disturbers of the peace, while friendship and ready access to the Peshâwur markets would be afforded to all who chose to live as good neighbours.

"Assurances of good will and promises of good behaviour were profuse on the part of the chiefs; but Edwardes well knew that these were to be relied on only as long as he could show himself equal to the task of compelling their fulfilment.

Plunderers. "He had not long to wait for proofs of the correctness of this opinion, for plundering expeditions by members of the different tribes continued to occur. Nor did the chiefs, when at their homes, appear willing or able to prevent these attacks on our territory. The depredators were safe when they escaped to their hills, and indeed were welcomed with their booty, especially by the Mohammedan priests, who shared in the prize.

"It was inconvenient, however, and expensive to move out a force from Peshâwur to attack the tribe and its allies to which the robbers belonged, and bring on, perhaps, a little war in order to avenge the insult or exact payment for its loss.

"Besides, the mischief done was often insufficient to warrant the exposure of men's lives in punishing the offence; and, like all high-minded soldiers, he put its true value on the sacredness of human life.

"He therefore tried the happy expedient of barring out the whole of the offending tribes from the Peshâwur market, thereby making the community suffer for its complicity in crime, or unwillingness to exert itself for its punishment and prevention.

New measures. "The sting of this punishment was, that the people, having to trade through the medium of their neighbours, only got their supplies after paying a heavy tax in the shape of loss through being cheated.

"Edwardes had not adopted this policy long before he had ample opportunity of testing its usefulness and showing the

Hill men that he was master of the position, and more than a match for them in resource and strength.

" One of these instances was in the case of the Sheranee tribe, a people living some distance up the Khyber.

" A member of this tribe had a personal quarrel with our native ambassador, who, he heard, was about to pass through the Sheranee territory on his way to Cabul. The man waited for him behind a rock at a sudden turn of the road, and fired a pistol close to him. The bullet, fortunately, struck on the hilt of the sword and glanced off, leaving his side bruised by the blow. The man escaped up the mountain and was soon safe among his people. An example. The Sheranees.

" The ambassador, however, wrote to Edwardes, complaining that he had been fired on by a Sheranee, and, as this was done to a representative of the Government, the insult and injury had to be atoned for.

" The tribe would not give up the offender, so Edwardes issued immediate orders of excommunication from Peshâwur against the whole of the Sheranees.

" This excommunication was kept up for a whole twelve-month, when, thoroughly worn out and disgusted with the distress of the situation, the tribe sent a greybeard to Edwardes to propose terms of accommodation.

" He was shown into the Commissioner's presence, who talked over the matter, and received from the greybeard the strongest assurance of the regret the tribe felt at the indignity shown to the Ambassador of the great Sircar (Government), and their anxiety that a friendly understanding should be resumed with them. Edwardes, thinking in his own mind that a fine would be the easiest way of settling the difficulty, asked how many matchlock-men the Sheranees could turn out in case of need ? The Asiatic greybeard, not thinking of the purpose of the question, and anxious to seize what he thought a favourable opening for the expression of a fine sentiment and devotion, replied that a thousand matchlock-men were at any hour ready to serve the British Government when required.

" Edwardes then said he would compromise the present difficulty by arranging that each matchlock-man should pay a fine of one rupee, and so the tribe would condone the insult to the Government of India.

"The old greybeard felt obliged to acquiesce in the mode suggested of settling the matter. It was a mode of raising money Edwardes knew was familiar to these men, as all matchlock-men were able-bodied, and equal to the payment of a rupee.

"The old man would have answered more discreetly as well as truly if he had said that three or four hundred men would be available from his tribe as allies of the Government in a difficulty. His desire, however, to magnify his tribe and speak largely, ruined his reputation as a wily diplomatist, and compelled his people to pay a sum, the loss of which would be heavily felt.

"The money was paid, and the Sherances have since been allowed to go and come to Peshâwur at their will.

"Another complication occurred with a different tribe, but connected with the same ambassador.

An expensive dose of quinine to the Kookee-Kheyl tribe.

"Shortly after going to Cabul, he fell sick with fever, and wrote to Edwardes, begging that some quinine might be sent up to him. Edwardes immediately procured an ounce of the precious medicine, paying sixteen rupees (or thirty-two shillings) for the same.

"He at once sent this off by a kossid, or native Queen's messenger, to the Elchee at Cabul. The kossid had to go by the Khyber Pass, the name of which is but too familiar to all of us, in connection with the disastrous retreat of our troops from Afghanistan. When the messenger reached the mouth of the pass, distant only some ten or twelve miles from Peshâwur, he was met by a party of young men belonging to the Kookee-Kheyls, a section of the great Afreedie tribe, who hold the pass and live in the neighbourhood.

"This party stopped the messenger, and asked him where he was going. He said he was taking a bottle of quinine to the Elchee at Cabul, from the Sircar at Peshâwur.

"They asked to see it, and, on being shown the bottle, took it from the kossid, saying that they knew it was good stuff for fever, and telling the man he need not trouble himself more about it. He could not resist them, and, indeed, was but too glad to get off with his life, for the usual policy of these men was to murder the people they plundered, and thereby escape notice. When out of their sight, he started

off at a run, and made for Peshâwur as quickly as he
could.

"On arriving at the magistrate's court-house, he rushed into
Edwardes's presence, flung himself on the ground at his feet,
and, in Oriental phrase, begged that his life should be taken, as,
after the loss of the quinine, he was no longer fit to live.

"Edwardes made him get up and tell what had happened,
and, on hearing the simple story of his having been robbed of
the quinine, and strange to say, unharmed in person, by the
Kookee-Kheyls, he quieted and comforted him. He then
called for all the moonshees (native writers) about the court,
and dictated an order, as many copies of which were written
on the spot as there were outposts and police-stations in the
neighbourhood.

"The order was to the effect that every man belonging to
the Kookee-Kheyl tribe who might be in Peshâwur, or within
the British border, should be caught and placed in confinement. A reward was at the same time offered, for each
common man of twenty rupees (£2), and fifty rupees (£5)
for a chief. So well was the order acted on that, before dark,
three hundred rupees worth of Kookee-Kheyls were safely
lodged in prison, of whom one was a chief.

"The story of the capture of the chief was instructive.
The chief of a neighbouring clan which had a feud with the
Kookee-Kheyls happened to be in Peshâwur. His knowledge
of the country led him to think his enemy would seek to fly
by an unfrequented route, which would avoid, too, the
frontier outposts. Taking some friends with him, he went
off, and, hiding in a ditch through which the road passed,
waited till after dark for his prey. As he calculated, the
Kookee-Kheyl chief, seeing no danger, walked straight into
the ambuscade, and was brought back to Peshâwur.

"Nothing was heard from the frontier that night; but
early the next morning a messenger came to say that the
greybeards of the Kookee-Kheyl tribe had come to Peshâwur,
and asked for an interview with the Sahib. This was at once
granted, and, on being introduced into Edwardes's presence,
the chief spokesman produced the bottle of quinine, which he
begged to return.

"He then began a long story about some unmannerly

and evil-minded young men of the tribe, who had disgraced
their body by taking a bottle of quinine from the kossid of
the great Government of Hindoostan.   The chiefs, he said,
had come in a body to return it, and to beg forgiveness, and
for a restoration of the good feeling which existed between
them, on the part of the great rulers of India.   Not a word
was said by them of their friends being locked up in the
Peshâwur Jail, as they handed back the quinine.   Nothing
was said, either, of a quarter of the bottle being empty.
Edwardes received it, and expressed his satisfaction at their
expressions of eternal friendship, and the proper feeling
which led them to return the quinine.   In an off-hand way
he remarked, however, that there was a little bill remaining
due by the Kookee-Kheyls to the great Sircar, and, until that
was settled, all could not be quite straight on the part of the
Kookee-Kheyls.

"Calling the treasurer, he asked what the amount was, and
found that three hundred rupees were due to his treasury.
Edwardes then told them what he had thought it necessary
to do in giving rewards for apprehending members of their
tribe, all of which he knew they had heard before, and on
that account had taken the trouble to come and humble
themselves before him.

"A man was sent off to the head-quarters of the tribe,
from which, in the course of the day, the money was with
more or less difficulty brought; and in the evening the £30
worth of prisoners left, safe and well, but wiser, for their
homes.

"The kossid was despatched again to Cabul with the
quinine, where he arrived unmolested.   The Kookee-Kheyls,
no doubt, thought it too expensive to give another £30 for
a quarter of an ounce of quinine, and did not care to spend
another night in the Peshâwur Jail, even though the quarters
were free.

"Edwardes was glad at the peaceful ending of the
business, for a little mismanagement might have led to a
more or less serious disturbance of the frontier.   He taught
a lesson also to this and to the other tribes; that without
bloodshed he could humble them, and make it worth their
while to be respectful and peaceable neighbours."

This sketch will serve the purpose of introducing us to the people among whom Edwardes has now come, and help us a little to understand the new surroundings.

Having made up his mind, as we have seen, to abandon the spy system, he resolved that the first thing to do was to bring about, if possible, a friendly feeling with Cabul, and to start with an open, honest, and straightforward policy towards them. *Spy system abandoned.*

He wrote to Lord Dalhousie, and explained his views to him fully, asking him to tell him how far they accorded with his own.

To state them broadly, in few words, they were to bring about an entirely new state of feeling between us and the Afghans, and to get a treaty signed on both sides, that " bygones should be bygones " between England and Cabul. *Opening of another proposal.*

Lord Dalhousie entirely concurred in these opinions, and wrote back cordially that he thought such a result would be most desirable, but most difficult to bring about, but added— *Lord Dalhousie's cordial acquiescence.*

" I give you *carte blanche,* and if you can only bring about such a result as you propose, it will be a feather even in your cap." *

His immediate superior in office, the Chief Commissioner of the Punjab (then Mr. John Lawrence), not participating in his views as to the importance of the case, and further thinking, and openly expressing his decided opinion, "that the thing was impossible to be done," the Governor-General wrote demi-officially to Colonel Edwardes, and desired him to correspond directly with himself, without sending the matter in the ordinary course through the Chief Commissioner at Lahore— *Difference of opinion in the Chief Commissioner.*

" In the same manner," Lord Dalhousie added, " as he has been in the habit of corresponding on political matters with his predecessor, Colonel Mackeson." *Lord Dalhousie's proposal for direct communication.*

* The " feather " was, oddly enough, placed in the cap of John Lawrence, who well deserved it for *other* services, but not for *this* policy, to which he was opposed throughout.

The Governor-General yields to Edwardes's suggestion.

But Colonel Edwardes submitted to Lord Dalhousie whether it might not be felt to be a discourtesy at Lahore; and he shrank from doing anything that could pain his friend. On these grounds, therefore, the Governor-General yielded, and the correspondence was carried on through Lahore, in the usual way. Edwardes preferred to take the risk of having an adverse opinion sent down to Calcutta on the margin of his letter, when forwarded on by the Chief Commissioner; for it suited best the generosity and openness of his character to have no dealings secret-from his chief.

Mr. Lawrence never approved of the undertaking, and used openly to express his opinion of its uselessness, and even went so far as to ridicule it. He used to say—

John Lawrence's reasons.

"I have two good reasons against it: (1) that you will never be able to *get* the Afghans to make a treaty; and (2) if they make it, they will not keep it."

Fortunately, this opinion could not interfere with Lord Dalhousie's *carte blanche;* and at all points of the long correspondence the Governor-General's opinion so entirely coincided with the Commissioner's, that the object was not hindered or interrupted, and Edwardes's arm was strengthened to go forward in the work.

The whole correspondence is very interesting, and a few extracts from it will not be out of place here.

Edwardes writes to Lord Dalhousie—

"Peshâwur, February 24, 1854.

Edwardes opens the subject in correspondence.

"It would contribute much to the security of this frontier if open relations of good will were established with Cabul.

"There is a sullenness in our present relations, as if both parties were brooding over the past and expecting an opportunity in the future. This keeps up excitement and unrest, and prevents our influence and institutions from striking root.

"I should be very glad to see a new account opened on the basis of an open treaty of friendship and alliance.

"In any event, our position is better than it ever was before, and no fear need be entertained of the result, if we are only true to ourselves and pursue a straightforward policy with vigour."

The remark of the Chief Commissioner to this was,[*] that he "doubted whether a treaty would be good policy with the Dost, who would only be bound by it as long as he liked."

Again Edwardes writes to the Governor-General—

"Of course, self-interest, and not affection for the English, or a remembrance of favours received from Lord Auckland, is at the bottom of Dost Mahommed's desire for amicable relations. Neither to him nor his people can we personally be otherwise than obnoxious. We might once have gained their esteem, but we preferred thrashing them into subjection.

"We succeeded in thrashing them, but not in subduing them, and the consequence is that we are not respected in Afghanistan. As a mass, the people hate us; but they also fear us. The war of 1849 has brought the conquerors of India to their door, and they cannot be insensible to their danger.

"Dost Mahommed is not alone in hoping we will come no farther. There is a large and influential party in Cabul who would resist any policy which would bring us, even as friends, to that capital, mainly because they would expect retaliation for their national defence. But I should anticipate that even these, as well as the people generally, would be relieved by a simple treaty of agreement to be friends and respect each other's boundaries. . . .

"Most cordially do I concur with your Lordship, that, if

Correspondence with Lord Dalhousie.

---

[*] Lord Dalhousie having agreed to Colonel Edwardes's proposal that their correspondence should go through Lahore. The Chief Commissioner's custom was to write his own remarks in pencil on the margin of Edwardes's letters, and they were invariably adverse to the idea of a treaty, as in this instance.

possible, there should be no detailed obligations in the
treaty. All that we want is, that Dost Mahommed should
respect our possessions and not ally himself with our enemies ;
and all that he ought to ask in return is, that we should do
the same.

"But should his alliance with us plunge him into difficulties . . . then, for our own interests, we should be obliged
to help him ; and what I would lay down beforehand as the
fundamental principle for such a contingency is, that the
help should be in money, and *not men or officers.*

"Neither our soldiers nor our officers can come into contact with the Afghans, even in a friendly way, without
reviving animosities and bringing unpopularity and disgrace on the cause to which they are attached." *

Edwardes from the first formed his own opinion of our
position on the frontier, and took a mental grasp of it, and
had a clear and definite policy, which seemed to him the
right and the safe one. In all his public work, as well as
his private concerns, he sought strength and guidance from
the Source of all wisdom and power; and this is the key to
much of the confidence and strength which were so conspicuous in him.

Writing to one of his family at home at this time of
anxiety at Peshâwur, he said (March 13, 1854) —

"Dost Mahommed sees us at his door, with a cantonment,
and a depôt, and a base of operations, ready for any campaign into which we may be forced.

"Common sense would dictate to him to side with us,
and not with Russia, in which case no irritation would
reach this frontier. But, of course, he *may* not take the
common-sense line . . . I should be very glad to see, openly,
amicable relations established between us and Cabul, and

Marginal note: Edwardes had a clear and definite policy for holding our fron-tier posi-tion.

* How wisely does this read in the light of the experience of later
years! Had counsels such as these been adhered to, how much bloodshed
might have been saved in 1878 !

expect that will be the happy result of this threatened war.

" Whichever way the chiefs and kings of Central Asia act, we are, I believe, quite safe in the camp of the Lord of Hosts ; and I really feel less anxiety than you might suppose in this position."

The treaty took a long time to negotiate, and the exercise of great wisdom, tact, kindness and forbearance, patience and skill to bring it to a successful termination ; but it was done at last, and it is but truth to say that both the wisdom to *conceive the plan* and the diplomatic skill to carry it out were Edwardes's own unaided work.

The full record of this tedious and difficult piece of diplomacy still exists, and is an interesting example of Oriental custom and wily circumlocution, contrasted with the straightforward honesty of a high-minded Englishman.

It may be only fair to give the adverse opinions that went down from Lahore on the margin of the papers, in forwarding them to the Government in Calcutta, from the Chief Commissioner.

John Lawrence, writing to Edwardes, says—

" I dare say you are right ; still, I cannot divest myself of the idea that it is a *mistake,* and will end in mixing us up in Afghan politics and affairs more than is desirable. The strength which a treaty can give us seems to be a delusion. It will be like the reed on which, if a man lean, it will break and pierce his hand." Opinions of John Lawrence.

Again—

" Nothing that we could do would make him a real ally and friend."

But Lord Dalhousie remarks to Edwardes—

" I do not agree with him. I think his views founded on a fallacy. It proceeds on the assumption that the Afghans are fools, whereas I think they are, in general, quite as clever fellows as we are." Opinions of Lord Dalhousie.

Again the Chief Commissioner writes to Edwardes—

" A treaty with the Afghans might be a dead letter so far as Russia and Persia are concerned. But while of no real value to us, it would, at home, be thought of some value, and might lead them into a mistaken line of policy.* . . .

John Lawrence kept to his own opinions.

" I so far agree with the Governor-General that I think all the merit of the affair, whatever it may be, is yours."

But, in spite of the Chief Commissioner's adverse criticism, the work went on successfully, and in 1855, a friendly treaty, that bygones should be bygones, being ready for signature, Dost Mahommed determined to entrust the honour and duty of representing himself and signing the treaty to his eldest and favourite son and heir-apparent, Sirdar Gholam Hydur Khan.

News came that the Sirdar would start from Cabul on January 17, accompanied by Foujdar Khan, to stay at Jellalabad until arrangements were made for the meeting at Peshawur with the British authorities.

Major Edwardes wrote to Lord Dalhousie—

Conclusion of the work.

" The visit is evidently looked upon as a trial of our feelings and sincerity, and the Ameer is desirous himself to come at some future time to meet your Lordship, if his son is well received."

Calcutta Government orders.

At this point of the proceedings, a public letter came from Calcutta from the Governor-General in Council, giving orders that as the whole work was his own from first to last, it was only right that Major Edwardes should be empowered to bring it to a conclusion himself; and full orders were given him to meet the Ameer's representative in full Durbar and sign the treaty on the part of Government, and thus put the finishing stroke to his own work.

---

* A letter from the Chief Commissioner to Edwardes at this time says, " I would determine nothing about the reception of Hydur Khan until the Government orders arrive."

Up to this time we see John Lawrence still unconvinced of any value in the treaty, and strenuously repudiating any connection with it.

The letter was couched in the most honourable and flattering terms, and may be quoted in this place, for the details are interesting.

From G. F. Edmonstone, Esq., Secretary to the Government of India, to John Lawrence, Esq., Chief Commissioner of the Punjab.

"Fort William, January 25, 1855.

"Sir,

"With my despatch, No. ——, dated November 14 last, I had the honour of forwarding to you the reply of the Most Noble the Governor-General to a letter which had been addressed to his Lordship by the Ameer of Cabul, Dost Mahommed Khan. The Ameer was thereby informed of the readiness of the Government of India to condone the past; he was assured of its good will; and he was invited to establish, by a formal treaty, those relations of friendship for the renewal of which he had expressed an earnest desire in his address to the Governor-General.

First letter from Calcutta with final orders.

"There is every probability that his Highness will meet the views of the Government of India, and will send an envoy to Peshâwur duly accredited for the negotiation of a treaty between the two States. It appears, therefore, to the Governor-General in Council expedient that, in order to avoid delay, an officer should be accredited on the part of the Government of India, and that he should be furnished with the draft of such a treaty as the Government would be willing to conclude, and with instructions for his guidance during the negotiations that may be carried on.

"The Governor-General in Council has resolved to entrust the duty of negotiating with the expected envoy from Cabul to Major Herbert Edwardes, C.B., the Commissioner of Peshâwur. He is the principal officer on the frontier, and is thus the person to whom such a duty would naturally and most conveniently be allotted. The well-known abilities of Major Edwardes, and the temper, discretion, and judgment he has shown during the demi-official negotiations which have been on foot for some months past, enable his Lordship in Council to feel perfect confidence that he will perform the duty to the entire satisfaction of the Government of India.

"The Government of India is bound, by the letter of the Governor-General to Dost Mahommed Khan, to conclude a simple treaty of friendship, should the Ameer depute a duly-accredited agent to Peshâwur for that purpose; but the Governor-General in Council deems it very desirable for every reason that the treaty, besides containing a promise of perpetual peace and friendship between the States, should provide also for the establishment of a mutual obligation upon each to respect the territories of the other, and for the imposition upon the Ameer, if possible, of an obligation to oppose to the utmost all the enemies of the British Government.

"Annexed to this despatch is the draft of a treaty which fulfils the following conditions, effects every object the Government of India has in view, and commits it to nothing which a cautious policy would require it to avoid."

Then follow directions, which need not be inserted here, and for which we have not space. A few extracts only will suffice.

"Fort William, January 25, 1855.

"Major Edwardes may be instructed in bringing forward the second article of the treaty for discussion, to advert to those representations of Nazir Khairoollah, and to point out that the article in question does substantially guarantee to the Ameer what he is said to have desired, excepting a promise that the Government of India shall never have a representative at the court of Cabul; and that it has been proposed for acceptance, with the express intention of meeting his wishes, as they are believed to have been represented by

the Nazir Khairoollah. The envoy may be assured at the
same time that the Government of India has no intention of
sending, and no wish to send, a representative to the Court
of Cabul; but it should be pointed out to him that this
Government could not in prudence bind itself *never* to
depute a representative to the Ameer; for if Russia or other
powers should be represented by envoys at Cabul, the
interests of the British Government would plainly suffer
injury if no envoy were present on its behalf. . . . Major
Edwardes may be authorized to deliver to the envoy, in the
event of his signing the treaty, a formal note which shall
explain that, in engaging (in the second article) not to interfere with the territories of the Ameer, the Government of
India intends to repudiate all desire to have a cantonment in
any part of his Highness's dominions; and that the Government in like manner intends, by that article, to repudiate all
desire to have any representative at the court of Cabul,
unless representatives from other powers should be admitted
there. . . .

"The communication of these facts, it seems to the
Governor-General in Council, may serve to reassure the
Ameer as to the security of his own position in Afghanistan, and to lessen the reluctance he possibly may exhibit to
conclude any treaty with the British Government which
does not include a guarantee against the hostility of
Persia. . . .

"The Governor-General in Council has every confidence
that the judgment and tact of Major Edwardes will enable
him to bring the negotiations, with which he is hereby
charged, to a successful issue.

"You are requested to forward to Major Edwardes, without any delay, copies of this despatch and of the draft which
is annexed to it.

"I have, etc.,
"G. F. EDMONSTONE,
"Secretary to the Government of India."

"DRAFT.

"Treaty between the British Government and His Highness Dost Mahommed Khan, Ameer of Cabul, concluded on the part of the British Government by Major Herbert Edwardes, C.B., in virtue of full powers vested in him by the Most Noble James Andrew, Marquis of Dalhousie, K.T., etc., Governor-General of India, and on the part of the Ameer of Cabul, Dost Mahommed Khan, by virtue of full authority granted to him by his Highness.

"ARTICLE I.

Treaty. "There shall be perpetual peace and friendship between the Honourable East India Company and his Highness Dost Mahommed Khan, the Ameer of Cabul, his heirs and successors.

"ARTICLE II.

"The Honourable East India Company engages to respect and never to interfere with the territories now in possession of his Highness the Ameer.

"ARTICLE III.

"His Highness Dost Mahommed Khan engages on his own part, and on the part of his heirs and successors, to respect the territories belonging to the Honourable East India Company, to be the friends of its friends and the enemy of its enemies.

"Done at Peshâwur, this, etc.

"(Signed)   G. F. EDMONSTONE,

"Secretary to the Governor of India."

Edwardes proposes John Lawrence be sent to sign the treaty. Not many men would be so entirely unselfish as to see any reason why *they* should not let honours due to them take their course; but it had come to Edwardes's knowledge, through Foujdar Khan,* that the Ameer was intending to send his eldest son and heir-apparent, and had even thought of going himself to Peshâwur, and had expressed to Foujdar Khân his opinion, that "it would have been a great advantage

---

* This is the same Foujdar Khan we have read of before as the faithful commander of the levies at Bunnoo.

for the treaty to be made in the presence of the Most Noble
the Governor-General of India himself, as there would then
be no occasion for reference to Calcutta, and no apprehension
that a succeeding Governor-General would annul the treaty
which had been made by his predecessor in person."

But being dissuaded by his brothers from going himself,
he decided to send his heir-apparent, and was anxious that
the greatest possible honour should be shown him.

Edwardes, being more anxious for the stability of the
work than for his own honour or any thought about
himself, the good of his country and the honour of his
Government being always first in his thoughts, considered
that it would give more importance to the treaty in the
Ameer's eyes if the chief authority in the Punjab were to
meet his son.

His disinterested views in doing so.

So, as he knew from private correspondence with Lord
Dalhousie that his lordship intended to appoint him to sign
the treaty, before the public letter came empowering him to
act alone as the signing power, Edwardes did what is worth
recording, for it is what only he and such as he would do—
he wrote to Lord Dalhousie, expressed his gratitude for his
kindness and his gratification at the flattering terms in
which his labours had been recognized by him "in Council"
at Calcutta, but suggested, for the Governor-General's consideration, whether it would not advance the stability and
importance of the treaty in the eyes of the Afghans if the
chief authority in the Punjab, the Chief Commissioner, were
ordered to Peshâwur to meet Hydur Khan, in conjunction
with himself.

Fresh proposal to Calcutta made by Edwardes.

The suggestion accepted.

This suggestion was considered, accepted, and acted upon;
and a fresh order was sent, directing the Chief Commissioner,
Mr. John Lawrence, to proceed to Peshâwur and sign the
treaty in conjunction with Major Edwardes.

Lord Dalhousie writes to him (privately)—

"Government House, Calcutta, January 30, 1855.

"MY DEAR EDWARDES,

"You had specially been named the negotiator. I
regret very much that the last letter should have rendered a

Second letter from the Governor-General.

change necessary, and compelled the Government—much against the wish of us all, to nominate the Chief Commissioner as the negotiator on our part."

And he goes on to say—

The Governor-General regrets the necessity.

"Nevertheless, I am exceedingly vexed that you should not have had, *as I intended you should*, the crowning credit of bringing to a close the negotiations you have conducted so well and so successfully to their present point. We have said something in this sense to you officially, which I hope will be pleasing to you.

" Believe me,
" Always yours sincerely,
" (Signed)   DALHOUSIE."

And John Lawrence wrote (privately)—

" Lahore, February 1, 1855.

" MY DEAR EDWARDES,

John Lawrence's letter.

" I have not received a line from the Governor-General on Cabul matters for a long time, and it is possible that he may prefer leaving all the arrangements to you. In this case, I would not, of course, go to Peshâwur, and you would do all that you think right and expedient. As far as my views go, I would say, treat him liberally and even handsomely, but not extravagantly, or it may turn the heads of him and his followers."

Up to this time the Chief Commissioner evidently supposed that Edwardes would be required to meet Hydur Khan, and to carry out the treaty alone. This shows that the idea originated with Edwardes, and that it was his own generosity that brought his chief at Lahore first on the scene.

Again John Lawrence writes (privately)—

" Lahore.

" The orders about the treaty arrived last night. In the letter of the 25th, containing the detailed instructions, *you* were to make the treaty; in one of the 30th, I am told to do it. Copies go to you. . . .

"I wish myself that you were to do it, sincerely."

Again—

"I so far agree with the Governor-General that I think all the merit of the affair, whatever it may be, is yours.

"Affectionately yours,

"JOHN LAWRENCE."

The signature of the treaty was the *first* stroke John Lawrence put to the work. But, after having "signed" it, the credit of it was given to him in England, and for this treaty he obtained his first honour of K.C.B., which has been, in after years, followed by so many others, then well earned by *former* years of labour and service, but not for *this* special service.

History seeks for *facts* and finds out the truth, or is itself valueless. And a recent author,* writing of the times of the Mutiny, has tracked the truth here through all the myths that have been raised up around it, and placed it, almost for the first time, before the public. *Holmes's "History of the Mutiny" reveals the truth.*

. . . "A later chapter of this history will show how triumphantly the policy that had led to the conclusion of this treaty was vindicated. The credit of that policy belonged, of right, to Herbert Edwardes alone. But years passed away, and the act to which he looked back with just pride as the most valuable service that he had been permitted to render to his country was *not* declared to be his. John Lawrence had, then, the opportunity of making a noble return for the self-abnegation which his lieutenant had practised towards him. It was for him to place the facts in their true light, and, standing boldly forward, to point to the man who would not utter a word to exalt himself at the cost of another, and to say 'Honour to whom honour is due.' Had he done so, he might, indeed, have lost some portion of his reputation for statesmanship; but he would have earned a glory as pure and imperishable as that which illuminates the self-sacrifice of

* Quoted from "The History of the Mutiny," by T. R. E. Holmes, p. 77.

Outram. But he preferred to claim for himself the credit of a policy which he had not only not originated, but had persistently opposed; and history, while acknowledging that part of his fame was indeed honestly won, is forced to expose the rottenness of the foundations upon which the other part is based."

These are strong words, but they show that their author had searched into and read the records for himself.

God writes history in the lives of men, and we may not alter *facts*.

And now we have only to add an extract from the Government orders from Calcutta, which finally came after this change in the arrangements was decided on.

From R. Temple, Esq., Secretary to Chief Commissioner of the Punjab, to Major H. B. Edwardes, C.B., Commissioner and Superintendent of Peshawur Division.

"Lahore, February 10, 1855.

"SIR,

"In reference to your letters regarding the relations of the British Government with his Highness the Ameer Dost Mahommed Khan, I am directed to forward for your information copies of two letters, conveying the instructions of the Government of India on this subject, and enclosing the draft of a proposed treaty with Cabul.

"You will see that the selection of the Most Noble the Governor-General in Council had originally fallen on yourself for the conduct of the negotiations with the Cabul Envoy, but that the information subsequently received regarding the delegation of Sirdar Gholam Hydur Khan, the Ameer's favourite son and designated heir, induced the Government to direct that the conferences should be carried on by the Chief Commissioner in person. The Chief Commissioner, however, trusts that the expressions which the Government have been pleased to convey in both the despatches now transmitted will prove highly satisfactory to you, and he desires me to state that it would have afforded him sincere gratification if the negotiations had devolved on you, as he is confident that your judgment and tact would have brought them to a successful issue.

"As ordered by Government, the Chief Commissioner will repair to Peshâwur to meet Sirdar Gholam Hydur Khan, with the least practicable delay, and expects to reach that place by the 10th proximo.

"I have, etc.,

"(Signed) R. TEMPLE,

"Secretary to Chief Commissioner."

From G. F. Edmonstone, Esq., Secretary to the Government of India, to John Lawrence, Esq., Chief Commissioner of the Punjab.

"Fort William, Calcutta, February 2, 1855.

"SIR,

"On the 25th ultimo, I had the honour of conveying to you, for communication to Major Herbert Edwardes, C.B., the instructions of the Most Noble the Governor-General in Council for the negotiations of a treaty with the envoy whom his Highness the Ameer of Cabul expected to depute for that purpose."

"I have since received your Secretary's despatch, dated 16th ultimo, with its enclosure from the Commissioner of Peshâwur, describing certain conversations held by the Ameer Dost Mahommed Khan with Foujdar Khan at Cabul, and having laid these communications before the Governor-General in Council, I have been directed to convey to you in reply the following observations and orders. . . .

"'The Ameer of Cabul has responded to the proposal of the Governor-General in Council, that an envoy should be sent to Peshâwur, by deputing Sirdar Gholam Khan, his favourite son and designated heir. Such an act deserves that it should be met in an equally friendly spirit by the Government of India. Moreover, the Ameer has specially expressed his wish that you should meet his son. If this wish were now to be disregarded, his Highness might fairly think that proper consideration had not been shown to himself or to his son, and the negotiation might be injuriously affected by the omission.

"Under these circumstances, the Governor-General in Council is of opinion that the duty of treating with the Ameer's envoy ought to be entrusted to you instead of Major Edwardes.

"I am accordingly directed to request that you will repair to Peshawur with all expedition, to meet Sirdar Hydur Khan, making known the probable date of your arrival there, as requested by Foujdar Khan.

"You are hereby invested with full powers to negotiate with the Sirdar, being guided in your proceedings strictly by the instructions which were addressed to you for communication to Major Edwardes, in my despatch dated 25th ultimo, above cited.

"You will be pleased to explain to Major Edwardes the cause of his supersession, and to express to him the regret of the Governor-General in Council that the political considerations above mentioned should have rendered it necessary to commit the duty, for which he was originally selected, to other hands.

"I have, etc.,

"(Signed)   G. F. EDMONSTONE,

"Secretary to the Government of India."

End of official correspondence.

We have now come to the end of the official correspondence, which has been curtailed as much as possible within the smallest limits. Nor would even so much have needed to be written had it not been made necessary by the many random assertions that have been lately published on this and other kindred subjects; and counter-*assertions* merely without proof can carry no weight with them at all.

The account here given is from actually existing records of the *facts*, which cannot be controverted.

There was a wonderful *fitness*, in the preparation of the life we are tracing, for the times we have come to now, and those which, though still hidden from our eyes in the undeveloped future, were nearer than we then thought.

The cementing of the bond of friendship between England and Afghanistan was thus put into the hands of the man who had gained a personal influence that few others had among the wild Mohammedan border tribes; and the brave commander-in-chief of the Bunnoo levies, Foujdar Khan, who had proved so true to Edwardes there, in those testing months of difficulty, and had found the master that he served so true to him, was now the British representative at the Court of Cabul. Placed there by the interest of his old master, and knowing that he owed to him all his honours and the high position that he now held, every motive that he had was engaged in his service, not the least valuable one being personal attachment.

How the past had prepared for the present times of difficulty and trust.

And thus the two could work together with certainty, and a confidence in each other which gave immense strength at such a time. We know, too, what a good report Foujdar Khan would give to the wily Afghans of the character of the man they had to deal with, of the security that there was in trusting to his word, and the certainty of detection and retribution if they attempted to deceive him. Yes; surely we can see, by the course of education in the life, how Bunnoo led on to the building up securely the great bulwark of our strength in 1857, that stood the test and tug, and held the Punjab like an anchor in the storm.

How much we owed to it in 1857.

As another frontier officer * writes to-day: "Often have I been told by Khans, Afghans, Beloochees, alike, that we should never have kept Peshawur (and with it the Punjab) without Edwardes. They would say, 'Yes, yes; Nicholson *was*, undoubtedly, a great man, but *he* wouldn't have kept us all true to Government. He was so stern; we feared him, but we didn't love him. Edwardes compelled us to like him better than any other Feringhee: and *see*, sahib, what he has left to our children—pensions, jagirs, etc."

Even John Lawrence, who could see no possible good in making this treaty, and was (privately) continually advising

* General Monro.

Edwardes to give it up altogether, and called it "waste of time," afterwards was brought to see its value, and admitted that, "as matters have turned out in Hindoostan, the late arrangements with the Ameer were very fortunate" (quoted from enclosures to secret letters from India, July 23, 1858).

On March 16, 1855, Sirdar Gholam Hydur Khan, the heir-apparent of the throne of Cabul, accompanied by Foujdar Khan Bahadoor, the British Envoy, who had been entrusted by Edwardes with the duties of ambassador, had completed their long and tedious march to the plain of the Peshâwur Valley.

And now they have arrived and pitched their tents; and the English camp moves out to meet them.

CHAPTER IX.

1855—1857.

THE AFGHAN TREATY RATIFIED—VIEWS UPON AFGHAN
POLITICS AND WAR.

" Peace hath her victories,
 Not less renowned than war."

CHAPTER IX.

It was a striking spectacle as these two camps, face to face First meeting of the two camps. once more, stood upon the plains of Peshâwur, and close to the very gate of the Khyber Pass—that same Pass so lately the scene of deadly strife, and treachery, and blood, now to witness the ratification of the engagement that "bygones should be bygones."

At this distance of time, as we look back upon the scene, Let bygones be bygones. past, present, and future seem all so mingled together in the vision that it is difficult to keep them apart. Presently it will be seen how well the engagement was kept, when it stood us in good stead; and we cannot forget even here, as we tell the tale in 1885, to wish that bygones had been bygones for ever!

But in this place we have to do only with the bright picture of the meeting, and we will tell it in the principal actor's own words.

"Peshâwur, March 17, 1855.

"My dear Lord Dalhousie,

"Yesterday Sirdar Hydur Khan pitched his tents at old Jumrood, our threshold of the Khyber.

"This morning I rode out there, and was with him at six o'clock. Crawford Chamberlain's 1st Irregular Cavalry went with me.

"The Sirdar's Cavalry and regular companies formed Sirdar Hydur Khan, the heir-apparent. a zigzag kind of street, up and down the hillocks, at the furthest end of which was seen the exact image of Henry VIII. seated in a tent, and surrounded by a small court—all on chairs in the English fashion.

"There was an evident excitement in the Afghan force when we arrived ; a thrill and restlessness ran through them all, and they quite waved about, and many Mohammedan exclamations burst forth.

"Our Cavalry closed, and clashed in, and we were saluted ; and officers of the Sirdar's camp were busy, thrusting back all kinds of blackguards ; and altogether it was a moment of considerable feeling, as if the two nations had once more come face to face.

"Dismounting at the Sirdar's tent, he came forth with a heavy rolling gait, but cheerful face, and led me in ; and after he had asked twenty-five times after the Chief Commissioner, and fifty times after the Governor-General ; and I had asked twenty-five times after his health, and fifty times after the Ameer's, we took to horse, and set out for British territory.

"Another thrill and crash ensued ; and I saw the Sirdar order all his Cavalry to the rear, till we got into open ground, when the Afghans lined out to the left, and the British Cavalry to the right of us ; and so, chatting, we jogged over the stones to his camp at our frontier police-tower. Here the Queen's 24th Foot and a troop of Horse Artillery saluted the Sirdar ; and I left him at his tent.

"It went off very well, and has broken the ice.

"Now ziyáfuts (presents) and supplies are pouring in to him.

"On Monday the Sirdar visits Mr. Lawrence in full Durbar, and Mr. Lawrence returns it on Tuesday. After which business will commence, and the Sirdar will probably come nearer to us.

"Believe me,

"Your Lordship's most obediently,

"HERBERT B. EDWARDES.

Again the account continues—

Letter to
Lord
Dalhousie.

" Yesterday, at half-past seven a.m., the Sirdar came to our Durbar in the cantonments. Tho brigadier and all his staff and myself received him at the boundary; and a street of soldiers and a troop of Horse Artillery saluted him; and a band played, and the Union Jack went up to the masthead; and Mr. Lawrence met him at the canopy, and led him up through the Durbar of British officers in full dress, and Peshāwur chiefs, in all their blaze of gold, and jewels, and bright colours, and he presented the letters from his father, and they were read aloud, calling the Sirdar his ' heir-apparent' in a very marked manner; and after an hour's friendly colloquy, he was conducted home again—with more guns, more noise, and more honours of all kinds.

" This morning, the Chief Commissioner and all the civil staff, and the brigadier and all his staff, returned the visit at the Sirdar's camp; and he produced bundles of presents—furs from Russia and Bokhâra, fine swords and Cabul manufactures, which gave us plenty of conversation, geographical and commercial.

" The most curious, perhaps, of the presents were some dromedaries from the Great Kuzzâuk Desert—creatures with deep hanging frills of dark brown wool, and large lustrous eyes—such as the Queen of Sheba may have brought King Solomon, and Salvator Rosa only could have painted.

" There were horses, too, who had seen their best days; and a few split-eared ponies. The Sirdar forced his own riding horse upon the Chief Commissioner—a noble beast, I do not think I ever saw a better in a chief's possession.

" Altogether the visits have passed off very well, and made a kindly feeling on both sides.

" To-morrow, the Sirdar brings his camp to the boundary of the cantonments, and the day after the conferences will commence.

" We have heard that the Sirdar's line is to ask for nothing whatever—' mere friendship,' he gives out. But

I dare say he will find an opportunity of hinting any objects the Ameer has at heart."

Conclusion of negotiations.

And so the work was brought successfully to an end and the Treaty signed; and Lord Dalhousie writes to Edwardes—

"I congratulate you and myself, and all else concerned, on this successful issue of negotiations, which have now lasted just a year."

And Edwardes writes in reply—

"I am glad your Lordship was pleased with the treaty. It went off well after much wrestling. Hydur's perspiration

A FAINT SHADOW OF THE HEIR-APPARENT, SIRDAR GHOLAM HYDUR KHAN,
HOLDING IN HIS HAND THE PESH WUR TREATY.
From a pen-and-ink sketch by Sir Herbert Edwardes.

at some points of the contest was great. Once in an agony at not getting his father declared 'Walee of Afghanistan,' he screamed for 'a cheroot!' and smoked in awful silence

for a quarter of an hour. Another time, he calmed himself
with a tune on my wife's piano, and firing off a few lucifer
matches.

"Very unfortunately there was no artist at hand to make
a picture of the Sirdar; but I drew a rough sketch myself,
while his vast form was still heavy on my memory."

On March 17 these two camps met, and on the 30th the
negotiations were brought to a satisfactory conclusion by the
signing of the treaty; and then tents were struck, the
pageants all melted away in the glow of the coming heat,
the hubbub died out, and ordinary work was resumed, while
all parties concerned rejoiced that the strain was over, "and
we had leisure to reap the advantages of the improved relations
of friendliness with our neighbours across the borders."

The next notice that appears in the records is a letter dated *Honour to*
March 24, 1855 (same year), that shows that the Governor- *John Law-*
General had long wished to ask some honour for the Chief *rence.*
Commissioner from his Queen, as Lord Dalhousie explains,
"well earned before for other times and other services;" but
this was thought a fitting cause to bring his name forward,
"because the great political importance of the entire change
in the relations between England and Afghanistan would be
well understood by her Majesty's advisers at home." And so
the stepping-stone was laid which led on to many others, as
the reader knows.

And two months were too short a time for the Chief Commissioner to have forgotten how it came to him; for he writes
in this private letter (asking Edwardes's advice as to what
honour would suit him best, as a choice was proposed to him)—

"I cannot conclude this note without saying that, in
fighting to get you made Commissioner of Peshâwur, it
turns out that, like the bandy-legged smith in the 'Fair
Maid of Perth,' I was fighting for my own hand."

Not much "fighting," however, was needed, for we have
already seen how cordially and spontaneously the appointment was given by Lord Dalhousie's own selection.

" I may say," John Lawrence adds, " with perfect truth, that I consider you deserve at least as much, if not more, for the late treaty than I do."

This was naturally and genially spoken at the moment of elation—and privately—and it was all that Edwardes ever heard of it or of gratitude.

But this did not stay his hand nor hinder his work ; for what could repay him better than to find the *success* of his labours, and to *prove* the wisdom of his judgment and of his policy ? And this his experience did most fully prove.

This treaty of March, 1855, was followed up at the close of 1856 by Edwardes recommending that more active aid should be given to the Ameer when difficulties with Persia had assumed alarming proportions, and Persia's designs upon Herat alarmed Dost Mahommed, and made him see very clearly the advantages of a friendly alliance with the English.

The Ameer was invited to a second conference at Peshâwur. He accepted the invitation, and came this time himself. He marched down with two of his sons, some of his chosen councillors, and a body of picked troops, to the frontier.

The first day of the new year, 1857, saw this second meeting.

The second meeting, 1857.

The Ameer pitched his tents at the mouth of the Khyber Pass ; and on the plain of Jumrood the British camp was again pitched, where the Ameer was received with friendly honour.

Our troops formed a street more than a mile long. Kaye describes the scene : " They marched past the Ameer and his host in review order after the Durbar was over. More than seven thousand British fighting men were assembled there, and among them were three complete European regiments, whose steady discipline, and solidity, and fine soldierly bearing made a strong impression on the minds of the Afghan visitors —from the aged Ameer himself to the youngest trooper of his escort."

Second treaty

On January 27, 1857, the conferences were brought to a conclusion, and this second treaty was signed at Peshâwur in

March, 1857 ; and, two months afterwards, the mutiny of the Indian army, which shook British India to its centre, broke out. signed at Peshâwur.

This time of our difficulty fully *tested* the value of the treaty. Dost Mahommed *stood by his engagement;* and *this* it was that prevented him from sweeping down upon us with his hordes at Peshâwur, when we should have been quite unable to resist him. The testing time of the value of the treaty.

His own people could not understand why he, a Mohammedan, did not catch at the opportunity to destroy the "infidels ;" and frequently, in open Durbar, they would come to him, and, flinging down their turbans at his feet, would say, "Hear the news from Delhi ! See the difficulties the Feringhees are in down below ! Are you a Mohammedan ? Why don't you lead us on to take advantage of them, and win back Peshâwur again ?"

But Dost Mahommed stood by the treaty honourably. And so was the fallacy *proved* of *both* the reasons that the Chief Commissioner always expressed *against* the policy, namely, first, "that Edwardes would never be able to bring the Afghans to sign a treaty," and second, "that if they signed it they wouldn't *keep* it." (Rather like the Irishman's defence on his trial for murder, first, "that he didn't do it," and second, "that, if he did, the man *deserved* it !") Dost Mahommed stood faithful to his part in the treaty.

However, so it was in truth (for this is but a simple record of *facts*). The treaty was both made and kept, and happy was Edwardes to be the instrument of so much blessing. He did his work to God, and not to man ; and he was blessed in it by success. He had the satisfaction of seeing the great importance and value of that work which he had been allowed to perform. And those who were on the frontier at Peshâwur understood how much the security of that important frontier of India was owing to Edwardes in 1857. Great value of the work.

He used to say himself that he thought it, perhaps, the most important piece of service which he had been permitted to render to his country and his Queen.

But it was a service for which he never even received a "thank you" in *public* acknowledgment, or recognition that Totally unacknowledged.

the work was his own. Probably had Lord Dalhousie lived, it might have been different.*

But Lord Dalhousie did not live to see fully the value of the policy that he had so steadily and cordially supported. In February, 1856, he resigned the burden of Government, which had been too heavy for his enfeebled health, and took his departure from India.

Before he left the country, he wrote a kindly farewell to Peshâwur.

"Government House, Calcutta, February 21, 1856.

"MY DEAR EDWARDES,

"The time has now come when I must bid you, too, farewell. I do it with sincere regret.

"I thank you most heartily and most warmly for the very able, and successful, and willing services by which you have aided me in the administration of this great land, and I trust you will always hold me in recollection as one who witnessed and applauded your early rise, who has been grateful for your aid, and who looks confidently to your future progress in the path of honour, and who hopes to be regarded always as a friend.

"Believe me, my dear Edwardes,

"Sincerely yours,

"(Signed)   DALHOUSIE."

To Lord Dalhousie all the details of the matter were entirely known, and he valued the treaty so highly that he counted it among the successes of his administration of the government of India in his formal "review" of his labours on

In the left margin: Lord Dalhousie's farewell and departure.

In the left margin: LordElgin's inquiry.

* In proof of how completely the facts of these negotiations had been obscured, we may remark here that, in after years (in 1863), when Lord Elgin was Governor-General and came up to the Punjab, and was in conversation frequently with Edwardes, he asked him one day "if he could tell him how those treaties with Dost Mahommed, that had brought such good result, had been brought about?" It was quite *news* to him when he heard all the *facts* of the case.—E. E.

his departure. Possibly, when his papers come out (sealed up by his will for fifty years), the facts will be made better known.

His successor, Lord Canning, knew the circumstances well enough to think it necessary to write privately to Edwardes on January 19.

"Government House, Calcutta, January 19, 1857.

"MY DEAR SIR,

"I must ask you to accept my best thanks for the part you have taken in the recent negotiations, and for their satisfactory issue.

Letter of Lord Canning.

"I feel the more bound to do this because the first suggestion of a meeting came from you, and so far as I can judge from the reports as yet received, and from the tone of the discussion shown in them, I believe that the suggestion has proved a very wise and useful one.

"It would be a good thing for us if all diplomatic conferences were conducted so satisfactorily, and set forth as lucidly as these have been.

"Believe me, my dear Sir,

"Yours very faithfully,

"(Signed)   CANNING."

A portion of the text of this second treaty may be given here—

"TREATY."

"Between the Honourable East India Company and his Highness Ameer Dost Mahommed Khan, Walee of Cabul and of those countries now in his possession, and the heirs of the said Ameer, there shall be perpetual peace and friendship.

"The Honourable East India Company engages to respect those territories of Afghanistan now in his Highness's possession, and never to interfere therein.

"His Highness Ameer Dost Mahommed Khan, Walee of

Cabul and of those countries of Afghanistan now in his possession, engages, on his own part and on the part of his heirs, to respect the territories of the Honourable East India Company, and never to interfere therein, and to be the friends of the friends and enemy of the enemies of the Honourable East India Company."

This further treaty, made in 1857, was signed January 26. We were then at war with Persia, and the greater part of the treaty has reference to the exigencies of that war.

Amongst other things it provided that a lakh of rupees (£10,000) per month should be paid by the Company to Dost Mahommed, for military purposes; and that British officers should reside in Candahar to see that the subsidy was properly applied, and to keep the Government of India informed of all affairs, but not to advise or interfere with the Cabul Government.

The sixth and seventh articles are as follows :—

" 6. The subsidy of one lakh per mensem shall cease from the date on which peace is made between the British and Persian Governments, or at any previous time at the will and pleasure of the Governor-General of India.

" 7. Whenever the subsidy shall cease, the British officers shall be withdrawn from the Ameer's country ; but, at the pleasure of the British Government, a vakeel, *not a European officer*, shall remain at Cabul on the part of the Government, and one at Peshâwur on the part of the Government of Cabul."

The officers who were selected by Government to fulfil the duties of these last articles were Major Harry Lumsden * (who commanded the Guides at that time), his brother, then Lieutenant Peter S. Lumsden * (of the Quartermaster-General's department), and Dr. Bellew, and they were accompanied by Foujdar Khan and Gholam Sirwur Khan Khaghwanee, and attended by a suitable escort.

They proceeded to Candahar, and carried on their delicate and difficult mission with great success, and to the great satisfaction of Government. Less able men could not have been trusted with so delicate a piece of diplomacy; but men of such weight and value could ill be spared from India in

* Now General Sir Harry Lumsden and General Sir Peter S. Lumsden.

such difficulties as those which arose in 1857, after they had
entered on their mission in Candahar.

Edwardes bears testimony to their services in his " Mutiny
Report " in the following terms :—

"And here I would beg to acknowledge the very great
services of our officers in Afghanistan during the late crisis.
At Candahar, with the heir-apparent, were Major Harry
Lumsden, Lieutenant Peter Lumsden, and Dr. Bellew,
accompanied by Gholam Sirwur Khan Khaghwanee. At
Cabul, in the Ameer's Court, was Nawáb Foujdar Khan
Bahadoor, our vakeel. It was thought to be a service of
great enterprise, for the English officers especially, when
they set out for Candahar, even in a time of peace ; and
their situation became one of decided peril when India was
in a blaze with a Mohammedan struggle. But these officers
and Khans, by a soldierly equanimity, by a fortitude equal
to the occasion, by a calm trust in the cause of England, by
the good feeling which their previous demeanour had created,
and by keeping the Cabul Government candidly and truth-
fully informed of real events, and thus disarming monstrous
exaggerations of our disasters, preserved the confidence of
the Ameer and his best counsellors, and were largely instrumental in maintaining those friendly relations which were of
such vital importance to our success.

"I would venture to solicit for all these officers and
Khans some mark of honourable distinction from Govern-
ment."—(Extract from letter from Major Edwardes, the
Commissioner and Superintendent of the Peshawur division
to the Judicial Commissioner for the Punjab. No. 64.
Dated March 2, 1858.)

Sir John Kaye, in his " History of the Sepoy War," touches
with his graphic pen many of the incidents of this important
piece of history : but the facts were either not all before him
or were obscured.

There is a note in Edwardes's handwriting that corrects what is deficient in Sir John Kaye's narrative, and is too valuable to be omitted here. It runs thus—

"The author, Sir John Kaye, in pp. 428-445, vol. i., seems only partially informed. In February, 1854, when Commissioner of Peshâwur, I proposed to Lord Dalhousie to change our policy towards Cabul, and I asked leave to bring about friendly relations.

Note of Edwardes's on a passage in Sir John Kaye's history of the events.

"Sir John Lawrence, the Chief Commissioner of the Punjab, opposed the proposal, but the Governor-General and Council, at Calcutta, approved of it; and before the close of 1854, I led the Afghans to come forward with the most honourable overtures, seeking for pardon.

"The result was the treaty of March, 1855, which Kaye treats too lightly and inaccurately, speaking at p. 428 thus : 'For some time there had been going on between the Governor-General of India and the ruler of Cabul certain passages of diplomatic coquetry, which had resulted rather in a promise of a close alliance, a kind of indefinite betrothal, than in the actual accomplishment of the fact.'

"It bound the Afghans to be 'friends of our friends and enemies of our enemies.' I followed this up at close of 1856, by recommending the active aid given to the Ameer and the interview of January, 1857, which Sir John Lawrence equally opposed. I regard this change of policy, effected in the time of our prosperity, and so invaluable in 1857, as the greatest service I have ever been able to render to my country. This is the first public notice of it.

"For Sir John Kaye goes on to say at p. 445, vol. i.—

"'Lord Canning, too, was more than well satisfied with the manner in which the negotiations had been conducted, and with the apparent result . . . and both in private and in public letters he cordially thanked the Commissioners, even before their work was done, for the admirable judgment and good tact which they had displayed at the conferences, giving an especial word of thanks to Edwardes as the original suggestor of the meeting, and, it might have been added, the *originator of the new policy* which had more recently been observed towards the Afghans. . . . For *the policy was emphatically Edwardes's policy;* he had been the first to recommend, in Lord Dalhousie's time, that we should try the effect of trusting the Afghans, and his recommendations had resulted in the general compact of 1855.'

"Sir John Kaye proceeds—

"'So Dost Mahommed set his face towards Cabul, and Sir John Lawrence returned to Lahore. It need be no subject of surprise if the latter, as he went about his work, thinking of all that had been done at Peshâwur, sometimes asked himself, What good? and wished that the monthly lakh of rupees to be expended on the Afghan army were available for the improvement of the province under his charge; for he had never liked the project from the beginning. He had no faith in Dost Mahommed, and he doubted whether the subsidy would produce any tangible results. . . . In the mean while, Lord Canning, though he had slowly come to this point, believed that the subsidising the Ameer was not a bad stroke of policy. *Extract from Sir John Kaye.*

"'It bound the Afghan ruler by strong ties of self-interest to remain faithful to the British Government. Even neutrality was a great gain, at a time when Persia was doing her best to raise a fervour of religious hatred against the English throughout all the countries of Central Asia. The very knowledge, indeed, of the fact that Dost Mahommed had gone down to Peshâwur to negotiate a closer alliance with the British must have had a moral effect at Teheran.' —(See Sir John Kaye's 'History of the Sepoy War,' vol. i. p. 447.)

"What was the result?" Edwardes goes on to say. "In *Edwardes's*

1863 the Ameer, unaided, except by our friendship, took Herat by siege!

"And what shall we say to the fidelity of Dost Mahommed? Did he prove himself worthy of the trust reposed in his word when he said, 'Now I have made an alliance with the British Government, and, come what may, I will keep it till death'?

"(Signed)   H. B. E."

This promise was kept and that alliance was never broken by him, even when the storm of the mutiny must have been a strong temptation to Mohammedan fanaticism, urged on, as we have seen he was, by the voice of his own people, who would have been only too glad, if he would have led them on, to take back their dearly-loved Peshâwur again, and strike a blow at the English in their hour of weakness.

One clause of this treaty was, that we should never send an *English* embassy to Cabul, but allow our relations to be carried on by the native envoy whom we chose to appoint.*

Who can say how much of the calamity of the second Cabul War of 1878–79 might have been spared had this clause been more respected?

The service to the country of this Afghan Treaty was thought so important, because it healed up the wounds left by the old Cabul War, and relieved England of anxiety when, in a few months, there was mutiny, and bloodshed, and distress from one end of India to another, and no native troops could be relied upon. Had our relations with the Afghans *then* not been friendly, we should not have held our frontier against them.

As it was, Colonel Edwardes was personally well known

---

* Dost Mahommed used to say, "I ask you, for the sake of friendship, not to send an English embassy into my country. *Personally,* I would receive him with honour, and desire that he should be honourably treated by all, but I cannot answer for it that some ruffian will not pull out his pistol and shoot him on the road; and then it brings me into difficulty with your Government, and I should be held as having broken my pledge. So, for the sake of *friendship,* I say, do not send an Englishman."

and trusted by the Ameer, and he kept up cordial relations with him, and held his post as Commissioner of the Peshàwur frontier throughout the whole of the mutiny; and it is not too much to say that it was greatly owing to his *personal* influence and command that Peshàwur stood in 1857.

Having spoken already of one act of that noble *self-forgetting*, which was a conspicuous feature of his character (the constant action of his mind and nature), this may not be an unsuitable place to mention another instance of it, as it was in connection with the same Governor-General, Lord Dalhousie.

After the Mooltân campaign, and when on his way to England in 1849, Edwardes met with Lord Dalhousie, who had watched his work at Bunnoo, and had very highly approved it; and, in a personal interview on that occasion, Lord Dalhousie said to him, after thanking him warmly for all he had done at Bunnoo and Mooltân, and praising his work in flattering terms—

"Now, Edwardes, I want to ask you to tell me what honours I shall ask for you from the Queen; for your services have been so great that I could not ask for greater honours than they would deserve?"

Edwardes's answer was, thanking him for all his kind approval—

"My Lord, the reward that I would ask, and that would please me best, is that the native officers who have served me so faithfully may be well rewarded—Foujdar Khan and Sirwur Khan—and I would ask you to give Foujdar Khan a jageer* in perpetuity and a suitable title; and to Sirwur Khan a similar and suitable reward."

The Governor-General replied, "You may rely upon it that your wishes will be attended to." And it was done, as we have seen in a former chapter.

* A *jageer* is a grant of land.

The request was characteristic of the noble nature from which it came; but how few men, at such a moment and with such an opportunity, would have asked for *nothing for himself!* No; like Wordsworth's "Happy Warrior," his honours "must fall like showers of manna, if they come at all!"

He instinctively acted out the rare virtue of (Rom. xii.) "in honour preferring one another" on all occasions.

The title given to Foujdar Khan at this time was that of Khan Bahadoor. This was in 1849. Later on, after the mutiny of 1857, this same Foujdar Khan was rewarded for his services with the higher title of Nawâb.

The following letter, written to a relative in England about this time, has an interest, as bearing upon this subject, before we pass on to other scenes.

From Colonel Edwardes.

"Camp, Upper Meranzye, April 20, 1855.

"I see how anxiously you are looking out for the result of Foujdar Khan's mission to Cabul. He took a kind but dignified answer from Lord Dalhousie, accepting the hand of friendship stretched out somewhat timorously by Dost Mahommed Khan. Foujdar was received with marked honour by the old Ameer (Emir, as it is spelt in the 'Arabian Nights').

"And it must have been a moment of honest pride to Foujdar Khan (who was only leader of four and twenty Horse when I first knew him), when the King of Cabul rose from his seat in full Durbar, and embraced him in the frank but often treacherous manner of Afghanistan. He bore himself as bravely in the fierce and factious Court as ever he did in battle; saw much, said little, but greatly to the point; and did not return without the heir-apparent to the throne. Altogether a successful campaign.

"The papers will have told you that Sirdar Hydur Khan, the chosen successor of Dost Mahommed, came down through

the Khyber with about two thousand men, and made peace
between his nation and ours, after sixteen years' hostility and
ill will.

"You will be interested to know that the Governor-
General and the Supreme Council had appointed me to negotiate the treaty with this young prince, as a kind acknowledgment of a whole year's anxious labour in bringing matters to
this point. (For the proposal to bury the past and its mutual
injuries and revert to a friendly policy, if the overtures could
be obtained from Cabul, originated with me in the beginning
of 1851, and elicited from Lord Dalhousie a *carte blanche* to
do so. And you may well imagine the anxiety and labour it
has occasioned me, in addition to the regular duties of my
post.) But after the instructions to me to make the treaty
had been drafted, Dost Mahommed expressed a hope to
Foujdar that the second greatest man in India would go to
meet his son and heir. And so the instructions were handed
over to Mr. John Lawrence, more to my delight than his; for
he thought I ought to have the honour, and I thought he
ought to give weight and dignity to the act, if it was to produce an instrument of any national importance. I tell you
these little matters because you will be interested in my
welfare and honour, and I should wish you to know that
nothing but kind appreciation has fallen to my lot. Most
sincerely, too, did I think the right course had been pursued. My heart was in the treaty, and not in the name of it;
and John Lawrence has had the most cordial and hearty
assistance from me in the conferences and negotiations at
Peshàwur. This he knows and feels. And there was to me
an inward pleasure and satisfaction which I cannot tell you,
in this closing task of helping one who has been so good
to me. . . . All ended well. We engaged never to interfere
in Afghanistan; and the Ameer and his heir engaged not
only to respect our territories, but to be the friend of our
friends and the enemy of our enemies.

"Thus it was offensive and defensive on their part, but not on ours. We pledged ourselves to nothing but an honest and peaceful policy. And after mutual exchange of numerous visits and presents, we sent the hungry prince and courtiers back, well pleased with their reception, and with the solid guarantee they had obtained for the safety of their country.

"The event is now ringing through Central Asia, and will, I believe, have a lasting influence on the current of events on that great theatre of struggle, in which Mohammedanism will, one day, be crushed between the Greek and Protestant Christians. . . .

"This affair being settled, I was ordered off here to accompany a force sent to enforce submission in an outlying valley, called Meranzye, which lies on the borders of Kohat and the kingdom of Cabul.

Meranzye affairs.

"It had not paid tribute to the Ameer for three years, leisure not having been found to send a force before. . . . Hitherto all our objects have been peacefully accomplished, as I pray they may continue to be." *

The Crimean War was going on at home, and Edwardes adds—

Remarks on the Crimean War.

"I look for an early modification of the present crisis; but Sebastopol must go down first, and the English nation must remodel its army. If peace comes suddenly, these lessons will be forgotten, glossed over by all parties in Parliament, and another war will come on us again and still find us without an educated staff, or a general who could crack a nut, much less a fortress.

"What pages and pages of humiliating records have we been reading every mail for the last six months! But *one* quality survives our brilliant reputation—PLUCK—a quality found very largely in the brute creation.

* The Meranzye expedition ended in the revenue being collected without firing a shot. The thermometer generally 110° in tents.

"And then the outcry of the people against Govern-   On preparedness for war.
ment seems to me very one-sided. Our disasters, calmly
considered, resolve themselves into bad arrangements. How
is Government to make military arrangements? They are
conceived, and proposed, and carried out by a body constituted for that purpose, and called 'the staff.' If you have
a good staff you have good arrangements, and if you have a
bad staff you have bad arrangements. This is the long and
short of the matter. Now a good staff is a highly-intelligent
and complicated piece of machinery, and is not to be put
together in a hurry. It must be educated through long
years of peace as the nucleus of an army in time of war; and
the people must consent to pay for it, and to see large
charges in the annual estimates for a body of men who are
apparently doing nothing.

"But this is just what the Duke of Wellington wanted
at the close of the war with France, and the English people,
headed by Mr. Hume, would not have it. They said it was
expensive. And now they have gone to war with their own
cheap staff, and ruined an expedition, and clouded our glory,
and squandered millions to no purpose. And the French
army lies alongside of ours, rejoicing in a perfect organization produced by a scientific staff. In all this I see more
blame to the English people (who hate soldiers till they
want them) than to the Government.

"What is Government? A selection of English gentlemen absorbed in party-struggles in Parliament, necessarily
ignorant of all military matters. I quite pity their position
when I think how they must feel their own utter incapacity
to organize a war in these days, when war is essentially a
science. But when I see that none of them admit it, and
don't tell the people the plain truth, then I despise them.
And the poor drowning people, catching at straws, and calling
out first for one Indian officer and then another, as if they
had some talisman in their pockets to charm away the
blunders of forty years!

" It is one of the most remarkable things of this war, that no man seems to have been drawn out from the Queen's army by the occasion. I hear no name mentioned. The eyes of the regiments at Sebastopol seem to fix on no one.

" But if a Wellington arose, he would want two campaigns, at least, in which to organize his army. The mischief *is done*, and there is no short road out of it, except a sudden peace. And then, mark my words, the country will go to sleep again, and Cobden and Bright will stuff its ears with cotton, and we shall have all the tom-noddyism of the Peace Society over again."

To return to the treaty with Dost Mahommed and the honours awarded to the Chief Commissioner for a work in which he had no part, the beautiful spirit with which Edwardes submitted to be ignored in his own work is such an example of Christian forbearance and true humility, that it may be useful to many a young man in public life to study it. Nor was it a mere passing impulse of acquiescence to be succeeded by a chronic discontent.

Long afterwards, in replying to some remonstrances that were urged upon him to make his own share in the Afghan frontier operations better known and understood, Edwardes wrote—

" I have lost all wish for fame. I have not lost the natural desire for the approval of those I serve, and, after them, of all good men.

" But we are very apt to overrate our own services, and it is the office and duty of Government to discern their value and put the stamp on. If so done, the stamp is doubly prized ; if not, a man had better possess his soul in patience.

" Not a finger will I move in the matter. We all think it a defect in John Lawrence that he praises no one. But I acquit him of all mean and selfish motive in it. It is not that he *wishes* to keep the credit to himself, though practically it has that effect. It is a *principle* of his *not* to praise public servants, for fear of its 'putting wind into their heads,' as he expresses it !

"This is, I think, a mistaken argument ; for there is a higher necessity—in justice, to praise the good men do, as well as blame their evil.

"John Lawrence's blame is an ever-impending thunder-bolt, but he is a Jupiter-Tonans who never smiles upon his world.

"I am as indignant as any one about it, when it touches a friend like John Nicholson, and I have had a hot corre-spondence with J. L. on this subject. But it does not do any good. He is emphatically a hard man in public matters, and so all one has to do is to love him in private and respect him in public.

"Most unquestionably he is a great public servant, and England would do well to make him Governor-General of India. Of course he could not be fit for such a post without being a lord ; but lords are easily made. They might first qualify him with a peerage, and then use his human nature.

"I nearly forgot what I began all this about, viz., to beg you not to blow a single blast, however gentle and musical, on the alt-horn of Fame for me. . . .

" Yours, etc.,
" H. B. E."

" 1858."

We have been carried on from 1853 to 1857, because it was impossible to break the thread of the story of the Afghan Treaty, which was only *concluded* two months before the great mutiny of the native army broke out, and which then became of such immense importance to us.

The timeliness of the treaty.

It was brought about little by little, with great skill, tact, and patience. At first sight it may seem long to have been engaged upon one work, but not in reality long when it is considered what important results were accomplished—nothing less than the entire change of relations between England and Afghanistan; so great as the difference between hatred and bloodshed and a friendly alliance, to let "bygones be bygones."

Who can doubt what would have been our position in the Punjab if, at Peshâwur, the frontier had been invaded by the Afghans when we were in extremities in 1857? and if our frontier relations had they remained as they were when Colonel Edwardes first took charge at Peshâwur in 1853, what could have restrained them?

Review of the past.

We see, then, how timely was the change.

In a review of the history of past years, a strange, mysteriously weird feeling comes over us, and great events stand out and seem to repeat themselves; and we seem far away, as if we were looking on them from another world, and we only see their points mapped out at long intervals, and almost forget what lies between them!

And now we stand on the *other* side of another Cabul War, that of 1878, and it is impossible to touch upon this much-vexed question of Afghan politics without a sad retrospect; for we then saw this treaty, with which we have been engaged from its birth to its completion, set aside, and the scene reversed, but only for a time.

The present time.

Again, in 1885 we see another meeting at Rawul Pindee between *another* Ameer and *another* Governor-General, his Highness Ameer Abdul Rahuman Khan, and his Excellency Lord Dufferin, at which, received with honour and courteously entertained by so worthy a representative of England's greatness and England's nobility, the bonds of friendship were cemented afresh as in 1855–57, by Abdul Rahuman, the present Ameer.*

From Herbert Edwardes's own pen we may extract here some remarks on this subject, which show his views of the

---

* At this moment the public papers bring us the report of this interview, in which the Ameer says, " In return for this kindness and favour, I am ready with my army and my people to render any services which may be required of me or of the Afghan nation. As the British Government has declared it will assist me in repelling any foreign enemy, so it is right and proper that Afghanistan should unite in the firmest manner and stand side by side with the British Government."

policy of friendship with Afghanistan, which he had laboured
to bring about.

"The most withering condemnation which has ever been
passed upon the whole policy of the old Cabul War was
fulminated by Lord Ellenborough in his memorable proclamation, dated Simla, October 1, 1842, written, as the
historian reminds us, at the same place, in the same house,
nay, 'in the very room,* and on the same day of the same
month as Lord Auckland's unjustifiable manifesto of 1838.'
And it was followed in January, 1843, by the free release
from captivity of Dost Mahommed Khan, whom we had
spent fifteen millions sterling of the revenues of India to
dethrone without a cause.

"Is it wonderful that six years later, when British India
was in the throe of its struggle with the brave Sikh nation,
this same Dost Mahommed Khan should have yielded to the
temptation of joining the Sikhs against us?

"The author of this Paper feels it one of the greatest
satisfactions of his life, and the most useful incident of his
service, that he has since then been enabled to heal those
open wounds, and be the peacemaker between that ill-used
ruler and the Government of India.

"When Commissioner of Peshâwur, in 1854, he sought
and obtained the permission of Lord Dalhousie to bring
about that hearty reconciliation which was expressed in the
first friendly treaty of March 30, 1855, and subsequently
(with the equally cordial approval of Lord Canning) was
substantially consolidated by the treaty of January 26,
1857.†

"At this latter juncture, the Shah of Persia had seized
Herat, and was threatening Candahar. England was herself
attacking Persia in the Gulf, and the Indian Government

Extracts
from
"Papers"
by Herbert
Edwardes
on Afghan
politics in
1858.

* Kaye, chap. iv. book viii.
† See Aitchison's valuable collection of Indian Treaties, vol. ii. pp.
430-433.

now gave to its old enemy at Cabul (worse than enemy, the man whom it had deeply injured) eight thousand stand of arms, and a subsidy of £10,000 a month, so long as the Persian War should last.

"We did this, as the treaty truly said, 'out of friendship.' What a fearful satire on the Cabul War!

"We did it, too, in the plenitude of our power and high-noon of that treacherous security which smiled on India in January, 1857. How little, as we set our seals to that treaty, did we know that in May, the English in India, from Peshàwur to the sea, would be fighting for empire and their lives, and that God's mercy was 'stopping the mouths of lions' against our hour of need!

"To the honour of Dost Mahommed Khan, let it be recorded that throughout the Sepoy War, under the greatest temptation from events and the constant taunts of the fanatical priests of Cabul, he remained true to the treaty, and abstained from raising the green flag of Islam and marching down on the Punjab. Had he done so, no man who was in India in those dreadful days of September before John Nicholson stormed Delhi will for a moment doubt that the English would have been driven to their ships —*towards* them, rather. How many would have reached them is another matter.

"And this being so, it is but historic justice to the Ameer's memory to conclude that had his overtures of 1837–38 been accepted by Lord Auckland, his fidelity would have been the same,* and the Cabul War, with all its

---

* "A curious parallel may be mentioned in illustration. In December, 1837, while Alexander Burns was at Cabul, forwarding to Lord Auckland the entreaties of Dost Mahommed Khan to be taken into alliance with the English, a Russian envoy named Wiktewitch, but commonly called Vicovitch, arrived with a letter from the Emperor of Russia.

"Dost Mahommed consulted Burns about admitting him, and then gave up the letter which he brought to Burns. But, on Lord Auckland's declining Dost Mahommed's alliance, the Ameer in despair turned to

sorrows and disgraces, and other wars and other sorrows which have followed in the train of our lost prestige, would never have darkened the history of England."

But this was in the past. The war of 1878 has come and gone too, and it is only in connection with this treaty, upon which our thoughts have been occupied, that we have anything to do with it here. But before we leave the subject, we may enter a little more fully upon this interesting discussion, and give a few more thoughts of Colonel Edwardes at this time upon the question, What is our best frontier line?

"The question which gives interest to all speculations on Afghanistan (the core, as one may say, of Central Asian politics) is, What ought England to do about the north-west frontier of her Indian Empire? . . . After the doubts and lessons of the last five years,* which, with Afghan alliances, Russian encroachments and intrigues, a Persian war about Herat itself, and an Indian revolution, have been unusually fertile in experience, I have myself arrived very decidedly at the conclusion that our true military position is on our side of the passes just where an enemy must debouch on the plain."

What is our best frontier line?

With these passes strengthened, and Peshâwur, Kohat, and Sindh brought by railroads and steamers into direct and rapid communication with the sea, which is our real base— possessed of these strategical points and communications, with a judiciously-located European and well-organized native army, both Edwardes and Major Harry Lumsden agree in thinking "that the 'keys of India' would be grasped."

Wiktewitch and accepted the Russian offers. And the Cabul War was the result.

"In the Crisis of 1857-58, another Russian envoy, as a matter of course, was despatched to Cabul. The Ameer was now an ally of the English, and, true to the stipulation of the treaty, that he should be 'the friend of the friends and the enemy of the enemies of the Honourable East India Company,' he stopped the Russian envoy at Candahar, and declined to receive him at his Court."—H. B. E.

* This was written in 1858. Extracts from a memorandum on Major Harry Lumsden's "Report on the Candahar Mission," by Lieutenant-Colonel Herbert B. Edwardes.

Edwardes goes on to say :—

Two great forces rushing to meet.

" Whether led on solely by ambition and jealousy, as some think, or driven by that Higher Power which works out its decree by human passions, it is clear that two great Christian forces are hurrying from the Caspian and the Indian Ocean towards some common centre, and rolling up the Hindoo and Mohammedan world between them. No one doubts that they will meet. All that seems doubtful is the point of meeting and the result of collision. The intervening space is growing narrower, and the question becomes more intensely interesting every year. Each power has left to it, in this as in other matters, a wide discretion ; and each is bound, in reason and prudence, to survey the battle-field and choose its vantage ground. Looking at it from this purely selfish and strategical point of view, and putting out of the discussion for the moment all moral arguments, reflection and observation have satisfied me that it would not be wise for England to choose her battle-field above the *Afghan difficulties.* passes. Afghanistan must be admitted to be a great physical difficulty. It is difficult to conquer, difficult to hold, difficult to sustain an army in, and most difficult of all to leave. The very native Government of the country lives from hand to mouth, and is savage with its own embarrassments. Finding such a country between us and Russia, why should we divide the difficulty ?

" Every mile that we advance beyond the present British border * is a relief to the enemy, and is taking on our own shoulders a share of the burden which the invader ought *Question of resources* to bear. After all, every contest is a question of resources. Experience has shown us that military operations in Afghanistan can, from the nature of the country, only be carried on at an enormous sacrifice of money.

---

* In 1858, before the scheme was proposed of a " rectified frontier," or " scientific frontier."

" To take that expenditure on ourselves would surely be a blunder; and to throw it on the enemy the most obvious dictate of strategy. If defending a fortress, before which lay a vast morass, we certainly should not plunge into the morass ourselves, but allow the besiegers to exhaust half their strength and lose half their material in its toils, and then assail them as they emerged. The point would be of no moment if it involved a difference of only thousands of pounds in a great war; but it seems to me to be a question of millions, which neither England nor Russia can afford to throw away. If England were once to adopt the moderate and purely defensive policy here advocated, there is little doubt that Russia would push on her schemes in Central Asia with greatly-increased vigour. But if she considered it wise and justifiable to absorb what still remains of Persian independence—Khiva, Bokhara, Kokan, Herat, and Afghanistan—I have come to think that there would be nothing in it which, as Englishmen, we should fear or, as philanthropists, regret. For supposing her to be entirely successful, Specula-tions. can any one doubt that to substitute Russian rule for the anarchy and man-stealing of Khiva, the dark tyranny of Bokhara, the nomad barbarism of Kokan, the effeteness and corruption of Persia, and the fanatical devilry of Afghanistan, would be anything but a great gain to mankind? And if we had ourselves, meanwhile, prepared our own frontier for defence, I do not see that we should go to war with Russia on any future occasion with any diminution of advantages. To make a diversion of any consequence in Asia, Russia must detach proportionally more of her strength than we to repel it; and the operations would be close to our base, and far from hers.

" One reason that we had for removing our struggles with Russia as far from India as possible has, please God, been removed, by the convulsions of 1857–58. Our internal power in India must now be placed on the basis of conquest, and if secure in our reorganization, we need not fear the announcement of a European enemy in the defiles of Afghanistan.

"But it is a very violent assumption to suppose that Russia could soon succeed in becoming our imperial neighbour, and I conceive that the policy now advocated would tend to retard such a result. Russia, being herself a half-caste Tartar power, has amalgamated readily with the cognate races of Asia, where they were either idolatrous, or Christian, or Armenian. In her early history, too, she forced both her yoke and her religion upon the Mohammedan tribes between the Black Sea and the Caspian. But the achievements of Ivan the Terrible have not been, nor are likely to be, rivalled in our day.

"The struggle in the Caucasus has undoubtedly been prolonged very greatly by the fanaticism of the followers of Schamyl, who do not call themselves his soldiers, but his disciples. And whatever success may attend Russia, in organizing the nomad tribes of the Kipchak Desert and of Turkistan, I do not think she would find the Afghans at all an easier prey than the Circassians. The best way to prevent it is to show them we ourselves want nothing in Afghanistan, by neither annexing, occupying, nor interfering in that country; and so, encouraging them to regard us as their friends, that in the hour of danger they may turn to us for pecuniary assistance.

"The surest way, on the other hand, to throw the Afghans into the arms of Russia would be to fix our battle-field above the passes, and seek for strategical points in countries which do not belong to us.

Opinions concerning the occupation of Quetta, 1858.

"Within the last few months I have learnt, with regret and astonishment, that the authorities in Sindh have advocated the friendly occupation of Quetta, above the Bolan Pass, as a preliminary to subsidising the Afghan nation and ultimately occupying Herat. So vast a pile of impracticable

schemes seems more like some dream of conquest than a
sober system of imperial defence.

"The meaning of distance, the necessity of support, the
physical difficulties of countries, the moral difficulties of
races, the future outlay involved, and the present financial
position of India seem alike defied or ignored in such
astounding speculations. In the name of common sense let
us deal with the difficulties and responsibilities which we
have already, and economize the means which are still left
at our disposal.

"There is not in the East a more independent people
than the Afghans, or one with a stronger country; and no
foreign power can enter it, whether English or Russian,
without being an object of bitter hatred and prolonged
resistance.

"From a policy that would throw these difficulties on
us instead of Russia, the minds of many will revert to the
more practical plan of strengthening the defences of our
north-west frontier.

"Can we do better than accept the position which
Providence has given us? Let us neither take more territory nor give up what we have. The mountain frontier
which happened to us in 1849 has stood the strain of an
imperial convulsion. It is still more capable, I believe, of
repelling an invasion.

Result.
Accept our
mountain
frontier.

"While our empire in India was expanding and advancing from the twenty-four pergunnahs and the sea to
the Punjab and its mountain wall, instinct seemed to tell us
not to stop and strive after a finality of frontier by building
forts midway in vast plains. But as there must be limits to
empire, as to other things, no one can, I think, take a broad
view of the map of Asia and not be satisfied that the
Himalaya and the Sulimanee range are Nature's frontier of
Hindoostan. Quit it, and we shall find no other definite
frontier in Central Asia.

Fortify the
frontier.

"At last, then, we may betake ourselves to setting up
and fencing in our boundaries, to the securing of a definite
and completed conquest, by a system of imperial forts and
military communications worthy of the great interests to be
guarded and the great dangers to be met.

"The Grand Trunk lines of railroad from the ports of
Calcutta, Madras, Bombay, and Kurrachee, to Lahore and
Peshâwur, which have already been decided and partially
executed,* are equally necessary for holding India and developing its wealth. All that remains, therefore, is to crown
these lines with a chain of forts from Peshâwur to Kurrachee,
and unite them to the railway by good roads, a bridge at
Attock,† and an effective flotilla of river-steamers on the
Indus.

"My own impression is, that the strength of the defence
may be concentrated upon the Peshâwur and Shikarpoor
borders, and that very subordinate measures will suffice
along the majority of the line; for, assuredly, an army
adequate to the invasion of India must pour its masses
through the Khyber or Bolan, or both, though its auxiliaries
may scramble through the Peywur, Gwylerec, and still more
difficult passes in the districts of Dera Ghazee Khan and
Sindh.

"I believe that the adoption of this policy and the
erection of such defensive works would go far to assure the
minds of our neighbours, not only in Afghanistan and
Beloochistan, but also in Persia and Russia, that we had
finally chosen our frontier and meant to advance no further.

"It would help Afghans and Beloochees to believe that
our interests as regards invasion from the west are really
one with their own; whereas, nothing could throw such
discredit on our professions of non-interference as an occupation (which we call friendly) of Quetta, which Beloochees

* And now are completed, 1884.
† Now completed.

must, in their hearts, regard as an intrusion, Afghans as a menace, and Persians and Russians as a blunder which would justify an encroachment of their own.

"No military occupation of a foreign soil or nearer approach of outposts to an independent neighbour can ever tend to real friendship. What were the feelings of Shah Soojah and the Suddozie party (to say nothing of the national party) during our stay in Afghanistan? And what were the feelings of the Romans towards the French? Surely nothing but resentment, smothered till it can be smothered no longer."

These were Colonel Edwardes's views expressed in 1858; and later on, when he had left India, he was led again to express himself (in writing to his friend John Lawrence, who was then Governor-General) upon the subject that he had so much at heart, although he had no longer any official charge; for ill-health had brought him home from India in 1865, and it seemed but little likely that he would be able to return there.

But the question of frontier politics was one that very deeply interested him. Edwardes foresaw the great advances Russia would make, which have come with such rapid strides in later years, and he felt convinced that nothing would prevent the two nations from rolling up together. The question was, *how to be best prepared for the meeting?* *

Letter on the subject of Russia and British India, written from England, to Sir John Lawrence.

Edwardes's letter to John Lawrence in 1865.

"July 2, 1866.

"I see that the Russians are busy in Bokhara, and doubtless their boundary will soon be on the Oxus. In time of

Later views, 1868.

---

* It is still a question of the very deepest interest, the extension of the Anglo-Saxon and the Russian power over Asia. If the ancestors of the English and the Russians more than three thousand years ago lived together in central Asia, and subsequently emigrated, some towards the rising and some towards the setting sun, the Slavonic race settling in Russia, and the forefathers of the Anglo-Saxon (a kindred Aryan one) in England, does it seem that, after a variety of revolutions, both branches of the great Aryan race are again to be near neighbours in Central Asia?

peace they would be better neighbours to us than Asiatics; but in time of difficulty in India or Europe, *much the reverse;* and however good for humanity would be the gain of bringing Khaurism under Russia, the loss to humanity would be immensely greater if British India were disturbed.

"I should counsel, therefore, two things: first, coming to a diplomatic understanding with Russia, that she might come up to the Oxus if she liked, and be welcome, so long as she left our Cabul ally alone; and, second, taking some steps to mediate between the contending children of Dost Mahommed, so as to patch up their government as seemed most feasible to those on the spot, either by all keeping their old provinces or otherwise. Were I on the spot, I would volunteer for the job. It is one which either Becher, or Harry Lumsden, or Neville Chamberlain, or Norman, is up to. Somehow or other, I do not think you fully care enough for keeping Afghanistan *as neutral ground between us and Russia,* which can only be done by keeping her *friendly and independent.*

Advocates Afghanistan being kept friendly and independent.

"My own feeling and judgment are clear as to the good policy of doing so. But *time is precious.* The time was when men pooh-poohed 'the Russian bugbear' on the ground that Russia had no idea of extending her boundary towards India. Now that Russia *has* done so, and is next door but one in the same street we live in, these same men turn round and say that 'it does not matter.' Of course, this is a matter of opinion; but my own opinion is, that some day we shall find it matters a good deal. 1867 + Russia would not be easily endured.

"Is there any bridge yet at Attock? *Do* it in your own time. It will be a noble mark. It will never be done until you take some one man, like Purdon, and order him to do it; and don't let it be thrown into the slow cauldron of the department. . . . I see the papers talk of a railroad to Peshâwur. Politically, it will be invaluable.*

"Yours affectionately,

"HERBERT B. EDWARDES."

A few extracts, condensed from the very able paper that has been alluded to already ("Report on the Candahar Mission, by Sir Harry Lumsden "), are quoted by permission, and throw light on a subject which only increases in interest every day. The views of this very able and accomplished officer are of permanent use and interest, and the unanimity of opinion between Edwardes and Lumsden gives them a natural place here.

Extracts from Sir Harry Lumsden's memorandum.

"Muscovite policy has now (1857–78) reached Kokán; Mongolia is her province, and her legions are rapidly closing on China. Afghanistan, therefore, stands isolated, as the only country free of the Russian taint, and to keep her so should be our great aim; but how to attain such a result naturally becomes the question, and one on which I am fully aware that many of our ablest diplomatists have greatly differed.

"My own conviction is that this object will be best obtained by having as little to say to Afghans as possible, beyond maintaining friendly and intimate intercourse with the *de facto* Government; by never on any occasion, interfering with the internal politics of the country, nor assisting any particular faction, but honestly leaving Afghans to manage their own affairs in the way that suits them best. We should endeavour to prevent the interference of Persia or any other power in these matters, and be careful that all our political agents on the frontier are fully instructed in the views of Government and carrying out a common policy. . . .

How to keep Afghanistan strong and independent.

"Unless under the most pressing danger to Afghanistan, and at the spontaneous and urgent demand of that Government itself, no proposition involving the deputing of British officers in the country should for a moment be entertained; for, after the example of Burns, all such missions will ever be looked on with the greatest suspicion, no matter how able the officers to be so employed or what their object.

Non-interference.

* These advantages are now accomplished facts, for both the bridge at Attock and the railroad at Peshâwur are completed.—E. E., 1885.

If the rulers really wish for the services of such men, they will be quick enough in asking for them; for modesty has never been an Afghan weakness. . . .

A strong
frontier.
"Providence has blessed us with a strong line of frontier, covered by rugged and barren hills, through which there are but a limited number of passes by which any army could approach India; and the military art teaches us that the best position for the defence of such ground is on our own side of the passes, just where an army must debouch on the plain. . . .

"Here, then, is our true position, which we are, of course, in common prudence, bound to strengthen in every possible way. . . . The most important and first to be attended to is the opening up of our communications with the real base of all military operations in India—the sea, and connecting these
Supports.
distant points with it by rail and steamers. With Peshâwur, Kohat, and Sindh in our possession, and the communications with our Indian provinces open by rail, and steamers on the Indus, and a strong force of Europeans located in healthy cantonments all over the country, supported by a well-organized native army, I consider that we should really have the keys of India in our own pockets, and be in a position to lock the doors in the face of all enemies, black or white. . . .

"At the same time I would strongly advocate the carrying out a conciliatory policy towards our hill neighbours, but bearing in mind the real Puthân character, whom the touch of money only renders more rapacious, who will swear anything for filthy lucre, but only respect that power which shows ability to punish with the one hand and reward with the other. . . .

Success of
the con-
ciliatory
policy of
the
Peshâwur
authorities.
"Our Peshâwur authorities have, ever since the Punjab became ours, pursued a policy towards the Afreedee tribes, the fruits of which are already ripening, and which in a few more years must lead to happiest results.—H. B. L."

Some letters have just come out in a periodical print, called "Jottings on Afghanistan, by a Khyberee," which touch the subject in a concise way, and, as evidence on the spot, may close these remarks.

A Khy-
beree's
views of
affairs in
1885.
"It can hardly be expected that a poor traveller, whose time has been spent in the rocky defiles of the Khyber, can possibly have any definite views of Afghan policy. Such

regions are not favourable to intellectual growth. But we in
the Khyber have seen some changes within the last eighty
years, and no mistake.

"We have seen Shah Shoojah, then a handsome young
fellow of thirty years of age, march through an inhospitable
pass to welcome the gorgeous mission of Mountstuart Elphinstone in 1809.

"This was the 'alarmist policy.' Then came the 'med-
dling policy' in 1832, when Secundar Burns passed through
on his 'commercial mission;' and again in 1838, when
General Keane advanced into Afghanistan. The British
frontier was then at Ferozepore, some three hundred miles
from the Afghan frontier. The Punjab had not been annexed. A powerful native chief ruled the province. And
yet, in the face of all these difficulties, a British army invaded Afghanistan simply to dethrone a popular Barakzaie
chief, Dost Mahommed, and to place on the throne a mere
puppet of a king. The Cabul disasters are well known.

"In 1848 the Punjab was annexed. The frontier line of
British India was moved from Ferozepore to the Khyber Pass.
Then it was that the whole political situation became changed.
Cabul was being governed by a truly great and popular
ruler, the Dost whom England had dethroned and restored.

"It was then that a state policy became really necessary,
and it was one of 'masterly activity.' Dost Mahommed, in
1854, concluded a treaty of alliance with his old enemies.
The treaty had three articles."

(We have seen it made, and followed its course in the
preceding pages.)

"Some would tell us that this policy of masterly activity
was inaugurated by Sir John Lawrence, but there is positive
proof that it was Sir Herbert Edwardes who brought about
the treaty.

"John Lawrence, it is true, signed it, but his correspondence with Colonel Edwardes shows that he did not
believe in its utility.

"Dost Mahommed kept that treaty, and during the Indian
Mutiny of 1857–58 the whole Afghan frontier was tranquil.
Our best allies before Delhi, next to the Sikhs, were Edwardes's
Afghan levies and Derâjat ones.

" Sir John Lawrence's real policy was that of ' masterly inactivity.' John Lawrence was a noble character, true and good. He was a great administrator, but he was not a statesman. He ruled India very much as our American cousins ' run a store.' Lord Lawrence thought the River Indus, rather than the great passes, the best frontier of India.

" His policy with regard to Afghanistan was to recognize the *de facto* ruler of Cabul ; consequently he had a word of encouragement, not only for Shere Ali when he reigned in peace, but also for his rival brothers, Afzul and Azim, when they seized their brother's throne. It pleased no one ; it offended both parties. But, unfortunately, this policy did not expire with his term of office.

" In the mean time Russia annexed Bokhara, Kokân, and Khiva. . . .

" In 1873 Shere Ali became alarmed at the Russian progress, and sought the aid of the English Government. But to the Ameer's appeal for help the Liberal Government replied, ' We do not share his alarm ; there is no cause for it.' This drove Shere Ali, the Ameer of Cabul, into the arms of Russia.

" When Disraeli came into power, an attempt was made to begin a policy of ' masterly determination ;' but it was too late. What the policy was may be seen from the draft of the treaty presented by Sir Lewis Pelly at the Peshâwur conference. . . . But Shere Ali was already driven into the arms of the Russian rival.

" An Afghan war was the result. . . . When the Liberals came into power, then began the ' scuttling-out policy.' The rails of the Quetta railway were, according to our last Indian authority, sold for old iron in the Indian bazaars. . . .

" What will be the future policy of England regarding Afghanistan it is impossible to say. With a man like Lord Dufferin at the helm in India, it seems likely that Afghan affairs will now cease to be a matter of party strife."

And here we close the Kyberee's thoughts and jottings, and the reader will take them for what he thinks them worth on this much-vexed question of Afghan politics.

Some thoughts of Edwardes's, culled from other sources and relating to this frontier question, are put together, and will close this chapter.

On the "Destiny of the Anglo-Saxons."

"It is commonly asserted to be the 'destiny' of the Anglo-Saxons to overrun Central Asia and other eastern countries. Is it presumption to undertake to interpret it? The tempting theory is called in the *Friend of India*, the right of the sane man over the insane. Who is to decide between? The sane man, even in Europe, does not confine himself always to putting the insane man under restraint, but takes the insane man's property for his own use! It is *the next heir* who is usually possessed with the humane design of putting the madman in confinement.

"The doctrine has its allurements, and so have the kindred cries of Chartists, Socialists, and Mormons; but we ourselves think it smacks of dishonesty.

"'Fools rush in where angels fear to tread.' We 'rushed in' once as far as Cabul and Herat, and might well 'fear to tread' that destiny again. If our destiny—of course we shall go.

"Meanwhile, let us watch reverently to see what this same 'destiny' has undeniably put under our charge —India. Let us attend to its well administration and Christianizing, which is the object for which it has been given to us.

"And first, to remedy the defects of our present organization, especially the native army.

"It may not unlikely prove that our destiny is *not* to take us beyond the Sulimanee range, which is the natural wall of India. Once go beyond that, and we see no well-defined boundary before us. We are launched on Central Asia.

"The *Westminster Review* says, 'The day must come when Cabul and the Hindoo Koosh will be our boundary;' and if so, it will not be for long. It is no boundary at all. Even Dost Mahommed Khan has crossed it and annexed

Bulkh, and holds both as parts of a whole, looking askance at Bokhara and Herat."

" Russia has a great advantage in the unity and constancy of her designs. It is a common saying that Peter the Great laid down the foreign policy of Russia, and common observation that his successors have adhered to it. She has doubtless laid down the boundary she intends to have, whether it rest on the Persian Gulf, the Sulimanee range, the Bay of Bengal, or the Pacific Ocean. There is nothing indefinite in *her* plans, and she fills them in as ladies do worsted-work—a bit at a time, often laying the canvas down when there are other things to do, but taking it up again in the first leisure moment and inserting a wreath, a flower, a single leaf, a needleful of wool—but all according to the pattern.

" The policy of England wants this breadth and fixedness of purpose. We have lived from hand to mouth in our career. This did not matter when Russia was at Orenberg and England on the Sutlej. The question becomes pressing *now*. Where do we mean to fix the British boundary in Central Asia—if *we can?*

" Let it be considered fully, and a policy adopted and acted on. Let the frontier we mean to stand by be fortified by our soldiers in times of peace.

" If there is anything like a conclusion of policy traceable in our proceedings, it is to make Afghanistan a ' buffer' between India and every danger. In 1808 we made an offensive and defensive treaty with Shah Shoojah on his throne. In 1838 we failed to come to terms with Dost Mahommed Khan, and we undertook to depose him, and to rethrone Shah Shoojah. In 1842 we released Dost Mahommed from prison, in order that he might re-occupy the throne of Cabul as our friend. In 1848 Dost Mahommed Khan joined our enemies the Sikhs, and all Afghans expected us to add Cabul to the Punjab; yet in 1854 we again reverted to the policy of the ' buffer,' and forgave Dost Mahommed's enmities."

" The *Friend of India* has lately contemplated, if not actually advocated, the occupation of Afghanistan as a better policy.

" There are three possible policies—

" 1. To take and hold Afghanistan in our own interest.

" 2. Never to take it; but, whenever necessary, occupy it as friends, and fight Russia on the Persian or Turcoman frontier.

" 3. To resolve to stick to our present frontier, and fight Russia, whenever Russia assails us, at the eastern mouths of the passes.

" On the threshold of this question we hold that we could not adopt this first policy without first having fair cause of quarrel ; and we protest against the brigand doctrine, that the white man has a vested right to take the country of the black, brown, or whitey-brown man. . . .

" Advancing to the eastern boundary of Afghanistan, as in policy No. 2, would be dividing the difficulties with Russia, bringing on us the enormous expense of transporting military stores so far, making enemies of the Afghans, and departing so far from our base of operations and railroads. . . .

" By waiting on our present frontier, we husband our money, organize our line of defence, rest upon our base and railroads, save our troops from fatigue, and bring our heaviest artillery into the field ; while the enemy can only bring light guns over the passes, has to bribe and fight his way across Afghanistan, wears out and decimates his army, exhausts his treasure and carriage, and, when defeated, has to retreat through the passes and over all Afghanistan—plundered at every march by tribes who would as soon cut the throat of a Russian as an English kafir ; perhaps sooner, for there is a distinct feeling

Three possible policies discussed.

The first rejected.

The second also.

The third preferred.

throughout Afghanistan that the Russians are not so trustworthy as the English."

" The dangers of a defensive policy are to be considered—risings behind us. Above all, we have to fear the native army, unless placed on a sounder footing.*

Dangers considered.

" The opinions of many as to the disaffection of the secularly-educated natives is a danger. It must be so, unless corrected by Christianity.

" On this subject, too, legislation should be broad and far-seeing, recognizing the probability that when we have taught the natives how to govern themselves they may wish to do so.

Aims compared.

" If we keep this in mind, our measures will aim at parting friends. If we ignore it and aim at the retention of India for our own national benefit, our legislation must become more repressive and harsh year by year, as knowledge spreads among the natives.

" Assuming policy No. 3 to be adopted, the subordinate question arises whether we should cultivate friendly and defensive relations with the countries beyond us, encouraging and aiding them to some extent in resisting Russian or pro-Russian encroachments, and so delaying the day of conterminous Russian and British boundary, or should abstain from anything further than civility and good neighbourhood, distinctly giving the outside chiefs to understand that they must make their own arrangements."

" Abstractedly it would be far better that Russia should rule in Persia, Cabul, Khiva, Bokhara, and Kokân, than the present native sovereigns. It would be a gain to mankind. (See Colonel Sutherland's Sketches and Ferrier's account of the internal administration of Persia and Afghanistan and the slave-dealing Turcoman states. I think Kaye in

---

* This was written before the mutiny of the native army of 1857, and shows how truly Edwardes estimated the dangerous organization of that army before that terrible catastrophe.

his 'History of Afghanistan' gives strong opinions of Conolly's on this point.)

"These considerations would seem to point to the propriety of not opposing the march of civilization from whatever quarter it may approach; and of coming to an amicable understanding with Russia, communicating to her the boundary we meant to maintain for British India, and renouncing all intention of interfering beyond that limit, leaving Russia to deal with the intermediate countries according to her own sense of justice or interest.

"But though we do not deem such a policy Utopian, and hope to see the day when it may be acted on with safety, yet, unfortunately, we are not prepared to recommend it now. It would demand either implicit confidence in Russia's objects or in the strength of our own position. We have neither.

"The Vicovitch history, the invasion of Kokán, the Menschikoff War with Turkey, Czar Nicholas's overtures to Sir Horace Seymour, Czar Alexander's fulfilment of the Treaty of Paris, have all left painful impressions that cannot easily be effaced."

"We class Russia for the future, by virtue both of extraction and morality, under the head, not of European but of Asiatic powers.

"The policy of Russia, however, would matter little to England if secure in her own position in India.—H. B. E."

CHAPTER X.

1853—1854.

THE PESHÂWUR MISSION TO THE AFGHANS.

" Such incense as of right belongs
     To the true shrine,
Where stands the *Healer of all wrongs*
     In light divine ;
The golden censer in His hand,
He offers hearts from every land,
Tied to His own by gentlest band
     Of silent Love ;
About Him wingèd blessings stand
     In act to move."

KEBLE.

CHAPTER X.

In the preceding chapters our attention has been fixed upon Afghan politics, and the thread of the story could not be broken to trace the origin of the Christian mission, which was first established at Peshâwur in 1853.

There can be no mission in any part of the world which can reach a lengthened existence without exhibiting in its history many interesting events. The position of the Peshâwur mission gives it an especial claim to interest.

Peshâwur being geographically a part of Afghanistan, the picket to British India, the people who inhabit it are Afghans. On the east is the river Indus; on the western side, the Sulimanee range of mountains, in which stands the Khyber Pass. From that pass to the Indus is about fifty miles; and on the south side stands the Kohat Pass. The hills of Swât shut in the north. Peshâwur geographically Afghanistan.

The valley lying between these ranges and the river Indus is most fertile, and produces crops and fruits in luxuriant abundance. For this valley the tribes have all contended for ages past, and the tribes that inhabit those mountain ranges are the fiercest clans that can be found anywhere on the face of the globe.

Edwardes says—

"I do not think that finer specimens of physical human nature can be found. Nurtured on those hills, with very little to support them, they have been reared in constant warfare. Each man is armed to the teeth, and goes forth with his hand against every man, prepared to meet every man's hand against him. Edwardes's description of Peshâwur.

"Whatever truth or whatever falsehood there may be in Lord Macaulay's description of the mountain-clans of our own north, I must say that if you were to take those pages and apply them to the inhabitants of the Khyber Pass and Afghan Mountains, you would find it suit exactly.* They possess every vice with which human nature is afflicted; but they have their virtues too.

"They have the great virtue of manly courage, and they have the great virtue of hospitality. When the English soldier is brought in contact with them, it is a refreshment, after coming from the slavish plains, to meet a race able to struggle with him for empire."

If you were to look over the map of Asia, certainly over the map of British India, and were to select the spot most uncongenial for the establishment of a mission, you would put your finger on Peshâwur.

The founder was a military officer, one of the best and most consistent and earnest among our Indian Christians, Colonel Martin, of the 9th Bengal Native Infantry. He had formed a desire to devote £1000 to the purpose of establishing a Christian mission in the Punjab. This officer's

---

* At present the principles by which Puthâns especially are guided in their intercourse with each other are those of retaliation—blood for blood, injury for injury, "an eye for an eye, and a tooth for a tooth."

An amusing instance of this occurred in a visit Edwardes paid one day in the hills. His host, a man of gigantic stature, to do honour to his visitor drew out his bed for a seat; and Edwardes was in his own mind amused for some time at the ridiculous disproportion of its size, being a very short one. At last he said to his host, "It surprises me how you, so tall a man, can lie upon a bed so very short." "Oh," said he, "I have a short bed in order to oblige me to sleep with my knees up, that I may sleep lightly! Do you see that smoke curling up from the hill below?" Edwardes looked where he pointed, and he saw a slight curl of smoke rising in the air. "That smoke is from the house of my enemy," said the man; "I am *two ahead of that man* now, and I must sleep lightly. If I were to stretch myself out straight upon my charpoy, I should sleep so soundly that he would catch me asleep; but by sleeping with my knees up, I wake easily!"

"Two ahead" meant that he had killed two members of the other man's family, that had to be paid off.—E. E.

regiment was stationed at Peshâwur, and this circumstance naturally localized his interest there.

He sent anonymously, and he thought secretly, Rs.10,000 to the Church Missionary Society, with the request that they would commence missionary work. But nothing of that kind could be done without the sanction and support of the chief civil authority on the spot, who was Colonel Mackeson, the Commissioner and Governor-General's Agent on the Peshâwur frontier.

When Colonel Martin asked for the Commissioner's permission, he met with a distinct refusal. Colonel Mackeson would not sanction it in any way, or even permit it; and he assured Colonel Martin that the first missionary who crossed the Indus at Attock to enter the Peshâwur Valley should be turned back by his orders.

Mission forbidden by the Commissioner, Colonel Mackeson.

Peshâwur is a large Mohammedan city, filled with Afghans and fanatical hill-tribes, with a population of not less than sixty thousand, and it had comparatively recently come under English rule; for, having been conquered from the Afghans by Runjeet Singh, the time was not so long distant when it had held its place in the map of Afghanistan.* Politically, therefore, Colonel Mackeson conceived that it was a dangerous experiment to plant a Christian mission there. The proposal was necessarily dropped.

But Colonel Martin was still at Peshâwur at the time of Colonel Mackeson's assassination and of Colonel Edwardes's arrival to succeed him. He lost no time in bringing the matter before Edwardes, and sounding him to discover what his views were.

Edwardes knew nothing of the previous attempt or previous failure; but, on being asked for his support, he warmly gave the right hand of fellowship to Colonel

Support given by Colonel Edwardes.

---

* Peshâwur is much celebrated for its schools of Mohammedan learning, and also as a commercial centre. Those who resort thither for these purposes are brought into direct contact with Christianity. And there is now a mission church, where the gospel is preached, in which a portion is railed off for their accommodation, where natives are allowed to come in at their will and listen to the preaching in their own tongue. And there many are often seen. This is an interesting feature of the Peshâwur mission.

Martin, and assured him that he would heartily support and approve it, and not be ashamed to own himself a Christian ; that, privately, he and his wife would assist the mission with their purse, and publicly, he would give the missionaries the protection which they could rightly claim, and which was extended to every other religion.

Mission resolved upon.

This was all that was required or asked, and a meeting was called of the European residents at Peshâwur, at which Colonel Edwardes presided, and the mission was established. The Church Missionary Society in Salisbury Square was invited to send fit men to start it.

Colonel Edwardes's own words, in addressing this meeting on December 19, 1853, will best explain his thoughts, and show that it was not alone as a true *Christian* that he supported missions (having regard to the command of his Master), but also as a *statesman*, with his own independent views of frontier rule, "that we are much *safer* if we do our duty." He said—

Edwardes's speech.

"Ladies and gentlemen,—It is my duty to state briefly the object of this meeting, but happily, it is not necessary to enlarge much either on that or on the general duty of assisting missions. A full sense of both brings us here to-day. A few practical resolutions will be proposed for your adoption or correction, and I will not occupy time by travelling over the same ground as the speakers who will move and second them. But, as Commissioner of this frontier, it is natural that of all in this room I should be the one to view the question in its public light, and I wish to state what I understand to be the mutual relations of the Christian Government and Christian missions of this country—our duties as public and private men in religious matters.

"That man must have a very narrow mind who thinks that this immense India has been given to our little England for no other purpose than for our own aggrandizement—for the sake of cadetships for our poor relations.

"Such might be the case if God did not guide the world's

affairs ; for England, like any other land, if left to its own selfishness and its own strength, would seize all it could.

"But the conquests and wars of the world all happen as the world's Creator wills them ; and empires come into existence for purposes of His, however blindly intent we may be upon our own.

"And what may we suppose His purposes to be ? Are they of the earth, earthy ? Have they no higher object than the spread of vernacular education, the reduction of taxes, the erection of bridges, the digging of canals, the increase of commerce, the introduction of electric telegraphs, and the laying down of grand lines of railroad ? Do they look no further than these temporal triumphs of civilization, and see nothing better in the distance than the physical improvement of a decaying world ?

"We cannot think so meanly of Him with whom ' one day is as a thousand years, and a thousand years as one day.' All His plans and purposes must look through time into eternity ; and we may rest assured that the East has been given to our country for a mission, neither to the minds nor bodies, but to the souls of men.

"And can we doubt what that mission is ? Why should England be selected for this charge from the other countries of Europe ?

"The Portuguese preceded us, and the French followed us here. The Pope of Rome gave India to the one, and the God of War was invoked to give it to the other. Yet our Protestant power triumphed over both ; and it is a remarkable coincidence, that the East India Company was founded just two years after the great reformation of the English Church. I believe, therefore, firmly, and I trust not uncharitably, that the reason why India has been given to England is because England has made the greatest efforts to preserve the Christian religion in its purest apostolic form, has most stoutly protested against idolatry in any shape, and sought no other mediator than the one revealed in the Bible.

"Our mission, then, in India is to do for other nations what we have done for our own. To the Hindoos we have to preach one God, and to the Mohammedans to preach one Mediator.

"And how is this to be done? By state armies and state persecutions? By demolishing Hindoo temples, as Máhmud of Ghuznee did? Or by defiling mosques with Mohammedan blood, as Runjeet Singh did?

"It is obvious that we could not, if we would, follow such barbarous examples. The thirty thousand Englishmen in India would never have been seen ruling over two hundred millions of Hindoos and Mohammedans, if they had tried to force Christianity upon them with the sword.

"The British Government has wisely maintained a strict neutrality in religious matters; and Hindoos and Mohammedans, secure of our impartiality, have filled our armies and built up our empire.

"It is not the duty of the Government, as a Government, to proselytize India. Let us rejoice that it is not; let us rejoice that pure and impure motives, religious zeal and worldly ambition, are not so lamentably mixed up.

"The duty of evangelizing India lies at the door of private Christians; the appeal is to private consciences, private effort, private zeal, and private example. Every Englishman and Englishwoman in India—every one now in this room—is answerable to do what he can towards fulfilling it.

"And this day we are met to do so—to provide the best means we can for spreading the gospel to the countries around us. They happen to be Mohammedan countries of peculiar bigotry.

"Sad instances of fanaticism have occurred under our eyes: and it might be feared, perhaps, in human judgment, that greater opposition would meet us here than elsewhere. But I do not anticipate it. The gospel of peace will bear its own fruit and justify its name. Experience, too, teaches us not to fear.

"The great city of Benares was a far more bigoted capital of Hindooism than Peshawur is of Mohammedanism; yet it is now filled with our schools and colleges and mission, and its pundits are sitting at the feet of our professors, earnestly and peacefully, though doubtless sadly, searching after truth.

"There is a circumstance in the movement now going on at Benares which is well worth our notice here. It had been the usual practice of European teachers to ignore all Hindoo philosophy, to tell the natives that they had no science of their own, and then to invite them to begin from the beginning in European method.

"There was something very unconciliatory, almost insulting, in thus treating a people who knew how to calculate the stars in ages when our own ancestors were painting themselves blue, and worshipping the oak and the mistletoe in the forest with the most barbarous and inhuman rites. Dr. Ballantyne has, I am told, pursued a very different process. He first went to school to the pundits, and then asked the pundits to come to school to him. He learned all their science, and sounded all their philosophy; and then, taking them up at the point where they could go no farther, he opened to them regions beyond, and led them forward to the light of truth. . . .

"If this could be done with the Polytheists of Benares, what may we not hope to do with the Afghans? *They* have much more in common with us—a one and a living God; Mosaic tradition; nay, a belief in Christ. There are good grounds for supposing that the Afghans are the descendants of Israel. And if that supposition be true, what a world of common sympathy and common hopes does it open out between us! How strikingly applicable will then be the passage, 'For if thou wert cut out of the olive tree which is wild by nature, and wert graffed contrary to nature into a good olive tree: how much more shall these, which be the natural branches, be graffed into their own olive tree?'

"For these reasons, I say plainly that I have no fear that the establishment of a Christian mission at Peshâwur will tend to disturb the peace.

"It is, of course, incumbent upon us to be prudent, to lay stress upon the selection of discreet men for missionaries, to begin quietly with schools, and wait the proper time for preaching. But having done that, I should fear nothing.

"In this crowded city we may hear the Brahmin in his temple sound his shunkh and gong; the Muezzin on his lofty minaret fill the air with the azan; and the civil Government, which protects them both, will take upon itself the duty of protecting the Christian missionary who goes forth to preach the gospel.

"Above all, we may be quite sure that we are much safer if we do our duty than if we neglect it, and that He who has brought us here with His own right arm will shield and bless us if, in simple reliance upon Him, we try to do His will." *

---

* The Rev. Robert Clark was present at this meeting. He writes, "I was invited to Peshâwur in the winter of 1853, and on December 9 a public meeting was held.

"Few meetings like this have ever, we believe, either before or since, been held in India. It was the day of the Peshâwur races, and it was suggested that the day which had been fixed for the missionary meeting should be deferred.

"'Put off the work of God for a steeplechase?' exclaimed our friend Colonel Martin, fresh from his closet of prayer. 'Never!'

"The meeting was not postponed on account of the races, but was held on the appointed day. There were comparatively few present, but God's Spirit has been invited by prayer, and He was present, and He made His presence unmistakably felt, and men's hearts, and women's hearts, too, then burned within them, as they spake one to another, and heard the words of Sir Herbert Edwardes, which seemed to be almost inspired, when he took the chair at the meeting. His speech, which at

Brave, noble words, but yet so simply spoken; for they were but spoken out of the fulness of a noble heart, that *feared not* to honour God.

The grounds for supposing the Afghans to be the descendants of Israel seem of too much interest to be altogether omitted; and yet, the question being one of such differing opinions, it would occupy too much of our space here.

But the broad subject of Englishmen and English statesmen supporting missions is of general interest and importance, and it is well to mark and observe *who* were the men who have gained the *most* influence among the natives of India, and who have induced the greatest amount of good service to the British Government.

The Oriental is religious, and he admires a man who holds his faith fast and lives an earnest and a religious life. Some of the most prominent characters in Anglo-Indian history have been men of decidedly religious feelings: D'Arcy Todd, who held Herat; Colin Mackenzie, in our Cabul disasters long ago. And in later times it would be almost invidious to *try* to name the men, who are so many, whom the Mutiny brought out, who showed their colours as true Christians and did the noblest work, but we may name such men as Henry Lawrence and his brothers, Robert Montgomery, and Donald McLeod, whom the natives called a ferishta (angel), Hope Grant, Henry Durand, Bartle Frere, and William Muir, whom all will agree to honour, to illustrate the remark. It is a mistake to suppose that the Mohammedans respect a man who is ashamed of his religion, and false to his God. Herbert Edwardes's open support of the mission never lost him a native friend. The natives *understood him.* And when the news reached the frontier of his *death*, the remark was made by them, "God cannot mean *good for India* if He has taken away such a man as Herbert Edwardes!" They loved as well as feared him.

the time 'thrilled through all India,' we give above. After the meeting the following words were read: 'Not unto us, O Lord, not unto us, but unto Thy Name give the praise, for Thy mercy and for Thy truth's sake. Wherefore should the heathen say, Where is now their God? As for our God, He is in heaven.'

"So was started this great work."

It was not the natives on this frontier that were alarmed at the proposal to establish a Christian mission. Bold, warlike, brave, and independent, they were very different races to any other amongst whom our missionaries had laboured in other parts of India; but, with care in the selection of the missionaries to be sent, Edwardes had no misgivings.

The large city of Peshâwur is, next to Cabul, the most important city in Afghanistan. There is a large military cantonment and a strong force of troops.

Of course, in a large society, opinions would be divided; worldly men would not approve, and timid men would fear. And so, when the subscription list went round, some captain thought it a good joke to put his name down for "one rupee towards a Colt's revolver for the first missionary;" and then his juniors followed the lead, or varied the joke as best they could. But, nevertheless, the offering was made, and God accepted it; and the mission was planted, and was watered with "His blessing that maketh rich."

Two good men were chosen—Dr. Pfander, the able Mohammedan controversialist; and the Rev. Robert Clark, so much respected and well-beloved, and who is still engaged in mission work in the Punjab. With them was associated the Christian officer, Colonel Martin, who had resigned the army and was now engaged in mission work in Peshâwur. A better selection could not have been made, for these men were cautious and wise as well as able.

We may quote from the words of Rev. Valpy French, now Bishop of Lahore, who spoke in 1869 at Murree, in the Punjab.

The Bishop of Lahore on Dr. Pfander.

"My friend, Dr. Pfander, a man of most revered memory, gave the key-note and first vigorous impulse to the Peshâwur mission. A man of the true missionary type, and for forty years invariably and dauntlessly standing in the breach, first in Persia; next, and for the greater part of his life, in India; last of all, and to the very death, in Constantinople unfurling the gospel banner with a burning love to souls, his heart immovably fixed and set on one aim—the preaching that word whose entrance giveth light, and enduring affliction with the gospel, according to the power of God.

"There was Herbert Edwardes, too, placed by God's

providence in very different circumstances, yet of a kindred spirit, of like courage, boldness, endurance, singleness of aim, his loins girded to like ventures of faith,—the heroic, chivalrous Christian champion. Few men have died more wept and regretted. Many a man, even proud, hardly Puthàns, were seen to shake their heads at the tidings of his early removal, as if to say that it was an ill day which lost to themselves and the empire a man of such eminence and promise, such manliness, purity, simplicity, and truth. He, too, had no small hand in the foundation of the Peshàwur mission.

Herbert Edwardes.

"And Clark, too, whom we all love and honour, and delight to follow; and so I might go on supplementing Heb. xi. out of the annals of the Peshàwur mission."

Robert Clark.

Such a total absence was there of fanatical opposition, that even during the testing time of the Mutiny of 1857–58, which tried so many of our Christian missionary stations, the work was little interfered with at Peshàwur. Once only, and that but for a day or two, did the children fail to come to the school; after that, they returned again as usual.

The missionaries were able to open their Bible in the city and preach the gospel, as they had been accustomed to do before, throughout the whole of that trying period.

Thus the truth of those words was *proved*, that "we are *safer* if we do our duty than if we neglect it."

To his wife, four years later, in the midst of the Mutiny, Colonel Edwardes was able to write as follows :—

"It is of no use to talk of wise or vigorous measures, though in General Sydney Cotton we have had the best of commanders.

"But providence, God's mercy, has alone kept this frontier in the wonderful state of peace that it has enjoyed since this Mutiny invited the very worms to come out of the earth. I assure you I never thought we could have got through this summer without a bloody conflict. Often and often we have been on the verge of it; but is it not a perfect miracle that, while all the Bengal Presidency is convulsed, Peshâwur has had less crime than was known in it before?

"I have no sort of doubt that we have been honoured because we honoured God in establishing the mission."

So the fears of the timid came to nought, the requisition was accepted by the society at home, and a favourable response was returned to Peshâwur. The missionaries arrived, and the mission began its work.

On February 12, 1855, another meeting was called at Peshâwur on the same subject, and Colonel Edwardes said—

Second
speech at
Peshâwur.

"Little more than a year has passed since we met in this room and addressed a requisition to the committee of the Church Missionary Society of London, for help in the establishment of a Christian mission at Peshâwur; and we then pledged ourselves to use our utmost efforts to further the objects of the mission of that society, by soliciting both contributions and subscriptions for its support. We now meet again together to see how our requisition has been answered and how our pledges have been kept.

"And now, on February 12, 1855, we see two ordained and one lay missionary present here among us.

"The actual selection of the missionaries for this post was left to the local authorities in India, and I cannot but believe that the choice has been wisely guided by His hand who is ever on the watch to help those who serve Him.

Mr.
Pfander.

"The Rev. Mr. Pfander has been a missionary for thirty years in the Russian provinces of the Caucasus and Georgia, in Persia, in Turkey, and in India, and the result is a rare knowledge of the principles and practice of the Mohammedan nations of the world.

"At his last station, Agra, Mr. Pfander had found a wide sphere of usefulness, and the learned Mohammedans there were taking a deep interest in his writings.

"I believe that the controversial works of no missionary

in India have yet aroused such misgivings and made such
an impression on thinking Mohammedan minds as those of
Mr. Pfander, because he knew their own books and met
them on their own ground.

"While, however, we must regard it as a great privilege
that he has been given to us, I think that we may fairly
add that no mission had so great a claim upon him as the
mission to the Afghans, which is addressed to a purely
Mohammedan nation, and whose standard is planted at the
outpost of British India and the door of Central Asia.

"Some happy incidents have marked his coming.
The first native Christian baptized at Peshâwur (and
now here present) is a Persian youth, who left his native
country and came to Peshâwur in consequence of reading
Mr. Pfander's 'Mizân-ul-hâqq.' Another Persian, the editor
of the Peshâwur native newspaper, remembers him and his
labours at Shirâz, and congratulates his readers on the
arrival of one so learned and so good. And lastly, the war
now raging between Russia and our country is marked by
this happy episode—that Russia banished this same preacher
of the gospel twenty years ago from Central Asia, and, after
a circuit of many thousand miles, England brings him back
to it again, and says the Bible is free wherever there is
British rule.

"Nor is Mr. Pfander less fortunate in his colleagues
than they in him. Mr. Clark and Colonel Martin were the
fathers and founders of the mission, and they will watch
over it with the more love and care that they first called it
into existence.

"I think it would be impossible to combine deep knowledge, mature experience, ardent missionary zeal, and valuable local knowledge more completely in any three men
than in Mr. Pfander, Mr. Clark, and Colonel Martin; and we
have reason to be grateful to the society for a selection so
entirely in accordance with our requisition of last year.

Mr.
Pfander's
colleagues.

"And now let us see if our own pledges to collect funds in aid have been equally well kept.

"You are aware that a full report of our last meeting was printed and circulated throughout India, and no sooner was it received than it was responded to from all quarters with a readiness and liberality perhaps seldom experienced by any Indian mission.

"The commander-in-chief and Lady Gomm gave £100, and a glance at the list of the subscribers will show what numerous and what liberal friends of missions the army and civil service of India contain. I would especially mention one who is a bright example of the Christian use of influence and high position—Mr. Henry Carre Tucker, the Commissioner of Benares.

"This gentleman not only gave us a large donation himself, but he circulated our report in every district in his large division; and to show what one man can do if he is in earnest, it deserves to be stated that the sums remitted to me by Mr. Tucker alone amounted to Rs.1843. . . .

"The Church Missionary Society, then, will acknowledge, and we have all the satisfaction of feeling, that we have done our part hitherto in this great work. Let us now take care to do the same in future, and prove that we have not been actuated by a momentary enthusiasm, but by steady and lasting principle. . . .

"It is now my gratifying duty to announce to you a contribution whose value is beyond money.

"When last we met, the great desideratum of the mission to the Afghans was to get the Bible in the Afghan tongue. It was supposed never to have been translated into Pushtoo, and two or three officers at Peshâwur had undertaken to translate some of the Gospels.

Discovery of a Pushtoo Bible.

"I at once remembered that in the year 1848, while acting for the Government of the Maharajah Dhuleep Singh, in the Derâjat, I had seen a Pushtoo Testament in the posses-

sion of a fine old Puthān chief, who had received it in his
youth at the Hurdwar Fair, where he had gone to sell horses,
from an English missionary, who told him that if he took
care of it, and preserved it from fire and water, it would
certainly be of use to him some day, when the English
should come to his country.   'That day,' said the old chief,
' has now come ; and here is the book, uninjured by fire or
water ! '

   " So saying, he unrolled it from many wrappers, and I
found that it had been printed at the Serampoor mission,
in 1818.   I read a few lines of it, and saw that it was Pushtoo, in the Persian character.   I asked him if he had ever
read it.   He said, ' Our moollah has read it, and says it is
a very good book, and quite correct ; for Father Abraham
and Father Moses are mentioned in it.'   I returned the
volume to the old man ; and though I fear it was for the
noble qualities of himself and his son, and not for the sake
of the Bible, yet certain it is that Ali Khan Kolachee never
had cause to regret that the English came into his country.

   " Well, this incident flashed across my mind at once,
when I heard everybody wondering what was to be done
to translate the Scriptures into Pushtoo, and I mentioned
it to Colonel Martin.   Application was, I believe, made to
the mission library at Serampoor ; but, strange to say, not
a copy could then be found.

   " I then wrote to my old friend Ali Khan, and recovered
the precious volume ; and I think it is impossible to consider this incident without being struck with awe and
humbled at the long foresight of that omniscient and constant God, who deposits His sealed-up purposes with unconscious man, and tells Futurity the hour to open and to read
them.

   " Thus was one mission at Calcutta, to be established in
1818, made to provide a translation of the Scriptures for
another mission at Peshāwur, to be established in 1855 ;

an Afghan chief was made to preserve one copy of this
message to his countrymen for twenty years, when all others
had either been lost or forgotten ; and I was shown where
that copy was hid, because five years after I was to fill this
chair.   These are startling things ; and may it please God
that none of us try to turn aside from the things He wills
us to accomplish.

"The Pushtoo Testament thus found was placed by
Colonel Martin in the hands of the Afghan branch of the
Bible Society, and they most generously undertook to reprint
and present to this mission three thousand copies of the
Gospels of Luke and John, the Acts of the Apostles, and
the Epistle to the Ephesians.

"There are several exceptional letters in Pushtoo which
differ from the Persian, and, before the reprint could be
effected, new type for all these letters had to be founded.
Captain James furnished the models for these types, and is
now actually engaged in correcting the proof-sheets of this
reprint ; and I claim the gratitude of the meeting both to
the munificent society which has furnished our mission with
three thousand copies of these sacred books, and to Captain
James for the benefit which has been derived so often from
his scholarship and knowledge.

"There is only one more occurrence of the past year
which requires to be reported, and it is one of considerable
interest.

"At the desire of Lord Shaftesbury, who is the president
of the Society for the Conversion of the Jews, a member of
that society addressed to me inquiries 'as to the groundwork
which exists for a mission to Peshawur on the society's
part.'

"I replied that I thought Captain James's researches
rendered it in the highest degree probable that the Afghans
are what they call themselves—sons of Israel ; but that still
it is not certain, and until it is certain I would not advise

diverting the funds of that society from labours among the
thousands of known Jews in other parts of the world.

"I know not, however, what decision the Jews' Society
may come to. A great deal, I should say, would rest on
Captain James's fuller exposition of his own researches ; and
as he is about to leave us for a short visit to England, he
will doubtless find there the leisure which is unattainable
here.

" Whether the Afghans are Jews or not, they are Mohammedans, and, regarding them in that broad light, the Church
Missionary Society has occupied the field.

" They are one of those nations to whom eighteen hundred
years ago our Lord ordered the Gospel to be preached.

" There is a record kept of how that order is obeyed.
Men fill it up themselves, and the world has no volume of
more vital interest ; for the leaves of that Book and the
years of the world will come to an end together. As mission
after mission is sent forth, page after page is turned.

" The blank pages are very few ; and it is a solemn
thought, that on one of those few leaves we ourselves are
now recording that a mission to the Afghans has been
established. Let us see that we write it down in no doubtful
characters, but in bold decided lines ; and may God bless
this mission, for His sake who ordered, and bless this
station and our country's rule for the sake of all who
help it." *

With regard to the remark whether the Afghans are

---

* There is a note written by Edwardes at Abbottabad two years afterwards which comes across the scene now, and goes to show that the effect
was not so dangerous as some had feared, and that the trust and confidence were not misplaced.

"Abbottabad, July 19, 1856.

" I was delighted to hear Mr. Pfander had taken tea with a small party
of fanatics at Kazee Nujeeb's, and came away without a smash of the
teacups.

" It is really wonderful how the mission melts away opposition.

    " (Signed)   H. B. E."

Jews or not, some information on the subject from Major Harry Lumsden will be interesting.

Origin of the Afghans (condensed by E. E.) from the Report of the Candahar Mission of Major Harry Lumsden, in 1857.

Origin
of the
Afghans.

"The Afghans call themselves 'Beni Israel,' or 'children of Israel,' and claim descent in a direct line from Saul, the Benjamite King of Israel. They adduce, however, no authentic evidence in support of their claim, which is not an exclusive one, since they admit all other Mohammedans, Jews, and Christians to be children of Israel, excluding only idol-worshippers and the heathen. . . .

"All the records of the Afghans (and they are mostly traditional) on the subject of their origin and descent are extremely vague and incongruous, without dates, and abounding in fabulous and distorted accounts of the deliverance of the Israelites from Egypt under Moses—of the ark of the covenant (Tábúti-sakiná), of their fights with the Amalekites, Philistines, etc.—and they are, moreover, so mixed up with Mohammedanism as to give the whole the appearance of fiction or uncertainty. . . . The traditions are numerous, but all have a close similitude to the Bible account of the ark and the Deluge, the ark of the covenant, the guiding of the pillar in the desert, the tables of the Law, and many other things. . . .

"Saul, they say, was of a great height. He had two sons, viz. Barakhia and Ramia, or Jeramiah. Jeramiah had a son called Afgháná. Then they have the tradition of the Captivity under Bhuka-u-nasr (Nebuchadnezzar). The tribe of Afgháná adhered to the religion of their forefathers, and on account of the obstinacy with which they resisted the idolatrous faith of their conquerors, were, after the massacre of many thousands of Israelites, for this reason banished from Palestine by order of Bhuka-n-nasr. After this they took refuge in the mountain of Ghor and the Koh-i-Ferózah. Here they were called by the neighbouring people 'Afghans' and 'Ben-i-Israel.' . . .

"At this time, and till the appearance of Mohammed, the

Afghans were readers of the Pentateuch, and observed the ordinances of the Mosaic Law. . . .

"In the ninth year after Mohammed announced himself as the prophet of God, and more than fifteen hundred years after the time of Solomon (this history dates upwards of a century ago), one Khálid-bin-Wálid, an inhabitant of Arabia and an Israelite, and one of the earliest disciples of the new prophet, sent and informed the Afghans of the advent of 'the last prophet of the times,' and exhorted them to accept his doctrine."

The whole subject is thoroughly worked out by Major H. B. Lumsden in his able "Report on the Candahar Mission," of which these are only scanty extracts. Without going further into the tradition for proof, it is easy to believe the fact, when we observe the striking physiognomic resemblance to the Jews and their customs, which are identical or nearly so, such as inheritance of land and its division by lot; offering of sacrifices and sprinkling the blood on the lintel and side-posts of the door to avert pestilence from a house; transferring the sins of a community to the head of a heifer, sheep, or goat, and then sending the animal out into the wilderness; a man marrying his deceased brother's widow; serving for a wife, as Jacob did; and many other such. The veneration for "ziárats," or high places, holy shrines, presided over by a faqir, or a moollah, and invested with false sanctity, and made places of meritorious pilgrimage. These all point to customs and sins of the people, with which the readers of the Old Testament are familiar.

Customs.

Though they will tell you they do not belong to the country, they know nothing of how they came there. "But," according to their own account, "after expulsion from Shám (Palestine) by Bhuka-u-nasr (Nebuchadnezzar), they took refuge in the mountains of Ghor and the 'Koh-i-Ferozah.' Here they were called by the neighbouring people Afghan and Beni-Israel. In these mountains they multiplied and increased greatly, and, after a protracted period of fighting, at length subdued the original inhabitants, and became possessors of the country, and gradually extended their borders towards the Kohistan-i-Cabul, Candahar, and Ghuznee.

"We know by 2 Kings xvii. 6 that 'in the ninth year of Hosea the King of Assyria took Samaria, and carried Israel away into Assyria, and placed them in Halar and Habor, and by the river of Gozan, and in the cities of the Medes.' This occurred under Shalmaneser, King of Assyria, about B.C. 722.

"Two years previously to this, Tiglath-Pileser took Gilead and Galilee, and all the land of Naphthali, and carried the Israelites into Assyria. And subsequently about B.C. 587, after a long series of adversities previously foretold, the Jewish nation was destroyed, and the Jews carried in captivity to Babylon by Nebuchadnezzar. In B.C. 536 Cyrus issued his famous edict, liberating the Jews and all Israelites.

"During the long period of one hundred and eighty-eight years that elapsed from the first carrying away of the Israelites by Tiglath-Pileser to their final restoration by Cyrus, it may be fairly assumed that they became distributed throughout the Medo-Persian empire. We know by Esth. iii. 8 and viii. 9 that the Jews were scattered throughout the provinces of the Medo-Persian empire, from India to Ethiopia."

Page 205 of Major H.B. Lumsden's memorandum.

These extracts from Major H. B. Lumsden's Report will help in tracing this interesting subject; and, without dogmatizing upon it, the idea is further confirmed in conversation with people of the present day, who, if you ask them, "You say you do not know where is your own country from which you came, how then will you know how to return to it?" will answer, "Oh, when the right time comes for us to go back to it, it will be shown us from heaven. The Prophet Esau Masih * will appear in heaven and lead us back to it, and show us the way."

Here we will leave this interesting subject for the present with the remark, "Several of the different hill tribes have no national or kindred affinity whatever with the Afghans, whilst others, though they resemble the Afghans in language, features, and many of their customs, are rejected by them as brethren, and assigned a separate origin, their names not being found in the genealogy of the Afghans.

"The earliest knowledge of them dates B.C. 536. The

* Esau Masih means "Jesus Messiah."

country was the eastern portion of the Medo-Persian kingdom founded by Cyrus, whose boundary was the Indus, beyond
which the world was supposed to terminate in a vast desert.
On the defeat of Darius by Alexander the Great, about B.C.
330, it became a satrapy of the Grecian monarchy. In A.D.
651 the Arabs or Saracens overran Afghanistan, with their
inevitable concomitants, the sword and the Korân. Mâhmud
of Ghuznee captured Delhi A.D. 1011, and brought the gates
of Somnauth (of sandalwood) in triumph from the temple at
Delhi.

"Ghuznee formed the metropolis of the empire, extending
from the Tigris on the west to the Ganges on the east.
The gates were placed at the entrance of his magnificent
mausoleum at Ghuznee," whence Lord Ellenborough eventually restored them to Hindostan again, as we all know.*

It adds to the interest of the narrative thus to trace the
changes that have passed over these people, and now new
prospects are opening to them.

It has been seen that all the community of Englishmen
at Peshâwur were not unanimously in favour of the mission,
and it is a fact to be remembered, while thinking upon
this subject, that the very officer who started the joke of
subscribing "one rupee for a revolver for the first missionary," and who was so alarmed at the "danger" of
bringing a Christian mission among the fanatical border
tribes, shortly afterwards was moved down to Meerut, in
what was considered the "quiet" part of India. He was
there with his regiment when the Mutiny of 1857 broke
out. His name was in the very first list of those who
suffered fearful atrocities at the hands of the Sepoys in the
first outbreak, and not only himself, but he had the unspeakable horror of seeing his wife and children cruelly killed
before his eyes, before his own life was taken.

We cannot forget these fearful things; nor is it well to
forget them! Rather it is wise to trace God's ruling hand,
and learn by His chastisements, as well as by His deliverances, that He is the Ruler of events, however long He may
be pleased to hide His hand, and allow men to carry out, as
it appears to them, their own way.

* They are now stowed away in a store-house in Agra.

A somewhat similar instance to this that we have mentioned above is given by Sir George Crawfurd in *tracing the origin of the "general order"* issued to all military chaplains in India, that they were not to speak at all to the native soldiery on the subject of religion—a prohibition which has remained in force ever since.

Sir George (then Rev. Mr. Crawfurd) was a chaplain at Allahabad in 1830, when the sepoys of the Native Infantry were in the habit, when on duty in the fort, of coming, uninvited, to the chaplain's quarters, and asking him to tell them about the Christian religion.

This he gladly did; and they invited him to come down to their own lines and preach to them, as it was only now and then that they were put on fort duty.

Mr. Crawfurd said he would come with pleasure if they really wished it; and he went, and they were greatly interested in the preaching of the gospel.

But one day, while the listening crowds were thus employed, a shadow crossed the circle, and the major of the regiment appeared. He was angry, and, confronting Mr. Crawfurd, said, " Sir, you are preaching to the sepoys! . You are exciting my men to insubordination. You'll cause an insurrection, sir! and we shall all be murdered at midnight!"

The chaplain said, "The sepoys invited me to come, and I am here by their desire."

" That *must* be false!" said the major.

The chaplain replied, " Ask the sepoys yourself, sir."

The assembly was dispersed quickly. But next day the general commanding the division sent for Mr. Crawfurd. He was a kind man, and was believed to have no objection himself to what had been done; but, yielding to the arguments of the major, he reproved the chaplain, and the matter had to be referred to the Governor-General (Lord William Bentinck); and this was the occasion that drew forth the " general standing orders" that the sepoys were not to be spoken to on the subject of religion.

What a strange retribution there seems to be in events! This same major, who was thus unhappily instrumental in getting this order first given (shutting out the teaching of the *true* nature and spirituality of the Christian faith

from the Sepoy), lived to rise to one of the highest ranks
of the Indian army; and in the great Mutiny of 1857, was
in command at Cawnpore. When the Sepoys rose because
they thought there was a conspiracy by the Government
"to make Christians of them" (by giving them a cartridge
to bite composed of fat that would destroy their caste—
pig's fat, the abomination of the Mohammedan; and bullock's
fat, that the Hindoo should be made to defile his god),
he and his wife and his whole family were the central
figures in a fearful tragedy that appalled all England, in
which numbers were murdered together in wholesale butchery
by the mutineers and the natives whom he had trusted!

If there was no connection between these events of 1830
and 1857, then we must say it was a strange coincidence.
We are not required to judge, but we may mark a lesson for
our own learning, to guide us in the future; and such experi-
ences as these serve to prove the truth of Edwardes's argument at the close of his opening speech at Peshâwur.

"Above all, we may be quite sure that we are much safer
if we do our duty than if we neglect it."

It may be a fitting close to this story of the first establishment of the mission to the Afghans at Peshâwur, to carry
on the record to the present year, 1885, in which this is
written. For thirty years have passed, and now a Christian
mission church stands in the heart of the city of Peshâwur.
It was opened on December 19, 1883, by the same Rev. Robert
Clark, who gives so full and interesting an account of it and
of the work at Peshâwur which has been carried on by the
Rev. T. P. Hughes for the last sixteen years, that it abundantly
shows that God has blessed and prospered the work begun
in 1853.

"OPENING OF THE C.M.S. MEMORIAL MISSION CHURCH
AT PESHÂWUR.*

"On December 19, 1853, it was my privilege, as the first
English missionary, I believe, who ever visited Peshâwur, to

* By the Rev. Robert Clark, M.A.

be present at the celebrated missionary meeting which took place at Peshâwur on the establishment of the Afghan mission. It was then that Sir Herbert Edwardes uttered his memorable speech, which, in the history of Indian missions, has since become historical. It was spoken almost immediately after the death of his predecessor by assassination; and it was under circumstances like these that he and Major Hugh James, Colonel Martin, Sir James Brind, Sir Henry Norman, Colonel Urmston, Colonel Bamfield, Dr. Baddeley, and Mr. Maltby, the chaplain, with other men, and many ladies also, met together to seek by prayer and effort, by God's grace, to commence missionary work amongst the Afghans at Peshâwur. The collection which was made for the mission soon amounted to Rs.30,000; of which Rs.10,000 were given to the parent society by an anonymous friend; Rs.5000 were given at the meeting through Mr. Urmston, also anonymously; Rs.1000 were collected after the Sunday service in the offertory collection; and the remainder was given by many friends in many places.

"After the meeting the following words were read : 'Not unto us, O Lord, not unto us, but unto Thy Name give the praise, for Thy mercy and for Thy truth's sake. Wherefore should the heathen say, Where is now their God? As for our God, He is in heaven.'

"Thirty years have passed, and I am again invited, this time by the Peshâwur missionaries, to visit Peshâwur, and to take part in an event the like of which has never yet taken place in Peshâwur since it was a city, although it is said to be one of the oldest cities in this part of Asia. I allude to the opening of a beautiful, and perhaps almost unique, Christian church in the midst of this great city of the Afghans.

"Well may we now repeat the inspired words of the psalmist, 'Not unto us, O Lord, not unto us, but unto Thy Name give the praise. . . . Wherefore should the heathen say, Where is now their God? As for our God, He is in heaven."

"Thirty years! And what changes have taken place in them in Peshâwur! It was considered then to be unsafe for a European to be seen outside the limits of the cantonments; and I remember, when walking one day a few hundred yards beyond them, how I was met by Sir John Lawrence, then Chief Commissioner of the Punjab, and Sir Herbert Edwardes, the Commissioner of Peshâwur, who were driving past with a large escort, and who, with many rebukes for my thoughtlessness, ordered me to enter their carriage, and to desist in the future from such dangerous practices. And now the whole country is so open and safe that the missionaries can go alone and unarmed to any village they will—a fact which shows not only the good will which the people bear to the missionaries, but shows also the effect of thirty years of English good government among headstrong and turbulent tribes. A school of more than four hundred scholars, many of whom belong to the highest classes of the Sirdars and Raises, is being carried on by the mission, in which God's Word is daily taught. A Christian congregation has been gathered together, and now, on the anniversary of the very Christmas week in which the first meeting was held, on December 19, 1853, after thirty years of steady, persevering, prayerful work of faith and labour of love, a beautiful church has been set apart to the service of God, and of His Son Jesus Christ, in the midst of the Afghan people. The mouth of opponents is silenced, for all have seen that this is God's work.

"It will be difficult to give a description of the church, or to do justice to it. We can only say that it is the most beautiful church, although, of course, it is very far from being the largest, that we have seen in India. It is situated in a public thoroughfare, very near to the Edwardes Memorial School, and close to one of the gates of the city. Instead of facing the east, it exactly faces Jerusalem, as the point to which all believers look for the second coming of the Lord. Its plan is cruciform, and its architecture is a successful adaptation of mosque architecture to the purposes of Christian worship. The symmetry and proportions of the columns and arches are almost perfect. At the end of the chancel is an exquisitely painted window, the gift of Lady Herbert Edwardes, in memory of her late husband. Above the chancel arch is another small painted window, erected by Mr. and Mrs. Worthington Jukes, to the memory of their little child. The transepts are separated from the nave by two carved screens, one of which is the gift of the Rev. C. M. Saunders, and the other of the Rev. A. Bridge, both chaplains of Peshâwur. One transept is set apart for purdah women, and in the other is the baptistery, the gift of Mr. Hughes, which is adapted for the administration of Holy Baptism by immersion. The carved pulpit is the gift of Mr. Jukes. The handsome brass lectern is the gift of Miss Milman, sister of the late Bishop of Calcutta, and bears the following inscription:—' In loving memory of Robert Milman, Bishop of Calcutta, who died March 15, 1876. He preached his last Urdu sermon to the native Christian congregation in the city of Peshâwur. His last English sermon was on behalf of the Peshâwur mission. His last public act was an address to the pupils of the Peshâwur Mission School. " I will very gladly spend and be spent for you." '

"The communion table is of Peshâwur carved wood-work. The book-desk on the holy table is the gift of Mr. Graves, who laid the foundation-stone of the church in 1882. The floor of the chancel is of Peshâwur pottery in different patterns. The kneeling cushion before the communion-rails was worked by Mrs. Freeman, who, together with her husband, was a large contributor to the church.

"The following text, in Persian, stands out in bold relief over the arch of the entrance-door, on the front of the church outside, from Rev. vii. 12 : 'Amen: Blessing, and glory, and wisdom, and thanksgiving, and honour, and power, and might, be unto our God for ever and ever. Amen.' Over the chancel arch inside appear the words in large letters, ' I will make them joyful in My house of prayer' (Isa. lvi. 7), words which were chosen by our bishop. Many other texts adorn the building, and especially the two following at the chancel end of the church : 'The salvation which is in Christ Jesus,' from 2 Tim. ii. 10 ; and, 'Jesus Christ the same yesterday, and to-day, and for ever,' from Heb. xiii. 8.

"But the chief feature of the church is the screen, beautifully carved in wood, of different native Peshâwur patterns, which divides the chancel from the ambulatory behind it. In this ambulatory are placed the mural tablets to the memory of deceased Peshâwur missionaries, on account of which the church is called All Saints' Memorial Church. The tablets are as follows :—The Rev. C. G. Pfander, D.D., 1855–1865 ;

died December 1, 1865, aged 62.   The Rev. T. Tuting, B.A.,
1857–1862; died October 27, 1862, aged 36.   The Rev. Roger
E. Clark, B.A., 1859–1863; died January 14, 1863, aged 28.
The Rev. Isidor Loewenthal, M.A., 1856–1864; died April
27, 1864, aged 38.   The Rev. J. Stevenson, 1864–1865; died
December 23, 1865, aged 26.   The Rev. J. W. Knott, M.A.,
1869–1870; died July 28, 1870, aged 40.   Alice Mary, wife
of the Rev. T. R. Wade; died October 8, 1871, aged 21.
Minnie and Alice, infant children of the Rev. T. P. Hughes.

"The dome-covered cupola of the tower is seen from a
great distance, and contains a fine-toned bell, which is heard
all over the city and neighbourhood, the gift, many years ago,
of the Rev. George Lea, and other friends in Birmingham, to
the Peshâwur mission, through Colonel Martin.   The cupola
is surmounted by a large gilt cross, showing the Christian
character of the building, and distinguishing it from other
public edifices in the city.

"Connected with the church is the parsonage-house, built
in native fashion, in the form of a square, and near to it the
large vestry-room and native library, two guest-rooms on an
upper story, below which are dwelling-places for the servants.
Everything is thus provided in connection with the church
for all purposes required.   The cost of the whole of the
buildings has been about Rs.25,000.   Rs.3000 are still
required to pay off the debt which has been necessarily
incurred, and we hope that the liberality of Christian friends
will speedily pay it, and that this sum will be soon forth-
coming, to remove all anxiety from those who are responsible
for it.

"At noon on December 27 (the Feast of St. John the
Evangelist), the day of the opening, the church was filled
from end to end by a very large and attentive audience.   The
two transepts were then filled with English officers, amongst
whom we noticed the Deputy-Commissioner.   One side of
the nave was occupied by native women, and by native and
English ladies; and the other side by the men and boys of
the congregation, and by the members of the Punjab Native
Church Council, who had received a hearty invitation from
Mr. Hughes and Mr. Jukes to be present at the opening of
the church, and to hold the eighth meeting of the Punjab

Native Church Council in Peshâwur. The completion of the Indus bridge at Attock and of the Punjab Northern State Railway to Peshâwur enabled them to accept the invitation; and many native friends from different parts of the province availed themselves of the true Afghan hospitality which our Peshâwur hosts so bountifully bestowed on us all.

" Fourteen clergymen, five of whom were natives, were present, and took part in the service; and in the absence of our beloved bishop at home, it devolved on us, as the senior missionary of the Church Missionary Society in the Punjab, by the invitation of the missionaries, to say such prayers at the opening service as could be taken by an ordinary clergyman. The lessons were read by the Rev. W. Jukes, and by the pastor of the church, the Rev. Imam Shah. A brief statement of the object of the service was made by the Rev. T. P. Hughes, who presented the pastor with a copy of the Holy Scriptures in the original languages, and with the sacramental vessels of the church, which were then reverently placed by him on the Lord's table. The sermon was then preached by the Rev. Moulvie Imad-úd-dín, chaplain to the Bishop of Lahore, from the words of our Lord, ' If I with the finger of God cast out devils, no doubt the kingdom of God is come upon you' (Luke xi. 20). The sound of the psalms and hymns swelled harmoniously through the church, and the service was concluded with praise, and thanksgiving, and prayer. The proceedings were very solemn, and verily God Himself was present with His people; and He made His presence felt, even as He had manifested His presence in an unmistakable manner at the first missionary meeting which had been held at Peshâwur thirty years before.

" But some of our C.M.S. supporters in India may perhaps ask, ' Why this apparent departure from some of the cherished traditions of the Church Missionary Society by the erection of this beautiful church in a C.M.S. station? The answer is very clear. It is no departure at all. The object of the Church Missionary Society is to build in every heathen land living temples to the Lord; whatever means will conduce to this end should be made use of. We wish to bring the people of this and of every land to the Cross of Christ. For nearly thirty years has the gospel been preached in the

bazaars, and streets, and the villages of Peshâwur city and
district; and it has been met with scorn, and derision, and
insult. For the last few years the policy of our Peshâwur
missionaries has been changed. The efforts which are now
made are those of conciliation and friendship within the
church, in the school, in the hujrah, and the anjumân. On
Thursday last were seen, perhaps for the first time in Peshâwur,
many leading native chiefs, who reverently sat behind the
red cord which separated the unbaptized from believers in
the faith of Christ, and who listened attentively to a Christian
moulvie as he preached to them boldly and very plainly the
gospel of Christ. There was no opposition at all; a leading
Khan of Eusufzai was there, with members of some royal
families. A Rajah from the frontier afterwards took his place
as a listener, if not a worshipper, in a Christian church. Expressions of approbation and congratulation were heard
from Mohammedans and Hindoos in Peshâwur. 'We serve
God in our way,' said they, 'and it is only right that you
should serve Him in yours.' Services of song and preaching
have since then been daily held, and for the first time in the
history of the Peshâwur mission has a Christian church been
thronged by people who are not Christians, and who are not
yet willing to listen quietly to Christian preaching when
delivered outside.

"We believe that it has been given to our friends, Mr.
Hughes and Mr. Jukes, to devise one more way to gain the
Afghans. The *hujrah* * is another. The school is another.
The *anjumân* † another. If religious services can be carried
on, and religious instruction can be given, without controversy
or noisy opposition and disputation, to Afghans in a beautiful
church, then let us have the church. We have seen in some
other places rooms in schools, in houses, or room-like—
so-called—churches, where services have been unattended,
except by a few paid agents of a mission. If the fault in a
church is merely that it is beautiful, then let us accept the
fault, if its consequences are the bringing in of souls to
Christ, or even if it is only the inducing heathen and
Mohammedan men and veiled women to listen to the gospel.
In this case the church is not an expensive one: Rs.21,000

* Guest-house.   † Answers to an assembly-house, or club.

is not a large sum for a well-finished, suitable, and com-
modious church; and even this sum has been in a great
measure given by private friends, who have presented most
of what is ornamental as a free gift.

"We believe that a new era in the history of the Afghan
mission has been entered on by the erection of this church in
the Peshâwur city. An onward movement has been made,
and although we know that a mere building is nothing without God's presence and blessing in it, yet if the cloud of glory
fills this house, even as it filled the tabernacle and the temple
of old, this building will not be without its special service in
the evangelization of the Afghans. Our earnest prayer is
that this new era may now be signalized by the coming in of
many Afghans into Christ's own fold; for 'unto Him shall
the gathering of the people be;' and He Himself has said,
'I will draw all men unto Me.'"

We will close this chapter with two sketches—one of an
early convert of this mission, the other of its first missionary.

Dilawur Khan.

"Dilawur Khan was a good specimen of the brave soldiers
on this frontier. He was a Subahdar in the Guide Corps.
Formerly a robber, and a plunderer, and a killer of infidels, he
joined the English as a soldier, 'because,' he said, 'he would
always be on the strongest side.' When he heard of Christian
missionaries, he went at once to confute them. But instead
of doing so, he himself became impressed that what they said
was right, and that the moollahs were wrong. He immediately
came over to the strongest side.

"He was once riding with Sir Herbert Edwardes between
Attock and Peshâwur, and he spoke to Sir Herbert of what
was nearest his heart, and asked him for 'some arguments
which would confound the moollahs.' Sir Herbert told him
of a Saviour's love, as Dilawur Khan had never heard of it
before, and so impressed him with the truth and self-satisfying
power of Christianity, that (as he described his feelings afterwards) his 'heart burned within him as he talked with him
by the way.'

"He was baptized by Mr. Fitzpatrick, and remained in his
regiment, doing excellent military service everywhere, and
especially at Delhi with the Guides. He was known through-

out the country as the Christian convert, or infidel who
' confounded the moollahs ' by his bluff, incisive words, every
one of which told against the Mohammedans.

"Mr. Hughes wrote, ' When Lord Mayo wished to send
some trusted native on very confidential service to Central
Asia, it was an Afghan convert of our mission who was
selected. Subahdar Dilawur Khan, who had served the English
well before the gates of Delhi, was sent on this secret mission
to Central Asia, where he died in the snows, a victim to the
treachery of the King of Chitral. His last words were, " Tell
the Government (Sircar) that I am glad to die in their service.
Give my salaam to the Commissioner of Peshâwur and the
Padre Sahib." ' " *

We have a sketch of Dr. Pfander, the first Peshâwur
missionary, from the pen of Herbert Edwardes, in 1866.

"During the three years 1855 to 1858, I knew much of Dr. Pfander.
Dr. Pfander and of his work, and have always looked back
to him as a chief in the mission band. Who that ever met
him can forget that burly Saxon figure and genial open face,
beaming with intellect, simplicity, and benevolence. He
had great natural gifts for a missionary, a large heart, a
powerful mind, high courage, and an indomitable good
humour; and to these, in a life of labour, he had added
great learning, practical wisdom in the conduct of missions,
and knowledge of Asiatics, especially Mohammedans.
Indeed, his mastery of the Mohammedan controversy was,
in India at least, unequalled. He had thoroughly explored
it, and acquired the happy power of treating it from Asiatic
points of view, in Oriental forms of thought and expression.
His refutations of Mohammedanism and exposition of
Christianity were all cast in native moulds, and had nothing
of the European about them. They might have been
written by a moollah, and yet moollahs found that they set

* Extracted from "The Punjab and Sindh Missions," by the Rev.
Robert Clark, 1885.

up the cross and threw the crescent into eclipse. The
Moslem doctors of Turkey, Persia, Afghanistan, and India
have never had such a bone to pick as Pfander's ' Mizân-
ul-Hâqq ' (or the ' Balance of Truth ').

   " It was in the Indian Mutiny, however, that the
character of Pfander appeared at the height of Christian
dignity. The city of Peshâwur, with its sixty thousand
bigots from Central Asia, was at no time a pleasant place for
the messenger of Christ; and in 1857, when the fanaticism
of both Mohammedans and Hindoos was stirred up from the
very dregs, it required something of the courage that ' fought
with beasts at Ephesus ' to go down into that arena, with no
weapon but the Bible. Yet Pfander never suspended his
preachings in the open street throughout that dreadful
time. Bible in hand, as usual, he took his stand on a bridge
or in a thoroughfare, and, alike without boasting and without
fear, proclaimed the truth and beauty of Christianity, while
the empire of the Christians in India was trembling in
the balance. On no occasion was any violence offered to
him. . . .

   " Sir John Lawrence, when Chief Commissioner, used to
say, with reference to discussions about the policy of missions in India, that ' nothing but good could come from
the presence of a man like Dr. Pfander anywhere;' and
General Nicholson, who was in charge of the district of
Peshâwur till called on to take command of the Punjab
Flying Column during the Mutiny, and who had every
opportunity of knowing the feeling of the people, gave Dr.
Pfander a confidence that was usually hard to win."

CHAPTER XI.

——⟡——

1856 1857.

JOHN NICHOLSON—JOURNEY TO CALCUTTA AND RETURN
TO PESHÂWUR.

" High nature amorous of the good,
    But touch'd with no ascetic gloom ;
    And passion pure in snowy bloom
Thro' all the years of April blood ; . . .

" And manhood fused with female grace
    In such a sort, the child would twine
    A trustful hand, unask'd, in thine,
And find his comfort in thy face."

From TENNYSON'S *In Memoriam.*

CHAPTER XI.

ABOUT February, 1856, John Nicholson, who had been holding the post of Deputy-Commissioner at Bunnoo ever since he returned to India in 1852, had become very unhappy in his work there. Friction with his chief at Lahore was becoming more and more intolerable, and conceiving, not without reason, that he was treated unjustly, his noble nature and his own high integrity rose against it; and he was determined, if he could manage it, to leave the Punjab, or at least that part of it where the yoke had been made so insupportable to him.

He would have joined the war in Persia, or gladly have taken up a charge in Rajpootana under his former and beloved chief, Sir Henry Lawrence; but no vacancy occurred, and, much as Sir Henry would have delighted to have him with him, he had no appointment of sufficient importance to offer.

Nicholson applied to be sent to Peshawur, to take up the Deputy-Commissionership there under Colonel Edwardes; and the subordinate position was no drawback to him when it meant association with his dearest friend in India.

The two friends frequently urged the plan, for nothing could be happier, both publicly and privately; but the inexorable John Lawrence set his face against it for a long time and declared he "didn't want two top-sawyers in one place."

However, something had to be done, for John Nicholson would stay no longer in Bunnoo, and his services there had been so great, and he had brought the district into such perfect order, that he had some right to be listened to. And so, in May, 1856, he was allowed to leave it, and was given

Was given
summer
charge of
Cashmere,
1856.
Appointed
Deputy-
Commis-
sioner of
Peshâwur,
December,
1856.
the charge of Cashmere for six months, an English Resident being sent there annually for the summer season. When the six months were ended, he was allowed to proceed to Peshâwur as Deputy-Commissioner, and the two friends rejoiced exceedingly at being once more together.

Little did they then know the full importance and value of the move they had so long struggled to accomplish; for they could foresee nothing of the terrible times that were so near, in which their united strength would be of such value. The end of 1856 found them working heartily and happily together, sympathizing heart and soul in each other's views and objects, in frontier policy, and finding the utmost pleasure in each other's society. Never were two men more closely united in unbroken friendship and confidence throughout their whole lives. They loved each other deeply.

There is a sketch of John Nicholson, drawn by the pen of Herbert Edwardes, for Mr. Raikes's "Notes on the Revolt of the North-Western Provinces of India," which is inserted here, by Mr. Raikes's permission.

"Of what class is John Nicholson the type, then? Of none; for truly he stands alone. But he belongs essentially to the school of Henry Lawrence.

"I only knocked down the walls of the Bunnoo *forts*. John Nicholson has since reduced the *people* (the most ignorant, depraved, and bloodthirsty in the Punjab) to such a state of good order and respect for the laws that, in the last year of his charge, not only was there no murder, burglary, or highway robbery, but not an *attempt* at any of those crimes.

"The Bunnoochees, reflecting on their own metamorphosis, in the village gatherings under the vines, by the streams they once delighted so to fight for, have come to the conclusion that 'the good Mohammedans' of historic ages must have been 'just like Nikkul-Seyn!'

"They emphatically approve him as every inch a hakeem.*   And so he is.

* *Hakeem*, master or lord.

CASHMERE, LOOKING ACROSS THE "DULL LAKE." SIRINGGUR IN THE DISTANCE.

From a drawing by Colonel H. H. Prynton.

"It is difficult to describe him. He must be seen. Lord Dalhousie—no mean judge—perhaps, best summed up his high military and administrative qualities when he called him 'a tower of strength.' I can only say that I think him equally fit to be Commissioner of a division or general of an army.

"Of the strength of his personal character I will only tell two anecdotes.

"1. If you visit either the battle-field of Goojerat or Chillianwallah, the country people begin their narrative of the battle thus: 'Nikkul-Seyn stood just *there.*'

"2. A brotherhood of fakeers in Hazâra abandoned all forms of Asiatic monachism, and commenced the worship of Nikkul-Seyn, which they still continue.* Repeatedly they have met John Nicholson since, and fallen at his feet as their Gooroo.†

The Nikkul-Seynee fakeers.

"He has flogged them soundly on every occasion, and sometimes imprisoned them; but the sect of the Nikkul-Seynees remains as devoted as ever. *Sanguis martyrum est semen Ecclesiæ.*

"On the last whipping, John Nicholson released them on the condition that they would transfer their adoration to John Becher; but, arrived at their monastery in Hazâra, they once more resumed the worship of the relentless Nikkul-Seyn!"

When the sad news came from Delhi of John Nicholson's death, the head of the party in Hazâra was found digging a grave, and being asked what he was doing, replied, that "If his gooroo was dead, he could live no longer;" and he did pine away and die within a very short time.

We have seen in a former chapter how the beginning of 1857 witnessed the meeting of Dost Mahommed, the Ameer of Cabul, and the English authorities, once more face to face

* This was written in 1857.
† Religious or spiritual guide.

upon the plains of Peshâwur. This time the occasion was to sign the second treaty.

The increased anxieties of the Persian War made it desirable to the Afghans to draw still closer the bonds of friendship with the English ; and the Ameer himself came down to Peshâwur to sign the second treaty, of which we have already spoken.

Proposed journey to Calcutta. When this work was accomplished, and the treaty signed, and all the Afghans had retired beyond the mountains back into their own country, it became necessary for Edwardes to absent himself for a short time from Peshâwur, to take his wife down to Calcutta, for severe illness had made it necessary for her, very unwillingly, to go to England (for only six months as was intended); and the separation was rendered less unbearable by the two friends being left together at Peshâwur, and sharing one house till her return in October.

So the time seemed well chosen ; for who knew anything about the storm that was near, to burst upon India within two short months ?

True, indeed, it was that, years ago, in the happy days of the Resident and his Assistants at Lahore, Sir Henry Lawrence had been frequently in the habit of discussing the subject of the Sepoy army, and was of decided opinion that there were many elements of weakness and danger in the existing system of military organization, from which he feared bad results would follow; and he strove hard and wrote much, from time to time, to stir up the military authorities to look into them and reform them.

Fore-shadowings of danger. And so far back as 1845 there were many articles written in the *Calcutta Review* by Sir Henry, foreshadowing dangers, that afterwards proved too true. For Sir Henry Lawrence had the far-sight of genius in all he did, and a keen insight into military affairs. He was heart and soul a soldier, and loved his profession. And as he talked these questions out with the band of young men whom he had gathered round him, and encouraged them to look into these subjects, it is not to be wondered at that they caught an inspiration from his enthusiasm.

And the reader will remember that there was written, so long back as 1849, by Edwardes, a light sketch, suggested as the outline subject for a novel, thrown off in the idle moments of floating down the Indus, on his way home with John Nicholson (which we have already quoted in chapter vi.), which reads like a prophecy of what came true in 1857—eight years afterwards.

But for the present India was at rest, and dreamed not that it slumbered over a volcano.

Even the frontier, where disturbance was common enough (and, if it came, was indeed looked upon as a wholesome irritant, only tending to keep the rest of the body in a healthy state), was more restful than usual, with the sense of the new amicable relations just completed with the Cabul ruler.

And so it seemed that the journey to Calcutta might be undertaken in safety, with the reins left in John Nicholson's hands during the Commissioner's absence.

There were some advantages to be had by a trip to Calcutta. It was well to come face to face with the new Governor-General, Lord Canning, and plans could be discussed in a few interviews in a way that letters could never accomplish; and it is very refreshing to see many old friends again.

Then Edwardes was glad to be able to bring the claims of his dear friend, John Nicholson, before Lord Canning; for he was still anxious to leave the Punjab altogether, and Edwardes was desirous that the Governor-General should know his merits and understand his value. So he pressed very urgently upon Lord Canning Nicholson's great qualities, and the irreparable loss he would be to the Punjab, as one of the best district officers in the province, and one of the finest soldiers in the army; and wound up his description of his friend by saying—

"If your Lordship ever has a thing of real difficulty to be done, I would answer for it, John Nicholson is the man to do it."

And Lord Canning kindled with interest, and smilingly replied—

"I will remember what you say, and I will take you for Major Nicholson's godfather."

Only too soon was this last proved true!

After a short stay together at Calcutta, the sad parting came; and, having seen his wife on board the steamer on March 23, 1857, and stood on the shore till the form of the *Ava* was lost in the distant haze of the river, Edwardes turned to prepare for his solitary journey back to Peshawur;

"and" he writes, "I felt that we had really *parted*. What a serious and sad word it is! May our kind heavenly Father watch over you, my beloved, and bring you back to me, crowned with the mercy of restored and enduring health! When coming away, I found I had been standing under a pretty evergreen tree with red berries, on whose leaves there seemed to be a constant contention going on, the smoky steamers trying to blacken them, and the thick dew wiping them again. I gathered a spray as a good omen, and send you a few leaves. The worst was coming back to the old room, strewed with the disorder of our packing-up. The wretchedness of the room was dreadful!"

That wretched parting now is looked back to as the beginning of sorrows!

It would be impossible to give anything like a true picture of him whose life this attempts to sketch, and to leave out *entirely* that tenderness and devotion in his home which was one of the lovely qualities of his heart and mind, and which shone out conspicuously in every word and action of his beautiful life.

Great as he was in his public life, in administrative power, and in his influence in curbing wild races (it was, even there, the iron hand in a velvet glove), great in eloquence, and strong in resolve and fertility of resource in difficulties, it was in his private life that all the refinement and true loveliness of his character came out fully; and his nobleness and gentleness of soul beautified every action of his daily life. The one who knew him best, and could tell the most of his *inner* life, and was privileged to share his deepest thoughts, is the one who can tell best from how *pure a source* flowed out the noble acts that the world saw. To know him truly was to see him in his home, where his natural brilliancy was unfettered, and his presence was always sunshine.

Unlike some, who look fair in public and adorn society, but who exhaust the charms of their mind on strangers, Herbert Edwardes's strong heart was full of love; and that *at all times*, and this light from heaven itself shone out the brightest on the one the nearest to catch the ray.

There all the poetry and romance of his nature came out in its richest pathos, and he wanted no other audience than those he loved best to display his richest treasures. His tenderness of sympathy for others would often lead him to acts of generous help to those who were in trouble, that no one heard of but his wife; and many can testify to, or may have passed away to thank him in heaven for all, the kind things he did continually. Sometimes a soldier had heavy debts he could not pay, or a wife who was sick, and he could not give her the luxuries she needed; or perhaps the soldier may have had a girl he loved at home, who would come out to be his wife if he could only pay her way. All such cases as these, when he proved them *real*, won a ready sympathy from his chivalrous heart.

All his life he had done these things, even when he was a subaltern with his regiment, and many were the voices that would bless him. And as his means increased, his *charities* expanded, and he gave away with large-hearted munificence.*

And to complete the picture, it must be told (and may be added here) how courteous he was in little things as

---

* A humorous instance of confidence in his readiness to help occurred at this time. The widow of a clerk who had been in his office and died some years before was very ill; and, expecting to die one day, said to her doctor, "Now I shall die, I am sure; I shall make over my two girls to Colonel Edwardes." And he says laughingly, in telling the story, " I heartily wish the good lady a long life!" But, had the occasion occurred, he would have been quite equal to it !

well as great. In Scotland, in the last year of his life, he
would delight to visit a poor old woman in a cottage, often
carrying a jug of soup to her with his own hands; and he
would enter her cottage door with as much deference and
courtesy as if it were a palace, and sit by her chimney-corner
and talk to her with such a kindly interest and grace that
he won her heart to believe in anything he had to say to her.

If he passed along the road another day, she would get
up from her chimney-corner and go to her door, and say,
"It does me good to see him only walk along the road!"

A rather amusing illustration of this feature of his
character occurred once when Edwardes was on his way
home. He went one day from Paris to Versailles, to visit
one of his Punjab friends (one of the frontier officers in high
command in India), and as he walked along from the station
to his friend's house, he overtook an old woman who was
tottering under the weight of a large bundle she was trying
to carry along. He stopped and spoke to her, and, finding
that their roads lay in the same direction, he said, "Give
me your bundle, my good woman, and I'll carry it for
you, and we will walk along together." And so they did;
and the friends on the look-out for him were greatly wondering if it were he, coming along the avenue, carrying a large
bundle in his arms, and an old Frenchwoman by his side.

She little knew to whom she was indebted for smoothing
her path that day. To him it was simply the natural
impulse of his genial, courteous, and sympathetic nature; and
he thought nothing of it, and gave the bundle back to her with
a courteous regret that he could carry it no further for her.

But this is a digression, and we must go back to the
point we started from. This little parenthesis will have
served to show the reader only a glimpse of the truth that
to be torn away from *such* a home was indeed the beginning
of sorrows to both.

And yet, when the fury of the storm had burst, and the
horrors of the Mutiny were being enacted in almost every
station in India, the kindness of the Providential care was
seen and recognized, that had removed his wife to a safe
place, and left him free, without distraction of private
anxieties, to devote his mind and his energies to the public

duties which were about to press so heavily and so anxiously
upon him in the Peshawur frontier charge, towards which
Edwardes was now to wend his way back with a very heavy
heart.

But before he did so, he stayed a few days in Calcutta,
to give opportunity for interviews with the Governor-General ;
and many were their meetings, and many the anxious conversations on burning questions of public interest.

There was much that Lord Canning wanted to talk over
of Peshawur matters and frontier policy—the Lumsden
mission (which he wished to correspond directly with the
Calcutta Government through Edwardes) and other questions
which Lord Canning discussed at great length, keeping
Edwardes long after all the guests had disappeared, and
asking him to come again the next morning and renew the
discussions.

Being somewhat new to India, Lord Canning seemed
anxious to think out questions for himself and form his
views ; and, in order to do so, to hear the opinions of public
men who had already given time and thought to them, and
had had experience by which to test them.

And there was no difficulty in drawing Lord Canning's
attention to the military questions and the state of the
army, which had so long and often engaged Edwardes's own
thoughts, and the dangers to our Indian Empire to which we
have already alluded in discussing the training which Sir
Henry Lawrence gave to his Assistants at Lahore. For
already there seem to have been felt the rumblings of the
coming storm of disaffection in the native army.

Even during this short time of Edwardes's visit to
Calcutta came the first signs of the Mutiny, and the 19th
Regiment of Native Infantry was quietly disbanded at
Barrackpore, without any disturbance. And although no
one could foretell the whole course of atrocities and rebellion,
peril and disaster, that would so soon follow upon this first
thunder-clap, till our very empire itself should reel under the
blow, still this opportunity was not lost by Colonel
Edwardes in pressing upon Lord Canning not to allow the
warning note that was sounding so loudly in his ears, so near
to him as Barrackpore, to pass unheeded. It brought home

First signs
of the
coming
storm.

his arguments with telling power to his Lordship's mind ; for, even now, blood had been spilt. The story was this—

Arguments brought home.

"A sad thing took place in the 34th Native Infantry at Barrackpore. A Sepoy, a Brahmin, got drunk with bhang, took his musket and a sword, and called on the other sepoys to join him in going to the ghat and preventing the European soldiers from landing ; of course knowing that they had been sent for to keep peace at the disbandment of the 19th, or perhaps suspecting harsher measures.

"The adjutant, Lieutenant Baugh, went down to the parade, and his horse was shot under him by the Brahmin. Baugh drew a pistol and fired at him to prevent his reloading, but missed, and the Brahmin closed with him, with his sword. A fight ensued, in which the native tulwar proved better than the Birmingham blade, and Baugh was terribly wounded. This was before all the men of the regiment, and only one sepoy came to Baugh's assistance. The sergeant-major seems to have been helping, for he got killed.

"This is the substance of a letter just received from an officer of the 34th, who does not hesitate to say that his regiment is in a worse state than the 19th, that *all* the European officers have lost confidence in their men, and that he hopes all sorts of things will be done by Government. . . . The army is in a state of lax discipline, and wants radical reform, which we seem to have no statesman to undertake. These regiments at Barrackpore have probably been tampered with by the dethroned Princes who are still in exile at the capital.*—H. B. E." (Extract from diary letters to his wife.)

* In confirmation of the truth of this idea, we may put into a note here a letter received at Peshâwur some months further on, when apprehensions had become certainties, and facts so much worse than apprehensions : "—— has had a letter from some friend in Calcutta, who evidently is behind the scenes ; for he says Government is in possession of information which shows that the Mutiny was preconcerted by Mohammedans.

"It was to have taken place on the Queen's birthday all over the

But these first symptoms at Barrackpore were not, at the time, generally thought of much consequence, and did not attract much attention. In disbanding the 19th Regiment, it was considered that the Mutiny was at an end, and that the offenders had met with the punishment they deserved.

But it is not a great stretch of imagination to suppose that afterwards, when the plots thickened, these earnest conversations, and warnings too, would come back to Lord Canning's mind, and would help to give him confidence in the man who held the reins at the frontier post at Peshâwur, and *held*, as it were, the anchor by which the great ship was able to outride the storm.

Maybe, too, it gave some force to the determination that enabled Lord Canning to give the casting vote *with Edwardes*, which was all-important at the time when it should come to pass, in after-days of difficulty, that the question actually was hanging in the balance, *whether or not* they should let slip the anchor.

Looking back, we can often trace the tiny links that help to make the chain of great and important events with which we could never have guessed that they had any connection.

In the return journey up the country many friends were visited at the different stations, in interchange of thought with whom Edwardes found much refreshment.

It was always interesting to him to study, too, the tone of native thought and feeling in the parts of India so far away from his own province; and an opportunity was unexpectedly afforded him in the journey as soon as he left Calcutta.

country, when the troops were on parade. The cartridge question came up accidentally, and offered so good an opportunity, uniting the Hindoo sepoy with the Mohammedan one, that it was seized upon, and took fire rapidly through the army, and the Cavalry at Meerut got so excited that they precipitated the matter.

"The King of Delhi was to have his old imperium, the Nawâb of Moorshedabad was to be Viceroy of Oude; and the late King of Oude, Viceroy of Bengal and Behar. I have no doubt that these three potentates were at the bottom of it, for an Oude subahdar of the Kilat-i-Ghilzie Regiment told me two months ago that the more we saw of the Mutiny, the clearer it would be that the two Nawâbs (of Moorshedabad and Oude) and the King of Delhi had planned it all.—H. B. E."

Extract from private letters to his wife—

"April, 1857.

"At night I got into the railroad again, and turned my face once more to that troubled post, Peshâwur. . . . A well-dressed native got into the carriage with a writing-desk, took out a Bible, and began to read by the light of the lamp over his head. I entered into talk with him, and asked if he was a Christian. 'Not exactly; that is, I have not declared myself.' Did he approve and believe Christianity? 'Yes; I have given up all *modern* Hindooism, but I adhere to pure deism, and agree with your English Unitarians.'

"'It was impossible,' I said, 'to read the Bible and not acknowledge that it came from God.' 'Yes,' he said, 'the Bible is the only religious system I know of that tells men to love their enemies and do good to those that despitefully use you. It certainly spiritualizes all the relations of life.' I asked him why so many young Baboos become infidels; and he said he could only suppose it was because 'The fool hath said in his heart, There is no God.' I looked into his Bible, and found it copiously annotated in pencil. It had been given him by a clergyman of the Free Church named Milne."

Meeting with this Bible-reading Bengalee in the railway carriage was a great opportunity of studying a live specimen of Young Bengal, and the subject which had always interested him greatly, viz., the effect and probable end of our educational measures upon India.

So long ago as January 25, 1845, we find, in "Brahminee Bull's letters in India, to his cousin John Bull in England"—

"The Cabul War was a crisis, if you like; but you made it yourself. There will be another crisis some years hence in India, when your Education Order has worked its way and self-knowledge begets the wish and the ability of self-government. But 'sufficient for the day is the evil thereof.'

You and I will scarce live to see the crisis that will re-generate India ; and if we do, let us hope that, among other books, history will be read, and therein men of all new opinions will read that belief is as free as thought, that the Hindoo persecuted the Mussulman, and the Mussulman persecuted the Hindoo, but that *you* tolerated them both.''

And if he was interested in these subjects in those early days, how much more should we expect to find it so when his mind became more ripened and his experience enlarged !

And so it was. His large and capacious mind was continually exercising itself upon all such subjects affecting the ultimate good of the people and the responsibilities of the governing race concerning them ; and, like all truly great men, he was humble, and neither narrow nor self-opinionated ; and he was glad to listen deferentially to the opinions of men older than himself, whom he respected and admired, and to ventilate his own opinions with theirs. This he had been able to do freely in Calcutta, for he found there many congenial spirits.

Dr. Duff was in Calcutta at the time, and, with his large **Dr. Duff.** views and expanded philanthropy, Edwardes could always feel great sympathy ; and personally, he felt great love and respect for him, as the veteran champion of all that was right and good.* This admiration and sympathy was mutual, for a letter in Dr. Duff's handwriting, written to a third party in the Punjab in 1859, says, " Is that noble, lion-hearted, Christian man, Colonel Edwardes, to leave the Punjab soon ? "

* In conversation with Dr. Duff, these questions were earnestly discussed. He said " there were numbers of Hindoos of good family who were Christians in belief, and who meet regularly for prayer, but will not openly profess. The educated Bengalees who are not Christians appear to be very disaffected to Government, and to talk freely of what they will do with India when they have got rid of us."

Dr. Duff and Mr. Beadon seemed to think that " the severance of India must be contemplated as the probable end of our educational measures, and all that we could do was to strive so to govern meanwhile as to part friends."

Mr. Wylie thinks it is not intended that the Anglo-Saxons should ever **Duty not a** lose India. In any case, I think the duty is clear of communicating to **question of** those whom Providence has placed in our charge all the light we possess **results.** ourselves, whatever the result may be.—See *Friend of India*, April 16, 1857, editorial headed " Patria Cara Carior Libertos."

Different
opinions
upon
educational
measures. Upon this subject, of the effect of our educational measures upon India, there is a passage in Kaye's " History of the Administration of the East India Company's Service " which we may extract here; for it is interesting to mark the views of different public men upon a question of such vital importance and interest. Kaye says, " The admission of the natives of India to the higher offices of the state is simply a question of time."

" I believe," said a distinguished member of the Company's service (Mr. Halliday), before the Committee of the House of Commons, " that our mission in India is to qualify them for governing themselves. I say also," he continued, " that the measures of Government, for a number of years past, have been advisedly directed to so qualifying them without the slightest reference to any remote consequences upon our administration."

Kaye proceeds : " Long before it became their duty to review the clauses of the Act of 1833, the Court of Directors had continually exhorted its servants in India to prepare, through the agency of improved systems of education, the natives of the country for higher official positions than they had yet been qualified to hold.

" And these exhortations had not been thrown away. What the ultimate effect of their general educational measures must be, it is not difficult to conjecture.

" Our mission will be fulfilled sooner or later. The only question is a question of time.

> " ' There is a divinity that shapes our ends,
> Rough-hew them how we will.' "

At Benares, Henry Carre Tucker was visited; and Sir William Muir, Mr. Charles Raikes, Dr. Farquhar, at Agra (where there was a crowd of good men and true); and at Cawnpore, Edwardes turned aside to Lucknow, where was now his beloved friend Sir Henry Lawrence, whom he had not seen since they parted at Jullundur, where he and his wife stayed on their way down to Rajpootana on leaving the Punjab to his brother John. It was then (in 1853), amidst the regrets and lamentations of all his many friends, that he parted from them; and those regrets had never died away in the hearts of the many who loved Sir Henry, and who delighted to serve under him. Rarely has there been found in public life a man who so oiled the wheels of the ponderous machine of Government, and was so able to carry men with him, attaching them at the same time to their work and to himself personally, and inspiring them with the devotion that he felt himself.

It is impossible to say how much it was this harmony of spirit with their chief that gave an impetus to the Government that Sir Henry left behind him. For deeply as he felt leaving his province, Sir Henry's Christian chivalry rose to the occasion, and, in the midst of his own personal grief at quitting Lahore, the *last act* of him and his noble-hearted wife before they left the Government House was to kneel down together and ask God to bless the Punjab, and to bless and prosper his brother John's rule over it, for the good of the people and of himself.

Brotherly forgiveness and Christian largeness of heart prompted it, and his true love for the Punjab would make him forget all personal feelings, and desire only the prosperity of the province which was his own from the first, and where he had laboured so devotedly. It was the true *testing-time* of the character of all his work; and the noble band of brave spirits that he had gathered together, and who felt he was their leader, could do nothing less than try to catch the influence of his parting example, that did but stamp deeper into their hearts the lessons of self-sacrifice which he had taught them so long.

They knew, too, that nothing would *please* him better than that they should give all their strength to the work that lay so near his heart. But none can say whose heart was the *most* heavily burdened—he who turned his back upon the Punjab, or those who stayed there without him.

Time showed how well these men braced themselves up to their work again; how every one of them came out as a strength and power in the great earthquake of the Mutiny, now so nearly at hand.

Sir Henry Lawrence had lately arrived at Lucknow, called upon by Lord Canning to take up the Government of the newly-annexed province of Oude, just as he was about to proceed to England for furlough, and had even sent on his little daughter and sister to Bombay to wait for him to join them there.

He had had a great trial in Rajpootana, for there he had been called to give up the dear wife who was the joy of his heart. Lady Lawrence had died at Mount Aboo in 1854.

Honoria Lawrence.She was a worthy helpmate for him, able to throw herself heart and soul into all *his* life and share it with him, helping him in his literary work very much, and cheering him at all times with her ready sympathy and love ; for she felt with him in everything. As with all good wives, the dearest thing to her was her husband's honour and truest happiness, and leaving the Punjab had been almost as deep a wound to her as it was to him. She used to say " it was one she could only keep her finger tightly pressed upon, or the bleeding would start out afresh."

But she braced herself up to cheer and support her noble husband, and hers was always the hand that pointed heavenwards and cheered him on, even from her sick-bed.

The following is a picture of Henry Lawrence at Lucknow, from Edwardes's private letters—

From Herbert Edwardes to his wife.

"Lucknow, April 4, 1857.

Sir Henry Lawrence at Lucknow, 1857."I got here to breakfast yesterday, and found Henry Lawrence in decidedly better health than when he parted from us at Jullundur in 1853. He says he was in very indifferent health at Agra before coming here, but has been *much better* since he came to Oude.

" This is characteristic of him. He is roused out of the very pit, as it were, by any call to work ; like a war-horse, ever ready for the battle. The only change is that he is *much* greyer ; no vestige now of brown in beard or hair— all grey, and the grey passing into white. This morning I was so lucky as to get two photographs of him done by a native gentleman here, and I enc'ose them for your great delight. . . . Dear Sir Henry is evidently *happy* in this new appointment. He says so and looks so. By as much as he felt injured and depressed by Lord D——'s removal of him from Lahore, by exactly so much does he go up again, now that Lord Canning has taken off the weight, and conferred exactly the same charge on him that John has got. And I believe he will do a great deal of good here. He comes in as a peacemaker. . . . And he is already winning golden opinions among the nobles and people also by his kindness and sympathy. Hitherto there seems to have been no sort of sympathy for the chiefs and heads of the native society; nothing but a rush of nukshas, nukshas,* to reduce the new province as soon as possible to the standard plan. I feel much more hopeful of Sir Henry *doing* well and *keeping* well since I have seen the state of things.

"This morning we rode through the city. It is an immense place, occupying about eighteen square miles, and containing from five to seven hundred thousand souls. There are many *pretentious* buildings—beautiful in design and grand in scale, but miserable in material; like a stuccoed club-house in London. The river Goomtee runs through the city, and bridges unite the banks. This gives a most picturesque appearance, and puts one in mind of Europe. Sir Henry has two houses—one in town and one in the outskirts. Of course he is living in the hottest himself, and has lent the coolest to the brigadier. *Description of Lucknow.*

" *The Residency,* in which we now are, has, I think, four stories—an immense pile. . . .

"Sir Henry has his old runaway Ladâkh pony still, and he rode him this morning. He says he keeps him to prevent his losing his nerve on horseback. This morning he read a chapter of the Bible to George † and me. And then he prayed with great earnestness. He laid great

---

* Official forms.

† His nephew, who was a Deputy-Commissioner in Oude before he came.

stress on 'Enable us to live in love with many and charity
to all.' The whole prayer was for peace and forbearance
and good-will, and the help of Christ Himself in our whole
lives.

"What a dear good man he is! Occasionally we have
such hearty laughs together, till the rooms echo again, quite
like old times! I have not yet asked to see dear Lady
L.——'s picture, as I do not know how he may feel it; so
I wait till to-morrow (Sunday), when the house will be
quiet. . . .

"Christian and Mrs. Christian arrived this morning. . . .
Then ensued a grand search for a double bed; and last a
despairing hunt for sheets to fit the bed. This all put me
so in mind of the old Residency at Lahore, where Sir Henry
and I slept, ate, and worked in one small room for the first
year, and when a brigadier came to stay for a night (Sir
Colin Campbell), we put a charpoy * for him between our
two, and thought we were all handsomely provided. What
queer creatures the earnest-working Englishmen in India
would become, if there were no ladies to put their houses in
order! . . . He wants me to stay a week, but I must really
go on Monday or Tuesday.

"Last evening we drove out to see the Martinière College.
Claude Martin was, I believe, a Swiss, and came out to India,
as a common soldier [as is written on his tomb]. Afterwards he entered the Oude service, and became a general.
He seems to have become a kind of commission agent for
the Kings of Lucknow, importing European luxuries for the
Court, and charging a handsome profit. Thus he amassed
great wealth. Among other speculations, he built a palace,
thinking the King would buy it; but the King refused to
give the price, and thought it would be cheaper to confiscate
the building when the old man died. General Martin, therefore, ordered his body to be buried in a vault in the centre of

_____
* Hindostanee for "bed;" literally, "four feet."

the house ; and thus turned it into a tomb, which it would Palace
turned
tomb. be a defilement for a Mohammedan to live in. The body was embalmed, and for many years was exposed to view in the vault. Now it is covered over with the monumental slab, with a marble bust of the general on one niche at the head of the tomb, and two plaster of Paris busts at the sides. Round the tomb stand four painted figures of soldiers leaning on their muskets. The heart, when removed at the embalming, was buried in a tank in front of the mansion, and a monumental pillar erected over it. This palace-turned-tomb was finally bequeathed as a college for children of all religions, and last night we heard about a hundred and forty piebald boys sing the evening hymn with much *voice*, at all events.

" In the opposite wing were as many pure blacks, but I don't know if they are taught to sing of Mohammed and Krishna. The mixture of faiths under one roof pleases me less and less the more I think of it ; but Sir Henry, with his large heart, goes on liking it.

" I stayed at Lucknow till Good Friday evening, so that altogether I was eight days with him. One day he got sick from a change of weather, and was feeble from it all the rest of the time I was there, so that after all I fear his health is but uncertain. . . .

" I believe that Council is the sphere where his wide and general views on all subjects, especially military and political, will be able to effect most good for India, and therefore I heartily hope he may be selected for an expected vacancy. I was very glad to have seen so much of him, and left Lucknow with regret.

And so the two friends parted, never to meet again on Edwardes
leaves
Lucknow. earth,—their next meeting would be in heaven ; and we are like children playing about among the shadows, compared with the light *up there*, in which they see things *now !*

The next stay was at Agra. There he found much to Agra.

interest—Mr. French and his college, where he examined
two of his upper classes in Acts ii. and iii., and Milton's
" Paradise Lost ; " and says—

" I suppose he is doing too much good here to be given
up to us for Pesháwur ; otherwise he is the very man ! "

(His merits have now found a wider field, for he is the
Bishop of Lahore.)

" Last evening we had a starlight party at the Táj. What
a peerless building it is ! It is more lovely every time one
sees it. Dr. Murray lit up the interior for us, and I wondered anew at the marvellous delicacy of the mosaic and
marble fretwork. I am glad this building was in honour of
a woman."

Edwardes delighted to meet again Mr. Charles Raikes
and Sir William Muir, and found refreshing talk of the many
things that lay nearest to their hearts in public matters.
How refreshing public life in India is, mixed up so closely as
it often is in friendship and sympathy ! Mr. Raikes was
recommending some modifications in the North-West Provinces administration ; and

Sketches of the Assistants. " holding up the school of Sir Henry Lawrence and his old
Assistants, as examples of out-of-door and open-air Governors,
who settled more cases under green trees than under fly-
blown punkahs. To lighten the subject, he wanted to throw
in a few sketches of Sir Henry's staff, and I was engaged for
some hours yesterday in penning him some notes on Arthur
Cocks, George Lawrence, George McGregor, Edward Lake,
James Abbott, Harry Lumsden, Reynell Taylor, John
Nicholson, and John Becher."

Himself left out. (This explains the reason why, in Mr. Raikes's book,
called " The Revolt of the North-Western Provinces of India,"
there is a sketch of all the staff of Sir Henry except of

Edwardes himself; for, of course, he could not write of himself!)

We might linger longer over the pleasant sketch of this very genial visit; but, as night set in, the journey has to be pursued, and one friend starts to walk ever so far along the road with him, unwilling to say farewell.

From Agra he hurried on to Umballa, and took a look at the Lawrence Asylum, at Sanâwur, on the way. This was the first of the soldiers' children's schools in the hills, started by Sir Henry Lawrence, and first proposed by him in January, 1845, by the offer of Rs.3000 from his private purse. It was a scheme very dear to his heart from that time; and he continued to support and extend it all his life, and established one at Mount Aboo and at other hill stations; and in his will he bequeathed them, with a sum of money, to the Government, and called them his "elder daughter." *Asylum at Sanâwur.*

But Sanâwur was the first, and had been started in the early days of his first going to Lahore, and Edwardes had a particular interest in it, having had much to do in assisting Sir Henry Lawrence in the work; and it was a great pleasure to him to have an opportunity of seeing for himself how it prospered.

"At night I started from Umballa for the asylum, got to Kalka about eight a.m., breakfasted and rode up the hill, every stone and tree in the winding road seeming familiar to me. *Diary letters continued.*

"With the asylum I was quite delighted. It has expanded into a perfect parish, clustering round a most English-looking church. The discipline and order of the whole institution are very remarkable, as well as the health and strength of the boys and girls. Above all, I was pleased with Mr. Parker. He is a dark-complexioned man, with a large coal-black eye and well-cut features full of resolution. His universal ability is exhibited at every turn. He has both planned and executed everything. The children evidently regard him with that mingling of confidence and fear which is inspired by a really good schoolmaster. . . .

"Mr. Parker told me that the Romish priest's congregation had dwindled to two children, at which point the priest abandoned the institution and retired to Agra, whence the bishop has since fulminated a sentence of condemnation. On the whole, I enjoyed this visit to the well-known hills extremely, . . . and I could see dear old Subâthoo slumbering like a flock of white sheep on a distant hill.

"There is something much more charming to me in these hills than in any that we have about us in Hazâra and Murree, but perhaps it is from old associations." *

The Lawrence Asylums. This benevolent scheme of Sir Henry Lawrence's is an unspeakable boon to the English soldiers in India, providing a safe and healthy place of education for their children, and a refuge from the contaminating air of barrack life, which is both physically and morally injurious to them.

Another sign of disaffection in the native army crops up at Umballa. Edwardes writes—

"At Umballa the disaffected portion of the sepoys were giving trouble, burning the houses of those sepoys who agreed to do their duty, and Government barracks, and some empty bungalows."

It seems like the flashes of lightning that often precede a heavy storm.

A day with Edward Lake at Jullundur, and a ride from midnight to midday in the mail-cart, brought him to Lahore. He says—

"John Lawrence is looking out of health. He is now suffering from a pain in the side of his head, which he calls 'neuralgia,' but I should think was hard work. He can only still it by constant application of chloroform. He has more than ever resolved to go home next January. . . .

"The terms of the peace with Persia have just been sent

---

* It will be remembered that, when a subaltern with his regiment, he was stationed here.

to John Lawrence by Lord Canning, with permission to show them to me. They are better than I hoped for, but I am anxious as to the future settlement of Herat, as to who is to get it. The articles only provide that Persia leaves and abandons it."

A day's visit to Lady (John) Lawrence, at Rawul Pindee, on the way, and the journey was brought to an end at Peshâwur, May 5, 1857.

To his wife—

"The difference of temperature between Calcutta and Peshâwur is quite extraordinary. You remember how impossible it was to do without punkahs in Calcutta, more than six weeks ago. Here none are yet thought of.

"Nicholson is looking much better than when we left him. He has been in camp, moving round the district, and this has done him good. Nicholson's society in the house is a great comfort to me in this great desolate house, where your books lie about where you last laid them, and our mutual words seem hanging entranced in the air, and coming back on me like echoes. It is both sad and sweet. It is like the thorn that they say the nightingale leans on."

He found heavy work awaiting him at Peshâwur, and

"that the political work, in consequence of our connection with the Afghans, is on the increase continually. It will become impossible to carry it on as well as the civil work of the frontier; and before John Lawrence goes home, or I go myself, I think I shall state my opinion to that effect, and advise a separate political agent for Central-Asian matters.

"It is very unsatisfactory to be able to give only a moiety of time and thought to great international questions which might well absorb the whole.

"A letter from Henderson gives such a delightful ac-

Diary letters. Return to Peshâwur.

Heavy work at Peshâwur.

count of Meranzye, where things are settling down into
established peace. He manages his district admirably, and
is a great comfort to me."

Edwardes's thoughts naturally turned homewards, and
his views about life, and choosing our own path, come out at
this time.

Views of
life's duty.
"I feel that England's homes are very beautiful and
dear, and that the climate there gives so much more zest
to life and occupation; and as a dream, if allowed to dream,
nothing can I fancy more happy on earth. . . . But I doubt
as to the duty.

"It is a low view of life to regard it as our own and
do with it what seems pleasantest. That cannot be what
God meant us to do. He must be supposed to wish us to
remain unhomed, pilgrims ever, while on earth, seeking to
be placed only where we can do most for Him. And it is
at this point that conscience finds such a hard case put
before it. '*Where* can we do most good?' . . . But after
all, if we can really bring ourselves to make sincere *self-
surrender*, and say, 'Lord, what wilt Thou have me to do?'
it is probable that we shall not be deceived in coming to our
conclusions, but be guided into right plans by God's own
Spirit."

Again, about training of boys —

Advice to
mothers on
training
boys.
"It is shameful and horrible how boys are *let alone!*
Mothers cannot keep their hold on their boys too long.
These young years when the little things adore their own
mother, and look up to all heaven through the windows
of her eyes, will soon fleet away. Seize them, mothers, and
write the knowledge of God all over them in a sweet, acceptable, happy, bright-lettered way. It will never, never be
erased, let man, or woman, or evil spirit try their worst.

" Keep their hearts soft and their minds pure as long as ever you can. It is a Moloch creed which says the sooner they are hardened the better. When they must leave you and go into the world and meet sin, let it at all events *shock* them, and find them prepared with a boyhood of good convictions. Even if they err, let them have something to come back to."

CHAPTER XII.

1857.

LEVIES—FIRST OPENING OF THE MUTINY.

"Arm, warriors, arm for fight; the foe at hand,
. . . each on himself relied,
As only in his arm the moment lay
Of victory."

MILTON.

CHAPTER XII.

AND now comes the first thunder-clap of the great storm that was impending, of which we have seen a few warnings at Barrackpore and Umballa. Already Edwardes had written to his wife—

" Monday night, May 11, 1857.

"All day I have been very busy buying guns and pistols for the Lumsden's 'Toshakhanah' at Candahar; and you know what a troublesome job that is in the midst of sessions-cases. The political work is sensibly increasing here, and is swelled by these odds and ends of jobs to an extent which quite alarms me. I do not know how I shall be able to carry on both works much longer. . . .

First burst of the Mutiny.

" The telegraph officer has just sent me a sad piece of news from Delhi, that the Sepoys from Meerut had come over and burnt the bungalows there, and killed several Europeans !' This is serious, and we must expect the Mutiny to spread to every station, if not put down with the bayonet at some one cantonment. If it comes here, we shall, please God, make short work of the mutineers, for we have three European regiments in the valley, and all the Artillery is European. . . .

" *May* 12.—The plot is thickening. This morning we got the following telegraphic message from the Deputy-Adjutant-General at Meerut, dated twelve at night of May 10 :— ' Native troops in open mutiny. Cantonments south of Mall burnt. Several European officers killed. European troops

under arms, defending barracks. Electric telegraph wire
cut.' Of course that means no *Calcutta wire.* . . .

Advice.

"This has forced us to make our own preparations, and
I have advised John Lawrence, by telegraph, to collect
and bring into the field at once a movable column, to move
on any station in the Punjab where disaffection shows itself,
and put it down with the bayonet. This matter cannot be
talked down; it must be *put* down. How very thankful
I am that you are in safety! I have now no care here, and
I hope to be useful, with Nicholson and our fine old
brigadier, Sydney Cotton, and Chamberlain, at this crisis.

"*Midnight.*—I have been sitting up with three moonshees
and two pundits, perusing the correspondence of the sepoys,
which came in this evening's post. We found nothing
disloyal! But there are a great number of their letters,
written neither in Persian nor Hindee, but in a character
called Kâyuthee—and this we none of us were able to
decipher. These mutineers are likely to entail trouble
enough on us before we have done with them.

"We have got the notorious 64th Native Infantry here,
and I have thought it best to move it out of cantonments,
on pretence of strengthening the forts on the Mohmund
frontier, where they can do little mischief. Here their
lines were next to the guns; and Major Barr, who was
senior officer of the Artillery, was, I hear, very anxious
about them. All this puts me so in mind of the last Sikh
War!"

At this first sounding of the key-note of the blast of the
Mutiny, Edwardes writes a long letter to Sir John Lawrence,
and telegraphs the outline of his letter the same night.

"Peshâwur, May 12, 1857.

"MY DEAR JOHN,

"I have not heard yet whether you are at
Pindee or Murree, but as we have received here the tele-

graphic news of May 10 from Meerut, that the 'native troops were in open mutiny, and Europeans on the defensive only,' I write a line to tell you that Nicholson and I are of opinion that a strong movable column of reliable troops (Europeans and irregulars) should take the field in the Punjab at once; and move on the first station that stirs next, and bring the matter, without further delay, *to the bayonet.* This disaffection will never be talked down now. It must be put down."

Then follow some military proposals, which we will not enter into in detail, and he proceeds—

" Further, we would advise you to raise a body of a thousand Mooltânee Horse at once, to act as Cavalry with this movable column, or in any other way that may be required during this mutiny.

" Depend upon it, there will be plenty to do, and you cannot act too promptly in getting together such men as you can trust to. The Cavalry of the irregular force are little better than our old Cavalry. The Mooltânees may be relied on. Their present leaders, the Ressaldars, might be told to double or treble their numbers, in the quickest way they could.

" Nicholson desires me to tell you that he would be ready to take command of them; and I need not add the pleasure it would give me to do the same. We are both at your disposal, remember; and, if this business goes far, it will soon come to a question of personal influence and exertion.

" Either of us could raise a serviceable body out of the Derájat, in a short time.

" We have written to ask Chamberlain to ride over and consult with Brigadier Cotton how they could co-operate to give you a movable force.

" As to this place, it will be just as in 1848, the last

to go; and not go at all if the intermediate country be occupied by a good field force, engaged in making stern examples. . . .

"Nicholson has just arranged with the brigadier to move the 64th out to the forts on the Mohmund frontier, as if an attack were there expected; thus removing them from the other troops, *and the guns*, to which they are nearest."

Then follow other proposals concerning the formation of the proposed movable column,

"as also the thousand Mooltânees. This would be something to move down the Punjab with; and, in the hands of a good man (I should say Chamberlain), might do the country an important service.

"But there is no time to be lost. If you wish for the Mooltânees, let us know by telegraph, and we will issue the perwannuhs."

Again—

"What you do about a movable force, *do at once.* There is no time to be lost in getting to the struggle which is to settle the matter. . . .

"Believe me,

"Affectionately yours,

"(Signed)   HERBERT B. EDWARDES."

The public letter follows next day—

From Colonel H. B. Edwardes, Commissioner of Peshâwur, to Captain H. B. James, Officiating Secretary to Chief Commissioner.

"Peshâwur, May 13, 1857.

"SIR,

"Yesterday, telegraphic news reached this cantonment from Major Waterfield, Adjutant-General of the

Meerut Division, that the troops at Meerut were on the 10th instant in open mutiny, and the European troops on the defensive.

"The night before we had received telegraphic news from Delhi of the bungalows having been burnt and several Europeans killed by mutinous Sepoys from Meerut.

"These news seemed to indicate so serious a state of affairs south of the Sutlej, that Colonel Nicholson and myself visited Brigadier Sydney Cotton, commanding the Peshâwur Brigade, and advocated the formation of a movable column of picked troops, to put down mutiny in the Punjab.

"There was one regiment of native Infantry in the Peshâwur garrison (64th Native Infantry) whose present feeling was generally rumoured to be disloyal, and whose past history was notoriously mutinous. It was desirable, therefore, to move it away from the other native troops, especially as its lines were nearest to the guns. . . .

"In the afternoon of yesterday I had the honour to telegraph to the Chief Commissioner our proposal for a movable column, of which the Queen's 27th and 24th, the Guide Corps, and some other irregular troops should form part.

"Later in the day Brigadier Cotton and Major-General Reed, commanding the division, decided on organizing the movable column, and orders were issued by them and myself for the Guides to make over the Fort of Murdan to the 55th Native Infantry from Nowshera, and join her Majesty's 27th at the latter station.

"Brigadier Neville Chamberlain, who commands the Punjab Irregular Force, and happened fortunately to be at Kohât, was invited over to Peshâwur for consultation as to further measures, and he rode in this morning at an early hour.

"At 10.30 a.m. to-day I had the honour of receiving your

Measures taken at Peshâwur.

telegraphic reply to my message of yesterday, in which you
announced that the native Infantry were disarmed this
morning at Mecan-Meer, and the Cavalry of their sabres.

Council of
war.

"At 11 a.m., by the invitation of General Reed, a
council of war was assembled at his quarters, consisting of
the general himself, Brigadier Cotton, Brigadier Chamberlain, Colonel Nicholson, and myself; and I have the
honour now to forward for the Chief Commissioner's information a copy of the resolutions which were unanimously
taken.

"General Reed will leave Peshàwur to-morrow for
Rawul Pindee, and unite his own head-quarters with those
of the Chief Commissioner, which will facilitate prompt
action at this crisis.

"Brigadier Chamberlain will also proceed to Rawul
Pindee, to consult with the Chief Commissioner.

"Major-General Reed has asked me to place the services
of Lieutenant-Colonel Nicholson at his disposal, as civil
and political officer with the movable column; and as that
officer, from his great local knowledge of the country between
Lahore and the Indus, in which he served with such distinction during the war of 1848–49, his combined experience of the regular and irregular armies, his rare talent
for acquiring information in the field, and the general force
and ability of his character, was undoubtedly the fittest
officer that I knew of for that duty, I have at once acceded
to the general's request, considering that at such a time as
this, our civil administration is dependent on the peace of
the Punjab.

"Among other measures to be advocated, I suggest to
the Chief Commissioner the advisability of authorizing
some of the best of the commanding officers of the Punjab
Irregular Force to enlist men of the Punjab and British
frontier. It will add immediately to our strength, it will
absorb the best of the floating candidates for military

service, and it will ultimately supply the gaps made in our native army by the present mutiny.

"I would also strongly recommend that each of the Ressaldars of the Mooltânee Horse in the Derajat be authorized to double the number of his men from the same race of Mooltânee Puthâns, than whom experience has shown we have none more thoroughly reliable in the Punjab.

"Trusting that these measures which have been taken here to-day will strengthen the Chief Commissioner's hands,

"I have, etc.,

"(Signed) HERBERT B. EDWARDES."

This letter was the first suggestion for the formation of the "movable column" and of the "levies," both of which proved such important features of the Punjab arrangements. And the memorandum of these arrangements that were decided on at the council of war was, "First, General Reed, as senior officer in the Punjab, assumes chief military command; and it is hereby resolved to organize a movable column instantly of thoroughly reliable troops to take the field, and get between the stations that *have* mutinied and those that have *not*, and move on any point in the Punjab where mutiny has to be put down by force of arms."

When the Chief Commissioner's answer came, it was a mild approval of the idea of the advantages of such a course, but by no means entering into the urgency of the case.

John Lawrence's answer is—

"I have written to the commander-in-chief, proposing it (!) . . . I believe that the Irregular Cavalry and the native Artillery will prove faithful. I would not raise Mooltânee Horse without the orders from Government, nor *do I think they are necessary*, at any rate at present." The Chief Commissioner's opinions and reply.

And on the 14th, his secretary writes to Edwardes—

"The Chief Commissioner does not consider that the emergency is of such a nature as to require immediate

Prompt
measures
discoun-
tenanced
by the
C. C.
measures being adopted. . . . The Chief Commissioner does not see the necessity for enlisting local horsemen at Kohat, and I am to request that for the present this may not be done. Indeed, a question of this kind might have been referred in the first instance."

He saw the necessity on May 28, but the fact is, he had not yet woke up to the real urgency of the case. Further on, he says again—

"It appears to the Chief Commissioner that the troops are sufficient, and that prompt action alone is wanted to crush mutiny and rebellion wherever it may arise."

Was this opinion justified by the result?

Sir John Lawrence wrote also to the military authorities at Peshàwur, disapproving of the vigorous measures set on foot by the council of war. General Reed writes to Edwardes—

"I have just received the accompanying despatch from the Chief Commissioner. It places me in a difficult position, the move having been decided ' in council.' Do you think it would be attended with any risk, delaying the execution of the order, as Sir John Lawrence requests?

"Yours very truly,

"(Signed)   THOMAS REED,

"Major-General."

Brigadier Sydney Cotton, who received a similar despatch, deals with it with characteristic decision. He writes to Colonel Edwardes—

"Peshàwur, May 14, 1857, 1 a.m.

"MY DEAR EDWARDES,

"I send you two letters received from Sir John Lawrence.

"Our arrangements of yesterday supersede, of course

those of the Chief Commissioner; and being at this moment
in operation, nothing more need be done.

"The arrangements of the council of war of yesterday *Sydney*
will, of course, be made known to the Chief Commissioner." *Cotton*
firm.

(And then the letter goes on to enter into arrangements
about the families, and the sick, of the men going on service.)

"Yours sincerely,

" (Signed)   SYDNEY COTTON,

"Brigadier."

Then came telegrams from the Chief Commissioner—

To Colonel Edwardes.

"May 14.

"The Chief Commissioner requests you will not raise
new troops anywhere without his instruction, and wishes that
Colonel Nicholson should remain at Peshâwur."

Again —

"If you have promised to let Futteh Khan have men, *Reluctant*
let the fewest number necessary be enlisted, provided they *assent*
granted.
are footmen; and report that number.*

"The enlistment of horsemen at Kohât should not be
authorized.

" (Signed)   H. B. JAMES,

" Officiating Secretary to Chief Commissioner."

These were the difficulties and hindrances that beset the
first raising of levies; nor was the need of them realized by
the Chief Commissioner, for he writes—

"May 14, 1857.

"I cannot conceive what has misled the Sepoys of the
native army. The cartridges, no doubt, began the mischief,

* A letter went down to the Chief Commissioner, dated May 16,
reporting the number of men allowed to Khan Bahadoor Futteh Khan
Kuttuck to levy, for the security of the Attock Bridge and Ferry: three
jummadars, ten havildars, a hundred sepoys, and one moonshee.

but what has carried on and intensified the ill feeling? There seems a general belief that we are about to convert them all; but some one must have worked on their minds.

"*I think one good example* would stop it all.

"We are, I believe, amply strong enough in the Punjab to put down all mischief.

"(Signed)   JOHN LAWRENCE."

We will resume the extracts from Edwardes's diary letters to his wife.

"May 15, 1857.

"It is a most critical time this, and I should deceive you if I wrote otherwise; but it must soon be decided one way or other. And, please God, the tide will soon turn in our favour when this splendid column gets together and comes smashing down upon the capital. The regiments to compose it are working nobly, and rushing to the rendezvous at Jhelum. I envy the man who is to command it—as yet, not known.

"As yet, *all is perfectly quiet in the Peshawur garrison,* and we have great advantages in our position over any other station.

"I offered to give up Nicholson as political officer for the movable column; but John Lawrence has prohibited it, and talks of going himself. Chamberlain rides to-night to Pindee, to consult with him.

"We are all deeply anxious about dear Sir Henry Lawrence. His position in Oude is the weakest in India. We can get no news from those parts; but we suppose the Delhi magazine to be in the hands of the mutineers; and hope that the commander-in-chief has descended from Simla, and has done in Upper India what we are doing for the Punjab.

"So long as the *people* do not rise against the civil Government, all will go well. The European troops, if

Anxious position of Oude.

they have time, will get together and smash the Sepoys;
. . . unless they get panic-stricken, in which case it will be
Cabul over again. But I don't believe it.

"It cannot be God's will; and you may rely on it we
shall gain the victory, though there must necessarily be a
frightful loss of blood. Who knows what dear friends we
may have lost ere this? . . . I write this very hurriedly, at
midnight. I am at work all day, and must send this off
to-morrow."

To the same——

" Peshawur, May 16, 1857.

"India has been convulsed by a mutiny of the Bengal
Native Army about those Enfield rifle cartridges; and when
the Delhi magazine was taken by the mutineers, the European
troops at Meerut on the defensive, with the native troops
in open mutiny, all native troops disarmed at Lahore,
another regiment disbanded at Barrackpore, and a third at
Lucknow by Sir Henry Lawrence,—you can easily conceive
that there was no communication between the Punjab and
North-West Provinces. . . .

"Since yesterday (my last), our intelligence has
brightened. The 45th Native Infantry at Ferozepore had
mutinied, and been annihilated by her Majesty's 61st, the
57th Native Infantry, not sympathizing, or rather not
fraternizing with the 45th, but giving up their arms; and
the 10th Light Cavalry (Wilkinson's) remaining staunch.
This was good. When men begin to *act*, clouds disperse
and success begins.

"Last night we heard that the commander-in-chief
(Anson) has come down from Simla, and is marching on
Delhi with a force, to recover that important point. . . .

"I scrawl these hurried lines, limiting them to telling
you generally how matters stand.

Progress of the Mutiny.

"Here, at Peshawur, we took time by the forelock, induced General Reed to assume chief command in the Punjab, and then issued orders in his name for the assembly of a field force of reliable troops, European and irregulars, to move down upon Lahore and crush mutiny wherever it showed its front. The prompt marching of these picked corps was unexampled in my experience. One feels proud of such fellows.

The Guide Corps.

"The Guide Corps made surprising efforts. Captain Daly * is worthy of them.

"The whole will soon be at Rawul Pindee, and thence march rapidly to Jhelum, if required; but it seems to have pleased God to turn the tide already, in the Punjab at all events. Our great anxiety is for the North-West Provinces and Oude. If the road *viâ* Agra be open, you will, of course, get public news from those parts of the latest date. But I much dread some terrible disasters there. The European corps are few and far between, and Benares, Nepâl, and Oude may each and all have thought their day was come for rising. We can only expect to hear of sad loss of life in every station; but pray that it may be otherwise.

Peshâwur quiet as yet.

At Peshâwur all is quiet, and we have taken all reasonable precautions. I offered to give up Nicholson to the movable column, as just the man to accompany the general, whoever he might be, on such a march; but John Lawrence has refused to let him go. . . .

Cheerful hopes.

"I am more than ever involved in labour and anxiety, of course; but am very well, thank God, and firmly believe that these troubles are not intended by the Ruler of events to shake, but to consolidate, our power.

"Nothing less would have brought about army reform.

"Nicholson is well and deeply interested, as you may

---

* Captain Daly was the officer in command of the Guides during the absence of Major Harry Lumsden, who, it will be remembered, had gone on special duty to Candahar.

suppose, in all that is going on. Chamberlain has gone down to Rawul Pindee, at our request, to John Lawrence."

We see how the first burst of the storm came upon Peshàwur, and how Edwardes and Nicholson were preparing to meet it. And the reader can fancy how heavily the disappointment fell upon these two brave hearts when they found their ideas were not taken up by Sir John Lawrence; that he did not at once see the necessity for immediate action.

In the plan of the movable column he concurred so far as " to propose it to the Commander-in-chief;" and to the raising of the levies he replied by warning Colonel Edwardes " to enlist no men without his sanction."

Thus time was lost that could not be regained; but Sir *Time lost.* John soon came to see that the levies were a wise and necessary measure. And, meanwhile, events rushed on so quickly that there was no time to wait for orders; and we shall see presently how action was taken, and the movable column formed, without further reference or delay.

It must not be supposed, because we frequently see a great difference of opinion and of judgment about public matters and the value of certain measures proposed, that the private and friendly relations between Lawrence and Edwardes were ever interrupted or interfered with. Both were public men, earnestly and sincerely working with all their strength, and giving all their brains and energies for the benefit of the country and the honour of their Queen's Government; and, their aims and objects being identical, their differences would only be (and that but occasionally) as to the best measures suitable at the moment to accomplish the result desired by both.

This has been already seen, for instance, in the Afghan treaties at Peshàwur; and again it reappears in the present emergencies which had risen up so suddenly; nor need it seem strange if the soldier-spirits of the land were found the most ready to face the fight and buckle on their swords.

Further differences will be seen as we proceed; but no differences of opinion ever for a moment interfered with the most intimate and affectionate private friendship; and often, in meeting together to talk over measures, differences would disappear.

Opposition ceases. It was so especially in the present instance of raising levies. On May 18, Sir John Lawrence summoned Colonel Edwardes down to Rawul Pindee for consultation. He stayed two days, and returned again to Peshâwur. And after the meeting together of the two friends at Rawul Pindee, John Lawrence was quite won over to the idea, and there was no more opposition.

Indeed, he afterwards became quite eager about the levies, and the readers of his recent biography would even suppose that he was the originator and inspiration of it all.

But a truer "History of the Mutiny" has been written since, by one who has earned the title of "historian" by a calm and careful research into records and official papers, before stating facts; and he tells us at page 331*—

Holmes's "History." "Edwardes also asked leave to raise levies among the Mooltânees of the Derajât, whom he had learnt to know and trust years before. Lawrence at first curtly refused his consent; but a few days later, convinced by the fiery eloquence of Edwardes that it was of vital importance to strengthen Peshâwur as far as possible, he gave way."

This is just an example of what we have been speaking of above.

Nicholson telegraphed urgently to Edwardes at Rawul Pindee, from Peshâwur, May 18, his wish to increase mounted levies two thousand, and also to raise foot levies.

"I give Mobarick Shah four hundred horse, and send him to join Coke or keep him under myself. If he is not on our side he will be against us."

Telegraphic reply comes from Edwardes—

"Rawul Pindee, May 18, 4.30 a.m.

"John Lawrence agrees to Mobarick Shah having two hundred horsemen, and to your raising six hundred to-

* "The History of the Mutiny" (in one vol.), by T. R. E. Holmes, published by Allen.

gether from the Peshâwur frontier, and fourteen hundred from the Derajât."

Again—

"This is written at noon of May 18. Sir John Lawrence sanctions two thousand Mooltânee horsemen, instead of a thousand. Order a thousand to join you at Peshâwur as fast as possible, five hundred to go to Lahore, and five hundred to remain at Dera Ishmael Khan, ready to go to Mooltân, if required. Let Meer Mobarick Shah join Major Coke quickly with one hundred Horse and fifty Foot, but no more."

On May 19, Edwardes telegraphed to Nicholson—

"The Commander-in-chief cannot spare Brigadier Cotton from Peshâwur, and has appointed Brigadier Chamberlain to command the movable column."

And so the telegrams went on, and orders came thick and fast. Colonel Edwardes telegraphs to Colonel Nicholson, May 19—

"Sir John Lawrence sanctions your raising two thousand Foot. I think the bridge of boats at Nowshera had better be broken up; and only single boats kept up at the ferries at the Cabul River."

The Chief Commissioner was now convinced, and he saw the necessity for levies; and there was, henceforth, no lack of energy in orders, nor any hindrances as before.

This important movement in the Punjab was one of the great measures for safety in these days, and no one would ever desire to crop a single laurel leaf from the brow of Sir John Lawrence because of his first opposition to it; for he was strenuous enough afterwards. But it is necessary to point out explicitly how the measure originated and came about, because of the unworthy pains taken by a biographer to

The raising of "levies" an important measure of defence in the Punjab.

misrepresent the truth, and actually to vilify the reputation
and the opinions of the very man by whom the idea was
conceived, and through whose energetic exertions the Chief
Commissioner was induced to withdraw his former opposition.

Afterwards the views of Edwardes and Nicholson were so
clearly proved to be sound ones, that there was no further
need for argument, and Lawrence was finally convinced.

Then we may mark the vigour with which orders came
from Rawul Pindee, to gather more levies and hurl them
down on India, until at last the same wise counsellor
(Edwardes) who had at first urged their despatch considered
the Punjab could spare no more, and called to stop.

Wisdom was in both counsels, as events showed. And
hundreds of officers on the frontier then and still living are
witnesses to the truth which the papers from which these
remarks are quoted fully prove.

It was well known then, and, in spite of recent mis-
representation, is not forgotten now; and so well known that
men (and women too) were not backward in expressing their
thankfulness that such men were at the front and at the
outpost of danger at Peshâwur.

A brave heart at Abbottabad (John Becher, Deputy-Commissioner of Hazâra) writes—

" I am very anxious to hear how matters go at Peshâwur
with you.   I think this vigorous determination of your
council to assemble at once a movable column will crush the
fiend.   In Chamberlain's letter to Rothney he said that I
should receive instructions to raise a levy of the country.   I
have not yet received any such instructions.   I think it will
be well to have some braderies.*   We have the wild reports
here in every shape; but the people care little about them,
and we are, perhaps, the quietest place in India.

---

* This word means "brotherhood," in English. It is called " braderie "
because the kind of levy thus alluded to is raised by chiefs from their own
clans, and the men of a frontier clan claim to be brothers, as being all
descended from the same stock.

"I am heartily glad we have such a ' three ' as Chamberlain, Nicholson, and you standing at the forecastle.

"Yours ever,

"JOHN R. BECHER."

And now Colonel Edwardes returns to Peshâwur and reports to the Secretary of the Chief Commissioner—

"Peshâwur, May 23, 1857.

"SIR,

"On my return to Peshâwur yesterday, from conferring with the Chief Commissioner at Pindee, I found affairs in a very discouraging state indeed. Lieutenant-Colonel Nicholson, with his usual energy, had left nothing untried to raise levies of Horse and Foot, to overawe the disaffected Hindostanee troops; but the time when this could have been done with effect has passed, and not a single chief responded as he ought to have done to the call of Government. Some inferior Mullicks had been next resorted to, with a prospect of success on a small scale."

The consequences of time lost.

Peshâwur chiefs did not respond to the call.

The tide had not been taken at the turn, and it was depressing enough.

There is no intention of writing here a history of the Mutiny, but only to present a glimpse of the course of events as they happened at Peshâwur, and of the spirit and views of the men engaged there; to furnish, in fact, a running commentary on the times and the place, which, in spite of all that has been written, partly indeed *because* of some things that have been written, is less superfluous.

To proceed then with extracts from letters. News came fast and thick from below of the spread of the rebellion of the native army.

"There is no doubt that the Delhi magazine has fallen into the hands of the mutineers; . . . that one of the native regiments there (the 54th) had murdered its own officers when called on to act ; . . . that the 38th Native

Infantry simultaneously fell on the troop of Artillery and captured four out of six guns. . . . The other two guns were worked by Captain De Teissier and his subalterns, for several hours; thus, apparently, covering the retreat of several ladies and women and children. But those who escaped must have been few; and we hear that awful atrocities were committed upon all Europeans, male and female, who fell into the hands of the mutineers."

On the 20th, he writes again—

"The occurrences at Delhi surprise no one, for there were no European troops there; and the risk of entrusting the arsenal of all Upper India to Sepoys only has, for many years, been a common topic of discourse in the army. But what we are all indignant at is the failure of the Meerut Division to do anything. The Mutiny broke out strongly there among the Sepoys; and eighteen hundred Europeans seem never to have struck a blow to put it down. All they have done is to stand on the defensive; and as this always demoralizes Englishmen, I dare say that by this time the European regiments at Meerut have no heart left. They are ' entrenching themselves and watching the natives.' * . . . The Commander-in-chief is with his army

---

* "It is clear God keeps us here in our place, not man!" An amusing paragraph appeared in a newspaper at that time. It shows the general feeling of the public.

" A COMMANDER-IN-CHIEF WANTED.

" *To the Editor of the Lahore Chronicle.*

"Dear Sir,—Will you oblige the Indian public by giving a prominent place to the following in your next issue? The exigency of the times requires it, and, I trust, you will not hesitate.

" Yours faithfully,

"   _____

"' A Card.

"' Lost, strayed, or stolen, the Commander-in-Chief of H.M.'s and the Company's forces in India. Any information that can be afforded as

at Umballa, where he has been since the 16th, and does not mean to move till the 22nd. All this time the Mutiny spreads, the country gets disorganized, small cantonments are exposed, and *the people* are tempted to rise.

"Had the Commander-in-chief made a move, the tide of disturbance would have been turned. It is but too evident that, though a great whist-player, he forgets the golden rule of Hoyle, 'When in doubt, play a trump!' We have urged action on him till we can urge no more. . . . Yesterday we heard good news from down-country—that Agra was still safe, with the fort held by a European regiment, and of course available as a last refuge for all the residents there. But how long will this be so if the Commander-in-chief does nothing? Lord Lake would have been at the gates of Delhi by this time, and the recreant mutineers swimming the Jumna for their lives. *Agra still safe.*

"Here in the Punjab we have acted promptly. Peshâwur took the lead (in calling the council of war and forming the movable column). . . .

"This column is now collecting, and in a few days it will be at Wuzeerabad. N. Chamberlain is to command, with the rank of brigadier-general. . . .

"The measures taken in the Punjab have been manly and vigorous in every place, and our officers have come out well. Robert Montgomery (then the Judicial Commissioner at Lahore) has behaved like a thorough soldier—prompt, cool, resolute, vigilant, unexcited, cheerful—the life and soul of all the capital. It is to him we owe the disarming of the sepoy regiments at Lahore, with the cordial co-operation of General Corbett, who was in military command of the station of Lahore. The same praise is *Vigorous measures at Lahore.*

to his whereabouts will be most gratefully received and handsomely acknowledged by the State.

"'The general supposition is that he has fallen into one of the trenches of the camp at Meerut, where, if a search is made, he will no doubt turn up.'"

due to Donald McLeod,* and the new Commissioner Roberts. The chiefs, too, of the country have come out well, and the people have shown no sort of sympathy with the insurgents. ... I am a little anxious about Peshâwur, and I think we can hardly get through the crisis without some outbreak on the part of the native troops there; and, in that case, the tribes about, who are so different in blood and feelings from the rest of the Punjab, might think it an opportunity for disturbance. But, please God, we shall put them all down. . . . Soon, I hope, we shall have some Mooltânees at Peshâwur, for Nicholson and myself to rely on. . . .

Uncertainty about Peshâwur's tranquillity.

"I ought to tell you that at Ferozepoor the 45th Native Infantry has mutinied, but been overpowered and dispersed. The number of armed mutineers now roving over the country must be very great. We have no news from Oude, and I continue to be very anxious about dear Sir Henry. He will, no doubt, be doing nobly. John Lawrence, too, is doing so. He is afflicted with excruciating tic-douloureux in his face; and the paroxysms of this add heavily to his troubles, poor fellow!

"We have advised the Governor-General to intercept the European troops now on their way to China, and bring them to India; for China is of very secondary importance when the Indian Empire is in the scale. . . . Certainly India has never seen the like of this before! The whole Sepoy army may be said to be against us. If the

---

* Then Financial Commissioner of the Punjab; in after years he became Sir Donald McLeod, and was Lieutenant-Governor of the Punjab in 1866.

He was a man greatly beloved and honoured by all who ever knew him. Kind and considerate to all, the natives so loved him that they used to say that there were two ferishtas (angels) among the English in the Punjab; that they were so good, that, if only all the English had been like them, the whole country would have become Christian, by seeing them and witnessing their actions, without the aid of any missionaries at all; and that these two ferishtas were Sir Donald McLeod, and General Reynell Taylor.—From Rev. R. Clark's "Thirty Years of Missionary Work."

Irregulars were to fail us, we could not possibly stand. I believe, however, that we have felt the worst of the storm, and that the time of action is about to begin. Equally confident am I that, however tried and troubled, God is on our side, and that we shall ultimately triumph. *Confident hopes of ultimate success.*

"But at this sad time how thankful am I that *you* are *in harbour!* It is the greatest source of comfort to me, and I thank God that we had the resolution to bear this separation; and did not give up the plans, as you wished, even in Calcutta. Whatever trouble we have now is light to what it would have been had you been at Peshâwur! . . .

"John Lawrence sends his love to you, and says we are all doing our best, and don't mean to be beaten. His wife is up at Murree, not well."

This was written on May 20, and the two friends were cheered and strengthened by meeting face to face, and discussing arrangements and consulting about plans. That very day came bad news from Nicholson at Peshâwur, of traitorous correspondence intercepted, and Edwardes determined to hasten back. Greatly were they both disappointed at the long delay in the Commander-in-chief's advance towards Delhi, to regain possession of which was necessary, as the only stroke that could stem the torrent of evil that was increasing everywhere through delay. *Edwardes returns to Peshâwur.*

But back to Peshâwur Edwardes hastened, and rode in by midday on the 21st. He writes—

"The heat was dreadful, and I was much fatigued. I found Nicholson immersed in cares and anxieties, everything looking as bad as it could look without an actual outbreak, the regiments talking big, and the natives of the district wearing that consciousness of impending difficulty to their European rulers which is so sure a herald of a crisis. *Threatening aspect of things at Peshâwur.*

"It was impossible to get any levies from the chiefs about Peshâwur.

Evil result
of delaying
the call for
levies.
" John Lawrence would not let us begin to raise men
when we could have done it, and now the day of our prestige
has passed for the present.

" The old Afghan Wuzeer, Nizâm-úd-dówlah, coolly told
Nicholson that this was a crisis in which we must rely upon
ourselves. All that day Nicholson and I were engaged in
using our influence with small Mullicks in the district to
raise men.

" I wrote also to Henderson at Kohât for us many as he
could send.

" It was generally believed that a conflict of some kind
must take place on the 22nd, and the object was to get into
cantonments a few men on whom we could rely."

Edwardes writes back to John Lawrence to acquaint him
with the state of things. A few extracts from his letters are
given here—hastily dashed off and hurried, for the pressure
was tremendous, and nights followed days in heavy work;
but such letters paint the picture vividly, and seem to bring
us back again face to face with the events they describe.

*To Sir John Lawrence, Rawul Pindee, Chief Commissioner
of the Punjab.*

" Peshâwur, May 27, 1857.

" My dear John,

" Enclosed is a letter from Lumsden, in cypher, of
which I suppose you have the key, for I have not.

" The messenger says all is well, so I suppose there is
nothing of importance in it. I could wish that we had both
the Lumsdens, and Foujdar Khan and Sirwur Khan here
now; but, on the whole, I think it is more important to
keep all those four pieces on the board where they are.

" It would unsettle Dost Mahommed if we showed any
doubts as to the result, or recalled our representatives from
around him. In thinking for him we are only thinking for
ourselves.

"Affairs are getting very arduous here. I send you some Peshawur
difficulties. letters of Nicholson's on the subject. Before receipt of them, I had heard of Ajoon Khan's move, and gone to the brigadier at night, and recommended much the same measures.

"So now we have put them all in operation, and to-morrow morning Nicholson will have a very nice little force collected at Nisûtta.

"I do hope that the gale will blow over without any insurrection of the tribes on the border, for when a fire is kindled in such an inflammable country, there is no saying where it may spread to.

"Things seem settling down in Hindostan, and to be pretty safe throughout the Punjab, and I think, if you could in any way manage it, it would only be prudent to throw some more strength upon this point; for Peshawur is a vital point, as it were, and if we conquer here we are safe every-where, whereas disaster here would roll down the Punjab.

"It was absolutely necessary to disarm the regiments,* and yet it recoils on us, for we want native troops. The Queen's 27th have been greatly fatigued by their trip to and fro, and we have sent out her Majesty's 70th in their stead.

"We must husband our Europeans, and we do so; we carry them about on elephants and carts, like children. If it comes to a post-chaise per man, they must have it. But they cannot do everything, and we feel the want of some organized natives greatly. I am lightening the duties with our levies as much as I can.

"Can you not think of any way to help us at this pinch? If you can, pray send us one, if not two, irregular Infantry corps or police corps (not Poorbeahs), and do it quickly.

"You were wrong to check me at first about levies. About
Peshawur
levies. We ought to have begun at the very first. *We lost the tide.* Time lost.

* The story will be told in the next chapter.

First in-
stalment of
Mooltânee
levies.
"We have only got ninety Mooltânees up here yet, and they are worth their weight in gold. Had we summoned them a few days sooner, we should now be in possession of three or four hundred.

"You know I am not an alarmist, and I dare say you will quite concur in what I urge, that, if all is looking well below, you should stretch several points to make things *triumphant* here. You know on what a nest of devils we stand. Once let us take our foot up, and we shall be stung to death.

Civil and
military
counsels
unanimous
at
Peshâwur.
"Happily we have no divided counsels here, and civil and military all work together cordially.

"What an extraordinary announcement is this of the Commander-in-chief's death! . . .

"I am beset with troubles, as you may imagine. Have you not got some Assistant who could come up here and put his hand to odd jobs?

"Is there never another in your quiver? . . .

"Henderson is doing finely, Nicholson nobly, Becher, too, famously and sweetly. One may thank God for such men. Adieu. Kind love to your wife. I often think of her amid the row.

"Ever affectionately yours,
"(Signed)   HERBERT B. EDWARDES."

CHAPTER XIII.

1857—1858.

AND LETTERS DURING THE MUTINY-TIMES AT PESHÂWUR (*Continued*).

" Let us, then, be up and doing,
With a heart for any fate,
Still achieving, still pursuing,
Learn to labour and to wait."

LONGFELLOW.

CHAPTER XIII.

THE crisis had now come. Edwardes and Nicholson were told that "they must rely upon themselves," and they felt it was true. The time seemed past for raising Peshâwur levies. Delay had increased their difficulties, and a conflict of some kind seemed to be at hand.

Letters to his wife—

"At night, much dispirited, we lay down in our clothes, prepared for any alarm; and, sure enough, at midnight we were aroused with an 'express,' announcing that some companies of the 55th Native Infantry, on duty at Nowshera, thirty miles from Peshâwur, were in open mutiny. The European regiment had been called away to join the movable column, and these companies of sepoys, together with the 10th Irregular Cavalry, were in charge of the station, with all the women and the children of the 27th Queen's at their mercy! Lieutenant Taylor,* of the Engineers, like Horatius of old, cut away the bridge of boats, and thus prevented the mutineers from being joined by the rest of the 55th Native Infantry from the Fort of Murdân, of which they were in charge during the absence of the Guide Corps.

"Things being in this state, Nicholson and I determined to advise the brigadier to take the initiative at Peshâwur,

Lieutenant Alexander Taylor, Engineers.

Council on the disarmament of Sepoys at Peshâwur.

* This is the same man whom we shall afterwards see so great in heroic deeds at Delhi—the engineer who planned the assault and siege of Delhi with John Nicholson the night before the assault, when Nicholson led the storming party up the scaling-ladders and through the breach of the walls of Delhi, and carried the assault on September 15.

and disarm nearly the whole of the native troops. We accordingly went over to the brigadier, who, at first, proposed to detach a force of Europeans to quell the mutiny at Nowshera. We pointed out the danger of dividing his European force here, while the native troops were in their state of disaffection; and he then concurred heartily, like a good old soldier as he is, in the propriety of disarming the corps here. All the commanding officers were accordingly summoned, and a most painful scene ensued. The commandants of those regiments which were to be disarmed unanimously and violently declared their implicit confidence in their men. One advised conciliation, and another threatened us that his men would resist and take the guns."

Nicholson and Edwardes had to take the odium of the proposition.

"The brigadier saw the need of decision, and, accepting the responsibility, he said, 'Gentlemen, no more discussion. These are my orders, and I must have them obeyed.'

Disarming parade at Peshâwur.

"This council lasted till 6 a.m.; and at 7 a.m. we brought out the troops, and ordered the bad regiments to lay down their arms. The regiments of European Infantry, with guns, were all ready to enforce obedience; but the Sepoys were completely cowed, and surrendered their arms without a word. It was a painful and affecting thing to see them putting their own firelocks into the Artillery waggons—weapons which they had used honourably for years. The officers of a Cavalry regiment, a very fine set of fellows, threw in their own swords with those of their men, and even tore off their spurs. It was impossible not to feel for and with them; but duty must be done, and I know that we shall never regret the counsel that we gave.

Result of disarming.

"The result was instantaneous. The air was cleared as if by a thunderstorm. We breathed freely again. On our return from the disarming parade, hundreds of Khans and Urbals, who stood aloof the day before, appeared, as thick as flies, and were profuse of offers of service. They had not calculated on our having so much pluck, and they shamelessly appeared at the very instant when their services were no longer wanted. I treated them very coldly indeed, and 1 believe they will be sorry for their want of calculation. Henderson's succours from Kohât soon came flowing in, and are still going on. Men are coming from Meranzye, which we were subduing last winter! Meranzye is now as quiet as a Bayswater tea-garden. . . .

" I was up at three o'clock, and threw a chain of Horse and Foot around the back of cantonments, so that, if the men of the 51st had attempted to mutiny, I should have cut them off. Happily, all passed off quietly. The subahdar-major of the 51st was made to walk round the whole paraded garrison; his desertion and sentence to death were explained; and he was then hanged before them all. This will have a great effect on the minds of the sepoys. It shows them that we will maintain discipline, and are strong enough to enforce it."

Again, to the same—

" Read the glorious speech of Sir Henry Lawrence to the soldiery at Lucknow. How it rings! True English! They should make him Commander-in-chief at this crisis, if they really want to reform the native army."

" *May* 31.—What anxious fears you will have, and not without cause! for indeed we have been passing through a fiery trial. Had the people of India been in a state of discontent, as some orators in Parliament assert, they would have risen along with the troops, and we must have been utterly exterminated. But it is most gratifying to observe that, except in one or two places, there has been no rising of the people; and we have, therefore, been at liberty to

The struggle is with the troops, not with the people.

struggle with the native troops as best we could. Even at Peshâwur, this has been the case; and when I called for levies of Horse or Foot, the villagers and mountain independent tribes have shown the greatest readiness to side with us against the Hindostance soldiery. But you can well understand what a difficult game it has been to play. No such danger has ever yet threatened India. Nor is it yet over. . . .

"Well, we are now picking up the fragments of this Mutiny. Last night at 11 o'clock Nicholson started with a small force of three hundred Europeans and eight guns, to reach Murdân in two marches by Dobundee Ferry line, and reduce the 55th Native Infantry to surrender. Horne has escaped out of the fort. (The mutineers threatened to roast him.) He is now with Kâdir Khan of Toroo, all right.

"The officers of the 55th * will be in a very painful position. The men say they will murder their officers as soon as any force comes against them. . . .

"I do feel so very thankful now that the trial, or rather mercy, of separation was sent to us. It has made my heart so light amid these cares, and enabled me to think more for others. The foresight of Almighty God, how wonderful it seems beside our beetle-vision!

Reflection on the situation.

"When all this Mutiny shall have been put down, it will still remain for Government to reconstruct its native army—a task not easy to perform. The system and confidence of a hundred years has passed away for ever like a breath. The Government never again can trust the Sepoys, nor the Sepoys believe themselves trusted. The wonderful spectacle of thirty or forty thousand Europeans ruling India will be seen no more. The natives have counted us at last. Fortunately, they never can equal us in character and in physique; and one Englishman will still go a long way. How Providence helps us, and confounds these rebels!

* At Murdân, in Euzofzye.

" Had they been unanimous, they could have murdered us in a day; but they have allowed us to deal with them in detail. And in this light there is great safety in the extended empire it is the fashion to deplore. One province or presidency may be surprised, but the remoter parts have time to prepare and give assistance. It is a most remarkable thing that the telegraph wire has never been cut throughout the Punjab, and so we have been able to effect the most rapid communication; without this instrument we might have been ruined. . . .

" The Mohammedans have, no doubt, been very active in this rebellion, but originally I believe it to have been a Hindoo movement of caste-apprehension of Christianity, seized upon, fostered, and taken advantage of by Moslems as a good opportunity of working their own ends. Had both creeds combined, and agreed to settle it between themselves, after expelling us, we *must* have been expelled; but God did not permit it. And I hear that a terrible religious strife broke out in Delhi between the Mohammedans and the Hindoos, as soon as ever the mutineers had murdered the Europeans. . . .

Absence of combination between the Mohammedans and Hindoos.

" The consoling feature of this terrific Mutiny is that the soldiery have met with very little sympathy indeed from the *people* of any part of the country. Here and there an apparent impunity of mutiny, and end of all government have raised the loose characters to plunder and licence. But as a rule the country has not stirred. This is a glorious reply to those who would fain make out that our rule is not a good one in India. . . . The Mohammedan element is the most dangerous we have to contend with. Our English rule found Hindoos oppressed, and brought them toleration. It found Mohammedans on the throne, and deposed them. As a broad remark, therefore, we stand in the light of friends to one race and enemies to the other.

" In the present Mutiny the panic was a sincere, though

ignorant, Hindoo feeling; but it has been fanned and aggra-
vated by Mohammedans for their own purposes. The
Hindoos have only just found it out when they saw a ‘King
of Delhi’ set up and persecution recommencing. . . .

"We had prayers in church this morning, to pray for
help in this national crisis, and to offer thanksgivings for
the mercies we have received at this station."

Diary letters continued—

Feasting
the levies.

"To-night is the ‘Eed,’ and I am preparing such heaps
of food to feast all our new levies, so that they may long
remember the year in which they came in to help us.* These
wild rascals frighten the sepoys out of their wits, and the
disarmed regiments are, I hear, quite in a panic about them.
It puts me so in mind of old times, in 1848. I feel quite at
home now the thing has come to military measures. I do
not understand it, for I always think I was meant for a
civilian; and yet it seems quite a holiday to have some
soldiering to do. Perhaps it is reaction after long years of
pen-and-ink work.

Good con-
duct of the
people.

"The police and people of the district are behaving
splendidly. They catch all the deserters from the regiments,
and bring them in with every rupee that was on them.
Yesterday they brought in a subahdar with nine hundred
rupees and a gold necklace. I wonder they did not kill and
rob him."

Derajât
levies come
from the
same stock
as at
Mooltân in
1848-49.

* "In the war of 1848-49 it was the whole length of the Derajât border
which gave us those levies of wild swordsmen, matchlock-men, and
cavalry which enabled us, in a season adverse to the march of European
troops, to shut up the rebel Dewan Moolraj in his fortress at Mooltân
and wrest from him one of the most fertile divisions of the Punjab. When
the next struggle came, in this terrible Sepoy Mutiny of 1857, the chiefs
of the Derajât instantly took up arms, raised Horse and Foot, and hurried
to our aid.

"From Peshâwur to Bengal these loyal men were once more found
fighting our battles, in spite of the taunts of the Mohammedans of India."
—(H. B. E.)

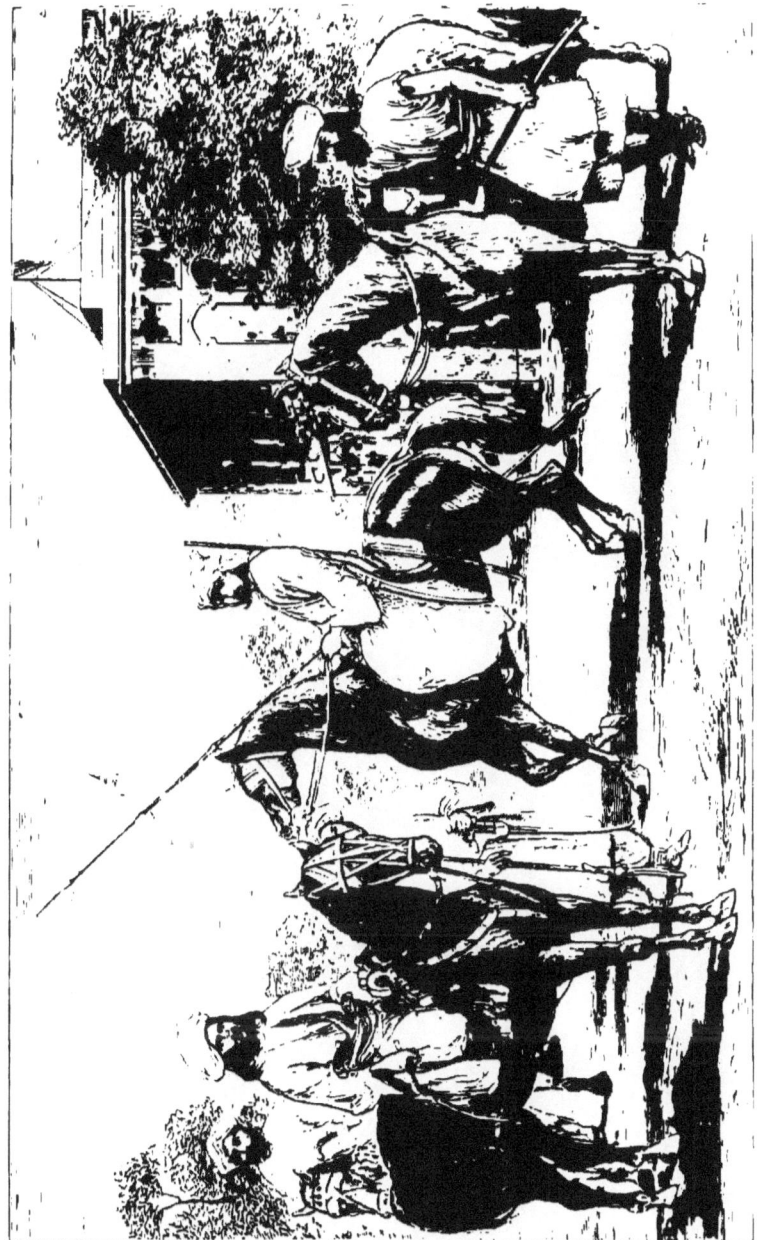

COLONEL EDWARDES' "LEVIES" AT PESHÁWUR, IN 1857, FROM MOOLTÁN AND THE DERAJÁT.

From a drawing by Colonel Rodney Brown, C.A.

We have seen Nicholson start to bring the 55th Regiment, at Murdân, to order; and we must follow him by the aid of the diary.

"When the column came in sight of the fort, all but a hundred and twenty men had mutinied, and marched off towards Swât. Colonel Spottiswood (their commandant), seeing what turn things had taken, blew his brains out with a pistol. He was an old and good officer, much beloved by sepoys, and he could not apparently bear the revulsion of the good feelings of a life. The few men who remained loyal came out with their officers, and were sent off to Nowshera. Then began the pursuit of the mutineers. They had got so great a start that the guns could not come up to them; and the pursuit fell entirely on the Cavalry, of which Nicholson had very few that were really trust-worthy. Mounted on his great grey, he nobly led the chase, was twenty hours in the saddle, and rode seventy miles.

Contrasted with the Sepoys of the 55th.

John Nicholson.

"The mutineers fought desperately whenever overtaken, but a hundred of them were killed, a hundred and fifty taken prisoners, and about four hundred got clear off into the hills. They are supposed now to be in Swât.

"The force is still out in the field, on the left bank of the Swât river; and will probably remain hovering about Aboozye till this crisis subsides. . . .

"The King of Delhi has certainly committed himself; and the notion of a Mohammedan King of Delhi has a very dangerous influence among these fanatical border tribes. Had the Commander-in-chief been a man of action, Delhi would probably have been recovered long ago, and that would have quieted India. As it is, General Anson has died. . . . General Reed succeeds to the command-in-chief of the army temporarily (by force of years), and Brigadier Cotton becomes General of the Peshâwur Division. . . . I have convinced John Lawrence that he must throw his

strength now upon Peshâwur, for it will not do to get into
any embarrassment here. He is sending us reinforcements.
I have got a very anxious and arduous post here, and all my
powers are taxed to the utmost.

"I hope the home Government is aware of what a
'crisis' this is. Twenty or thirty thousand men should
be sent to India, even if the Militia has to be called out
again. . . . You will be glad to hear that Mrs. Charles
Saunders and her husband have escaped safely, after riding
seventy miles. Some faithful native horsemen escorted them
all the way. Many chivalrous things, and heroic things, will
have to be told of these extraordinary natives, when all
comes out ; as well as many horrors—perhaps too sad to see
the light. One of the rebel troopers killed at Delhi was
found with Mrs. ——'s picture hanging round his filthy
neck !"

From Peshâwur, to his wife (continued)—

"June, 1857.

Levies
from the
surround-
ing hills.

"I am overwhelmed with offers of men for service
from every wild tribe on the surrounding hills. Doubtless it was fortunate that we invited these offers; for it
has drawn into our pay all those who, if idle, might have
been led into opposition. It must be a dull heart, indeed,
that does not acknowledge that nothing but God's mercy
has saved us. One turning-point in the crisis was the
persecuting spirit shown by the elated Mohammedans at
Delhi. The Hindoo Rajahs took alarm, bethought them of
former Mogul times, and rallied round John Company. So
the setting-up of the King excited the Mussulmans against
us and the Hindoos for us. The most seditious letters have
been intercepted, preaching the extermination of the infidels.
The devil has certainly done his best to get rid of us ; and,
depend upon it, it shows that Christianity is working at the
very foundations of Hindooism and Mohammedanism.

Religious fear and religious hatred have caused this frightful rebellion, and political causes will be sought in vain.

"All is well at Lucknow, we now hear. Sir Henry Lawrence has done more noble things than any one. We have overcome force with force. Sir Henry has *appealed* to the native regiments with success. He is as wise as he is good. They ought now to make him Commander-in-chief, and collect a Committee to reorganize the Indian army, while the lesson is fresh. . . . <!-- marginal note: Noble bearing of Henry Lawrence at Lucknow. -->

"We want about twenty more European regiments in India, the expense to be made up by getting rid of the useless number of English officers with the native corps. Let the native army be almost entirely a native army, with only three English officers in each corps; but have one European corps to every two or three native corps, so that the whites could thrash the blacks.

"Sir John Lawrence has steered his province through the storm with courage, and I hope the Punjab has set a good example to the rest of India. . . . <!-- marginal note: John Lawrence in the Punjab. -->

"It has been a struggle for empire. It was, I always thought, one of the standing wonders of the world that we held India by an Indian army. The fabric of a hundred years, piled up unreflectingly, province on province, kingdom on kingdom, on the bayonets of a single race, has subsided in a month, like a snow-palace in the sun, and nothing short of this dissolution would, I believe, have ever brought about the reorganization of the army of India on a more solid footing. So it's all for the best, but, alas! the price that has been paid. What mourning and grief there will be in England! It is a second Cabul—not quite so much blood; but really fifty times more danger. . . . <!-- marginal note: Struggle for empire. -->

"Dear Sir Henry was all right on June 1, but Oude in a fearful state. Worse in Rohilcund, where all our countrymen were obliged to fly to Nainée Tál and Meerut. <!-- marginal note: State of Oude. -->

"The Rohilla chief has actually 'executed' (I suppose

hanged) Dr. Hay, the Civil Surgeon of Bareilly (son-in-law of Mr. Thomason), also the judge, named Robertson, and two others. All the officers of the 18th Native Infantry at Bareilly are said to be murdered. The troops of the Bhurtpore Rajah refused to act against the rebels. John Lawrence is working very energetically to send down reinforcements to General Reed. Coke's and Rothney's regiments are on their way by forced marches. They are urgently wanted.

"*June* 19.—Our news from Delhi is not good. General Reed has only half as many men and only half as many guns as the enemy. . . . We shall evidently have as much as we can do to hold India till succours arrive from England; but if we are true to ourselves and act vigorously, with God's help always, we shall do it; and, however anxious and harassed I may be, I never for a moment admit the possibility of ultimate failure. Whatever trials we pass through, I feel quite sure we shall triumph. But it is a dreadful period to have to go through July, August, September, before any large reinforcements can reach India."

Confidence and hope.

There is a public letter from John Lawrence to Government at this time, in which he says, "The Chief Commissioner feels assured that, with three such officers at Peshâwur as Brigadier Sydney Cotton, Lieutenant-Colonel Edwardes, and Lieutenant-Colonel Nicholson, everything that is possible will be done to maintain order and security."

Commendation like this did not often come from this quarter; and it astonished them all. But it cheered the hard-pressed, struggling lives of these brave men, and was worth the effort. Days were too short for work, and nights could rarely be spared for sleep. Edwardes writes to his wife—

"You have no idea what a life I have led. From earliest dawn to latest night receiving reports, issuing orders, holding consultations, enlisting levies, writing innumerable letters and then aroused several times in the night to read 'expresses.'

"*June* 16.—There is nothing decisive yet from Delhi, and I almost fear our troops there are too few;—the old Mooltán story over again. . . . It is a great trial to lead this life of hot-and-cold fits of public news—enough to make one old and grey. There is more trial in this than in fighting!

"*June* 17.—The state of the country gets worse and worse daily; and John Lawrence tells me it is a matter of great difficulty to maintain the communication with General Reed and forward supplies. The head-quarters of the army are approaching Delhi, to recover it from the wretched creature who has declared himself a King. There is a great deal in the name of 'the King of Delhi,' and it has excited the imagination of the Mohammedans a great deal, especially hereabouts; so that the sooner this farthing rushlight is extinguished the better. No new atrocities have taken place since I last wrote, and the postal communications with different parts of the country are gradually being restored. At one time they were at an end. . . . There has been lamentably frequent want of energy. John Lawrence writes, 'There has been no vigour shown, except at Peshawur, (the same at Lahore)."

Things get worse.

Edwardes continues—

"I felt that it was not like an ordinary campaign, in which there is one army against another, and you feel reliance on your own and never doubt as to the issue. Here our own army was the enemy, and the issue very doubtful indeed. God only could have carried us through it. There is a sure refuge in our God, in faith and prayer."

In writing to John Lawrence, Edwardes says (June 13)—

"As to holding the Punjab by two grips—at Peshawur

Sydney
Cotton
proposed
by John
Lawrence
for promo-
tion to
brigadier-
general.

and Lahore, if you consider the matter, this is just what the Sikhs did. I am glad you have written to get Cotton made a brigadier-general. He is, indeed, a fine old fellow, and we are most fortunate in having had him here."

Extracts from diary letters (continued) to his wife—

Position of
affairs at
Peshâwur.

"It is the gravest crisis I have ever seen, though I have been in some trouble ere now. But I rely firmly on God's help and *will*, and believe that it is of little use for the heathen furiously to rage against the great Disposer of events. I have many sources of comfort and support, too. First, that *you*, my most precious possession, are not here in this Maëlstrom. What a relief is this! . . . Second, I have such a noble coadjutor in Nicholson. It was, doubtless, all

Unanimity
in council
at
Peshâwur.

Providential my labouring to get him here. Third, there is entire harmony between us and Brigadier Cotton; and the civil and military strength are united on every occasion. Fourth, God gives me good health throughout all this trial.

People of
Peshâwur
loyal.

Fifth, there seems no disposition of the *people* to rise against us, though, of course, if we got involved in a doubtful struggle with our own troops, bit by bit the people would be tempted into excesses and awaken all their religious passions. It is absolutely necessary for the safety of the Punjab that Peshâwur should be secure; and I am glad that John Lawrence has aroused himself to see it. He began by checking me for raising levies! Now we can hardly get enough of them!

"How valuable, too, is now our friendly policy with Afghanistan! Suppose we had been still on the terms I found existing at the close of 1853. We must have surely had Dost Mahommed Khan down upon us."

In a letter written to John Lawrence a little later on, dated September 12, when the test had been a little longer tried, Edwardes says—

"I am glad you will try and contrive to bring up one, if not two European corps into this neighbourhood (Pindee and Huttean or Shumshabad would be better than Peshawur itself) as soon as you can. Either we never wanted any force here or we are now trusting to a chapter of accidents. There is no help for it; and the policy we have adopted with Cabul has proved a perfect God-send to us; it keeps all above us quiet in a wonderful way. Still, we ought not to stand in this helpless position a week longer than we can help."

Value of the friendship with Cabul.

And, after giving instances of the effect of our relations with Cabul being friendly, he adds—

" It is clear that, if we had been on *bad* terms just now with Cabul, we should have lost, first Peshawur, and then the Punjab, and all India would have reeled under the blow.

" Does it strike you so ? And do you *now* regret the time and money given to our treaties and moolakâts ?

" Positively, God has provided for us, when we little saw the *full* force of what we were doing."

This gentle effort to point a moral is the only effort ever made by him to extort an acknowledgment from his chief of the value of the treaties which he so much opposed, and the only reply was, " But you didn't know when you made the treaty that the *Mutiny* was coming," to which Edwardes answered—

" Concerning our policy with Cabul, of course, we did not foresee this Mutiny when we made our treaties ; but the object of every treaty is to make friends against a day of difficulty, whatever that difficulty may be ; and it seems to me that our not foreseeing that the difficulty would be *a mutiny* does not affect the wisdom of the policy or the advantage of the result.

Letter to John Lawrence on Cabul treaties.

" When you put a paling round your garden, you do it

to save the flowers, and it will be impossible to say whether it will be your own donkey or your neighbour's which will break loose and try to get into the parterre.

" Yours affectionately,

" H. B. E."

This is a curious little episode, after all our past experience, and looks as if—

> " A man convinced against his will
> Is of the same opinion still."

It is of interest to know that the opinions of John Nicholson and Herbert Edwardes were identical on this subject, as on most political subjects. We find an entry here in Edwardes's diary letters to his wife—

Nicholson's opinion. " Nicholson was saying this morning he never thought we should live to derive such solid advantage from our alliance with Dost Mahommed as we are doing at this crisis, in the perfect peace of our border; so that we are left at liberty to contend with our own sepoys. There can be no question as to what must have happened had the Ameer of Cabul now been our foe, and moved down upon us while the army was in mutiny. You will understand how satisfactory this is to me."

Visit of three hundred outlaws. An exciting scene occurred about this time at Peshâwur, which will give a sample of the surroundings of Edwardes's life. One day, one of his men came running into his study, saying, " O Sahib ! a number of armed hill-men are coming into the cantonment, and calling out for your house. What are we to do ?" And so it truly was. " Nearly three hundred Afreedees, armed in every imaginable manner, came down from the hills, and asked me to enlist them as regular soldiers." They were " outlaws "—wild men who had committed crimes so many and so great that they had to take to their hills and hide from the pursuit of justice. And they thought, wisely, that *now* the time had come to get the score paid off in "service." So Edwardes made them sit down on the lawn and seated himself in their midst, and drew out the stories of their deeds of crime and "outlawry." And as they told them, he called his moonshee to bring out the "records" and compare the account.

And then he ruled what ready justice they were to perform, according to their own rude laws, to give such compensation as they could to the men they had injured. Rough-and-ready justice, such as became the times and the circumstances, was all that suited the occasion; but it was enough to show them that their crimes were not condoned until they had done their best to make restitution, and only then could their ban be taken off or their "services" be accepted by the Government they had defied.

"What a scene it was! It might have been an ambush as easily as anything else. They might have cut me in pieces and dispersed themselves immediately. At least, these thoughts occurred to me at the moment as among the possibilities. But the great secret of association with these utter barbarians is to take them as they come, like wild beasts, and show no fear of them. Habit has taught me this; and I went among them and picked out their youths, and enrolled them as recruits, then brought the older ones, weather-beaten, scarred, and scored with frays, into our willow-walk in the garden, sat them down in the shade, and, after talking to them, dismissed them to their hills again with a rupee each, quite satisfied that they had been honourably treated. I was not sorry, however, to get them out of the cantonments again.

"What short-sighted creatures these Hindostanee sepoys are! How many new races, like unworked mines, are ready to fill up the gaps in our native army!"

It was a great advantage to the peace of Peshâwur to give employment to these wild and turbulent spirits; and Edwardes says— *A field for turbulent spirits.*

"I am inviting a big blackguard, named Mokurrum

Khan (who is tired of Swât), to come with his followers and
go down to Delhi with Shazâdah Jumhoor's son. The old
Shazâdah proposed it, and I was delighted to agree. He is
a man of mettle, and his sowars too. They have bothered
us for six years, but never done unforgiveable things.
Swât is being a very good neighbour to us just now, by a
wonderful turn in the cards; and I hope this district will
send aid instead of being a trouble."

Amusing
incident.
Æsop's
Fables. There was an amusing incident with this Shazâdah.   One
day he asked for an interview, and, it being granted, he came
in and threw down his turban at Edwardes's feet.

"What is the matter?" said he.   "What does this
mean?"

"My Lord," he said, "I always knew you were a wise
man; but I never knew you were so great a man as I know
you to be now! I verily believe you are the author himself of
Æsop's Fables" (the highest pinnacle of wisdom in their eyes).

"Why, what do you mean?   What have I done?"

"Done?" said Shazâdah Jumhoor; "why, *see* what you've
done! This last stroke of policy is wisdom itself" (in having
sent down to Delhi a regiment of wild frontier men).   "See,
if they kill the enemy—*well;* if the enemy kills them—
better still! Now I know that you are the wisest man that
was ever known.   The peace of this frontier is secured whichever way it happens!"

About this time Edwardes writes—

Thoughts
on the
opium
trade. "Thinking over Job's prayer, 'Do not condemn me;
show me wherefore Thou contendest with me,' it strikes me
as a curious coincidence that the East India Company's
Government is shaken to its very foundations at the very
time that we are warring with China; which Indian legislation and English legislation together have been for several
years attacking and poisoning with opium, to the moral
degradation of millions of Chinese. The very troops that
England had upon the seas on their way to coerce Canton
are obliged to be intercepted and brought to the rescue of

India. In this, chastisement and mercy, trouble and remedy, are mixed together in the marvellous way that God's dealings delight in; but I cannot but think that the opium trade from China to India is one main reason for the national shock we are now enduring. I am *no* Cobdenite, and would certainly have voted with Lord Palmerston on the Chinese War question; but the melancholy thing is that we are morally in the wrong with reference to the Chinese; the opium injury lies at the root of all their hostilities against us. Our commerce is unholy in this matter, and I hope Lord Shaftesbury will carry his point with all my heart."

"*June* 10.—This morning there was a terrible execution parade. Out of one hundred and twenty men of the 55th Native Infantry taken prisoners in the fight and flight of May 25, at Murdán, one-third (or forty mutineers) were blown away from guns. I was out with all my levies, guarding the avenues of cantonments; so I did not witness it. But the general says it was a frightful spectacle. All this is very dreadful, but right and necessary." *

Military execution parade at Peshâwur.

This is the occasion taken by the biographer of Lord Lawrence lately to enlarge upon " Colonel Edwardes's blood-

---

* " The news of these executions and the mode adopted in carrying them into effect spread far and wide, and, even in the city of Cabul itself, were the subject of discussion and of astonishment. It was clear to all that discipline was upheld and maintained . . . and the Afghans, keenly watching the turn of events, on finding that the supremacy of the British Government had prevailed, were deterred from an aggressive movement. . . . The subsidy given by the British Commissioner to Dost Mahommed no doubt had some effect on the mind of that monarch; but the Afghans themselves, ever restless and unsettled, were thoroughly meditating an attack on the British frontier, and a rich harvest in Hindostan, and were alone deterred from the movement by the imposing attitude which had been assumed at Peshâwur; and it came to the author's knowledge afterwards that thirty thousand Afghans had shod their horses at one time, ready to invade our territory " (Cotton, pp. 174, 175. See also " Enclosures to Secret Letters from India," July 23, 1858, pp. 152, 169, 197.) " In a proclamation issued by the Persian Government, the Ameer was urged, as a Mohammedan, to side with the Persians against the English " (Ibid., p. 124).

Effect of vigorous action at Peshâwur felt in Cabul.

thirstiness;" and, of course, not understanding his character, he is not aware how entirely the opposite of truth is any such allegation; but he must also have forgotten (or be ignorant of) the relative duties of civil and political charge, and military command; for these trials were by *military court-martial*, and the punishments were *military* also, in which Colonel Edwardes could not interfere nor be in any way held responsible.

This is only remarked in passing, for by no one who knew Colonel Edwardes could the idea be ever entertained of his character for a moment; and it therefore does not call for further notice.

Brigadier Sydney Cotton expresses his opinion in a public letter on this matter.

Sydney Cotton's opinion.

"Peshâwur, April 20, 1858.

"With regard to the injunction placed on me by the Chief Commissioner not to carry into effect the execution of the hundred and forty criminals, but to take one-fourth or one-third of them, which latter I determined on. . . .

"I am of opinion, and I was at the time of the great execution of forty criminals blown away from guns, that mutiny was raging to such an extent throughout the country that no one ought to escape punishment (capital); and I now believe that if the hundred and forty men had been executed, as I intended, we should not have had the 51st affair at all.

"No doubt Sir John Lawrence's views were humane, *but it was not mercy in the end.* . . .

"(Signed)   SYDNEY COTTON."

While such exciting scenes were taking place at Peshâwur, it is refreshing to turn to the comparatively peaceful Hazâra, and read the report of it given by the pen of Major John R. Becher, who was doing good service there, and holding the people firmly, while he won their love and regard.

"Abbottabad, June 2, 1857.

"MY DEAR EDWARDES,

John Becher in Hazâra.

"I am very much obliged to you for your letter; it was most acceptable. I rejoice to see you thus riding on

the whirlwind and controlling the storm, and glad amidst
the thunder-clouds. The letter sounds like a clarion-blast,
full of vigour and self-reliance. And I am proud to see
you and Nicholson in this grand storm masters at your
work, right glad that Nicholson did not leave ; there was
work for his war-horse, and he is in his element, the first
who has struck a death-blow.

"And we may be proud of John Lawrence as a master-
spirit in these times.

"I long every hour to hear more of you at Peshâwur.
Here I am tranquil, only that, of course, there is excitement
among the people. Chiefs and people flock in. They are
in the most loyal spirit, desirous only to be employed more
than I can employ them. If I ask for two horsemen I get
ten supplied. I really feel very happy at seeing this good
disposition, and am very confident that it will endure.
Fûzul Khan has put some of his hawk-horse across the
river, and they have caught Poorbeas on their way to Sat-
tâna. I have placed posts at all the points of communication with Pindee or Cashmere, to intercept correspondence
or one black sheep of Poorbeas. . . .

"Hurrah for Sir Henry at Lucknow! What a good,
noble speech he has made! and how wise he is!

"Ever yours, my dear Edwardes,
"JOHN R. BECHER."

And John Lawrence, writing to Edwardes about the same
date, says—

"The Governor-General says that Henry has managed
admirably in Oude. He is just the man for such a crisis.
I wish we had another like him at Delhi.

"(Signed)   J. L."

From Sir John Lawrence to Colonel Edwardes.

"June 13, 1857.

"I have sent four kossids off from Umballa to Agra,

to get a message telegraphed that Cotton may be made a brigadier-general. He is an old 'trump.'

" Yours affectionately,

"(Signed)   JOHN LAWRENCE."

Here's a nice bit of friendship between Edwardes and Cotton, in a letter from the latter—

" Peshâwur, May 28, 1857.

" MY DEAR EDWARDES,

"I thank you very sincerely for your kind and cordial congratulations.

"I feel confident in the prevailing unanimity amongst us all, and pray for its continuance.

"I feel very proud of your expressions of confidence in me.

"We have had the experience of nearly four years together on this frontier.

" Believe me,
" Ever yours most sincerely,

"(Signed)   SYDNEY COTTON."

Unanimity and cordiality in council a strength in work. Such unanimity and cordiality of feeling between all the men on this frontier was a great strength and power, and made everything work well, all joining heart and hand together. Major Henderson, Deputy-Commissioner at Kohât, writes—

" Kohât, May 21, 1857.

" MY DEAR EDWARDES,

Major Henderson at Kohât. "It is of no use making any concealment any longer, so I'll move the treasure into the fort in the morning, and I have already garrisoned it with my own men. From to-morrow I will also mount a strong picket over the guns, and then, come what may, we need not fear for the result. If you want *more* men, tell me, and you shall have them at once."

And from Major Richard Pollock, then Deputy-Commissioner in Derajât—

"Dera Ghazee Khan.

"Nothing could really have been better than the feeling exhibited by the head-men of this district. They could hardly conceive that any one would dare perpetrate the enormities they heard of, but begged to be employed if they could be of use."

And there were ready hands to volunteer for commanding the new levies. As a sample, here is one—

"Kohât, May 16, 1857.

"MY DEAR COLONEL EDWARDES,

"I write to propose to you, if Government requires to raise a few men as a temporary measure, to offer my services.

"I could raise a regiment in a short time, and if a few of the disciplined trained Puthân troops were intermixed, a draft of ten from two or three of the regiments, a respectable regiment might be ready for immediate fighting at all events, if required. . . . Don't trouble yourself with answering this unless you like my proposal, as I know you have too much to do in these troubled, anxious times. But if I can be of use, here I am.

"Yours very truly,

"(Signed)   THOMAS KEYES."

It would give a very incomplete idea of the work done by the Commissioner of Peshâwur during these years we have been passing through, to tell only of the political work connected with the relations of England with Afghanistan, resulting in bringing about and concluding the Treaties with the Afghans, which, as we have seen, were signed in 1855 and 1857. Arduous as this political work with Cabul was, there was, besides it, a vast amount of labour and tact required in the delicate handling of all the many hill tribes that surround Peshâwur and form the border of the north-west frontier of British India. Quoting from Dr. Bellew, "It may be said to commence at the top of the Kaghan Valley adjoining the Chilas district. It skirts the range of the Black Mountain, which separates Kaghan from the Indus, and then, reaching that river, follows its left bank to Torbela, where, crossing once, it runs along the base of the hills encircling the Peshâwur Valley as far as the Khyber Pass. From this point the border is deflected back towards the Indus, and, passing round the Afreedie Hills to Kohât, thence proceeds westward up the Meranza Valley along the base of the Orukzai and Zwaeenakht Hills to the river Kûrrum. Here it is again turned back, and, passing round the Wuzuree Hills, strikes the Tukhti-Suleman range in the Dera Ismael Khan district. Our north-west frontier, as we received it from the Sikhs, extends in an irregular and ill-defined line along the base of the mountain region separating the Indus Valley from the Cabul Highlands. These mountains may be described in general terms as forming a continuous, though somewhat uneven chain, with a generally bare and rocky aspect towards the southern portion of the range, and with a more or less wooded or pine-clad surface in its northern portion. They are traversed by a series of passes leading down from the Cabul Highlands to the Indus Valley, and are inhabited by a number of different Pathân tribes, of whom those located on the western slopes are the subjects of the Cabul Government; whilst those occupying the eastern slopes, where the valleys mostly open directly on to the Indus Valley, and all either directly or indirectly drain into it, are, as regards government, taxes, and allegiance, thoroughly independent."

(margin note: Position of Peshâwur among the surrounding hill tribes, many of them subjects of Cabul, and many thoroughly independent.*)*

This sketch of the wild hills that surround Peshâwur will help the reader to understand that the wild inhabitants of such regions were but restless and dangerous neighbours in such troubled times as these, and would add greatly to the anxiety of the events that will follow.

END OF VOL. I.

PRINTED BY WILLIAM CLOWES AND SONS, LIMITED, LONDON AND BICCLES.

A LIST OF

KEGAN PAUL, TRENCH, & CO.'S

PUBLICATIONS.

1 *Paternoster Square,*
London.

A LIST OF

KEGAN PAUL, TRENCH, & CO.'S
PUBLICATIONS.

CONTENTS.

A. K. H. B.—FROM A QUIET PLACE. A New Volume of Sermons. Crown 8vo. 5s.

ALLEN (Rev. R.) M.A.—ABRAHAM; HIS LIFE, TIMES, AND TRAVELS, 3,800 years ago. With Map. Second Edition. Post 8vo. 6s.

ALLIES (T. W.) M.A.—PER CRUCEM AD LUCEM. The Result of a Life. 2 vols. Demy 8vo. 25s.

A LIFE'S DECISION. Crown 8vo. 7s. 6d.

ALLNATT (F. J. B.) B.D.—THE WITNESS OF ST. MATTHEW. An Inquiry into the Sequence of Inspired Thought pervading the First Gospel, and into its Result of Unity, Symmetry, and Completeness, as a Perfect Portrait of the Perfect Man. Crown 8vo. 5s.

AMOS (Prof. Sheldon)—THE HISTORY AND PRINCIPLES OF THE CIVIL LAW OF ROME. An aid to the study of Scientific and Comparative Jurisprudence. Demy 8vo. 16s.

ANCIENT and MODERN BRITONS: a Retrospect. 2 vols. demy 8vo. 24s.

ANDERDON (Rev. W. H.)—FASTI APOSTOLICI. A Chronology of the Years between the Ascension of Our Lord and the Martyrdom of SS. Peter and Paul. Second Edition Enlarged. Square 8vo. 5s.

EVENINGS WITH THE SAINTS. Crown 8vo. 5s.

ANDERSON (David)—'SCENES' IN THE COMMONS. Crown 8vo. 5s.

ARMSTRONG (Richard A.) B.A. — LATTER-DAY TEACHERS. Six Lectures. Small crown 8vo. 2s. 6d.

AUBERTIN (J. J.)—A FLIGHT TO MEXICO. With 7 full-page Illustrations and a Railway Map of Mexico. Crown 8vo. 7s. 6d.

BADGER (George Percy) D.C.L.—AN ENGLISH-ARABIC LEXICON. In which the equivalents for English Words and Idiomatic Sentences are rendered into literary and colloquial Arabic. Royal 4to. 80s.

BAGEHOT (Walter)—THE ENGLISH CONSTITUTION. New and Revised Edition. Crown 8vo. 7s. 6d.

LOMBARD STREET. A Description of the Money Market. Eighth Edition. Crown 8vo. 7s. 6d.

ESSAYS ON PARLIAMENTARY REFORM. Crown 8vo. 5s.

SOME ARTICLES ON THE DEPRECIATION OF SILVER, AND TOPICS CONNECTED WITH IT. Demy 8vo. 5s.

BAGENAL (Philip H.)—THE AMERICAN-IRISH AND THEIR INFLUENCE ON IRISH POLITICS. Crown 8vo. 5s.

BAGOT (Alan) C.E.—ACCIDENTS IN MINES : Their Causes and Prevention. Crown 8vo. 6s.

THE PRINCIPLES OF COLLIERY VENTILATION. Second Edition, greatly enlarged, crown 8vo. 5s.

THE PRINCIPLES OF CIVIL ENGINEERING IN ESTATE MANAGEMENT. Crown 8vo. 7s. 6d.

BAKER (Sir Sherston, Bart.)—THE LAWS RELATING TO QUARANTINE. Crown 8vo. 12s. 6d.

BALDWIN (Capt. J. H.)—THE LARGE AND SMALL GAME OF BENGAL AND THE NORTH-WESTERN PROVINCES OF INDIA. Small 4to. With 20 Illustrations. New and Cheaper Edition. Small 4to. 10s. 6d.

BALLIN (Ada S. and F. L.)—A HEBREW GRAMMAR. With Exercises selected from the Bible. Crown 8vo. 7s. 6d.

BARCLAY (Edgar) — MOUNTAIN LIFE IN ALGERIA. Crown 4to. With numerous Illustrations by Photogravure. 16s.

BARLOW (F. W.) M.A.—THE ULTIMATUM OF PESSIMISM. An Ethical Study. Demy 8vo. 6s.

BARNES (William)—OUTLINES OF REDECRAFT (LOGIC). With English Wording. Crown 8vo. 3s.

BAUR (Ferdinand) Dr. Ph., Professor in Maulbronn.—A PHILOLOGICAL INTRODUCTION TO GREEK AND LATIN FOR STUDENTS. Translated and adapted from the German by C. KEGAN PAUL, M.A., and the Rev. E. D. STONE, M.A. Third Edition. Crown 8vo. 6s.

BELLARS (Rev. W.)—THE TESTIMONY OF CONSCIENCE TO THE TRUTH AND DIVINE ORIGIN OF THE CHRISTIAN REVELATION. Burney Prize Essay. Small crown 8vo. 3s. 6d.

BELLASIS (Edward)—THE MONEY JAR OF PLAUTUS AT THE ORATORY SCHOOL : An Account of the Recent Representation. With Appendix and 16 Illustrations. Small 4to. 2s.

BELLINGHAM (Henry) M.P.—SOCIAL ASPECTS OF CATHOLICISM AND PROTESTANTISM IN THEIR CIVIL BEARING UPON NATIONS. Translated and adapted from the French of M. le Baron de Haulleville. With a Preface by his Eminence Cardinal Manning. Second and Cheaper Edition. Crown 8vo. 3s. 6d.

BELLINGHAM (H. Belsches Graham)—UPS AND DOWNS OF SPANISH TRAVEL. Second Edition. Crown 8vo. 5s.

BENN (Alfred W.) THE GREEK PHILOSOPHERS. 2 vols. Demy 8vo. 28s.

BENT (J. Theodore)—GENOA : How the Republic Rose and Fell. With 18 Illustrations. Demy 8vo. 18s.

BIBLE FOLK-LORE.—A Study in Comparative Mythology. Large crown 8vo. 10s. 6d.

BIRD (Charles) F.G.S.—Higher Education in Germany and England : Being a Brief Practical Account of the Organisation and Curriculum of the German Higher Schools. With Critical Remarks and Suggestions with reference to those of England. Small crown 8vo. 2s. 6d.

BLACKLEY (Rev. W. S.)—Essays on Pauperism. 16mo. cloth, 1s. 6d. ; sewed, 1s.

BLECKLY (Henry)—Socrates and the Athenians : an Apology. Crown 8vo. 2s. 6d.

BLOOMFIELD (The Lady)—Reminiscences of Court and Diplomatic Life. New and Cheaper Edition. With Frontispiece. Crown 8vo. 6s.

BLUNT (The Ven. Archdeacon)—The Divine Patriot, and other Sermons, Preached in Scarborough and in Cannes. New and Cheaper Edition. Crown 8vo. 4s. 6d.

BLUNT (Wilfrid S.)—The Future of Islam. Crown 8vo. 6s.

BODDY (Alexander A.)—To Kairwân the Holy. Scenes in Muhammedan Africa. With Route Map, and 8 Illustrations by A. F. Jacassey. Crown 8vo. 6s.

BOOLE (Mary)—Symbolical Methods of Study. Crown 8vo .5s.

BOUVERIE-PUSEY (S. E. B.)—Permanence and Evolution. An Inquiry into the supposed Mutability of Animal Types. Crown 8vo. 5s.

BOWEN (H. C.) M.A.—Studies in English, for the use of Modern Schools. 7th Thousand. Small crown 8vo. 1s. 6d.

English Grammar for Beginners. Fcp. 8vo. 1s.

Simple English Poems. English Literature for Junior Classes. In Four Parts. Parts I., II., and III. 6d. each ; Part IV. 1s. ; complete, 3s.

BRADLEY (F. H.)—The Principles of Logic. Demy 8vo. 16s.

BRIDGETT (Rev. T. E.)— History of the Holy Eucharist in Great Britain. 2 vols. Demy 8vo. 18s.

BRODRICK (The Hon. G. C.)—Political Studies. Demy 8vo. 14s.

BROOKE (Rev. S. A.)—Life and Letters of the Late Rev. F. W. Robertson, M.A. Edited by.
I. Uniform with Robertson's Sermons. 2 vols. With Steel Portrait, 7s. 6d.
II. Library Edition. 8vo. With Portrait, 12s.
III. A Popular Edition. In 1 vol. 8vo. 6s.

The Fight of Faith. Sermons preached on various occasions. Fifth Edition. Crown 8vo. 7s. 6d.

The Spirit of the Christian Life. Third Edition. Crown 8vo. 5s.

Theology in the English Poets.—Cowper, Coleridge, Wordsworth, and Burns. Fifth Edition. Post 8vo. 5s.

Christ in Modern Life. Sixteenth Edition. Crown 8vo. 5s.

Sermons. First Series. Thirteenth Edition. Crown 8vo. 5s.

Sermons. Second Series. Sixth Edition. Crown 8vo. 5s.

BROWN (Rev. J. Baldwin) B.A.—THE HIGHER LIFE: its Reality, Experience, and Destiny. Sixth Edition. Crown 8vo. 5*s.*

DOCTRINE OF ANNIHILATION IN THE LIGHT OF THE GOSPEL OF LOVE. Five Discourses. Fourth Edition. Crown 8vo. 2*s.* 6*d.*

THE CHRISTIAN POLICY OF LIFE. A Book for Young Men of Business. Third Edition. Crown 8vo. 3*s.* 6*d.*

BROWN (S. Borton) B.A.—THE FIRE BAPTISM OF ALL FLESH ; or, the Coming Spiritual Crisis of the Dispensation. Crown 8vo. 6*s.*

BROWN (Horatio F.)—LIFE ON THE LAGOONS. With two Illustrations and a Map. Crown 8vo. 6*s.*

BROWNBILL (John)—PRINCIPLES OF ENGLISH CANON LAW. Part I. General Introduction. Crown 8vo. 6*s.*

BROWNE (W. R.)—THE INSPIRATION OF THE NEW TESTAMENT. With a Preface by the Rev. J. P. NORRIS, D.D. Fcp. 8vo. 2*s.* 6*d.*

BURDETT (Henry C.)—HELP IN SICKNESS : Where to Go and What to Do. Crown 8vo. 1*s.* 6*d.*

HELPS TO HEALTH : The Habitation, The Nursery, The Schoolroom, and The Person. With a Chapter on Pleasure and Health Resorts. Crown 8vo. 1*s.* 6*d.*

BURTON (Mrs. Richard)—THE INNER LIFE OF SYRIA, PALESTINE, AND THE HOLY LAND. Post 8vo. 6*s.*

BUSBECQ (Ogier Ghiselin de)—HIS LIFE AND LETTERS. By CHARLES THORNTON FORSTER, M.A., and F. H. BLACKBURNE DANIELL, M.A. 2 vols. With Frontispieces. Demy 8vo. 24*s.*

CARPENTER (W. B.) LL.D., M.D., F.R.S., &c.—THE PRINCIPLES OF MENTAL PHYSIOLOGY. With their Applications to the Training and Discipline of the Mind, and the Study of its Morbid Conditions. Illustrated. Sixth Edition. 8vo. 12*s.*

CATHOLIC DICTIONARY-- Containing some account of the Doctrine, Discipline, Rites, Ceremonies, Councils, and Religious Orders of the Catholic Church. By WILLIAM E. ADDIS and THOMAS ARNOLD, M.A. Second Edition, demy 8vo. 21*s.*

CERVANTES—JOURNEY TO PARNASSUS. Spanish Text, with Translation into English Tercets, Preface, and Illustrative Notes, by JAMES Y. GIBSON. Crown 8vo. 12*s.*

CHEYNE (Rev. T. K.)—THE PROPHECIES OF ISAIAH. Translated with Critical Notes and Dissertations. 2 vols. Third Edition. Demy 8vo. 25*s.*

CHICHELE (Mary)—DOING AND UNDOING. A Story. 1 vol. Crown 8vo.

CLAIRAUT—ELEMENTS OF GEOMETRY. Translated by Dr. KAINES. With 145 Figures. Crown 8vo. 4*s.* 6*d.*

CLARKE (Rev. Henry James) A.K.C.—THE FUNDAMENTAL SCIENCE. Demy 8vo. 10*s.* 6*d.*

CLAYDEN (P. W.)—SAMUEL SHARPE—EGYPTOLOGIST AND TRANSLATOR OF THE BIBLE. Crown 8vo. 6*s.*

CLIFFORD (Samuel)—WHAT THINK YE OF THE CHRIST? Crown 8vo. 6*s.*

CLODD (Edward) F.R.A.S.—THE CHILDHOOD OF THE WORLD : a Simple Account of Man in Early Times. Seventh Edition. Crown 8vo. 3*s.* A Special Edition for Schools, 1*s.*

CLODD (*Edward*)—continued.

THE CHILDHOOD OF RELIGIONS.　Including a Simple Account of the Birth and Growth of Myths and Legends.　Eighth Thousand.　Crown 8vo. 5*s*.
A Special Edition for Schools. 1*s*. 6*d*.

JESUS OF NAZARETH.　With a brief sketch of Jewish History to the Time of His Birth.　Small crown 8vo. 6*s*.

COGHLAN (*J. Cole*) *D.D.*—THE MODERN PHARISEE, AND OTHER SERMONS.　Edited by the Very Rev. H. H. DICKINSON, D.D., Dean of Chapel Royal, Dublin.　New and Cheaper Edition.　Crown 8vo. 7*s*. 6*d*.

COLE (*George R. Fitz-Roy*)—THE PERUVIANS AT HOME.　Crown 8vo. 6*s*.

COLERIDGE (*Sara*)—MEMOIR AND LETTERS OF SARA COLERIDGE.　Edited by her Daughter.　With Index.　Cheap Edition.　With one Portrait. 7*s*. 6*d*.

COLLECTS EXEMPLIFIED (*The*) — Being Illustrations from the Old and New Testaments of the Collects for the Sundays after Trinity.　By the Author of ' A Commentary on the Epistles and Gospels.'　Edited by the Rev. JOSEPH JACKSON.　Crown 8vo. 5*s*.

CONNELL (*A. K.*)—DISCONTENT AND DANGER IN INDIA.　Small crown 8vo. 3*s*. 6*d*.

THE ECONOMIC REVOLUTION OF INDIA.　Crown 8vo. 4*s*. 6*d*.

CORY (*William*)—A GUIDE TO MODERN ENGLISH HISTORY.　Part I.— MDCCCXV.-MDCCCXXX.　Demy 8vo. 9*s*.　Part II.—MDCCCXXX.- MDCCCXXXV. 15*s*.

COTTERILL (*H. B.*)—AN INTRODUCTION TO THE STUDY OF POETRY.　Crown 8vo. 7*s*. 6*d*.

COUTTS (*Francis Burdett Money*)—THE TRAINING OF THE INSTINCT OF LOVE.　With a Preface by the Rev. EDWARD THRING, M.A.　Small crown 8vo. 2*s*. 6*d*.

COX (*Rev. Sir George W.*) *M.A., Bart.*—THE MYTHOLOGY OF THE ARYAN NATIONS.　New Edition.　Demy 8vo. 16*s*.

TALES OF ANCIENT GREECE.　New Edition.　Small crown 8vo. 6*s*.

A MANUAL OF MYTHOLOGY IN THE FORM OF QUESTION AND ANSWER.　New Edition.　Fcp. 8vo. 3*s*.

AN INTRODUCTION TO THE SCIENCE OF COMPARATIVE MYTHOLOGY AND FOLK-LORE.　Second Edition.　Crown 8vo. 7*s*. 6*d*.

COX (*Rev. Sir G. W.*) *M.A., Bart., and JONES* (*Eustace Hinton*)— POPULAR ROMANCES OF THE MIDDLE AGES.　Third Edition, in 1 vol.　Crown 8vo. 6*s*.

COX (*Rev. Samuel*) *D.D.*—A COMMENTARY ON THE BOOK OF JOB.　With a Translation.　Demy 8vo. 15*s*.

SALVATOR MUNDI ; or, Is Christ the Saviour of all Men?　Ninth Edition.　Crown 8vo. 5*s*.

THE LARGER HOPE : a Sequel to ' SALVATOR MUNDI.'　Second Edition. 16mo. 1*s*.

THE GENESIS OF EVIL, AND OTHER SERMONS, mainly expository.　Third Edition.　Crown 8vo. 6*s*.

COX (*Rev. Samuel*)—continued.
BALAAM : An Exposition and a Study. Crown 8vo. 5s.
MIRACLES. An Argument and a Challenge. Crown 8vo. 2s. 6d.

CRAVEN (*Mrs.*)—A YEAR'S MEDITATIONS. Crown 8vo. 6s.

CRAWFURD (*Oswald*)—PORTUGAL, OLD AND NEW. With Illustrations and Maps. New and Cheaper Edition. Crown 8vo. 6s.

CRIME OF CHRISTMAS DAY : A Tale of the Latin Quarter. By the Author of 'My Ducats and My Daughter.' 1s.

CROZIER (*John Beattie*) *M.B.*—THE RELIGION OF THE FUTURE. Crown 8vo. 6s.

DANIELL (*Clarmont*)—THE GOLD TREASURE OF INDIA : An Inquiry into its Amount, the Cause of its Accumulation, and the Proper Means of Using it as Money. Crown 8vo. 5s.

DANISH PARSONAGE. By an Angler. Crown 8vo. 6s.

DARKNESS AND DAWN. The Peaceful Birth of a New Age. Small crown 8vo. 2s. 6d.

DAVIDSON (*Rev. Samuel*) *D.D., LL.D.*—CANON OF THE BIBLE : Its Formation, History, and Fluctuations. Third and revised Edition. Small crown 8vo. 5s.
THE DOCTRINE OF LAST THINGS, contained in the New Testament, compared with the Notions of the Jews and the Statements of Church Creeds. Small crown 8vo. 3s. 6d.

DAVIDSON (*Thomas*)—THE PARTHENON FRIEZE, and other Essays. Crown 8vo. 6s.

DAWSON (*Geo.*) *M.A.*—PRAYERS, WITH A DISCOURSE ON PRAYER. Edited by his Wife. First Series. Eighth Edition. Crown 8vo. 6s.
    *** Also a New and Cheaper Edition. Crown 8vo. 3s. 6d.
PRAYERS, WITH A DISCOURSE ON PRAYER. Edited by GEORGE ST. CLAIR. Second Series. Crown 8vo. 6s.
SERMONS ON DISPUTED POINTS AND SPECIAL OCCASIONS. Edited by his Wife. Fourth Edition. Crown 8vo. 6s.
SERMONS ON DAILY LIFE AND DUTY. Edited by his Wife. Fourth Edition. Crown 8vo. 6s.
THE AUTHENTIC GOSPEL, and other Sermons. Edited by GEORGE ST. CLAIR. Third Edition. Crown 8vo. 6s.
THREE BOOKS OF GOD. Nature, History, and Scripture. Sermons, Edited by GEORGE ST. CLAIR. Crown 8vo. 6s.

DE JONCOURT (*Madame Marie*)—WHOLESOME COOKERY. Third Edition. Crown 8vo. 3s. 6d.

DE LONG (*Lieut.-Com. G. W.*)—THE VOYAGE OF THE 'JEANNETTE.' The Ship and Ice Journals of. Edited by his Wife, EMMA DE LONG. With Portraits, Maps, and many Illustrations on wood and stone. 2 vols. Demy 8vo. 36s.

DEMOCRACY IN THE OLD WORLD AND THE NEW. By the Author of 'The Suez Canal, the Eastern Question, and Abyssinia,' &c. Small crown 8vo. 2s. 6d.

DEVEREUX (*W. Cope*) *R.N., F.R.G.S.*—FAIR ITALY, THE RIVIERA AND MONTE CARLO. Comprising a Tour through North and South Italy and Sicily, with a short account of Malta. Crown 8vo. 6s.

DOING AND UNDOING. A Story. By MARY CHICHELE. 1 vol. Crown 8vo.

DOWDEN (Edward) LL.D.—SHAKSPERE : a Critical Study of his Mind and Art. Seventh Edition. Post 8vo. 12s.

STUDIES IN LITERATURE, 1789-1877. Third Edition. Large post 8vo. 6s.

DUFFIELD (A. J.)—DON QUIXOTE : HIS CRITICS AND COMMENTATORS With a brief account of the minor works of MIGUEL DE CERVANTES SAAVEDRA, and a statement of the aim and end of the greatest of them all. A handy book for general readers. Crown 8vo. 3s. 6d.

DU MONCEL (Count)—THE TELEPHONE, THE MICROPHONE, AND THE PHONOGRAPH. With 74 Illustrations. Second Edition. Small crown 8vo. 5s.

DURUY (Victor)—HISTORY OF ROME AND THE ROMAN PEOPLE. Edited by Professor MAHAFFY, with nearly 3,000 Illustrations. 4to. Vols. I., II., and III. in 6 Parts, 30s. each volume.

EDGEWORTH (F. Y.)—MATHEMATICAL PSYCHICS. An Essay on the Application of Mathematics to Social Science. Demy 8vo. 7s. 6d.

EDUCATIONAL CODE OF THE PRUSSIAN NATION, IN ITS PRESENT FORM. In accordance with the Decisions of the Common Provincial Law, and with those of Recent Legislation. Crown 8vo. 2s. 6d.

EDUCATION LIBRARY. Edited by PHILIP MAGNUS :—

AN INTRODUCTION TO THE HISTORY OF EDUCATIONAL THEORIES. By OSCAR BROWNING, M.A. Second Edition. 3s. 6d.

OLD GREEK EDUCATION. By the Rev. Prof. MAHAFFY, M.A. Second Edition. 3s. 6d.

SCHOOL MANAGEMENT ; including a General View of the Work of Education, Organization, and Discipline. By JOSEPH LANDON. Third Edition. Crown 8vo. 6s.

ELSDALE (Henry)—STUDIES IN TENNYSON'S IDYLLS. Crown 8vo. 5s.

ELYOT (Sir Thomas)—THE BOKE NAMED THE GOUERNOUR. Edited from the First Edition of 1531 by HENRY HERBERT STEPHEN CROFT, M.A., Barrister-at-Law. 2 vols. Fcp. 4to. 50s.

EMERSON'S (Ralph Waldo) LIFE. By OLIVER WENDELL HOLMES. [English Copyright Edition.] With Portrait. Crown 8vo. 6s.

ENOCH, THE PROPHET. The Book of. Archbishop Laurence's Translation. With an Introduction by the Author of the 'Evolution of Christianity.' Crown 8vo. 5s.

ERANUS. A COLLECTION OF EXERCISES IN THE ALCAIC AND SAPPHIC METRES. Edited by F. W. CORNISH, Assistant Master at Eton. Second Edition. Crown 8vo. 2s.

EVANS (Mark)—THE STORY OF OUR FATHER'S LOVE, told to Children. Sixth and Cheaper Edition. With Four Illustrations. Fcp. 8vo. 1s. 6d.

'*FAN KWAE*' AT CANTON BEFORE TREATY DAYS, 1825-1844. By AN OLD RESIDENT. With Frontispiece. Crown 8vo. 5s.

FEIS (Jacob)—SHAKSPERE AND MONTAIGNE : An Endeavour to Explain the Tendency of Hamlet from Allusions in Contemporary Works. Crown 8vo. 5s.

FLECKER (Rev. Eliezer)—SCRIPTURE ONOMATOLOGY. Being Critical Notes on the Septuagint and other versions. Second Edition. Crown 8vo. 3s. 6d.

FLOREDICE (W. H.)—A MONTH AMONG THE MERE IRISH. Small crown 8vo. 5s.

FOWLE (Rev. T. W.)—THE DIVINE LEGATION OF CHRIST. Crown 8vo. 7s.

FRANK LEWARD. Edited by CHARLES BAMPTON. Crown 8vo. 7s. 6d.

FULLER (Rev. Morris)—THE LORD'S DAY; or, Christian Sunday. Its Unity, History, Philosophy, and Perpetual Obligation. Sermons. Demy 8vo. 10s. 6d.

GARDINER (Samuel R.) and J. BASS MULLINGER, M.A.— INTRODUCTION TO THE STUDY OF ENGLISH HISTORY. Second Edition. Large crown 8vo. 9s.

GARDNER (Dorsey) — QUATRE BRAS, LIGNY, AND WATERLOO. A Narrative of the Campaign in Belgium, 1815. With Maps and Plans. Demy 8vo. 16s.

GENESIS IN ADVANCE OF PRESENT SCIENCE. A Critical Investigation of Chapters I. to IX. By a Septuagenarian Beneficed Presbyter. Demy 8vo. 10s. 6d.

GENNA (E.)—IRRESPONSIBLE PHILANTHROPISTS. Being some Chapters on the Employment of Gentlewomen. Small crown 8vo. 2s. 6d.

GEORGE (Henry)—PROGRESS AND POVERTY: an Inquiry into the Causes of Industrial Depressions, and of Increase of Want with Increase of Wealth. The Remedy. Fifth Library Edition. Post 8vo. 7s. 6d. Cabinet Edition, crown 8vo. 2s. 6d.

** Also a Cheap Edition, limp cloth, 1s. 6d.; paper covers, 1s.

SOCIAL PROBLEMS. Crown 8vo. 5s.

** Also a Cheap Edition, paper covers, 1s.

GIBSON (James Y.)—JOURNEY TO PARNASSUS. Composed by MIGUEL DE CERVANTES SAAVEDRA. Spanish Text, with Translation into English Tercets, Preface, and Illustrative Notes by. Crown 8vo. 12s.

GLOSSARY OF TERMS AND PHRASES. Edited by the Rev. H. PERCY SMITH and others. Medium 8vo. 12s.

GLOVER (F.) M.A.—EXEMPLA LATINA. A First Construing Book, with Short Notes, Lexicon, and an Introduction to the Analysis of Sentences. Second Edition. Fcp. 8vo. 2s.

GOLDSMID (Sir Francis Henry) Bart., Q.C., M.P.—MEMOIR OF. Second Edition, revised. Crown 8vo. 6s.

GOODENOUGH (Commodore J. G.)—MEMOIR OF, with Extracts from his Letters and Journals. Edited by his Widow. With Steel Engraved Portrait. Third Edition. Crown 8vo. 5s.

GOSSE (Edmund)—STUDIES IN THE LITERATURE OF NORTHERN EUROPE. New Edition. Large post 8vo. 6s.

SEVENTEENTH CENTURY STUDIES. A Contribution to the History of English Poetry. Demy 8vo. 10s. 6d.

GOULD (Rev. S. Baring) M.A.—GERMANY, PRESENT AND PAST. New and Cheaper Edition. Large crown 8vo. 7s. 6d.

GOWAN (Major Walter E.) — A. IVANOFF'S RUSSIAN GRAMMAR. (16th Edition). Translated, enlarged, and arranged for use of Students of the Russian Language. Demy 8vo. 6s.

GOWER (Lord Ronald)—MY REMINISCENCES. Cheap Edition, with Portrait, Large crown 8vo. 7s. 6d.

GRAHAM (William) M.A.—THE CREED OF SCIENCE, Religious, Moral, and Social. Second Edition, revised. Crown 8vo. 6s.

GREY (Rowland)—IN SUNNY SWITZERLAND. A Tale of Six Weeks. Small crown 8vo. 5s.

GRIFFITH (Thomas) A.M.—THE GOSPEL OF THE DIVINE LIFE: a Study of the Fourth Evangelist. Demy 8vo. 14s.

GRIMLEY (Rev. H. N.) M.A.—TREMADOC SERMONS, CHIEFLY ON THE SPIRITUAL BODY, THE UNSEEN WORLD, AND THE DIVINE HUMANITY. Fourth Edition. Crown 8vo. 6s.

G. S. B.—A STUDY OF THE PROLOGUE AND EPILOGUE IN ENGLISH LITERATURE, from Shakespeare to Dryden. Crown 8vo. 5s.

GUSTAFSON (Axel)—THE FOUNDATION OF DEATH. A Study of the Drink Question. Third Edition. Crown 8vo. 5s.

HAECKEL (Prof. Ernst)—THE HISTORY OF CREATION. Translation revised by Professor E. RAY LANKESTER, M.A., F.R.S. With Coloured Plates and Genealogical Trees of the various groups of both plants and animals. 2 vols. Third Edition. Post 8vo. 32s.

THE HISTORY OF THE EVOLUTION OF MAN. With numerous Illustrations. 2 vols. Post 8vo. 32s.

A VISIT TO CEYLON. Post 8vo. 7s. 6d.

FREEDOM IN SCIENCE AND TEACHING. With a Prefatory Note by T. H. HUXLEY, F.R.S. Crown 8vo. 5s.

HALF-CROWN SERIES :—

A LOST LOVE. By ANNA C. OGLE (Ashford Owen).

SISTER DORA : a Biography. By MARGARET LONSDALE.

TRUE WORDS FOR BRAVE MEN : a Book for Soldiers and Sailors. By the late CHARLES KINGSLEY.

NOTES OF TRAVEL : being Extracts from the Journals of Count VON MOLTKE.

ENGLISH SONNETS. Collected and Arranged by J. DENNIS.

LONDON LYRICS. By F. LOCKER.

HOME SONGS FOR QUIET HOURS. By the Rev. Canon R. H. BAYNES.

HARRIS (William)—THE HISTORY OF THE RADICAL PARTY IN PARLIAMENT. Demy 8vo. 15s.

HARROP (Robert)—BOLINGBROKE. A Political Study and Criticism. Demy 8vo. 14s.

HART (Rev. J. W. T.)—AUTOBIOGRAPHY OF JUDAS ISCARIOT. A Character-Study. Crown 8vo. 3s. 6d.

HAWEIS (Rev. H. R.) M.A.—CURRENT COIN. Materialism—The Devil — Crime — Drunkenness — Pauperism — Emotion — Recreation — The Sabbath. Fifth Edition. Crown 8vo. 5s.

ARROWS IN THE AIR. Fifth Edition. Crown 8vo. 5s.

SPEECH IN SEASON. Fifth Edition. Crown 8vo. 5s.

THOUGHTS FOR THE TIMES. Thirteenth Edition. Crown 8vo. 5s.

UNSECTARIAN FAMILY PRAYERS. New Edition. Fcp. 8vo. 1s. 6d.

HAWKINS (Edwards Comerford) — SPIRIT AND FORM. Sermons preached in the Parish Church of Leatherhead. Crown 8vo. 6s.

HAWTHORNE (Nathaniel)—WORKS. Complete in 12 vols. Large post 8vo. each vol. 7s. 6d.
    VOL. I. TWICE-TOLD TALES.
        II. MOSSES FROM AN OLD MANSE.
        III. THE HOUSE OF THE SEVEN GABLES, and THE SNOW IMAGE.
        IV. THE WONDER BOOK, TANGLEWOOD TALES, and GRANDFATHER'S CHAIR.
        V. THE SCARLET LETTER, and THE BLITHEDALE ROMANCE.
        VI. THE MARBLE FAUN. (Transformation.)
  VII. & VIII. OUR OLD HOME, and ENGLISH NOTE-BOOKS.
        IX. AMERICAN NOTE-BOOKS.
        X. FRENCH AND ITALIAN NOTE-BOOKS.
        XI. SEPTIMIUS FELTON, THE DOLLIVER ROMANCE, FANSHAWE, and, in an appendix, THE ANCESTRAL FOOTSTEP.
        XII. TALES AND ESSAYS, AND OTHER PAPERS, WITH A BIOGRAPHICAL SKETCH OF HAWTHORNE.

HAYES (A. A.) Jun.—NEW COLORADO AND THE SANTA FÉ TRAIL. With Map and 60 Illustrations. Square 8vo. 9s.

HENNESSY (Sir John Pope)—RALEGH IN IRELAND, WITH HIS LETTERS ON IRISH AFFAIRS AND SOME CONTEMPORARY DOCUMENTS. Large crown 8vo. printed on hand-made paper, parchment, 10s. 6d.

HENRY (Philip)—DIARIES AND LETTERS. Edited by MATTHEW HENRY LEE, M.A. Large crown 8vo. 7s. 6d.

HIDE (Albert)—THE AGE TO COME. Small crown 8vo. 2s. 6d.

HIME (Major H. W. L.) R.A.—WAGNERISM : a Protest. Crown 8vo. 2s. 6d.

HINTON (J.)—THE MYSTERY OF PAIN. New Edition. Fcp. 8vo. 1s.

    LIFE AND LETTERS. With an Introduction by Sir W. W. GULL, Bart., and Portrait engraved on Steel by C. H. JEENS. Fifth Edition. Crown 8vo. 8s. 6d.

    PHILOSOPHY AND RELIGION. Selections from the MSS. of the late JAMES HINTON. Edited by CAROLINE HADDON. Second Edition. Crown 8vo. 5s.

    THE LAW BREAKER AND THE COMING OF THE LAW. Edited by MARGARET HINTON. Crown 8vo. 6s.

HODSON OF HODSON'S HORSE ; or, Twelve Years of a Soldier's Life in India. Being Extracts from the Letters of the late Major W. S. R. Hodson. With a vindication from the attack of Mr. Bosworth Smith. Edited by his brother, G. H. HODSON, M.A. Fourth Edition. Large crown 8vo. 5s.

HOLTHAM (E. G.)—EIGHT YEARS IN JAPAN, 1873–1881. Work, Travel, and Recreation. With 3 Maps. Large crown 8vo. 9s.

HOMOLOGY OF ECONOMIC JUSTICE : An Essay by an EAST INDIA MERCHANT. Small crown 8vo. 5s.

HOOPER (Mary)—LITTLE DINNERS : HOW TO SERVE THEM WITH ELEGANCE AND ECONOMY. Eighteenth Edition. Crown 8vo. 2s. 6d.

    COOKERY FOR INVALIDS, PERSONS OF DELICATE DIGESTION, AND CHILDREN. Fourth Edition. Crown 8vo. 2s. 6d.

    EVERY-DAY MEALS. Being Economical and Wholesome Recipes for Breakfast, Luncheon, and Supper. Sixth Edition. Crown 8vo. 2s. 6d.

HOPKINS (Ellice)—WORK AMONGST WORKING MEN. Fifth Edition. Crown 8vo. 3*s*. 6*d*.

HOSPITALIER (E.)—THE MODERN APPLICATIONS OF ELECTRICITY. Translated and Enlarged by JULIUS MAIER, Ph.D. 2 vols. Second Edition, revised, with many additions and numerous Illustrations. Demy 8vo. 12*s*. 6*d*. each volume.

VOL. I.—Electric Generators, Electric Light.
II.—Telephone : Various Applications : Electrical Transmission of Energy.

HOUSEHOLD READINGS ON PROPHECY. By A LAYMAN. Small crown 8vo. 3*s*. 6*d*.

HUGHES (Henry)—THE REDEMPTION OF THE WORLD. Crown 8vo. 3*s*. 6*d*.

HUNTINGFORD (Rev. E.) D.C.L. — THE APOCALYPSE. With a Commentary and Introductory Essay. Demy 8vo. 9*s*.

HUTCHINSON (H.)—THOUGHT SYMBOLISM AND GRAMMATIC ILLU-SIONS : Being a Treatise on the Nature, Purpose, and Material of Speech. Crown 8vo. 5*s*.

HUTTON (Rev. Charles F.)—UNCONSCIOUS TESTIMONY ; OR, THE SILENT WITNESS OF THE HEBREW TO THE TRUTH OF THE HISTORICAL SCRIP-TURES. Crown 8vo. 2*s*. 6*d*.

HYNDMAN (H. M.) –THE HISTORICAL BASIS OF SOCIALISM IN ENGLAND. Large crown 8vo. 8*s*. 6*d*.

IM THURN (Everard F.)—AMONG THE INDIANS OF GUIANA. Being Sketches, chiefly Anthropologic, from the Interior of British Guiana. With 53 Illustrations and a Map. Demy 8vo. 18*s*.

JACCOUD (Prof. S.)—THE CURABILITY AND TREATMENT OF PULMO-NARY PHTHISIS. Translated and Edited by MONTAGU LUBBOCK, M.D. Demy 8vo. 15*s*.

JAUNT IN A JUNK : A Ten Days' Cruise in Indian Seas. Large crown 8vo. 7*s*. 6*d*.

JENKINS (E.) and RAYMOND (J.)—THE ARCHITECT'S LEGAL HANDBOOK. Third Edition, Revised. Crown 8vo. 6*s*.

JENNINGS (Mrs. Vaughan)— RAHEL : Her Life and Letters. Large post 8vo. 7*s*. 6*d*.

JERVIS (Rev. W. Henley)—THE GALLICAN CHURCH AND THE REVO-LUTION. A Sequel to the History of the Church of France, from the Con-cordat of Bologna to the Revolution. Demy 8vo. 18*s*.

JOEL (L.)—A CONSUL'S MANUAL AND SHIPOWNER'S AND SHIPMASTER'S PRACTICAL GUIDE IN THEIR TRANSACTIONS ABROAD. With Definitions of Nautical, Mercantile, and Legal Terms ; a Glossary of Mercantile Terms in English, French, German, Italian, and Spanish ; Tables of the Money, Weights, and Measures of the Principal Commercial Nations and their Equivalents in British Standards ; and Forms of Consular and Notarial Acts. Demy 8vo. 12*s*.

JOHNSTONE (C. F.) M.A.—HISTORICAL ABSTRACTS : being Outlines of the History of some of the less known States of Europe. Crown 8vo. 7*s*. 6*d*.

JOLLY (*William*) *F.R.S.E.* — JOHN DUNCAN, Scotch Weaver and Botanist. With Sketches of his Friends and Notices of his Times. With Portrait. Second Edition. Large crown 8vo. 9s.

JONES (*C. A.*)—THE FOREIGN FREAKS OF FIVE FRIENDS. With 30 Illustrations. Crown 8vo. 6s.

JOYCE (*P. W.*) *LL.D. &c.*—OLD CELTIC ROMANCES. Translated from the Gaelic. Crown 8vo. 7s. 6d.

KAUFMANN (*Rev. M.*) *B.A.*—SOCIALISM: its Nature, its Dangers, and its Remedies considered. Crown 8vo. 7s. 6d.

UTOPIAS; or, Schemes of Social Improvement, from Sir Thomas More to Karl Marx. Crown 8vo. 5s.

KAY (*David*)—EDUCATION AND EDUCATORS. Crown 8vo. 7s. 6d.

KAY (*Joseph*)—FREE TRADE IN LAND. Edited by his Widow. With Preface by the Right Hon. JOHN BRIGHT, M.P. Seventh Edition. Crown 8vo. 5s.

KEMPIS (*Thomas à*)—OF THE IMITATION OF CHRIST. Parchment Library Edition, parchment or cloth, 6s.; vellum, 7s. 6d. The Red Line Edition, fcp. 8vo. red edges, 2s. 6d. The Cabinet Edition, small 8vo. cloth limp, 1s.; or cloth boards, red edges, 1s. 6d. The Miniature Edition, 32mo. red edges, 1s.

** All the above Editions may be had in various extra bindings.

KENT (*C.*)—CORONA CATHOLICA AD PETRI SUCCESSORIS PEDES OBLATA. DE SUMMI PONTIFICIS LEONIS XIII. ASSUMPTIONE EPIGRAMMA. In Quinquaginta Linguis. Fcp. 4to. 15s.

KETTLEWELL (*Rev. S.*) *M.A.*—THOMAS À KEMPIS AND THE BROTHERS OF COMMON LIFE. 2 vols. With Frontispieces. Demy 8vo. 30s.

** Also an Abridged Edition in 1 vol. With Portrait. Crown 8vo. 7s. 6d.

KIDD (*Joseph*) *M.D.*—THE LAWS OF THERAPEUTICS; or, the Science and Art of Medicine. Second Edition. Crown 8vo. 6s.

KINGSFORD (*Anna*) *M.D.*—THE PERFECT WAY IN DIET. A Treatise advocating a Return to the Natural and Ancient Food of Race. Small crown 8vo. 2s.

KINGSLEY (*Charles*) *M.A.*—LETTERS AND MEMORIES OF HIS LIFE. Edited by his WIFE. With Two Steel Engraved Portraits and Vignettes. Fifteenth Cabinet Edition, in 2 vols. Crown 8vo. 12s.

** Also a People's Edition in 1 vol. With Portrait. Crown 8vo. 6s.

ALL SAINTS' DAY, and other Sermons. Edited by the Rev. W. HARRISON. Third Edition. Crown 8vo. 7s. 6d.

TRUE WORDS FOR BRAVE MEN. A Book for Soldiers' and Sailors' Libraries. Eleventh Edition. Crown 8vo. 2s. 6d.

KNOX (*Alexander A.*)—THE NEW PLAYGROUND; or, Wanderings in Algeria. New and Cheaper Edition. Large crown 8vo. 6s.

LANDON (*Joseph*)—SCHOOL MANAGEMENT; including a General View of the Work of Education, Organisation, and Discipline. Third Edition. Crown 8vo. 6s.

LAURIE (S. S.)—The Training of Teachers, and other Educational Papers. Crown 8vo. 7s. 6d.

LEE (Rev. F. G.) D.C.L.—The Other World; or, Glimpses of the Supernatural. 2 vols. A New Edition. Crown 8vo. 15s.

Letters from an Unknown Friend. By the Author of 'Charles Lowder.' With a Preface by the Rev. W. H. Cleaver. Fcp. 8vo. 1s.

Letters from a Young Emigrant in Manitoba. Second Edition. Small crown 8vo. 3s. 6d.

LEWARD (Frank)—Edited by Chas. Bampton. Crown 8vo. 7s. 6d.

LEWIS (Edward Dillon)—A Draft Code of Criminal Law and Procedure. Demy 8vo. 21s.

LILLIE (Arthur) M.R.A.S.—The Popular Life of Buddha. Containing an Answer to the Hibbert Lectures of 1881. With Illustrations. Crown 8vo. 6s. .

LLOYD (Walter)—The Hope of the World : An Essay on Universal Redemption. Crown 8vo. 5s.

LONSDALE (Margaret)—Sister Dora : a Biography. With Portrait. Cheap Edition. Crown 8vo. 2s. 6d.

LOUNSBURY (Thomas R.)—James Fenimore Cooper. With Portrait. Crown 8vo. 5s.

LOWDER (Charles)—A Biography. By the Author of 'St. Teresa.' New and Cheaper Edition. Crown 8vo. With Portrait. 3s. 6d.

LÜCKES (Eva C. E.)—Lectures on General Nursing, delivered to the Probationers of the London Hospital Training School for Nurses. Crown 8vo. 2s. 6d.

LYALL (William Rowe) D.D.—Propædeia Prophetica ; or, The Use and Design of the Old Testament Examined. New Edition, with Notices by George C. Pearson, M.A., Hon. Canon of Canterbury. Demy 8vo.

LYTTON (Edward Bulwer, Lord)—Life, Letters, and Literary Remains. By his Son the Earl of Lytton. With Portraits, Illustrations, and Facsimiles. Demy 8vo. cloth. Vols. I. and II. 32s.

MACAULAY (G. C.)—Francis Beaumont : A Critical Study. Crown 8vo. 5s.

MACCALLUM (M. W.)—Studies in Low German and High German Literature. Crown 8vo. 6s.

MACHIAVELLI (Niccolò)—His Life and Times. By Prof. Villari. Translated by Linda Villari. 4 vols. Large post 8vo. 48s.

Discourses on the First Decade of Titus Livius. Translated from the Italian by Ninian Hill Thomson, M.A. Large crown 8vo. 12s.

The Prince. Translated from the Italian by N. H. T. Small crown 8vo. printed on hand-made paper, bevelled boards, 6s.

MACKENZIE (Alexander)—How India is Governed. Being an Account of England's work in India. Small crown 8vo. 2s.

MACNAUGHT (Rev. John)—Cœna Domini : An Essay on the Lord's Supper, its Primitive Institution, Apostolic Uses, and Subsequent History. Demy 8vo. 14s.

MACWALTER (Rev. G. S.)—LIFE OF ANTONIO ROSMINI SERBATI (Founder of the Institute of Charity). 2 vols. Demy 8vo.
[Vol. I. now ready, 12s.

MAGNUS (Mrs.)—ABOUT THE JEWS SINCE BIBLE TIMES. From the Babylonian Exile till the English Exodus. Small crown 8vo. 6s.

MAIR (R. S.) M.D., F.R.C.S.E.—THE MEDICAL GUIDE FOR ANGLO-INDIANS. Being a Compendium of Advice to Europeans in India, relating to the Preservation and Regulation of Health. With a Supplement on the Management of Children in India. Second Edition. Crown 8vo. 3s. 6d.

MALDEN (Henry Elliot)—VIENNA, 1683. The History and Consequences of the Defeat of the Turks before Vienna, September 12, 1683, by John Sobieski, King of Poland, and Charles Leopold, Duke of Lorraine. Crown 8vo. 4s. 6d.

MANY VOICES.—A Volume of Extracts from the Religious Writers of Christendom, from the First to the Sixteenth Century. With Biographical Sketches. Crown 8vo. cloth extra, red edges, 6s.

MARKHAM (Capt. Albert Hastings) R.N.—THE GREAT FROZEN SEA : a Personal Narrative of the Voyage of the *Alert* during the Arctic Expedition of 1875-6. With Six Full-page Illustrations, Two Maps, and Twenty-seven Woodcuts. Sixth and Cheaper Edition. Crown 8vo. 6s.

MARRIAGE AND MATERNITY; or, Scripture Wives and Mothers. Small crown 8vo. 4s. 6d.

MARTINEAU (Gertrude)—OUTLINE LESSONS ON MORALS. Small crown 8vo. 3s. 6d.

MAUDSLEY (H.) M.D.—BODY AND WILL. Being an Essay Concerning Will, in its Metaphysical, Physiological, and Pathological Aspects. 8vo. 12s.

McGRATH (Terence)—PICTURES FROM IRELAND. New and Cheaper Edition. Crown 8vo. 2s.

MEREDITH (M. A.)—THEOTOKOS, THE EXAMPLE FOR WOMAN. Dedicated, by permission, to Lady AGNES WOOD. Revised by the Venerable Archdeacon DENISON. 32mo. 1s. 6d.

MILLER (Edward)—THE HISTORY AND DOCTRINES OF IRVINGISM ; or, the so-called Catholic and Apostolic Church. 2 vols. Large post 8vo. 25s.

THE CHURCH IN RELATION TO THE STATE. Large crown 8vo. 7s. 6d.

MINCHIN (J. G.)—BULGARIA SINCE THE WAR : Notes of a Tour in the Autumn of 1879. Small crown 8vo. 3s. 6d.

MITCHELL (Lucy M.)—A HISTORY OF ANCIENT SCULPTURE. With numerous Illustrations, including six Plates in Phototype. Super royal, 42s.
SELECTIONS FROM ANCIENT SCULPTURE. Being a Portfolio containing Reproductions in Phototype of 36 Masterpieces of Ancient Art, to illustrate Mrs. MITCHELL'S 'History of Ancient Sculpture.' 18s.

MITFORD (Bertram)—THROUGH THE ZULU COUNTRY. Its Battlefields and its People. With five Illustrations. Demy 8vo. 14s.

MOCKLER (E.)—A GRAMMAR OF THE BALOOCHEE LANGUAGE, as it is spoken in Makran (Ancient Gedrosia), in the Persia-Arabic and Roman characters. Fcp. 8vo. 5s.

MOLESWORTH (*H. Nassau*)—HISTORY OF THE CHURCH OF ENG-
LAND FROM 1660. Large crown 8vo. 7s. 6d.

MORELL (*J. R.*)—EUCLID SIMPLIFIED IN METHOD AND LANGUAGE.
Being a Manual of Geometry. Compiled from the most important French
Works, approved by the University of Paris and the Minister of Public
Instruction. Fcp. 8vo. 2s. 6d.

MORRIS (*George*)—THE DUALITY OF ALL DIVINE TRUTH IN OUR
LORD JESUS CHRIST : FOR GOD'S SELF-MANIFESTATION IN THE IMPAR-
TATION OF THE DIVINE NATURE TO MAN. Large Crown 8vo. 7s. 6d.

MORSE (*E. S.*) *Ph.D.*—FIRST BOOK OF ZOOLOGY. With numerous
Illustrations. New and Cheaper Edition. Crown 8vo. 2s. 6d.

MULL (*Matthias*)—PARADISE LOST. By JOHN MILTON. Books I.-VI.
The Mutilations of the Text Emended, the Punctuation Revised, and all Col-
lectively Presented, with Notes and Preface ; also a Short Essay on the
Intellectual Value of Milton's Works, &c. Demy 8vo. 6s.

MURPHY (*J. N.*)—THE CHAIR OF PETER ; or, the Papacy Considered
in its Institution, Development, and Organization, and in the Benefits which for
over Eighteen Centuries it has conferred on Mankind. Demy 8vo. 18s.

NELSON (*J. H.*) *M.A.*—A PROSPECTUS OF THE SCIENTIFIC STUDY OF
THE HINDÛ LAW. Demy 8vo. 9s.

NEWMAN (*Cardinal*)—CHARACTERISTICS FROM THE WRITINGS OF.
Being Selections from his various Works. Arranged with the Author's
personal Approval. Sixth Edition. With Portrait Crown 8vo. 6s.
₊ A Portrait of Cardinal Newman, mounted for framing, can be had, 2s. 6d.

NEWMAN (*Francis William*)—ESSAYS ON DIET. Small crown 8vo. 2s.
2s.

NEW TRUTH AND THE OLD FAITH : ARE THEY INCOMPATIBLE? By
a Scientific Layman. Demy 8vo. 10s. 6d.

NEW WERTHER. By LOKI. Small crown 8vo. 2s. 6d.

NICHOLSON (*Edward Byron*)—THE GOSPEL ACCORDING TO THE
HEBREWS. Its Fragments Translated and Annotated with a Critical Analysis of
the External and Internal Evidence relating to it. Demy 8vo. 9s. 6d.
A NEW COMMENTARY ON THE GOSPEL ACCORDING TO MATTHEW.
Demy 8vo. 12s.

NICOLS (*Arthur*) *F.G.S.*, *F.R.G.S.*—CHAPTERS FROM THE PHYSICAL
HISTORY OF THE EARTH : an Introduction to Geology and Palæontology
With numerous Illustrations. Crown 8vo. 5s.

NOPS (*Marianne*)—CLASS LESSONS ON EUCLID. Part I. containing the
First Two Books of the Elements. Crown 8vo. 2s. 6d.

NUCES : EXERCISES ON THE SYNTAX OF THE PUBLIC SCHOOL LATIN PRIMER.
New Edition in Three Parts. Crown 8vo. each 1s.
₊ The Three Parts can also be had bound together in cloth, 3s.

OATES (*Frank*) *F.R.G.S.*—MATABELE LAND AND THE VICTORIA FALLS.
A Naturalist's Wanderings in the Interior of South Africa. Edited by C. G.
OATES, B.A. With numerous Illustrations and 4 Maps. Demy 8vo. 21s.

OGLE (*W.*) *M.D.*, *F.R.C.P.*—ARISTOTLE ON THE PARTS OF ANIMALS.
Translated, with Introduction and Notes. Royal 8vo. 12s. 6d.

O'HAGAN (Lord) K.P.—OCCASIONAL PAPERS AND ADDRESSES. Large crown 8vo. 7s. 6d.

OKEN (Lorenz) Life of.—By ALEXANDER ECKER. With Explanatory Notes, Selections from Oken's Correspondence, and Portrait of the Professor. From the German by ALFRED TULK. Crown 8vo. 6s.

O'MEARA (Kathleen)—FREDERIC OZANAM, Professor of the Sorbonne : his Life and Work. Second Edition. Crown 8vo. 7s. 6d.

> HENRI PERREYVE AND HIS COUNSELS TO THE SICK. Small crown 8vo. 5s.

OSBORNE (Rev. W. A.)—THE REVISED VERSION OF THE NEW TESTA-MENT. A Critical Commentary, with Notes upon the Text. Crown 8vo. 5s.

OTTLEY (Henry Bickersteth)—THE GREAT DILEMMA : Christ His own Witness or His own Accuser. Six Lectures. Second Edition. Crown 8vo. 3s. 6d.

OUR PUBLIC SCHOOLS—ETON, HARROW, WINCHESTER, RUGBY, WEST-MINSTER, MARLBOROUGH, THE CHARTERHOUSE. Crown 8vo. 6s.

OWEN (F. M.)—JOHN KEATS : a Study. Crown 8vo. 6s.

> ACROSS THE HILLS. Small crown 8vo. 1s. 6d.

OWEN (Rev. Robert) B.D.—SANCTORALE CATHOLICUM ; or, Book of Saints. With Notes, Critical, Exegetical, and Historical. Demy 8vo. 18s.

OXENHAM (Rev. F. Nutcombe)—WHAT IS THE TRUTH AS TO EVER-LASTING PUNISHMENT? Part II. Being an Historical Enquiry into the Witness and Weight of certain Anti-Origenist Councils. Crown 8vo. 2s. 6d.

OXONIENSIS—ROMANISM, PROTESTANTISM, ANGLICANISM. Being a Layman's View of some Questions of the Day. Together with Remarks on Dr. Littledale's 'Plain Reasons against Joining the Church of Rome.' Small crown 8vo. 3s. 6d.

PALMER (the late William)—NOTES OF A VISIT TO RUSSIA IN 1840–41. Selected and arranged by JOHN H. CARDINAL NEWMAN. With Portrait. Crown 8vo. 8s. 6d.

> EARLY CHRISTIAN SYMBOLISM. A series of Compositions from Fresco-Paintings, Glasses, and Sculptured Sarcophagi. Edited by the Rev. PROVOST NORTHCOTE, D.D., and the Rev. CANON BROWNLOW, M.A. With Coloured Plates, folio, 42s. ; or with plain plates, folio, 25s.

PARCHMENT LIBRARY. Choicely printed on hand-made paper, limp parchment antique or cloth, 6s. ; vellum, 7s. 6d. each volume.

> SELECTIONS FROM THE PROSE WRITINGS OF JONATHAN SWIFT. With a Preface and Notes by STANLEY LANE-POOLE, and Portrait.

> ENGLISH SACRED LYRICS.

> SIR JOSHUA REYNOLDS' DISCOURSES. Edited by EDMUND GOSSE.

> SELECTIONS FROM MILTON'S PROSE WRITINGS. Edited by ERNEST MYERS.

> THE BOOK OF PSALMS. Translated by the Rev. T. K. CHEYNE, M.A.

> THE VICAR OF WAKEFIELD. With Preface and Notes by AUSTIN DOBSON.

> ENGLISH COMIC DRAMATISTS. Edited by OSWALD CRAWFURD.

> ENGLISH LYRICS.

B

PARCHMENT LIBRARY—continued.

THE SONNETS OF JOHN MILTON. Edited by MARK PATTISON.
With Portrait after Vertue.

FRENCH LYRICS. Selected and Annotated by GEORGE SAINTSBURY.
With miniature Frontispiece, designed and etched by H. G. Glindoni.

FABLES by MR. JOHN GAY. With Memoir by AUSTIN DOBSON,
and an etched Portrait from an unfinished Oil-sketch by Sir Godfrey Kneller.

SELECT LETTERS OF PERCY BYSSHE SHELLEY. Edited, with an Intro-
tion, by RICHARD GARNETT.

THE CHRISTIAN YEAR; Thoughts in Verse for the Sundays and
Holy Days throughout the Year. With etched Portrait of the Rev. J. Keble,
after the Drawing by G. Richmond, R.A.

SHAKSPERE'S WORKS. Complete in Twelve Volumes.

EIGHTEENTH CENTURY ESSAYS. Selected and Edited by AUSTIN
DOBSON. With a Miniature Frontispiece by R. Caldecott.

Q. HORATI FLACCI OPERA. Edited by F. A. CORNISH, Assistant
Master at Eton. With a Frontispiece after a design by L. ALMA TADEMA.
Etched by LEOPOLD LOWENSTAM.

EDGAR ALLAN POE'S POEMS. With an Essay on his Poetry by
ANDREW LANG, and a Frontispiece by Linley Sambourne.

SHAKSPERE'S SONNETS. Edited by EDWARD DOWDEN. With a
Frontispiece etched by Leopold Lowenstam, after the Death Mask.

ENGLISH ODES. Selected by EDMUND GOSSE. With Frontispiece on India paper by Hamo Thornycroft, A.R.A.

OF THE IMITATION OF CHRIST. By THOMAS À KEMPIS. A revised
Translation. With Frontispiece on India paper, from a Design by W. B.
Richmond.

POEMS : Selected from PERCY BYSSHE SHELLEY. Dedicated to Lady
Shelley. With Preface by RICHARD GARNET and a Miniature Frontispiece.
₊ The above Volumes may also be had in a variety of leather bindings.

PARSLOE (*Joseph*) — OUR RAILWAYS. Sketches, Historical and
Descriptive. With Practical Information as to Fares and Rates, &c., and a
Chapter on Railway Reform. Crown 8vo. 6s.

PASCAL (*Blaise*)—THE THOUGHTS OF. Translated from the Text of
AUGUSTE MOLINIER by C. KEGAN PAUL. Large crown 8vo. with Frontispiece,
printed on hand-made paper, parchment antique, or cloth, 12s. ; vellum, 15s.

PAUL (*C. Kegan*)—BIOGRAPHICAL SKETCHES. Printed on hand-made
paper, bound in buckram. Second Edition. Crown 8vo. 7s. 6d.

PAUL (*Alexander*)—SHORT PARLIAMENTS. A History of the National
Demand for Frequent General Elections. Small crown 8vo. 3s. 6d.

PEARSON (*Rev. S.*)—WEEK-DAY LIVING. A Book for Young Men
and Women. Second Edition. Crown 8vo. 5s.

PESCHEL (*Dr. Oscar*)—THE RACES OF MAN AND THEIR GEOGRAPHICAL
DISTRIBUTION. Second Edition, large crown 8vo. 9s.

PETERS (*F. H.*)—THE NICOMACHEAN ETHICS OF ARISTOTLE. Translated by. Crown 8vo. 6s.

PHIPSON (*E.*)—THE ANIMAL LORE OF SHAKSPEARE'S TIME. Including
Quadrupeds, Birds, Reptiles, Fish, and Insects. Large post 8vo. 9s.

PIDGEON (*D.*)—An Engineer's Holiday; or, Notes of a Round Trip from Long. 0° to 0°. New and Cheaper Edition. Large crown 8vo. 7*s.* 6*d.*

Old World Questions and New World Answers. Large crown 8vo. 7*s.* 6*d.*

Plain Thoughts for Men. Eight Lectures delivered at the Foresters' Hall, Clerkenwell, during the London Mission, 1884. Crown 8vo. 1*s.* 6*d.*; paper covers, 1*s.*

POE (*Edgar Allan*)—Works of. With an Introduction and a Memoir by Richard Henry Stoddard. In 6 vols. with Frontispieces and Vignettes. Large crown 8vo. 6*s.* each vol.

POPE (*J. Buckingham*)—Railway Rates and Radical Rule. Trade Questions as Election Tests. Crown 8vo. 2*s.* 6*d.*

PRICE (*Prof. Bonamy*)—Chapters on Practical Political Economy. Being the Substance of Lectures delivered before the University of Oxford. New and Cheaper Edition. Large post 8vo. 5*s.*

Pulpit Commentary (The). Old Testament Series. Edited by the Rev. J. S. Exell and the Rev. Canon H. D. M. Spence.

> Genesis. By Rev. T. Whitelaw, M.A. With Homilies by the Very Rev. J. F. Montgomery, D.D., Rev. Prof. R. A. Redford, M.A., LL.B., Rev. F. Hastings, Rev. W. Roberts, M.A.; an Introduction to the Study of the Old Testament by the Venerable Archdeacon Farrar, D.D., F.R.S.; and Introductions to the Pentateuch by the Right Rev. H. Cotterill, D.D., and Rev. T. Whitelaw, M.A. Eighth Edition. One vol. 15*s.*

> Exodus. By the Rev. Canon Rawlinson. With Homilies by Rev. J. Orr, Rev. D. Young, Rev. C. A. Goodhart, Rev. J. Urquhart, and Rev. H. T. Robjohns. Fourth Edition. Two vols. 18*s.*

> Leviticus. By the Rev. Prebendary Meyrick, M.A. With Introductions by Rev. R. Collins, Rev. Professor A. Cave, and Homilies by Rev. Prof. Redford, LL.B., Rev. J. A. Macdonald, Rev. W. Clarkson, Rev. S. R. Aldridge, LL.B., and Rev. McCheyne Edgar. Fourth Edition. 15*s.*

> Numbers. By the Rev R. Winterbotham, LL.B. With Homilies by the Rev. Professor W. Binnie, D.D., Rev. E. S. Prout, M.A., Rev. D. Young, Rev. J. Waite; and an Introduction by the Rev. Thomas Whitelaw, M.A. Fourth Edition. 15*s.*

> Deuteronomy. By Rev. W. L. Alexander, D.D. With Homilies by Rev. D. Davies, M.A., Rev. C. Clemance, D.D., Rev. J. Orr, B.D., and Rev. R. M. Edgar, M.A. Third Edition. 15*s.*

> Joshua. By Rev. J. J. Lias, M.A. With Homilies by Rev. S. R. Aldridge, LL.B., Rev. R. Glover, Rev. E. De Pressensé, D.D., Rev. J. Waite, B.A., Rev. F. W. Adeney, M.A.; and an Introduction by the Rev. A. Plummer, M.A. Fifth Edition. 12*s.* 6*d.*

> Judges and Ruth. By the Bishop of Bath and Wells and Rev. J. Morison, D.D. With Homilies by Rev. A. F. Muir, M.A., Rev. F. W. Adeney, M.A., Rev. W. M. Statham, and Rev. Professor J. Thomson, M.A. Fourth Edition. 10*s.* 6*d.*

> 1 Samuel. By the Very Rev. R. P. Smith, D.D. With Homilies by Rev. Donald Fraser, D.D., Rev. Prof. Chapman, and Rev. B. Dale. Sixth Edition. 15*s.*

B 2

PULPIT COMMENTARY ('THE). Old Testament Series—continued.

    1 KINGS. By the Rev. JOSEPH HAMMOND, LL.B. With Homilies by the Rev. E DE PRESSENSÉ, D.D., Rev. J. WAITE, B.A., Rev. A. ROWLAND, LL.B., Rev. J. A. MACDONALD, and Rev. J. URQUHART. Fourth Edition. 15*s.*

    1 CHRONICLES. By the Rev. Prof. P. C. BARKER, M.A., LL.B. With Homilies by Rev. Prof. J. R. THOMSON, M.A., Rev. R. TUCK, B.A., Rev. W. CLARKSON, B.A., Rev. F. WHITFIELD, M A., and Rev. RICHARD GLOVER. 15*s.*

    EZRA, NEHEMIAH, AND ESTHER. By Rev. Canon G. RAWLINSON, M.A. With Homilies by Rev. Prof. J. R. THOMSON, M.A., Rev. Prof. R. A. REDFORD, LL.B., M.A., Rev. W. S. LEWIS, M.A., Rev. J. A. MACDONALD, Rev. A. MACKENNAL, B.A., Rev. W. CLARKSON, B.A., Rev. F. HASTINGS, Rev. W. DINWIDDIE, LL.B., Rev. Prof. ROWLANDS, B.A., Rev. G. WOOD, B.A., Rev. Prof. P. C. BARKER, LL.B., M.A., and Rev. J. S. EXELL, M.A. Sixth Edition. One vol. 12*s.* 6*d.*

    JEREMIAH (Vol. I.). By the Rev. T. K. CHEYNE, M.A. With Homilies by the Rev. F. W. ADENEY, M.A., Rev. A. F. MUIR, M.A., Rev. S. CONWAY, B.A., Rev. J. WAITE, B.A., and Rev. D. YOUNG, B.A. Second Edition. 15*s.*

    JEREMIAH (Vol. II.), AND LAMENTATIONS. By Rev. T. K. CHEYNE, M.A. With Homilies by Rev. Prof. J. R. THOMSON, M.A., Rev. W. F. ADENEY, M.A., Rev. A. F. MUIR, M.A., Rev. S. CONWAY, B.A., Rev. D. YOUNG, B.A. 15*s.*

PULPIT COMMENTARY ('THE). New Testament Series.

    ST. MARK. By the Very Rev. E. BICKERSTETH, D.D., Dean of Lichfield. With Homilies by the Rev. Prof. THOMSON, M.A., Rev. Prof. GIVEN, M.A., Rev. Prof. JOHNSON, M.A., Rev. A. ROWLAND, LL.B., Rev. A. MUIR, M.A., and Rev. R. GREEN. Fourth Edition. 2 Vols. 21*s.*

    THE ACTS OF THE APOSTLES. By the Bishop of BATH AND WELLS. With Homilies by Rev. Prof. P. C. BARKER, M.A., Rev. Prof. E. JOHNSON, M.A., Rev. Prof. R. A. REDFORD, M.A., Rev. R. TUCK, B.A., Rev. W. CLARKSON, B.A. Second Edition. Two vols. 21*s.*

    1 CORINTHIANS. By the Ven. Archdeacon FARRAR, D.D. With Homilies by Rev. Ex-Chancellor LIPSCOMB, LL.D., Rev. DAVID THOMAS, D.D., Rev. DONALD FRASER, D.D., Rev. Prof. J. R. THOMSON, M.A., Rev. R. TUCK, B.A., Rev. E. HURNDALL, M.A., Rev. J. WAITE, B.A., Rev. H. BREMNER, B.D. Second Edition. 15*s.*

PUSEY (*Dr.*)—SERMONS FOR THE CHURCH'S SEASONS FROM ADVENT TO TRINITY. Selected from the published Sermons of the late EDWARD BOUVERIE PUSEY, D.D. Crown 8vo. 5*s.*

RADCLIFFE (*Frank R. Y.*)—THE NEW POLITICUS. Small crown 8vo. 2*s.* 6*d.*

RANKE (*Leopold von*)—UNIVERSAL HISTORY. The Oldest Historical Group of Nations and the Greeks. Edited by G. W. PROTHERO. Demy 8vo. 16*s.*

REALITIES OF THE FUTURE LIFE. Small crown 8vo. 1*s.* 6*d.*

RENDELL (*J. M.*)—CONCISE HANDBOOK OF THE ISLAND OF MADEIRA. With Plan of Funchal and Map of the Island. Fcp. 8vo. 1*s.* 6*d.*

REYNOLDS (Rev. J. W.)—THE SUPERNATURAL IN NATURE. A Verification by Free Use of Science. Third Edition, revised and enlarged. Demy 8vo. 14s.

THE MYSTERY OF MIRACLES. Third and Enlarged Edition. Crown 8vo. 6s.

THE MYSTERY OF THE UNIVERSE: Our Common Faith. Demy 8vo. 14s.

RIBOT (Prof. Th.)—HEREDITY: a Psychological Study on its Phenomena, its Laws, its Causes, and its Consequences. Second Edition. Large crown 8vo. 9s.

RIMMER (William) M.D.—ART ANATOMY: A Portfolio of 81 Plates. Folio, 70s. nett.

ROBERTSON (The late Rev. F. W.) M.A.—LIFE AND LETTERS OF. Edited by the Rev. Stopford Brooke, M.A.

   I. Two vols., uniform with the Sermons. With Steel Portrait. Crown 8vo. 7s. 6d.

   II. Library Edition, in demy 8vo. with Portrait. 12s.

   III. A Popular Edition, in 1 vol. Crown 8vo. 6s.

SERMONS. Four Series. Small crown 8vo. 3s. 6d.

THE HUMAN RACE, and other Sermons. Preached at Cheltenham, Oxford, and Brighton. New and Cheaper Edition. Small crown 8vo. 3s. 6d.

NOTES ON GENESIS. New and Cheaper Edition. Small crown 8vo. 3s. 6d.

EXPOSITORY LECTURES ON ST. PAUL'S EPISTLES TO THE CORINTHIANS. A New Edition. Small crown 8vo. 5s.

LECTURES AND ADDRESSES, with other Literary Remains. A New Edition. Small crown 8vo. 5s.

AN ANALYSIS OF TENNYSON'S 'IN MEMORIAM.' (Dedicated by Permission to the Poet-Laureate.) Fcp. 8vo. 2s.

THE EDUCATION OF THE HUMAN RACE. Translated from the German of Gotthold Ephraim Lessing. Fcp. 8vo. 2s. 6d.
    The above Works can also be had bound in half-morocco.
   . A Portrait of the late Rev. F. W. Robertson, mounted for framing, can be had, 2s. 6d.

ROMANES (G. J.)—MENTAL EVOLUTION IN ANIMALS. With a Posthumous Essay on Instinct, by CHARLES DARWIN, F.R.S. Demy 8vo. 12s.

ROSMINI SERBATI (A.) Founder of the Institute of Charity—LIFE. By G. STUART MACWALTER. 2 vols. 8vo. [Vol. I. now ready, 12s.

ROSMINI'S ORIGIN OF IDEAS. Translated from the Fifth Italian Edition of the Nuovo Saggio. *Sull' origine delle idee* 3 vols. Demy 8vo. 16s each.

ROSMINI'S PSYCHOLOGY. 3 vols. Demy 8vo. [Vol. I. now ready, 16s.

ROSMINI'S PHILOSOPHICAL SYSTEM. Translated, with a Sketch of the Author's Life, Bibliography, Introduction, and Notes, by THOMAS DAVIDSON. Demy 8vo. 16s.

RULE (Martin) M.A.—THE LIFE AND TIMES OF ST. ANSELM, ARCHBISHOP OF CANTERBURY AND PRIMATE OF THE BRITAINS. 2 vols. Demy 8vo. 32s.

SAMUEL (Sydney M.)—JEWISH LIFE IN THE EAST. Small crown 8vo. 3s. 6d.

SARTORIUS (Ernestine)—THREE MONTHS IN THE SOUDAN. With 11 Full-page Illustrations. Demy 8vo. 14s.

SAYCE (Rev. Archibald Henry)—INTRODUCTION TO THE SCIENCE OF LANGUAGE. 2 vols. Second Edition. Large post 8vo. 21s.

SCIENTIFIC LAYMAN. The New Truth and the Old Faith : are they Incompatible ? Demy 8vo. 10s. 6d.

SCOONES (W. Baptiste)—FOUR CENTURIES OF ENGLISH LETTERS : A Selection of 350 Letters by 150 Writers, from the Period of the Paston Letters to the Present Time. Third Edition. Large crown 8vo. 6s.

SÉE (Prof. Germain)—BACILLARY PHTHISIS OF THE LUNGS. Translated and Edited for English Practitioners, by WILLIAM HENRY WEDDELL, M.R.C.S. Demy 8vo.

SHILLITO (Rev. Joseph)—WOMANHOOD : its Duties, Temptations, and Privileges. A Book for Young Women. Third Edition. Crown 8vo. 3s. 6d.

SHIPLEY (Rev. Orby) M.A.—PRINCIPLES OF THE FAITH IN RELATION TO SIN. Topics for Thought in Times of Retreat. Eleven Addresses delivered during a Retreat of Three Days to Persons living in the World. Demy 8vo. 12s.

SIDNEY (Algernon)—A REVIEW. By GERTRUDE M. IRELAND BLACKBURNE. Crown 8vo. 6s.

SISTER AUGUSTINE, Superior of the Sisters of Charity at the St. Johannis Hospital at Bonn. Authorised Translation by HANS THARAU, from the German 'Memorials of AMALIE VON LASAULX.' Cheap Edition. Large crown 8vo. 4s. 6d.

SKINNER (JAMES). A Memoir. By the Author of 'Charles Lowder.' With a Preface by the Rev. Canon CARTER, and Portrait. Large crown 8vo. 7s. 6d.
   ** Also a Cheap Edition, with Portrait. Crown 8vo. 3s. 6d.

SMITH (Edward) M.D., LL.B., F.R.S.—TUBERCULAR CONSUMPTION IN ITS EARLY AND REMEDIABLE STAGES. Second Edition. Crown 8vo. 6s.

SPEDDING (James)—REVIEWS AND DISCUSSIONS, LITERARY, POLITICAL, AND HISTORICAL NOT RELATING TO BACON. Demy 8vo. 12s. 6d.

   EVENINGS WITH A REVIEWER ; or, Bacon and Macaulay. With a Prefatory Notice by G. S. VENABLES, Q.C. 2 vols. Demy 8vo. 18s.

STAPFER (Paul)—SHAKSPEARE AND CLASSICAL ANTIQUITY : Greek and Latin Antiquity as presented in Shakspeare's Plays. Translated by EMILY J. CAREY. Large post 8vo. 12s.

STATHAM (F. Reginald)—FREE THOUGHT AND TRUE THOUGHT. A Contribution to an Existing Argument. Crown 8vo. 6s.

STEVENSON (Rev. W. F.)—HYMNS FOR THE CHURCH AND HOME. Selected and Edited by the Rev. W. Fleming Stevenson.
   The Hymn Book consists of Three Parts :—I. For Public Worship.—II. For Family and Private Worship.—III. For Children.
   SMALL EDITION, cloth limp, 10d. ; cloth boards, 1s.
   LARGE TYPE EDITION, cloth limp, 1s. 3d. ; cloth boards, 1s. 6d.

STRAY PAPERS ON EDUCATION AND SCENES FROM SCHOOL LIFE. By B. H. Second Edition. Small crown 8vo. 3s. 6d.

STREATFEILD (Rev. G. S.) M.A.—LINCOLNSHIRE AND THE DANES. Large crown 8vo. 7s. 6d.

STRECKER-WISLICENUS—ORGANIC CHEMISTRY. Translated and Edited, with Extensive Additions, by W. R. HODGKINSON, Ph.D., and A. J. GREENAWAY, F.I.C. Demy 8vo. 21s.

STUDY OF THE PROLOGUE AND EPILOGUE IN ENGLISH LITERATURE, FROM SHAKESPEARE TO DRYDEN. By G. S. B. Crown 8vo. 5s.

SULLY (James) M.A.—PESSIMISM : a History and a Criticism. Second Edition. Demy 8vo. 14s.

SUTHERST (Thomas).—DEATH AND DISEASE BEHIND THE COUNTER. Crown 8vo. 1s. 6d. ; paper covers, 1s.

SWEDENBORG (Eman.)—DE CULTU ET AMORE DEI, UBI AGITUR DE TELLURIS ORTU, PARADISO ET VIVARIO, TUM DE PRIMOGENITI SEU ADAMI NATIVITATE, INFANTIA, ET AMORE. Crown 8vo. 6s.

SYME (David)—REPRESENTATIVE GOVERNMENT IN ENGLAND : its Faults and Failures. Second Edition. Large crown 8vo. 6s.

TACITUS'S AGRICOLA : A Translation. Small crown 8vo. 2s. 6d.

TAYLOR (Rev. Isaac)—THE ALPHABET. An Account of the Origin and Development of Letters. With numerous Tables and Facsimiles. 2 vols. Demy 8vo. 36s.

TAYLOR (Jeremy)—THE MARRIAGE RING. With Preface, Notes, and Appendices. Edited by FRANCIS BURDETT MONEY COUTTS. Small crown 8vo. 2s. 6d.

TAYLOR (Sedley)—PROFIT SHARING BETWEEN CAPITAL AND LABOUR. To which is added a Memorandum on the Industrial Partnership at the Whitwood Collieries, by ARCHIBALD and HENRY BRIGGS, with Remarks by SEDLEY TAYLOR. Crown 8vo. 2s. 6d.

THIRTY THOUSAND THOUGHTS. Edited by the Rev. Canon SPENCE, Rev. J. S. EXELL, and Rev. CHARLES NEIL. 6 vols. Super-royal 8vo.
[Vols. I., II., and III. now ready, 16s. each.

THOM (John Hamilton)—LAWS OF LIFE AFTER THE MIND OF CHRIST. Second Edition. Crown 8vo. 7s. 6d.

TIDMAN (Paul F.)—GOLD AND SILVER MONEY. Part I.—A Plain Statement. Part II.—Objections Answered. Third Edition. Crown 8vo. 1s.

TIPPLE (Rev. S. A.)—SUNDAY MORNINGS AT NORWOOD. Prayers and Sermons. Crown 8vo. 6s.

TODHUNTER (Dr. J.)—A STUDY OF SHELLEY. Crown 8vo. 7s.

TRANT (William)—TRADE UNIONS : Their Origin and Objects, Influence and Efficacy. Small crown 8vo. 1s. 6d. ; paper covers, 1s.

TREMENHEERE (H. Seymour) C.B.—A MANUAL OF THE PRINCIPLES OF GOVERNMENT AS SET FORTH BY THE AUTHORITIES OF ANCIENT AND MODERN TIMES. New and enlarged Edition. Crown 8vo. 3s. 6d.

TUKE (Daniel Hack) M.D.—CHAPTERS IN THE HISTORY OF THE INSANE IN THE BRITISH ISLES. With Four Illustrations. Large crown 8vo. 12s.

TWINING (Louisa)—WORKHOUSE VISITING AND MANAGEMENT DURING TWENTY-FIVE YEARS. Small crown 8vo. 2s.

TYLER (J.)—THE MYSTERY OF BEING; OR, WHAT DO WE KNOW?
Small crown 8vo. 3*s*. 6*d*.

UPTON (Major R. D.)—GLEANINGS FROM THE DESERT OF ARABIA.
Large post 8vo. 10*s*. 6*d*.

VACUUS VIATOR—FLYING SOUTH. Recollections of France and its
Littoral. Small crown 8vo. 3*s*. 6*d*.

VAUGHAN (H. Halford)—NEW READINGS AND RENDERINGS OF
SHAKESPEARE'S TRAGEDIES. 2 vols. Demy 8vo. 25*s*.

VILLARI (Professor)—NICCOLÒ MACHIAVELLI AND HIS TIMES. Translated by Linda Villari. 4 vols. Large crown 8vo. 48*s*.

VILLIERS (The Right Hon. C. P.)—FREE TRADE SPEECHES OF. With
Political Memoir. Edited by a Member of the Cobden Club. 2 vols. With
Portrait. Demy 8vo. 25*s*.

　*** Also a People's Edition, in 1 vol. crown 8vo. limp 2*s*. 6*d*.

VOGT (Lieut.-Col. Hermann)—THE EGYPTIAN WAR OF 1882. A Translation. With Map and Plans. Large crown 8vo. 6*s*.

VOLCKXSOM (E. W. v.)—CATECHISM OF ELEMENTARY MODERN
CHEMISTRY. Small crown 8vo. 3*s*.

VYNER (Lady Mary)—EVERY DAY A PORTION. Adapted from the
Bible and the Prayer Book, for the Private Devotions of those living in Widow-
hood. Collected and Edited by Lady Mary Vyner. Square crown 8vo. 5*s*.

WALDSTEIN (Charles) Ph.D.—THE BALANCE OF EMOTION AND
INTELLECT; an Introductory Essay to the Study of Philosophy. Crown 8vo. 6*s*.

WALLER (Rev. C. B.)—THE APOCALYPSE, reviewed under the Light of
the Doctrine of the Unfolding Ages, and the Restitution of All Things. Demy
8vo. 12*s*.

WALPOLE (Chas. George)—A SHORT HISTORY OF IRELAND FROM THE
EARLIEST TIMES TO THE UNION WITH GREAT BRITAIN. With 5 Maps and
Appendices. Second Edition. Crown 8vo. 6*s*.

WALSHE (Walter Hayle) M.D.—DRAMATIC SINGING PHYSIOLOGICALLY
ESTIMATED. Crown 8vo, cloth, price 3*s*. 6*d*.

WARD (William George) Ph.D. — ESSAYS ON THE PHILOSOPHY OF
THEISM. Edited, with an Introduction, by WILFRID WARD. 2 vols. demy
8vo. 21*s*.

WARD (Wilfrid)—THE WISH TO BELIEVE: A Discussion concerning
the Temper of Mind in which a reasonable Man should undertake Religious
Inquiry. Small crown 8vo. 5*s*.

WEDDERBURN (Sir David) Bart., M.P.—LIFE OF. Compiled from
his Journals and Writings by his Sister, Mrs. E. H. PERCIVAL. With etched
Portrait, and facsimiles of Pencil Sketches. Demy 8vo. 14*s*.

WEDMORE (Frederick)—THE MASTERS OF GENRE PAINTING. With
Sixteen Illustrations. Post 8vo. 7*s*. 6*d*.

WHAT TO DO AND HOW TO DO IT. A Manual of the Law affecting
the Housing and Sanitary Condition of Londoners, with Special Reference to
the Dwellings of the Poor. Issued by the Sanitary Laws Enforcement Society.
Demy 8vo. 1*s*.

WHEWELL (*William*) *D.D.*—His Life and Selections from his Correspondence. By Mrs. Stair Douglas. With a Portrait from a Painting by Samuel Laurence. Demy 8vo. 21*s.*

WHITNEY (*Prof. William Dwight*)—Essentials of English Grammar, for the Use of Schools. Second Edition, crown 8vo. 3*s.* 6*d.*

WILLIAMS (*Rowland*) *D.D.*—Psalms, Litanies, Counsels, and Collects for Devout Persons. Edited by his Widow. New and Popular Edition. Crown 8vo. 3*s.* 6*d.*

Stray Thoughts Collected from the Writings of the late Rowland Williams, D.D. Edited by his Widow. Crown 8vo. 3*s.* 6*d.*

WILSON (*Lieut.-Col. C. T.*)—The Duke of Berwick, Marshal of France, 1702–1734. Demy 8vo. 15*s.*

WILSON (*Mrs. R. F.*)—The Christian Brothers : their Origin and Work. With a Sketch of the Life of their Founder, the Ven. Jean Baptiste, de la Salle. Crown 8vo. 6*s.*

WOLTMANN (*Dr. Alfred*), *and WOERMANN* (*Dr. Karl*)—History of Painting. Edited by Sidney Colvin. Vol. I. Painting in Antiquity and the Middle Ages. With numerous Illustrations. Medium 8vo. 28*s.* ; bevelled boards, gilt leaves, 30*s.*

Word was Made Flesh. Short Family Readings on the Epistles for each Sunday of the Christian Year. Demy 8vo. 10*s.* 6*d.*

WREN (*Sir Christopher*)—His Family and his Times. With Original Letters, and a Discourse on Architecture hitherto unpublished. By Lucy Phillimore. Demy 8vo. 10*s.* 6*d.*

YOUMANS (*Eliza A.*)—First Book of Botany. Designed to cultivate the Observing Powers of Children. With 300 Engravings. New and Cheaper Edition. Crown 8vo. 2*s.* 6*d.*

YOUMANS (*Edward L.*) *M.D.*—A Class Book of Chemistry, on the Basis of the New System. With 200 Illustrations. Crown 8vo. 5*s.*

THE INTERNATIONAL SCIENTIFIC SERIES.

I. FORMS OF WATER : a Familiar Exposition of the Origin and Phenomena of Glaciers. By J. Tyndall, LL.D., F.R.S. With 25 Illustrations. Eighth Edition. Crown 8vo. 5*s*.

II. PHYSICS AND POLITICS ; or, Thoughts on the Application of the Principles of 'Natural Selection' and 'Inheritance' to Political Society. By Walter Bagehot. Sixth Edition. Crown 8vo. 4*s*.

III. FOODS. By Edward Smith, M.D., LL.B., F.R.S. With numerous Illustrations. Eighth Edition. Crown 8vo. 5*s*.

IV. MIND AND BODY : the Theories of their Relation. By Alexander Bain, LL.D. With Four Illustrations. Seventh Edition. Crown 8vo. 4*s*.

V. THE STUDY OF SOCIOLOGY. By Herbert Spencer. Eleventh Edition. Crown 8vo. 5*s*.

VI. ON THE CONSERVATION OF ENERGY. By Balfour Stewart, M.A., LL.D., F.R.S. With 14 Illustrations. Sixth Edition. Crown 8vo. 5*s*.

VII. ANIMAL LOCOMOTION ; or, Walking, Swimming, and Flying. By J. B. Pettigrew, M.D., F.R.S., &c. With 130 Illustrations. Third Edition. Crown 8vo. 5*s*.

VIII. RESPONSIBILITY IN MENTAL DISEASE. By Henry Maudsley, M.D. Fourth Edition. Crown 8vo. 5*s*.

IX. THE NEW CHEMISTRY. By Professor J. P. Cooke. With 31 Illustrations. Eighth Edition, remodelled and enlarged. Crown 8vo. 5*s*.

X. THE SCIENCE OF LAW. By Professor Sheldon Amos. Fifth Edition. Crown 8vo. 5*s*.

XI. ANIMAL MECHANISM : a Treatise on Terrestrial and Aërial Locomotion. By Professor E. J. Marey. With 117 Illustrations. Third Edition. Crown 8vo. 5*s*.

XII. THE DOCTRINE OF DESCENT AND DARWINISM. By Professor Oscar Schmidt. With 26 Illustrations. Sixth Edition. Crown 8vo. 5*s*.

XIII. THE HISTORY OF THE CONFLICT BETWEEN RELIGION AND SCIENCE. By J. W. Draper, M.D., LL.D. Eighteenth Edition. Crown 8vo. 5*s*.

XIV. FUNGI : their Nature, Influences, Uses, &c. By M. C. Cooke, M.D., LL.D. Edited by the Rev. M. J. Berkeley, M.A., F.L.S. With numerous Illustrations. Third Edition. Crown 8vo. 5*s*.

XV. THE CHEMICAL EFFECTS OF LIGHT AND PHOTOGRAPHY. By Dr. Hermann Vogel. Translation thoroughly revised. With 100 Illustrations. Fourth Edition. Crown 8vo. 5*s*.

XVI. THE LIFE AND GROWTH OF LANGUAGE. By Professor William Dwight Whitney. Fourth Edition. Crown 8vo. 5*s*.

XVII. MONEY AND THE MECHANISM OF EXCHANGE. By W. Stanley Jevons, M.A., F.R.S. Sixth Edition. Crown 8vo. 5*s*.

XVIII. THE NATURE OF LIGHT. With a General Account of Physical Optics. By Dr. Eugene Lommel. With 188 Illustrations and a Table of Spectra in Chromo-lithography. Third Edit. Crown 8vo. 5*s*.

XIX. ANIMAL PARASITES AND MESSMATES. By P. J. Van Beneden. With 83 Illustrations. Third Edition. Crown 8vo. 5*s*.

XX. FERMENTATION. By Professor Schützenberger. With 28 Illustrations. Fourth Edition. Crown 8vo. 5*s*.

XXI. THE FIVE SENSES OF MAN. By Professor Bernstein. With 91 Illustrations. Fourth Edition. Crown 8vo. 5*s*.

XXII. THE THEORY OF SOUND IN ITS RELATION TO MUSIC. By Professor Pietro Blaserna. With numerous Illustrations. Third Edition. Crown 8vo. 5*s*.

XXIII. STUDIES IN SPECTRUM ANALYSIS. By J. Norman Lockyer, F.R.S. Third Edition. With six Photographic Illustrations of Spectra, and numerous Engravings on Wood. Crown 8vo. 6*s*. 6*d*.

XXIV. A HISTORY OF THE GROWTH OF THE STEAM ENGINE. By Professor R. H. Thurston. With numerous Illustrations. Third Edition. Crown 8vo. 6s. 6d.

XXV. EDUCATION AS A SCIENCE. By Alexander Bain, LL.D. Fourth Edition. Crown 8vo. 5s.

XXVI. THE HUMAN SPECIES. By Prof. A. De Quatrefages. Third Edition. Crown 8vo. 5s.

XXVII. MODERN CHROMATICS. With Applications to Art and Industry. By Ogden N. Rood. With 130 original Illustrations. Second Edition. Crown 8vo. 5s.

XXVIII. THE CRAYFISH: an Introduction to the Study of Zoology. By Professor T. H. Huxley. With 82 Illustrations. Fourth Edition. Crown 8vo. 5s.

XXIX. THE BRAIN AS AN ORGAN OF MIND. By H. Charlton Bastian, M.D. With numerous Illustrations. Third Edition. Crown 8vo. 5s.

XXX. THE ATOMIC THEORY. By Prof. Wurtz. Translated by G. Cleminshaw, F.C.S. Third Edition. Crown 8vo. 5s.

XXXI. THE NATURAL CONDITIONS OF EXISTENCE AS THEY AFFECT ANIMAL LIFE. By Karl Semper. With 2 Maps and 106 Woodcuts. Third Edition. Crown 8vo. 5s.

XXXII. GENERAL PHYSIOLOGY OF MUSCLES AND NERVES. By Prof. J. Rosenthal. Third Edition. With Illustrations. Crown 8vo. 5s.

XXXIII. SIGHT: an Exposition of the Principles of Monocular and Binocular Vision. By Joseph Le Conte, LL.D. Second Edition. With 132 Illustrations. Crown 8vo. 5s.

XXXIV. ILLUSIONS: a Psychological Study. By James Sully. Second Edition. Crown 8vo. 5s.

XXXV. VOLCANOES: WHAT THEY ARE AND WHAT THEY TEACH. By Professor J. W. Judd, F.R.S. With 92 Illustrations on Wood. Third Edition. Crown 8vo. 5s.

XXXVI. SUICIDE: an Essay on Comparative Moral Statistics. By Prof. H. Morselli. Second Edition. With Diagrams. Crown 8vo. 5s.

XXXVII. THE BRAIN AND ITS FUNCTIONS. By J. Luys. Second Edition. With Illustrations. Crown 8vo. 5s.

XXXVIII. MYTH AND SCIENCE: an Essay. By Tito Vignoli. Second Edition. Crown 8vo. 5s.

XXXIX. THE SUN. By Professor Young. With Illustrations. Second Edition. Crown 8vo. 5s.

XL. ANTS, BEES, AND WASPS: a Record of Observations on the Habits of the Social Hymenoptera. By Sir John Lubbock, Bart., M.P. With 5 Chromolithographic Illustrations. Seventh Edition. Crown 8vo 5s.

XLI. ANIMAL INTELLIGENCE. By G. J. Romanes, LL.D., F.R.S. Third Edition. Crown 8vo. 5s.

XLII. THE CONCEPTS AND THEORIES OF MODERN PHYSICS. By J. B. Stallo. Third Edition. Crown 8vo. 5s.

XLIII. DISEASES OF MEMORY: an Essay in the Positive Psychology. By Prof. Th. Ribot. Second Edition. Crown 8vo. 5s.

XLIV. MAN BEFORE METALS. By N. Joly. Third Edition. Crown 8vo. 5s.

XLV. THE SCIENCE OF POLITICS. By Prof. Sheldon Amos. Third Edit. Crown. 8vo. 5s.

XLVI. ELEMENTARY METEOROLOGY. By Robert H. Scott. Third Edition. With numerous Illustrations. Crown 8vo. 5s.

XLVII. THE ORGANS OF SPEECH AND THEIR APPLICATION IN THE FORMATION OF ARTICULATE SOUNDS. By Georg Hermann von Meyer. With 47 Woodcuts. Crown 8vo. 5s.

XLVIII. FALLACIES: a View of Logic from the Practical Side. By Alfred Sidgwick. Crown 8vo. 5s.

XLIX. ORIGIN OF CULTIVATED PLANTS. By Alphonse de Candolle. Crown 8vo. 5s.

L. JELLY FISH, STAR FISH, AND SEA URCHINS. Being a Research on Primitive Nervous Systems. By G. J. Romanes. Crown 8vo. 5s.

MILITARY WORKS.

BARRINGTON (Capt. J. T.)—ENGLAND ON THE DEFENSIVE; or, the Problem of Invasion Critically Examined. Large crown 8vo. with Map, 7s. 6d.

BRACKENBURY (Col. C. B.) R.A. —MILITARY HANDBOOKS FOR REGIMENTAL OFFICERS:

I. MILITARY SKETCHING AND RECONNAISSANCE. By Colonel F. J. Hutchison and Major H. G. MacGregor. Fourth Edition. With 15 Plates. Small crown 8vo. 4s.

II. THE ELEMENTS OF MODERN TACTICS PRACTICALLY APPLIED TO ENGLISH FORMATIONS. By Lieut.-Col. Wilkinson Shaw. Fifth Edit. With 25 Plates and Maps. Small crown 8vo. 9s.

III. FIELD ARTILLERY : its Equipment, Organisation, and Tactics. By Major Sisson C. Pratt, R.A. With 12 Plates. Second Edition. Small crown 8vo. 6s.

IV. THE ELEMENTS OF MILITARY ADMINISTRATION. First Part : Permanent System of Administration. By Major J. W. Buxton. Small crown 8vo. 7s. 6d.

V. MILITARY LAW : its Procedure and Practice. By Major Sisson C. Pratt, R.A. Second Edition. Small crown 8vo. 4s. 6d.

VI. CAVALRY IN MODERN WAR. By Col. F. Chenevix Trench. Small crown 8vo. 6s.

VII. FIELD WORKS. Their Technical Construction and Tactical Application. By the Editor, Col. C. B. Brackenbury, R.A. Small crown 8vo.

BROOKE (Major C. K.)—A SYSTEM OF FIELD TRAINING. Small crown 8vo. 2s.

CLERY (C.) Lieut.-Col.—MINOR TACTICS. With 26 Maps and Plans. Sixth and cheaper Edition, revised. Crown 8vo. 9s.

COLVILE (Lieut.-Col. C. F.)—MILITARY TRIBUNALS. Sewed, 2s. 6d.

CRAUFURD (Capt. H. J.)—SUGGESTIONS FOR THE MILITARY TRAINING OF A COMPANY OF INFANTRY. Crown 8vo. 1s. 6d.

HARRISON (Lieut.-Col. R.) — THE OFFICER'S MEMORANDUM BOOK FOR PEACE AND WAR. Third Edition. Oblong 32mo. roan, with pencil, 3s. 6d.

NOTES ON CAVALRY TACTICS, ORGANISATION, &c. By a Cavalry Officer. With Diagrams. Demy 8vo. 12s.

PARR (Capt. H. Hallam) C.M.G.—THE DRESS, HORSES, AND EQUIPMENT OF INFANTRY AND STAFF OFFICERS. Crown 8vo. 1s.

SCHAW (Col. H.)—THE DEFENCE AND ATTACK OF POSITIONS AND LOCALITIES. Third Edition, revised and corrected. Crown 8vo. 3s. 6d.

WILKINSON (H. Spenser) Capt. 20th Lancashire R.V.—CITIZEN SOLDIERS. Essays towards the Improvement of the Volunteer Force. Crown 8vo. 2s. 6d.

POETRY.

ADAM OF ST. VICTOR—THE LITURGICAL POETRY OF ADAM OF ST. VICTOR. From the text of Gautier. With Translations into English in the Original Metres, and Short Explanatory Notes. By Digby S. Wrangham, M.A. 3 vols. Crown 8vo. printed on hand-made paper, boards, 21s.

AUCHMUTY (A. C.)—POEMS OF ENGLISH HEROISM : From Brunanburgh to Lucknow ; from Athelstan to Albert. Small crown 8vo. 1s. 6d.

AVIA—THE ODYSSEY OF HOMER. Done into English Verse by. Fcp. 4to. 15s.

BARING (*T. C.*), *M.P.*—THE SCHEME OF EPICURUS. A Rendering into English Verse of the Unfinished Poem of Lucretius, entitled, 'De Rerum Naturâ.' Fcp. 4to. 7s.

BARNES (*William*)—POEMS OF RURAL LIFE, IN THE DORSET DIALECT. New Edition, complete in one vol. Crown 8vo. 8s. 6d.

BAYNES (*Rev. Canon H. R.*)—HOME SONGS FOR QUIET HOURS. Fourth and cheaper Edition. Fcp. 8vo. 2s. 6d.

BENDALL (*Gerard*)—MUSA SILVESTRIS. 16mo. 1s. 6d.

BEVINGTON (*L. S.*)—KEY NOTES. Small crown 8vo. 5s.

BILLSON (*C. J.*)—THE ACHARNIANS OF ARISTOPHANES. Crown 8vo. 3s. 6d.

BLUNT (*Wilfrid Scawen*)—THE WIND AND THE WHIRLWIND. Demy 8vo. 1s. 6d.

BOWEN (*H. C.*) *M.A.*—SIMPLE ENGLISH POEMS. English Literature for Junior Classes. In Four Parts. Parts I. II. and III. 6d. each, and Part IV. 1s., complete 3s.

BRASHER (*Alfred*)—SOPHIA; or, the Viceroy of Valencia. A Comedy in Five Acts, Founded on a Story in Scarron. Small crown 8vo. 2s. 6d.

BRYANT (*W. C.*) — POEMS. Cheap Edition, with Frontispiece. Small crown 8vo. 3s. 6d.

BYRNNE (*E. Fairfax*)—MILICENT: a Poem. Small crown 8vo. 6s.

CAILLARD (*Emma Marie*) — CHARLOTTE CORDAY, and other Poems. Small crown 8vo. 3s. 6d.

CALDERON'S DRAMAS: the Wonderworking Magician—Life is a Dream —the Purgatory of St. Patrick. Translated by Denis Florence MacCarthy. Post 8vo. 10s.

CAMOENS LUSIADS. Portuguese Text with English Translation, by J. J. AUBERTIN. Second Edition. 2 vols. Crown 8vo. 12s.

CAMPBELL (*Lewis*)- SOPHOCLES. The Seven Plays in English Verse. Crown 8vo. 7s. 6d.

CASTILIAN BROTHERS (*The*) CHATEAUBRIANT, WALDEMAR, THREE TRAGEDIES, AND THE ROSE OF SICILY. A Drama. By the Author of 'Ginevra,' &c. Crown 8vo. 6s.

CHRISTIAN (*Owen*)—POEMS. Small crown 8vo. 2s. 6d.

CHRONICLES OF CHRISTOPHER COLUMBUS: a Poem in Twelve Cantos. By M. D. C. Crown 8vo. 7s. 6d.

CLARKE (*Mary Cowden*)—HONEY FROM THE WEED. Verses. Crown 8vo. 7s.

COSMO DE MEDICI, The False One, Agramont and Beaumont, Three Tragedies, and The Deformed. A Dramatic Sketch. By the Author of 'Ginevra,' &c. Crown 8vo. 5s.

COXHEAD (*Ethel*)—BIRDS AND BABIES. Imp. 16mo. With 33 Illustrations. 2s. 6d.

DAVID RIZZIO, BOTHWELL, AND THE WITCH LADY. Three Tragedies. By the Author of 'Ginevra,' &c. Crown 8vo. 6s.

DAVIE (*G. S.*) *M.D.*—THE GARDEN OF FRAGRANCE. Being a complete Translation of the Bóstan of Sádi, from the original Persian into English Verse. Crown 8vo. 7s. 6d.

DAVIES (*T. Hart*)—CATULLUS. Translated into English Verse. Crown 8vo. 6s.

DENNIS (*J.*) — ENGLISH SONNETS. Collected and Arranged by. Small crown 8vo. 2s. 6d.

DE VERE (*Aubrey*)—POETICAL WORKS:

    I. THE SEARCH AFTER PROSERPINE, &c. 6s.

    II. THE LEGENDS OF ST. PATRICK, &c. 6s.

    III. ALEXANDER THE GREAT, &c. 6s.

DE VERE (*Aubrey*)—continued.

　THE FORAY OF QUEEN MEAVE, and
　other Legends of Ireland's Heroic
　Age. Small crown 8vo. 5*s.*

　LEGENDS OF THE SAXON SAINTS.
　Small crown 8vo. 6*s.*

DILLON (*Arthur*)—RIVER SONGS and
　other Poems. With 13 Autotype
　Illustrations from designs by Margery
　May. Fcp. 4to. cloth extra, gilt
　leaves, 10*s. 6d.*

DOBELL (*Mrs. Horace*)—ETHELSTONE,
　EVELINE, and other Poems. Crown
　8vo. 6*s.*

DOBSON (*Austin*)—OLD WORLD IDYLLS,
　and other Verses. Fourth Edition.
　18mo. cloth extra, gilt tops, 6*s.*

DOMET (*Alfred*)—RANOLF AND AM-
　OHIA ; a Dream of Two Lives. New
　Edition revised. 2 vols. Crown 8vo.
　12*s.*

DOROTHY : a Country Story in Elegiac
　Verse. With Preface. Demy 8vo. 5*s.*

DOWDEN (*Edward*) LL.D.—SHAK-
　SPERE'S SONNETS. With Introduc-
　tion and Notes. Large post 8vo.
　7*s. 6d.*

DUTT (*Toru*)—A SHEAF GLEANED IN
　FRENCH FIELDS. New Edition.
　Demy 8vo. 10*s. 6d.*

EDMONDS (E. M.) — HESPERAS,
　Rhythm and Rhyme. Crown 8vo. 4*s.*

EDWARDS (*Miss Betham*) — POEMS.
　Small crown 8vo. 3*s. 6d.*

ELDRYTH (*Maud*)—MARGARET, and
　other Poems. Small crown 8vo. 3*s.6d.*

　ALL SOULS' EVE, 'NO GOD,' and other
　Poems. Fcp. 8vo. 3*s. 6d.*

ELLIOTT (*Ebenezer*), *The Corn Law
　Rhymer*—POEMS. Edited by his Son,
　the Rev. Edwin Elliott, of St. John's,
　Antigua. 2 vols. crown 8vo. 8*s.*

ENGLISH VERSE. Edited by W. J. LIN-
　TON and R. H. STODDARD. In 5
　vols. Crown 8vo. each 5*s.*

　1. CHAUCER TO BURNS.
　2. TRANSLATIONS.
　3. LYRICS OF THE NINETEENTH CEN-
　　TURY.
　4. DRAMATIC SCENES AND CHARAC-
　　TERS.
　5. BALLADS AND ROMANCES.

ENIS—GATHERED LEAVES. Small crown
　8vo.

EVANS (*Anne*)—POEMS AND MUSIC.
　With Memorial Preface by ANN
　THACKERAY RITCHIE. Large crown
　8vo. 7*s.*

FORSTER (*the late William*)—MIDAS.
　Crown 8vo. 5*s.*

GINNER (*Isaac B.*) - THE DEATH OF
　OTHO, and other Poems. Small
　crown 8vo. 5*s.*

GOODCHILD (*John A.*) — SOMNIA
　MEDICI. Small crown 8vo. 5*s.*

GOSSE (*Edmund W.*)—NEW POEMS.
　Crown 8vo. 7*s. 6d.*

GRAHAM (*William*) — TWO FANCIES,
　and other Poems. Crown 8vo. 5*s.*

GRINDROD (*Charles*) — PLAYS FROM
　ENGLISH HISTORY. Crown 8vo.
　7*s. 6d.*

　THE STRANGER'S STORY and his Poem,
　THE LAMENT OF LOVE: An Epi-
　sode of the Malvern Hills. Small
　crown 8vo. 2*s. 6d.*

GURNEY (*Rev. Alfred*)—THE VISION OF
　THE EUCHARIST, and other Poems.
　Crown 8vo. 5*s.*

　A CHRISTMAS FAGGOT. Small crown
　8vo. 5*s.*

HELLON (*H. G.*) · DAPHNIS: a Pastoral
　Poem. Small crown 8vo. 3*s. 6d.*

HENRY (*Daniel*) *junr.* — UNDER A
　FOOL'S CAP. Songs. Crown 8vo.
　bevelled boards, 5*s.*

HERMAN WALDGRAVE : a Life's Drama.
　By the Author of 'Ginevra,' &c.
　Crown 8vo. 6*s.*

HEYWOOD (*J.C.*) — HERODIAS. A
　Dramatic Poem. New Edition re-
　vised. Small crown 8vo. 5*s.*

HICKEY (*E. H.*)—A SCULPTOR, and
　other Poems. Small crown 8vo. 5*s.*

HONEYWOOD (*Patty*)—POEMS. Dedi-
　cated, by permission, to Lord Wolse-
　ley, G.C.B., &c. Small crown 8vo.
　2*s. 6d.*

JENKINS (*Rev. Canon*) — ALFONSO PETRUCCI, Cardinal and Conspirator: an Historical Tragedy in Five Acts. Small crown 8vo. 3s. 6d.

JOHNSON (*Ernie S. W.*)—ILARIA, and other Poems. Small crown 8vo. 3s. 6d.

KEATS (*John*) — POETICAL WORKS. Edited by W. T. ARNOLD. Large crown 8vo. choicely printed on hand-made paper, with Portrait in *eau forte*. Parchment, or cloth, 12s.; vellum, 15s.

KENNEDY (*Capt. Alexander W. M. Clark*) — ROBERT THE BRUCE. A Poem: Historical and Romantic. With 3 Illustrations by James Faed, Junr. Printed on hand-made paper, parchment, bevelled boards, crown 8vo. 10s. 6d.

KING (*Edward*)—ECHOES FROM THE ORIENT. With Miscellaneous Poems. Small crown 8vo. 3s. 6d.

KING (*Mrs. Hamilton*)—THE DISCIPLES. Sixth Edition, with Portrait and Notes. Crown 8vo. 5s.

A BOOK OF DREAMS. Crown 8vo. 3s. 6d.

KNOX (*The Hon. Mrs. O. N.*)—FOUR PICTURES FROM A LIFE, and other Poems. Small crown 8vo. 3s. 6d.

LANG (*A.*)—XXXII BALLADES IN BLUE CHINA. Elzevir 8vo. parchment, or cloth, 5s.

RHYMES À LA MODE. With Frontispiece by E. A. Abbey. 18mo. cloth extra, gilt tops, 5s.

LAWSON (*Right Hon. Mr. Justice*)— HYMNI USITATI LATINE REDDITI, with other Verses. Small 8vo. parchment, 5s.

LESSING'S NATHAN THE WISE. Translated by Eustace K. Corbett. Crown 8vo. 6s.

LIFE THOUGHTS. Small crown 8vo. 2s. 6d.

LIVING ENGLISH POETS. MDCCCLXXXII. With Frontispiece by Walter Crane. Second Edition. Large crown 8vo. printed on hand-made paper. Parchment, or cloth, 12s.; vellum, 15s.

LOCKER (*F.*)—LONDON LYRICS. New Edition, with Portrait. 18mo. cloth extra, gilt tops, 5s.

LOVE IN IDLENESS. A Volume of Poems. With an etching by W. B. Scott. Small crown 8vo. 5s.

LOVE SONNETS OF PROTEUS. With Frontispiece by the Author. Elzevir 8vo. 5s.

LUMSDEN (*Lieut.-Col. H. W.*) BEO-WULF: an Old English Poem. Translated into Modern Rhymes. Second and revised Edition. Small crown 8vo. 5s.

LYRE AND STAR. Poems by the Author of 'Ginevra,' &c. Crown 8vo. 5s.

MACGREGOR (*Duncan*)—CLOUDS AND SUNLIGHT. Poems. Small crown 8vo. 5s.

MAGNUSSON (*Eirikr*) *M.A.*, *and* PALMER (*E. H.*) *M.A.*—JOHAN LUDVIG RUNEBERG'S LYRICAL SONGS, IDYLLS, AND EPIGRAMS. Fcp. 8vo. 5s.

MDC. Chronicles of Christopher Columbus. A Poem in Twelve Cantos. Small crown 8vo. 7s. 6d.

MEREDITH (*Owen*) [*The Earl of Lytton*] LUCILE. New Edition. With 32 Illustrations. 16mo. 3s. 6d.; cloth extra, gilt edges, 4s. 6d.

MORRIS (*Lewis*) — POETICAL WORKS. New and Cheaper Editions, with Portrait, complete in 3 vols. 5s. each.

Vol. I. contains Songs of Two Worlds. Tenth Edition.

Vol. II. contains The Epic of Hades. Seventeenth Edition.

Vol. III. contains Gwen and the Ode of Life. Sixth Edition.

THE EPIC OF HADES. With 16 Autotype Illustrations after the drawings by the late George R. Chapman. 4to. cloth extra, gilt leaves, 21s.

THE EPIC OF HADES. Presentation Edition. 4to. cloth extra, gilt leaves, 10s. 6d.

SONGS UNSUNG. Fourth Edition. Fcp. 8vo. 6s.

THE LEWIS MORRIS BIRTHDAY BOOK. Edited by S. S. Copeman. With Frontispiece after a design by the late George R. Chapman. 32mo. cloth extra, gilt edges, 2s.; cloth limp, 1s. 6d.

MORSHEAD (*E. D. A.*)—THE HOUSE OF ATREUS. Being the Agamemnon, Libation-Bearers, and Furies of Æschylus. Translated into English Verse. Crown 8vo. 7s.

THE SUPPLIANT MAIDENS OF ÆSCHY-
LUS. Crown 8vo. 3s. 6d.

NADEN (*Constance W.*)—SONGS AND
SONNETS OF SPRING TIME. Small
crown 8vo. 5s.

NEWELL (*E. J.*)—THE SORROW OF
SIMONA, and Lyrical Verses. Small
crown 8vo. 3s. 6d.

NOEL (*The Hon. Roden*)—A LITTLE
CHILD'S   MONUMENT.   Third
Edition. Small crown 8vo. 3s. 6d.

THE RED FLAG, and other Poems.
New Edition. Small crown 8vo. 6s.

O'HAGAN (*John*) — THE SONG OF
ROLAND. Translated into English
Verse. New and Cheaper Edition.
Crown 8vo. 5s.

PFEIFFER (*Emily*)—THE RHYME OF
THE LADY OF THE ROCK AND HOW
IT GREW. Small crown 8vo. 3s. 6d.

GERARD'S MONUMENT, and other Poems.
Second Edition. Crown 8vo. 6s.

UNDER THE ASPENS: Lyrical and
Dramatic. With Portrait. Crown
8vo. 6s.

PIATT (*J. J.*)—IDYLS AND LYRICS OF
THE OHIO VALLEY. Crown 8vo. 5s.

RAFFALOVICH (*Mark André*)—CYRIL
AND LIONEL, and other Poems. A
Volume of Sentimental Studies. Small
crown 8vo. 3s. 6d.

RARE POEMS OF THE 16TH AND 17TH
CENTURIES. Edited by W. J. Linton.
Crown 8vo. 5s.

RHOADES (*James*)—THE GEORGICS OF
VIRGIL. Translated into English
Verse. Small crown 8vo. 5s.

ROBINSON (*A. Mary F.*)—A HANDFUL
OF HONEYSUCKLE. Fcp. 8vo. 3s. 6d.

THE CROWNED HIPPOLYTUS. Translated from Euripides. With New
Poems. Small crown 8vo. cloth, 5s.

ROUS (*Lieut.-Col.*)—CONRADIN. Small
crown 8vo. 2s.

SCHILLER'S MARY STUART. German
Text with English Translation on
opposite page. By Leedham White.
Crown 8vo. 6s.

SCOTT (*E. J. L.*) THE ECLOGUES OF
VIRGIL. Translated into English
Verse. Small crown 8vo. 3s. 6d.

SCOTT (*George F. E.*)—THEODORA, and
other Poems. Small crown 8vo. 3s.6d.

SEAL (*W. H.*) IONE, and other
Poems. Second and cheaper edition,
revised, crown 8vo. 3s. 6d.

SELKIRK (*J. B.*)—POEMS. Crown 8vo.
7s. 6d.

SHARP (*William*) — EUPHRENIA ; or,
The Test of Love. A Poem. Crown
8vo. 5s.

SKINNER (*H. J.*)—THE LILY OF THE
LYN, and other Poems. Small crown
8vo. 3s. 6d.

SLADEN (*Douglas B. W.*)—FRITHJOF
AND INGEBJORG, and other Poems.
Small crown 8vo. 5s.

SMITH (*J. W. Gilbart*)—THE LOVES OF
VANDYCK : a Tale of Genoa. Small
crown 8vo. 2s. 6d.

THE LOG O' THE 'NORSEMAN,' Small
crown 8vo. 5s.

SOPHOCLES : The Seven Plays in English
Verse. Translated by Lewis Campbell. Crown 8vo. 7s. 6d.

SPICER (*Henry*)—HASKA : a Drama in
Three Acts (as represented at the
Theatre Royal, Drury Lane, March
10th, 1877). Third Edition, crown
8vo. 3s. 6d.

SYMONDS (*John Addington*) — VAGA-
BUNDULI LIBELLUS Crown 8vo. 6s.

TARES. Crown vo. s. 6d.

TASSO'S JERUSALEM DELIVERED. Translated by Sir John Kingston James,
Bart. 2 vols. printed on hand-made
paper, parchment, bevelled boards,
large crown 8vo. 21s.

TAYLOR (*Sir H.*)—Works Complete in
Five Volumes. Crown 8vo. 30s.

PHILIP VAN ARTEVELDE. Fcp. 8vo.
3s. 6d.

THE VIRGIN WIDOW, &c. Fcp. 8vo.
3s. 6d.

THE STATESMAN. Fcp. 8vo. 3s. 6d.

TAYLOR (*Augustus*) — POEMS. Fcp.
8vo. 5s.

TAYLOR (Margaret Scott) — 'BOYS TOGETHER,' and other Poems. Small crown 8vo. 6s.

THORNTON (L. M.)—THE SON OF SHELOMITH. Small crown 8vo. 3s. 6d.

TODHUNTER (Dr. J.) — LAURELLA, and other Poems. Crown 8vo. 6s. 6d.

FOREST SONGS. Small crown 8vo. 3s. 6d.

THE TRUE TRAGEDY OF RIENZI: a Drama. Crown 8vo. 3s. 6d.

ALCESTIS: a Dramatic Poem. Extra fcp. 8vo. 5s.

TYLER (M. C.) — ANNE BOLEYN: a Tragedy in Six Acts. Small crown 8vo. 2s. 6d.

WALTERS (Sophia Lydia) — A DREAMER'S SKETCH BOOK. With 21 Illustrations by Percival Skelton, R. P. Leitch, W. H. J. Boot, and T. R. Pritchett. Engraved by J. D. Cooper. Fcp. 4to. 12s. 6d.

WANDERING ECHOES. By J. E. D. G. In Four Parts. Small crown 8vo. 5s.

WATTS (Alaric Alfred and Emma Mary Howitt) — AURORA: a Medley of Verse. Fcp. 8vo. cloth, bevelled boards, 5s.

WEBSTER (Augusta)—IN A DAY: a Drama. Small crown 8vo. 2s. 6d.

DISGUISES: a Drama. Small crown 8vo. 5s.

WET DAYS. By a Farmer. Small crown 8vo. 6s.

WILLIAMS (J.)- A STORY OF THREE YEARS, and other Poems. Small crown 8vo. 3s. 6d.

WORDSWORTH BIRTHDAY BOOK, THE. Edited by ADELAIDE and VIOLET WORDSWORTH. 32mo. limp cloth, 1s. 6d.; cloth extra, 2s.

YOUNGMAN (Thomas George)—POEMS. Small crown 8vo. 5s.

YOUNGS (Ella Sharpe)—PAPHUS, and other Poems. Small crown 8vo. 3s. 6d.

A HEARTS LIFE, SARPEDON, and other Poems. Small crown 8vo. 3s. 6d.

WORKS OF FICTION IN ONE VOLUME.

BANKS (Mrs. G. L.)—GOD'S PROVIDENCE HOUSE. New Edition. Crown 8vo. 3s. 6d.

HUNTER (Hay)—CRIME OF CHRISTMAS DAY. A Tale of the Latin Quarter. By the Author of 'My Ducats and My Daughter.' 1s.

HUNTER (Hay) and WHYTE (Walter) MY DUCATS AND MY DAUGHTER. New and Cheaper Edition. With Frontispiece. Crown 8vo. 6s.

INGELOW (Jean)—OFF THE SKELLIGS. A Novel. With Frontispiece. Second Edition. Crown 8vo. 6s.

KIELLAND (Alexander L.)—GARMAN AND WORSE. A Norwegian Novel. Authorised Translation by W. W. Kettlewell. Crown 8vo. 6s.

MACDONALD (G.)—DONAL GRANT. A Novel. New and Cheap Edition, with Frontispiece. Crown 8vo. 6s.

CASTLE WARLOCK. A Novel. New and Cheaper Edition. Crown 8vo. 9s.

MALCOLM. With Portrait of the Author engraved on Steel. Sixth Edition. Crown 8vo. 6s.

THE MARQUIS OF LOSSIE. Fifth Edition. With Frontispiece. Crown 8vo. 6s.

ST. GEORGE AND ST. MICHAEL. Fourth Edition. With Frontispiece. Crown 8vo. 6s.

PALGRAVE (W. Gifford)—HERMANN AGHA: an Eastern Narrative. Third Edition. Crown 8vo. 6s.

SHAW (Flora L.)—CASTLE BLAIR; a Story of Youthful Days. New and Cheaper Edition. Crown 8vo. 3s. 6d.

STRETTON (Hesba) — THROUGH A NEEDLE'S EYE. A Story. New and Cheaper Edition, with Frontispiece. Crown 8vo. 6s.

TAYLOR (Col. Meadows) C.S.I., M.R.I.A.

SEETA. A Novel. New and Cheaper Edition. With Frontispiece. Crown 8vo. 6s.

TIPPOO SULTAUN: a Tale of the Mysore War. New Edition, with Frontispiece. Crown 8vo. 6s.

RALPH DARNELL. New and Cheaper Edition. With Frontispiece. Crown 8vo. 6s.

C

TAYLOR—continued.

A NOBLE QUEEN. New and Cheaper Edition. With Frontispiece. Crown 8vo. 6s.

THE CONFESSIONS OF A THUG. Crown 8vo. 6s.

TAYLOR—continued.

TARA: a Mahratta Tale. Crown 8vo. 6s.

WITHIN SOUND OF THE SEA. New and Cheaper Edition, with Frontispiece. Crown 8vo. 6s.

BOOKS FOR THE YOUNG.

BRAVE MEN'S FOOTSTEPS. A Book of Example and Anecdote for Young People. By the Editor of 'Men who have Risen.' With Four Illustrations by C. Doyle. Eighth Edition. Crown 8vo. 3s. 6d.

COXHEAD (Ethel)—BIRDS AND BABIES. With 33 Illustrations. Imp. 16mo. cloth gilt, 2s. 6d.

DAVIES (G. Christopher) — RAMBLES AND ADVENTURES OF OUR SCHOOL FIELD CLUB. With Four Illustrations. New and Cheaper Edition. Crown 8vo. 3s. 6d.

EDMONDS (Herbert) — WELL-SPENT LIVES: a Series of Modern Biographies. New and Cheaper Edition. Crown 8vo. 3s. 6d.

EVANS (Mark)—THE STORY OF OUR FATHER'S LOVE, told to Children. Sixth and Cheaper Edition of Theology for Children. With Four Illustrations. Fcp. 8vo. 1s. 6d.

JOHNSON (Virginia W.)—THE CATSKILL FAIRIES. Illustrated by ALFRED FREDERICKS. 5s.

MAC KENNA (S. J.)—PLUCKY FELLOWS. A Book for Boys. With Six Illustrations. Fifth Edition. Crown 8vo. 3s. 6d.

REANEY (Mrs. G. S.)—WAKING AND WORKING; or, From Girlhood to Womanhood. New and Cheaper Edition. With a Frontispiece. Cr. 8vo. 3s. 6d.

BLESSING AND BLESSED: a Sketch of Girl Life. New and Cheaper Edition. Crown 8vo. 3s. 6d.

REANEY (Mrs. G. S.)—continued.

ROSE GURNEY'S DISCOVERY. A Book for Girls. Dedicated to their Mothers. Crown 8vo. 3s. 6d.

ENGLISH GIRLS: Their Place and Power. With Preface by the Rev. R. W. Dale. Fourth Edition. Fcp. 8vo. 2s. 6d.

JUST ANYONE, and other Stories. Three Illustrations. Royal 16mo. 1s. 6d.

SUNBEAM WILLIE, and other Stories. Three Illustrations. Royal 16mo. 1s. 6d.

SUNSHINE JENNY, and other Stories. Three Illustrations. Royal 16mo. 1s. 6d.

STOCKTON (Frank R.)—A JOLLY FELLOWSHIP. With 20 Illustrations. Crown 8vo. 5s.

STORR (Francis) and TURNER (Hawes). CANTERBURY CHIMES; or, Chaucer Tales Re-told to Children. With Six Illustrations from the Ellesmere MS. Third Edition. Fcp. 8vo. 3s. 6d.

STRETTON (Hesba)—DAVID LLOYD'S LAST WILL. With Four Illustrations. New Edition. Royal 16mo. 2s. 6d.

TALES FROM ARIOSTO RE-TOLD FOR CHILDREN. By a Lady. With Three Illustrations. Crown 8vo. 4s. 6d.

WHITAKER (Florence)—CHRISTY'S INHERITANCE: A London Story. Illustrated. Royal 16mo. 1s. 6d.

LONDON: PRINTED BY
SPOTTISWOODE AND CO., NEW-STREET SQUARE
AND PARLIAMENT STREET